William Sparrow Simpson

S. Paul's cathedral library

A catalogue of Bibles, rituals, and rare books; works relating to London and

especially to S. Paul's cathedral

William Sparrow Simpson

S. Paul's cathedral library
A catalogue of Bibles, rituals, and rare books; works relating to London and especially to S. Paul's cathedral

ISBN/EAN: 9783337104788

Printed in Europe, USA, Canada, Australia, Japan

Cover: Foto ©Lupo / pixelio.de

More available books at **www.hansebooks.com**

S. PAUL'S CATHEDRAL LIBRARY.

A CATALOGUE

OF BIBLES, RITUALS, AND RARE BOOKS;
WORKS RELATING TO LONDON AND ESPECIALLY TO S. PAUL'S
CATHEDRAL, INCLUDING A LARGE COLLECTION
OF PAUL'S CROSS SERMONS;
MAPS, PLANS, AND VIEWS OF LONDON AND OF
S. PAUL'S CATHEDRAL.

BY

W. SPARROW SIMPSON, D.D., F.S.A.,

SUB-DEAN AND LIBRARIAN OF S. PAUL'S,
SOME OF THE HONORARY LIBRARIANS OF THE UNDER THE ARCHBISHOP OF CANTERBURY.

LONDON:
ELLIOT STOCK, 62, PATERNOSTER ROW, E.C.
1893.

PREFACE.

I DESIRE to state at once what will be found and what will not be found in the present volume. It is not a catalogue of the entire Cathedral library. That will at once be understood when I mention that the library contains about

10,446 volumes of printed books,
10,730 separate pamphlets,

making a gross total of about 21,176 volumes.

But it is a catalogue of certain sections of the library, as will be seen from the title-page, from the full table of contents, and from the following brief narrative :

On January 16, 1862, to my great pleasure, Dean Milman offered me the post of librarian of S. Paul's Cathedral. I had been librarian of my college at Cambridge, had always been a lover of books, and had taken interest in their arrangement and safe keeping. I had, of course, views of my own as to the method which should be adopted in dealing with such a collection of books as that which I found upon the shelves of the Cathedral. It was obviously useless to attempt to vie with any of the great libraries, or to struggle vainly to gather together miscellaneous works on general literature. I thought it better to make the collection of books illustrating the history of the cathedral my speciality. I arrived at this decision at a very early period in my tenure of office, for, on searching the catalogue, I found that, with the single exception of a copy of the second edition of Dugdale's *History of S. Paul's Cathedral*, there was hardly a book in the library which bore directly upon this subject.

Since October, 1872, the Dean and Chapter have been so good as to place in my hands a certain annual sum, to be used at my own discretion for the purposes of the Library. Binding and repairs form, in a City library, a serious item of regular outlay, and subscriptions

to a few of the learned societies absorb another portion of the amount
at my disposal, but the remaining portion has been available for my
special object.

The result has been that I have been able to gather together what I
venture to consider a valuable mass of material for the history of S.
Paul's Cathedral.   I point, with no little satisfaction, to the series of
Paul's Cross Sermons which I have collected.[1]   All who know the
place which Paul's Cross occupied in the political and civil, no less
than in the religious, history of the times, will appreciate the im-
portance of the collection.   For certainly in these vigorous discourses
the men of the past age stand before us in their habit as they lived.

> 'There is no Past, so long as Books shall live,
> A disinterr'd Pompeii wakes again
> For him who seeks you well,
> Ye make the Past our heritage and home.'[2]

I am aware that the series is far from being complete; and, with
a view to its enlargement, I have printed a list of Paul's Cross
Sermons[3] which are in the British Museum, but of which, at present,
I have not been able to obtain copies.   And I am hopeful that, in
the course of years, many of these, by gift or by purchase, may
find their way to the Cathedral.

Second in interest to the Paul's Cross Sermons, but still with a
certain historical value, is the series of sermons preached not at the
Cross, but within the walls of the Cathedral.[4]   These also throw
considerable light upon the manners and customs of our forefathers
in the great City.   Attention may be specially directed to the annual
services held in the Cathedral, at which the 'Native Citizens of
London,'[5] or the 'Natives of S. Martin-in-the-Fields,'[6] or the
'Gentlemen of Cheshire,'[7] or the 'Gentlemen of Wiltshire,'[8] met
together on the occasion of their annual feast.   In like manner, the
Gentlemen educated at S. Paul's School,[9] or at Eton,[10] were accus-
tomed to keep an anniversary, and to mark it by a religious service.
The numerous sermons preached on occasions of public thanksgiving reflect the temper of the times, and the changing political
sentiment of the restless seventeenth century.   A few examples will
serve to illustrate my meaning.

In 1639 Dr. Valentine preaches on the 'day of His Majesties most

---

[1] See pp. 85-97.
[2] Lord Lytton. (In *Ballads of Books*, edited by Andrew Lang, 1885.)
[3] See *Appendix*, pp. 232-237.   [4] See pp. 97-114.   [5] In 1656, 1657, and 1658.
[6] In 1684.   [7] In 1655.   [8] In 1658.
[9] In 1697-98, 1699, 1711, 1717-18, 1728, 1755, 1757.   [10] In 1702.

happy Inauguration, and of His Northerne Expedition.' In 1645 Simeon Ash preaches at a 'Publike Thanksgiving for the taking in of the Towns and Castles of Caermarthen and Mounmouth in Wales.' In 1648 Jo. Geree anxiously endeavours to clear himself from 'Malignancy imputed to him by some ill-eared Auditors,' and preaches about 'the Red Horse, or the Bloodines of War.' In 1651 Joseph Carryl commemorates the 'wonderfull Victorie to the Parliament Forces before Worcester, in the total defeat of the Enemie.' In 1660 Dr. Gauden rejoices over the restoring of 'the Secluded Members of Parliament to the House of Commons;' and the 'Door of Hope thereby opened to the fulness and freedom of future Parliaments, the most probable means under God for healing the hurts and recovering the health of these three Brittish Kingdomes.' In 1660 Richard Baxter discourses at the thanksgiving 'for God raising up and succeeding his Excellency, and other Instruments, in order to his Majesties Restoration and the settlement of these Nations.' In 1661 Henry Hibbert declares 'His Majesties most wonderful glorious, peaceable, and joyful Restauration to the actual possession of his undoubted, hereditary, Sovereign, and actual authority;' the day being also his Majesty's 'most memorable Birth-Day.' The Lord Mayor attends the ministry of this master of adjectives. One more example only must be quoted, when, in the same year, Samuel Stone is the preacher, at 'the Initial of the Reverend Dr. John Barwick, Dean; at the first Celebrity of Divine Service with the Organ and Choristers, which the Lord Maior himself Solemniz'd with his Personal presence from the very beginning.'

Puritan ascendancy had passed away, and once more it was lawful to mention *Saint* Paul; whereas, of late, preachers had described themselves as Ministers of the Gospell at Magnus, Pastour of Christopher Le Stocks, minister of Mary Wolnoth, and the like.

Queen Anne was a frequent visitor to the Cathedral, coming to return thanks for the great victories achieved under Marlborough. A series of sermons, preached on occasion of these thanksgivings, will be found recorded here.

One notable and rare sermon, by Dean Feckenham, 'at the celebration of the exequies of the righte excellent and famous princesse, lady Jane, Queene of Spayne, Sicilie, & Navarre,' in 1555, deserves especial notice. As does also 'the sermon of doctor Colete, made to the Convocation of Paulos.' The copy is, alas, imperfect; the only perfect copy known forms one of the many gems of the Lambeth Library.

Specially interesting also is the little collection of plays acted by the Children of Paul's.[1] In my *Gleanings in Old S. Paul's* I have devoted a chapter to the subject of these **plays**, and have attempted to draw up a list, no doubt an imperfect one, of the various pieces enacted by the young players. I do not repeat the list in the present volume, but I will venture to express a hope that generous donors may be found **who will** enrich this curious collection.

In the more **general class** of books relating to the history of the Cathedral[2] I **have** been an insatiable collector; the largest folio or the thinnest pamphlet, the great work of some illustrious genius or the ephemeral production of some obscure pamphleteer, has been welcome. Nothing can be too large, nothing too small, to find a **place** in such a series. The almost worthless pamphlet of to-day may, a few years hence, supply a date **or a fact** worth recording, and would then probably be sought for in vain.

I have included in the Catalogue a few tracts relating to Sir Christopher Wren,[3] even though they record, to the lasting disgrace of the perpetrators, the hard measure meted out to the illustrious architect by those who ought to have known better.

The Sacheverell controversy occupies a small place in my list, not from any great interest now attaching to the subject, but because the sermon from which it originated was preached within the walls of the Cathedral.

In the series of pamphlets, broadsides, and views which I have gathered together,[4] the story of the funerals of Nelson and of Wellington is told in great detail.

From the history of S. Paul's to that of the great City which it **adorns** is an easy and natural transition. Sketches of the history of S. Paul's are found in every important *History* or *Survey* of London; and hence books of this kind soon came to be included in my search. Any experienced collector will readily observe that many valuable works are wanting; but this department of the Library will certainly grow. The City Fathers have been generous givers, and have placed upon our shelves the important works issued from time to time by the Guildhall Library Committee.

A fair number of scarce tracts will be found **in** this section of the Catalogue, together with many quaint and curious little books, not

---

[1] See pp. 120, 121.   [2] See pp. 71-85.   [3] See pp. 121, 122.
[4] See pp. 125, 126; and also pp. 200-202.

easily to be obtained, such as D. Lupton's *London and the Countrey
Carbonadoed, The Sermon and Prophecie of Mr. James Hunt of the
Countie of Kent*, or the *Strange News from New-Gate*, the latter illustrating the remarkable and most instructive outbreak of fanaticism in
the middle of the seventeenth century; the tract *Three Looks over
London*, with its interesting woodcut of Paul's Cross as it appeared
in 1643; the pamphlet called *News from the Dead*, showing that the
Barber-Surgeons' Company was still in possession of its dissecting-
room in 1740 (illustrative details will be found in Mr. Sidney Young's
admirable *Annals of the Barber Surgeons*. The entry on p. 419 :[1]

> '1740.   Paid for mending the windows broke upon bringing the
>   last Body from Tyburn   .   .   .   o 6 o'

refers to some popular tumult on this very occasion. The beadles
of the company were apt to meet with rough usage when claiming
and removing the bodies of executed malefactors); Mr. Herbert
Croft's satirical tract, *The Wreck of Westminster Abbey*; and many
another illustration of the history of the past.

It is much to be wished that some future Librarian may augment
the sections relating to the City Parishes and to the Livery Companies.[2]   Dr. Freshfield has greatly enriched the former section by
presenting copies of his privately printed volumes, and several of the
Livery Companies have generously sent us records of their history—
a history of the highest interest to the student of municipal institutions.   It is difficult to gather together the scattered notices of City
parishes which have from time to time appeared—often privately
printed—sometimes consisting only of a very few leaves, and liable,
therefore, to perish in the using, though they frequently deserve a
better fate: whilst the histories of the City companies are costly and
often sumptuous volumes, severely taxing the resources of the
Library.

Attention may be specially directed to the series of tracts relating
to Mr. Henry Burton,[3] the very notorious Rector of S. Matthew,
Friday Street, who, in consequence of a sermon preached in this
church, was condemned to stand in the pillory in the Palace Yard
at Westminster, to lose his ears, to pay a fine of £5,000 to the king,
and to be imprisoned for life. He suffered part of his sentence, but
in 1640 was released by order of Parliament. Fuller says 'that he
rather took a snap than any meat in any University.' He afterward

---

[1] See also *Annals of the Barber Surgeons' Company*, pp. 358, 359.
[2] See pp. 145-155.   [3] See pp. 150, 151.

turned Independent, and set up a separatist congregation of his own.
The circumstance that I am Rector of the parish of S. Matthew,
Friday Street,[1] has led me to pay special attention to this subject.

Not least in interest is the curious series of tracts[2] which tell the
story of Cheapside Cross and those which supply accounts of the
Plague and the Great Fire.[3]

I have also gathered together by the process of slow and laborious
accumulation a large collection (amounting to about 951 plates) of
Maps, Plans, and Views of London and of S. Paul's Cathedral. To
these are added a few illustrations relating to Chertsey, Barking,
Fulham, and other places whose story is interwoven with that of
S. Paul's.[4]

These Plans and Views are for the most part mounted uniformly
on 530 sheets,[5] and are placed in a series of Solander cases, after
a plan suggested to me by the late Mr. Fagan, whose efficient
conduct of his department in the British Museum is well-known to
all students.   These cases are arranged as follows :

LONDON : Maps and Plans.   (Two cases.)
                  General Views.   (Three cases.)
S. PAUL'S : The Old Cathedral.
                  The Present Building :
                  Interior.
                  Exterior.   (Two Cases.)
PAGEANTS : Including   Public   Thanksgivings,   Ceremonials,
                  Funerals, etc.   (Two cases.)
MISCELLANEOUS.

I desire to acknowledge the great care and personal interest which
Mr. Walter V. Daniell[6] has taken in arranging and mounting this
large mass of material, and also in compiling the catalogue of this
portion of the collection, which is large and varied, the result of the
labours of many years, comprising some very rare maps, plans, and

[1] The parish is now united with S. Vedast, Foster Lane.
[2] See pp. 155, 156.   [3] See pp. 156-158.
[4] This enumeration does not include :
      28 old views of London in a separate quarto volume.
      50 wood-cuts from Longman's *History of S. Paul's.*
      51 sheets of the Ordnance Maps of London.
      120 Photographs of the Society for Photographing Relics of Old London.
      24 sheets Horwood's Map of London.
      226 Drawings and Tracings by Mr. W. Burges, in a portfolio.
      Rocque's, Visscher's, and Hollar's Maps of London, in separate cases.
[5] Each sheet measuring 31½ inches by 21¾ inches.
[6] Of Mortimer Street.

views, together with a multitude of familiar engravings known to every collector. The general views of London have almost always been selected because they show some aspect of S. Paul's Cathedral. The magnificent church, dominating the City, as it does still, notwithstanding the lofty buildings which have grown up around it in recent times, has had a great fascination for me, and has caused me to add many a general view to the series.

Then follow detailed lists of two series of Plates, the first series taken from Mr. William Longman's *History of the Three Cathedrals Dedicated to S. Paul in London;* and the second series, being a complete set of the photographs issued by the *Society for Photographing Relics of Old London,* the latter the gift of Mrs. Church.

These are succeeded by a list (a somewhat scanty one) of Engraved Portraits of Bishops of London, Deans of S. Paul's, and Canons of the Cathedral. After this section comes a catalogue of casts of Seals of many of the Bishops of London, and of the Dean and Chapter; together with a list of Medals which in some way or other illustrate the history of S. Paul's, and a short notice of some miscellaneous objects of interest exhibited in glass cases in the Library.

An Appendix follows, which contains a list of DESIDERATA. This will tend to give more completeness to what was the leading idea with which I commenced the Catalogue; namely, to make it an attempt, however humble, at a Bibliography of S. Paul's.

This purpose, always present in my mind, will explain the inclusion in the Catalogue of many books which, at first sight, may seem to have no relation to the Cathedral. Thus *The Army's Martyr*[1] is included because it records the tragical story of the death of Robert Lockier, shot in S. Paul's Churchyard. Everyone will remember Carlyle's allusion to the incident : ' Trooper Lockyer is shot in Paul's Churchyard. A very brave young man, they say. Though but three and twenty, "he has served seven years in these Wars," ever since the Wars began. "Religious," too, of excellent parts, and much beloved.'[2] With more detail in his graphic manner. The *Brief Relation of the Persecutions and Cruelties that have been acted upon the people called Quakers*[3] finds place because it relates a strange fanatical exhibition which took place within the church itself. Two Quaker women having entered S. Paul's during service time, the one of them ' vvith her face made black, and her hair down

---

[1] Pp. 73, 74.   [2] *Letters and Speeches of Oliver Cromwell.*   [3] Pp. 74, 75.

vvith blood poured in it, vvich ran dovvn upon her sackcloth vvich she had on, and she poured also some blood dovvn upon the Altar, and spoke some vvords.'[1] R. Keach's *War with the Devil*[2] occurs only because it has a view of *London in Flames*, in which the Cathedral is to be seen ; whilst, even, certain *Select Fables of Æsop and other Fabulists*[3] are included, only because one of the fables is entitled *The Fly in S. Paul's Cupola ;* and Bishop Earle's quaint *Microcosmography,*[4] because of its vivid account of Paul's Walk.

These examples will suffice to show that any allusion to S. Paul's Cathedral which can be regarded as of the very smallest historical value suffices, in my judgment, to entitle a book to a place in the collection.

The Catalogue concludes with three long Lists of Preachers at the anniversary meetings of three great religious societies, held for the most part in the Cathedral. These three societies, the outcome of a deep and widespread movement on the part of some of the most loyal sons of the English Church, year by year gathered their supporters within the sacred walls, and listened to the great masters of religious eloquence as they advocated the claims of these associations for the spread of vital religion. Many of their sermons are to be found on the shelves of the Library. The sermons on behalf of the Society for Promoting Christian Knowledge were usually preached on the occasions on which the children educated in what were called the *Charity Schools* of London were massed together under the vast dome of S. Paul's. Many readers will remember the picturesque scene —the quaint dresses of the children, with the occasional brilliant patches of colour where the girls were dressed in scarlet, the glowing colour relieved by the snow-white caps and aprons, and, above all, the almost overpowering effect when the combined voices of the great multitude of children burst forth in singing 'All people that on earth do dwell,' or united in the grand choruses of the Coronation anthem.

I had intended to have limited the present volume to a Catalogue of the Books, Maps, Plans, and Views already enumerated. But the Dean of S. Paul's suggested to me that it would be well to add a list of the Bibles and other rare books *in Archivis ;* and this has accordingly been done. The Bibles and New Testaments[5] formed a special subject, requiring much bibliographical knowledge, and in

---

[1] *Gleanings from Old S. Paul's*, p. 284.   [2] P. 76.   [3] P. 77.
[4] P. 77.   [5] See pp. 3-32.

this portion of the work I have called in the skilled help of Mr. Henry Guppy, one of the assistant librarians at Sion College, who threw himself very heartily into the work, and who is mainly responsible for pp. 3 to 55.

I need hardly draw the attention of the student of Bibles to our great treasures, the Tyndale *New Testament*, the Tyndale *Pentateuch*, and the Large Paper Walton's *Polyglot*; books which are in themselves sufficient to give a character to any library.

Amongst the Office Books and Liturgies,[1] which follow the Bibles, special mention may be made of the books *Secundum usum Sarum*, the *Ordinal* and *Order of Communion* of 1548; the copy of the *Sealed Book*; and Bishop Compton's own beautiful copy of the same edition of the Prayer-Book, once clothed in a sumptuous silver binding.[2]

I have thought it well to add an extended list of Rituals, especially of a series of service-books of the Greek Church, and a brief enumeration of a few liturgical reprints, which, though not to be classed amongst rare books, may yet add a little more completeness to this interesting section of the Catalogue.

Under each section the books enumerated will be found arranged, as far as possible, in chronological order; the early books are fully entered, but the later and less important works appear under condensed and shortened titles.

It must be remembered that the primary intention of this volume is to supply the members of the Cathedral body with a guide to the treasures which might otherwise be unknown upon the shelves.

If there is one thing more than another to be desired in such a work as this it is minute, literal accuracy. It is easier to aim at accuracy than to attain to it. I have heard it said that the librarian who prints a catalogue must from that moment bid farewell to happiness, as it will be the special occupation of the great mass of his acquaintance to point out errors in his work.

Well, I have run the risk.

Errors, no doubt, will be found. It is almost impossible to avoid them. Each librarian would certainly adopt his own system of classification, and I can well understand that his system might not be my own. But I have tried to make my system clear by a full table of contents and by a large and ample index (containing about

---

[1] See pp. 35-68.   [2] P. 47.

2,694 entries), by means of which I hope that any book included in the list may readily be found.

But every year that I live convinces me more fully that one's own methods are not necessarily the most perfect ; and I am sure that I cannot do better than adopt the words lately used by the learned Dean of Winchester :

' In a work so full of details there must be many errors and short-comings. There are many traps for the unwary ; wherein when I have been caught, I would pray the wiser critics, who stand safe, to be not scornful, but pitiful.'

I beg to acknowledge the courtesy of Mr. Bedford Lemere in granting me permission to use the very interesting photograph which forms the frontispiece to this volume.

One welcome duty alone remains, and that is to record my thanks to my loving and patient wife, who has saved my weary eyes many a strain by her help in the tedious labour of correcting the proofs.

IN Dugdale's *History of S. Paul's Cathedral* that laborious antiquary gives a catalogue of the contents of the Library in the year 1458. Walter Shiryngton, clerk, had founded the Library, and his executors had carried out his pious intentions by erecting a suitable building over the cloister which surrounded Pardon-chirche-hawe on the north side of the grand Church. The catalogue fills eight folio pages in the first edition of Dugdale. Of all these manuscripts only three are known to exist : one is still at S. Paul's, the second is at Aberdeen, the third is at Lambeth. As for the rest, it seems probable that the fire of 1561 may have destroyed very many, and that if any survived they fell victims to the zeal of civil or ecclesiastical iconoclasts, receiving a final *coup de grâce* in the terrible conflagration of 1666.

The Records of the Cathedral happily escaped. No doubt a great number of deeds and documents have been purloined and destroyed; but a very large mass still remains, as may be seen in Mr. Maxwell Lyte's excellent *Calendar* in the *Historical Manuscripts Commission Reports.*

The Library itself is a noble room, lined with oak presses, and surrounded by a gallery supported by exceedingly fine brackets carved by Grinling Gibbons. Lord Lytton's words may well be taken to describe it :

> ' Sit here and muse! —It is an antique Room ;
> High-roof'd, with casement, through whose purple panes
> Unwilling Daylight steals amidst the gloom
> Shy as a fearful Stranger.
> Hark ! while we muse, without the walls is heard
> The various murmur of the labouring crowd.
> How still, within those archive cells interr'd,
> The Calm Ones reign.'

Henry Compton, Bishop of London during the rebuilding of the Cathedral, was the founder of the present Library. He bequeathed no less than 1,892 volumes to form the nucleus of a collection.

Partly by gift and partly by purchase, the books of Dr. Thomas

Mangey, Prebendary of Durham, and of his son, the Rev. John Mangey, Prebendary of S. Paul's, were acquired in 1783.

I have given some account of the growth of the collection in my *Gleanings from Old S. Paul's*, and it is unnecessary to repeat in this place what has there been said.

There is a manuscript catalogue of the printed books, which form the staple of the collection, and I have compiled a catalogue, also in manuscript, of the 10,000 pamphlets which I have purchased for the Cathedral during my tenure of office. These pamphlets include 6,348 separate tracts, gathered together by Bishop Sumner, who presided over the Diocese of Winchester from 1827 to 1869; and the 1,405 tracts of Archdeacon Hale, Archdeacon of London from 1842 to 1870; together with the smaller, but yet important collection, made by Dr. Irons, late Prebendary, and presented to the Cathedral by his widow.

The Cathedral Clergy responded with great liberality to an appeal which I ventured to address to them some years ago, and have added to our stores, at my especial request, copies of works of which they have themselves been the authors. Amongst the more generous donations, I may mention that the families of Dean Milman, Dean Mansel, and Dean Church have greatly enriched the Library ; Dean Church during his lifetime having been also a great benefactor. Dr. Wace, amongst other important gifts, has contributed a copy of his *Dictionary of Christian Biography;* Dr. Freshfield, a series of his interesting volumes on parochial history; and the Rev. W. H. Milman, a set of the *Quarterly Review* from its commencement. The latest accession has been a bequest by Archdeacon Hessey of his complete set of the *Bampton Lectures.*

The Library is, as might be expected, rich in councils, patristic literature, and theology. The publications of the *Surtees Society,* the *Camden Society,* the *Palæographical Society,* the youthful but vigorous *Henry Bradshaw Society,* the *Ecclesiastical History Society,* the *London and Middlesex Archæological Society,* the *S. Paul's Ecclesiological Society* (which has already done some excellent work), the large series of *Chronicles* issued by the Master of the Rolls, the *Calendars of the State Papers,* and if last, certainly not least, the *Acta Sanctorum* of the Bollandists, find place upon the shelves.

I have lately enriched the Library by the purchase of a valuable series of original manuscripts, once the property of the learned Bishop Gibson, many of them in his own handwriting. Amongst the manuscripts is a Vow made by Charles I., and signed with his own hand ;

and the draft of a Letter from the King to Queen Henrietta Maria, which is entirely in his own handwriting. A facsimile of the Vow and a copy of the Letter will be found in the *Archæologia*, vol. liii., pp. 155-160.

Amongst those who have laboured lovingly in the Cathedral Library should be especially commemorated the brilliant author of the *Ingoldsby Legends*, Richard Harris Barham, of most facetious memory. He found the Library in a sadly neglected condition, and 'it pitied him to see it in the dust.' His carefully-written reports, which are still extant, led to the repair of many volumes which might else have perished. He was much more than a mere wit. He was an ardent bibliographer, as some notes in his fine, clear hand in many of the rarer books still testify.

May there never be wanting loving hands and hearts to deal with the treasures stored within these walls : and to transmit to others

'The Love of Books the Golden Key
That opens the Enchanted Door.'

CONTENTS.

S. Paul's Cathedral.

London.

Maps, Plans, and Views of London, and especially of S. Paul's Cathedral.

APPENDIX.

CONTENTS.

BIBLES.

1569-73. **Biblia Sacra.** Hebraice, Chaldaice, Græce et Latine. Edited by Arias MONTANUS. Antverpiæ, Chris. Plantinus. 8 vols. Folio (varying in size from 15-10½ to 15⅞-10½ inches). 1569-1573.
[2 B 2-9.]

*** Volumes 1 to 5, containing the text, are uniform in size, (15-10½ inches), but vols. 6 to 8, comprising the appendices, are somewhat taller.

This Bible was produced under the auspices and at the expense of Philip II. of Spain.

1599. **Sacra Biblia, Hebraice, Graece, et Latine.** Cum annotationibus Francisci Vatabli Hebraicæ linguæ quondam Professoris Regii Lutetiæ. Latina interpretatio duplex est, altera vetus, altera nova. Omnia cum editione Complutensi diligenter collata, additis in margine, quos Vatablus in suis annotationibus nonnunquam omiserat, idiotismis, verborumque difficiliorum radicibus.

Editio postrema, multo quàm antehac emendatior : cui etiam nunc accessit, ne quid in ea desiderari posset.

Novum Testamentum Græcolatinum Ben. Ariæ Montani Hispalensis. Ex officina Commeliniana. 1599. 2 vols. Folio (15$\frac{11}{16}$-10⅛ inches).
[27 B 11-12.]

1629-45. **Biblia.** 1, Hebraica ; 2, Samaritana ; 3, Chaldaica ; 4, Græca ; 5, Syriaca ; 6, Latina ; 7, Arabica. Quibus textus originales totius Scripturæ Sacræ, quorum pars in editione Complvtensi, deinde in Antverpiensi regiis sumptibus extat, nunc integri, ex manuscriptis toto ferè orbe quæsitas exemplaribus, exhibentur. Lutetiæ Parisiorum, Antonius Vitrè. 9 vols. in 10 (vol. 5 in 2 parts). Folio (19½-13½ inches). 1629-1645.
[19 A 1-10.]

*** A very fine copy, on large paper, in the original binding.

1657-69. **Biblia Sacra Polyglotta** complectentia textus originales, Hebraicum, cum Pentateucho Samaritano, Chaldaicum, Græcum, versionumque antiquarum, Samaritanæ, Græcæ LXXII. Interp., Chaldaicæ, Syriacæ, Arabicæ, Æthiopicæ, Persicæ, Vulg. Lat., etc. Edited by Brian WALTON. 6 vols. bound in 12. With the Lexicon Heptaglotton Edmundi CASTELLI, in 2 vols. Londini, Thomas Roycroft. 8 vols. in 14. Folio (measuring : Bible, 19¼-13½, and **Lexicon,** 19⅝-14 inches). 1657-1669.

[Case B.]

✱✱✱ Upon large paper, this work is of great rarity. This copy is exceptionally fine and tall and in a perfect state, except that the engraved title and portrait of Walton have been slightly cut down in the process of remounting. On the sides, JACOBVS. DVX. EBOR. This copy has the royal dedication. In the second volume of the Lexicon the first 32 pages have been very neatly inlaid.

1657. **Biblia Sacra Polyglotta.** . . . Edited by Brian WALTON. Two small-paper copies of the preceding, but without the Lexicon. 6 vols. Folio (17½-11 inches). 1657.
[3 A 3-8 and 47 A 7-12.]

HEBREW TEXTS.

1566. **Biblia Hebraica,** cum punctis. Antverpiæ ex officina Christ. Plantini, 1566. Quarto (8$\frac{7}{16}$-5⅜ inches).

[9 E 19.]

✱✱✱ Printed with great care, by command of Bomberg, the great publisher of Hebrew books.

1571-72. **Hebraicorum Bibliorum.** Veteris Testamenti Latina interpretatio, opera olim Xantis Pagnini Lucensis : nunc verò Ben. Ariæ Montani Hispalësis ; Francisci Raphelengii Alnetani, Guidonis et Nicolai Fabriciorum Boderianorum fratrum collato studio ad Hebraicam dictionem diligentissimè expensa—Novum Testamentum Græce cum Vulgata interpretatione Latina Græci contextus lineis inserta, atque alia Ben Ariæ Montani Hispalensis operâ. Antverpiæ, Chris. Plantinus. 2 vols. in 1. Folio (15¼-14¼ inches). **1571-1572.**
[2 B 8.]

1573. **Biblia Hebraica cum notis criticis et versione Latina ad notas criticas facta,** accedunt Libri Græci, qui Deuterocanonici vocantur in tres classes distributi. Autore Carolo Francisco HOUBIGANT, O.J.S. Lutetiæ Parisiorum, A. C. **Briasson** et L. Durand. 4 vols. Folio (15½-10 inches). 1753.
[2 B 10-13.]

✱✱✱ A very fine and clean copy.

GREEK VERSIONS.

1545. **Biblia Græca**. Divinae Scripturae, Veteris ac Novi Testamenti, omnia, innumeris locis nunc demum, & optimorum librorum collatione, & doctorum uirorum operâ, multo quàm unquam antea emendatiora in lucem edita. Cum Cæs. Maiest. gratia et privilegio ad quinquennium. Basiliæ per Joan. Hervagium 1545. Folio (18-7⅛ inches).
[43 B. 25.]

  ** The preface of this edition, which is said to surpass in correctness both the Strasburg and Venetian editions, is by Melancthon. The edition is very little known and is rare.

1628. **Vetus Testamentum [Græcum]**. Secundum LXX et ex auctoritate Sixti. V. Pont. Max. Editum nunc primum e regione textus Græci apposita est Latina translatio. Versuum quoque numeri qui antea nulli erant, ad collationem Latinæ vulgatæ, in margine, quoad fieri potuit, inscripti sunt. Lutetiæ Parisiorum, apud Claudium Sonnium. 2 vols. Folio (14¼-9½ inches). 1628.
[19 C 16-17.]

1707-9. **Vetus Testamentum Septuaginta Interpretum.** Ex antiquissimo MS. Codice Alexandrino accuratè descriptum. Edidit Joannes Ernestus GRABE, S.T.P. Oxonii, Theatro Sheldoniano, Rich. Smith. Vols. 1 and 4 only. Folio (17¾-11 inches). 1707-1709.
[3 A 9-10.]

  ** Tomus 1, continens Octateuchum. Tomus [4] Ultimus, continens Psalmorum, Jobi, ac tres Salomonis libros, cum Apocrypha ejusdem, nec non Siracidæ Sapientia.

LATIN VERSIONS.

1495. [Biblia Integra : summata : distincta : accuratius re-emendata : utriusque testamenti concordantiis illustrata.] Basileæ, Johannem Froben de Hamelburgk. 8vo. (6⅞-4 inches). 1495.
Imperfect, wanting four leaves, title and three following leaves (a1 to a4).
[38 B 18.]

1497. **Biblia cum summariis concordantiis : divisionibus : quattuor** repertoriis ppositis : numerique foliorum distinctione : **terse** et fidelit impssa. [Parisiis], Franciscus Fradin et Johānes Piuard. Folio (10½-6⅞ inches). 1497.
[38 B 15.]

  ** The Acts of the Apostles in this version follows the Epistle to the Hebrews. This copy is quite perfect and in excellent condition, but for a small hole piercing ten leaves in the Acts.

1526. Sacra Biblia **ad LXX Interpretum** fidem diligentissime trålata. Basileæ, per **Andream Cratandrum.** Quarto (8¼-5¾ inches). 1526.
[38 B 17.]

** The title **and** first leaf **are** soiled, and the **volume** is slightly wormed in **parts ;** otherwise a clean copy.

1597. Biblia Sacra, sive, Libri Canonici Priscæ Judæorum Ecclesiæ à Deo traditi, Latini recèns ex Hebræo facti, brevibusque Scholiis illustrati ab Immanuele Tremellio & Francisco Junio. Accesserunt Libri qui vulgo dicuntur Apocryphi, Latinè redditi, & notis quibusdam aucti à Francisco Junio. Multo omnes quàm antè emendatius editi & aucti locis innumeris : quibus etiam adjunximus Novi Testamenti libros ex sermone Syro ab eodem Tremellio & ex Græco à Theodoro Beza in Latinum versos, notisque **itidem illustratos.**

Tertia **et** omnium quæ hodiè **extant novissima cura Francisci** Junii cujus æmula ad verbum **nuper Hanoviæ impressa, sed** longè inferior.

Londini, Excudebat **G. B., R. N., and R. B., Anno Dom.** 1597. Folio (11¾-8 inches).
[28 D 7.]

1618. Biblia Sacra Vulgatæ Editionis. Sixti. V. Pont. Max. jussu recognita atque edita. Antverpiæ, Ex Officina Plantiniana apud Balthasarem et Joannem Moretos fratres. 3 vols. Quarto (9½-7 inches). 1618.
[3 E 4-6.]

1618. Biblia Latina Vulgata. To which is appended ' Romanæ correctionis in Latinis Bibliis editionis Vulgatæ jussu Sixti. V. Pont. Max. recognitis **loca** insigniora observata à Francisco LUCA. Lutetiæ Parisiorum, R. Fouët, N. Buon, S. Cramoisy. Folio (15½-9¾ inches). 1618.

Imperfect, wanting two leaves : **title and ā2.**
[3 B 3.]

GERMAN VERSION.

1586. Biblia, Das ist : Die gantze heilige Schrifft Deudsch. **D. Mart. Luth.** Begnadet mit Churfürstlicher zu Sachssen Freyheit. Wittemberg Gedruckt durch Zacharias Lehman 1586. Quarto (7½-4¾ inches).
[36 B 31.]

DUTCH VERSION.

1616. Biblia Dat is de Gantsche Heijlighe Schriftuere **voortijts bij Jacob van Liesvelt** ootgegaen na de alderoudtste ende corectste copijen die gedruckt zijn. Arnhem, Jan Janssen. Folio (11⅝-7⅝ inches). 1616.
[38 B **14.**]

SPANISH VERSION.

1569. La Biblia que es, los sacros libros **del** viejo y nuevo **Testamento.** Trasladada en Español [por CASIODORO DE

REYNA]. Without place or name of printer. Folio (9⅝-7⅝ inches). 1569.
[38 B 16.]

⁎⁎⁎ This Bible is popularly known as the 'Bear Bible,' on account of the cut upon the title-page, which represents a bear sucking honey from a tree. The title is the genuine original, with the 1569 imprint, and not the reprinted title of 1622.

ENGLISH VERSIONS.
Arranged chronologically.

1535. **Reprint of the Coverdale Bible.** 'The Holy Scriptures, Faithfully and truly translated, By Myles COVERDALE, Bishop of Exeter 1535.' Reprinted from the copy in the library of his Royal Highness the Duke of Sussex for Samuel Bagster, 15, Paternoster Row, London. Folio (12½-10 inches). 1838.
[38 B 19.]

⁎⁎⁎ A reprint of the first edition of the entire Bible in English, which is now generally believed to have been printed at Antwerp by Jacob van Meteren. The seven preliminary leaves, which are in a different type, are supposed to have been printed by James Nicholson, of Southwark, who was probably the publisher of the volume.

1537. **The Bible.** MATTHEW'S (partly Tyndale's and partly Coverdale's Versions). [Probably printed at Antwerp by Jacob van Meteren] at the expense of Richard Grafton and Edward Whitchurch, in the year 1537. Folio (12½-9 inches).
Imperfect, wanting twenty-one leaves: title, first leaf of Kalendar, To the Chrysten Readers and A Table (thirteen leaves), Names of Books, etc. (one leaf), and Gg1 of part 1, title of New Testament (which is in facsimile), N8, O6, O8.
[38 A 1.]

⁎⁎⁎ This Bible, which is popularly known as 'Matthew's,' or 'the Bugge Bible,' was published by John Rogers, the first martyr under Queen Mary, under the assumed name of Thomas Matthew. The Old Testament to the end of the Book of Chronicles is Tyndale's translation, thence to the end of the Apocrypha Coverdale's, and the whole of the New Testament Tyndale's. The rendering of Psalm xci. 5, 'so that thou shalt not nede to be afrayed for eny bugges by nyght,' is common to Coverdale's, Matthew's, and Taverner's versions.

1539. **The Bible.** Published under the auspices of Thomas Lord Cromwell. Printed [partly in Paris, finished in London] by Rychard Grafton and Edward Whitchurch; fynisshed in Apryll, 1539. Folio (14⅞-9⅝ inches).
Imperfect, wanting three leaves: title of part 3 (AA1) and the two last leaves of the volume (NN7, NN8). The first title, which is imperfect, has been made up in facsimile; many other leaves are mutilated and partly missing.
[38 A 2.]

*** Although this **edition** was **commonly** called the first
edition of Cranmer's Great Bible, **Ames** says that the Archbishop had no hand whatever in it. It was put forth **by** Lord
Cromwell, who employed Coverdale to revise the then existing
translation. The woodcut titles and illustrations are attributed
to Hans Holbein.

1540. **The Bible**. 'Cranmer's, or the Great Bible,' with Cranmer's Prologue. Printed at London by Edward Whitchurch,
April and July, 1540. Folio (14⅝-9½ inches).
    Imperfect, wanting eight leaves : first title and five following
leaves and the two last leaves of the volume (NN7 and NN8).
A few other leaves are slightly damaged. A facsimile title,
supplied by Mr. George Offor, has been **appended to this**
copy.
[38 A 3.]
    *** The prologue of this copy begins with a large **flourished**
initial letter of twelve lines deep, and has the Latin quotations
in italic type, which features are peculiar to the July impression,
whilst the rendering of the first verse of Job xli. shows the text
to be of the April impression (or **first** edition of Cranmer's Bible).
This copy is probably made up of the two editions.

1540. **The Bible**. The Great **Bible**. **Printed at London by**
Thomas Petyt and Robert **Redman for Thomas Berthelet.**
Finisshed in Apryll, Anno **1540**. Folio (12 3/16-8⅜ inches).
    Imperfect, wanting **two leaves : first title and** second leaf of
calendar.
[38 A 4.]
    *** This is a reprint, or second edition, of the Bible printed
in 1539, and popularly, but erroneously, called the first edition
of Cranmer. One peculiarity of this edition is in Psalm xiv.,
of which seven lines commencing 'Their throte,' etc., is printed
in Roman type, and not in black letter, as the body of the text.

1541. **The Bible**. Cranmer's. Printed at London by Edwarde
Whitchurche and Fynyshed in November, 1541. Folio (15¼-10
inches).
[38 A 6.]
    *** An exceedingly fine and quite perfect copy, having **the**
rare leaf (CC8) at the end of the Book **of** Psalms, which **is**
seldom to be met with in a perfect state.
    This is the first edition of the Bible that was **ordered to be**
chained in **the** churches.

1541. **The Bible**. Cranmer's. **An imperfect** copy of the preceding. Fynyshed in November, 1541. **Folio** (15¼-10 inches).
    Wanting six leaves : the five leaves immediately following
title and CC8 (the rare leaf of the Psalms). Several other leaves
are repaired.
[38 **A** 5.]

1541. The Bible. Cranmer's. Another imperfect copy of the preceding. **Fynyshed in** November, **1541.** Folio ($15\frac{3}{16}$-$10\frac{1}{2}$ inches).

Wanting seventeen **leaves** : all before b1, b8, c1, and the last leaf of table (Mm6).
[38 A 7.]

1547. The Bible. Matthew's Version, revised by Edmund Becke. Printed at London by John Daye and W. Seres, **1547.** Folio ($11\frac{7}{16}$-7 inches).

Imperfect, wanting title **and** all before BB1, F5, G1 (of part 1), and all after T6, except U4 (of New Testament).
[38 B 1.]

.*. The title prefixed **to this** copy does not belong to it, but to Barker's Version of **1589,** popularly known as ' the Breeches Bible.'

1547. The Bible. Matthew's Version, revised by Edmund Becke. **Another copy of** the preceding. **1547.** ($11\frac{7}{16}$-7 inches).

Imperfect, wanting title and all before E1, F2 **to F5** (of part 1); A1 **to A8, B1 and all after R6** (of the New Testament).
[38 B 2.]

1549. The Bible. Matthew's. [A faulty reprint of the **1537** edition.] Printed at London by Wylliam Hyll and **Thomas** Raynaldes. 1549. Folio ($12\frac{7}{8}$-$7\frac{1}{2}$ inches).

Imperfect, wanting only the first title.
[38 B 3.]

.*. So erratic is the numbering of the leaves, that it is useless as a guide to the sequence of the **pages.**

1550. The Bible. Coverdale's. [Probably printed at Zurich by Christopher Froschover] for Andrew Hester, of London, 1550. Quarto ($8\frac{3}{4}$-7 inches).

Imperfect, wanting three leaves at end, comprising table of the Gospels and Epistles, concluding with the colophon.
[38 A 15.]

.*. This second foreign **edition of the** Coverdale Bible is printed in an angular German type, similar to the **1535** edition, but smaller, and is now believed to have come from the press of Chris. Froschover, at Zurich. **The** preliminary leaves, which are in a small black-letter type, **were** evidently printed in England.

The original title is imperfect ; the missing parts have **been** supplied in facsimile.

The volume has been judiciously rebound, the original sides with a beautifully-tooled lace edging carefully preserved.

1550. The Bible. Cranmer's. Printed at London by Edward Whytchurche. Quarto ($8\frac{5}{16}$-$5\frac{7}{8}$ inches), 1550.

Very imperfect, wanting the whole Book of Psalms, Ruth, part of Joshua, and the New Testament after the First Epistle to the Corinthians, as well as many other isolated sheets.
[38 A 10.]

1550. **The Bible.** CRANMER'S. **Another copy of the preceding.**
Quarto (8$\frac{8}{16}$-5$\frac{5}{8}$ inches). **1550.**
Imperfect, wanting **A1, D6, and all after Nn7, which ends**
the First Epistle of S. **John.**
[38 A 9.]

1551. **The Bible.** MATTHEW'S Version, revised by Edmund
BECKE. Printed at London by John Daye. Folio (10$\frac{11}{16}$-7$\frac{1}{8}$
inches). 1551.
Imperfect, wanting title, AA1, and the six last leaves (Uuuu3
to Uuuu8).
[38 B 4.]
  *** This Bible contains the Third Book of Machabees.

1551. **The Bible.** MATTHEW'S. Printed at London by Nicolas
Hyll for Thomas Petyt. Folio (11$\frac{3}{16}$-7$\frac{6}{16}$ inches). **1551.**
Imperfect, wanting only the last leaf, which has **been supplied**
in facsimile; certain other leaves have been repaired.
[38 B 5.]
  *** This edition is very badly printed; the broken and im-
perfect letters, which are almost innumerable, have in this copy
been filled in with pen and ink.

1551. **The Bible.** MATTHEW'S. Another copy of the **preceding.**
Folio (11$\frac{3}{16}$-7$\frac{6}{8}$ inches). 1551.
Imperfect, wanting all before aiiii, **a1, Aa1, Hh4, Qq8, AA1,**
AAa1, TTt2-TTt6.
[38 B 6.]
  *** Although in all other respects **this copy is** identical with
the preceding, there are certain variations in the signatures,
which prove it to be of another impression. N5 is here missigned M5; MMiii, and PPpii are likewise missigned; but in
the preceding copy these faults do not occur. The present copy
is probably an earlier impression than the former.

1553. **The Bible.** COVERDALE'S. Printed [at Zurich by Ch.
Froschover for] Richard Jugge. Quarto (9$\frac{1}{8}$-7 inches). 1553.
Imperfect, wanting mm8, nn1, pp8, qq1-qq4, and the three
leaves (table and colophon) at the end of New Testament.
[38 A 16.]
  *** Although this edition bears the name of Jugge as printer,
he is only responsible for the preliminary leaves; the text is
identical with that of 1550, which was printed for Hester by
Froschover. Jugge, who was less scrupulous than Hester, states
that this edition was printed *by* him; Hester states *for* him.
That the editions are identical is proved by the fault in the head-
line of folio 26, which in both copies reads ' Genesis,' instead of
' Exodus.'

1553. **The Bible.** COVERDALE'S. Another copy of the preceding.
Very imperfect, wanting the first eight leaves of Prolegomena,
including title, A1 to Cii, and all after OO7 (Heb. xiii.).
[38 A 17.]

$*_*$ Sheets of Barker and Bill's Bible of 1630 have been bound up at the commencement, in order to complete the text of Genesis.

1553. **The Bible.** CRANMER'S. Printed at London by Edwarde Whytchurche. Folio (12⅝-8⅝ inches). 1553.
[38 A 11.]
$*_*$ According to the MS. note in the British Museum copy, 'It has been said that Queen Mary destroyed the greater part of this impression.'

1553. **The Bible.** CRANMER'S. Printed at London by Richard Grafton. Quarto (7⅛-5⅛ inches). 1553.
Imperfect, wanting two leaves : title, and following leaf.
Appended to this volume are eleven leaves, comprising Calendar, the title to the Psalter, the order how the Psalter is appointed to be read, and the Table of Proper Lessons. Printed by W. Seres. 1567.
[38 A 12.]

1553. **The Bible.** CRANMER'S. Another copy of the preceding, but less perfect. Quarto (6½-5 inches). 1553.
Wanting seven leaves : title and following leaf (A1, A2), and three leaves at the end (M6 to M8).
[38 A 13.]

1562. **The Bible.** CRANMER'S. Printed at London by Richard Harrison. Folio (12¼-8¼ inches). 1562.
Imperfect, wanting all after P8 (Rev. xx.), portions of LL8, of Part 2, and the first two leaves (A1-2) of the New Testament have been torn away.
[38 A 18.]
$*_*$ The title, which has been remounted, is the same beautiful woodcut as that used in the 1537 Matthew Bible ; the central shield bearing the title has been cut away, and is now replaced by a manuscript facsimile.

1562. **The Bible.** CRANMER'S. Another copy of the preceding. Folio (12¼-8 inches). 1562.
Imperfect, wanting all before A1 (part of which is torn away), DD7, the title of New Testament, M3, P1, and all after P2 ; several other leaves are mutilated.
[38 A 19.]

1562. **The Bible.** CRANMER'S. Another copy of the preceding. Folio (12 6/16-8½ inches). 1562.
Imperfect, wanting many leaves ; a poor and mutilated copy.
[38 A 20.]

1566. **The Bible.** CRANMER'S. Printed at Rouen by C. Hamilton, at the cost and charges of Richard Carmarden. Folio (14⅝-9⅝ inches). 1566.
Imperfect, wanting four leaves : title, Aa2, Aa3, and the last leaf (table).
[38 A 8.]

。*。 This volume, which is beautifully printed in a large and clean type on fine thick paper, is in excellent state.

1568. **The Bible.** PARKER'S, or the BISHOPS' BIBLE.   Printed at London by Richard Jugge.   Folio (15-10½ inches).   1568.

Very imperfect, wanting : title, prolegomena, all before G7, A2, F7 and F8 of Part 3 ; P3 to P7 of the Apocrypha ; and A1 and all after N8 of the New Testament.   Many other leaves are mutilated.

[38 B 7.]

。*。 This is the first edition of the Bishops' Version, copies of which are rarely found in a perfect state.

1569. **The Bible.** CRANMER'S.   Printed at **London by Jhon** Cawood.   Quarto (7⅝-5⅝ inches).   [1569.]

Imperfect, wanting : title and prolegomena, SS7, SS8, TT8, Ddd7, R4 (Rev. xxii.), and the following two leaves, which are unsigned, being the Table to the Epistles and Gospels.

[38 A 14.]

。*。 This edition is sometimes confused with that of 1561 ; it may, however, be identified by **the** numbering of the folios, which is in ordinary figures ; in the 1561 edition it is in Roman figures.

1573. **The Bible.** PARKER'S or the BISHOPS' BIBLE.   Printed at London by Richard Jugge.   Quarto (8¼-6¼ inches).   1573.

Imperfect, wanting : title and first eleven leaves of prolegomena, A1, F1, L4, N8, P1, Y3, Y4 ; I3, V8 ; A2, A4, K5, K6, and all after O7 (of the New Testament) ; portions of a number of other leaves are missing.

[38 B 8.]

1577. **The Bible.** PARKER'S or the BISHOPS' BIBLE.   [Probably printed by Richard Jugge.]   Quarto (7-5 inches).   1577.

Imperfect, wanting only title and last leaf with colophon, otherwise complete.

Appended to this volume and preceding the Bible is 'Proper Lessons and Calendar,' forming eight leaves, and the Book of Common Prayer in the same type as the Bible. Following the Bible is the Psalter, by Sternhold, Hopkins, **etc.** Printed by John Daye, London.   **1579.**

Imperfect, wanting all after H4.

[38 B 10.]

1583. **The Bible.** GENEVAN VERSION.   'The Third **Part of the** Bible (after some Division), conteining fiue excellent **bookes,** most commodious for all Christians.   .'   Printed at London **by** Christopher Barker.   In 8vo. (4⅞-2⅝ inches).   1583.

Imperfect ; the title is mutilated and the preface to the reader wanting.

The volume also contains TOMSON'S New Testament of 1583, which is described under New Testaments.

[38 **C** 18.]

*** This is a portion of one of the Bibles popularly known as the Breeches Bible.

1637. **The Bible.** Known as the Royal or AUTHORIZED VERSION appointed to be read in Churches. Printed by Thomas Buck and Roger Daniel, printers to the University of Cambridge. Quarto (8¼-6¼ inches). 1637.

The Bible has been divided into three volumes and interleaved with old paper.

[38 B 11-13.]

*** The dedication is to the High and Mighty Prince James.

1640. **The Bible.** The Royal or AUTHORIZED VERSION. Printed at London by R. Barker and the assignes of John Bill. Folio (17⅜-11 inches). 1640.

[Case B.]

*** This is Bishop COMPTON'S copy, which was originally bound in silver and placed upon the altar on all the great festivals. When the cathedral was robbed in December, 1810, the massive covers were carried off by the thieves.

The volume in its original condition is thus described in Malcolm's *Londinium Redivivum*, III., 144: 'A Bible, with a silver gilt cover, representing a temple, with Moses and Aaron in the intervals between the columns, and Jacob's dream on one side, with the inscription, *Verbum Domini manet in æternum*. On the other leaf, the prophet fed by a raven, and *Habent Moysen et Prophetas: audiant illos.*'

1659-60. **The Bible.** The Royal or AUTHORIZED VERSION. Printed at Cambridge by John Field. Folio (17-11¼ inches). 1659-1660.

[38 B 9.]

*** A very fine and perfect copy. The first title bears the 1660 imprint, but the title of the New Testament and the colophon have 1659.

The volume is bound in morocco, and on either side bears the following inscription:

'Donvm Mariæ HORNE vid: Relict: Roberti.
Horne civis et bibliopolæ Lond:
dicatum Altari Ecclesiæ Cathedralis.
Divi Pauli Lond: Anno Salutis.
Christianæ MDCCIIIII.'

1819. **The Holy Bible.** Two volumes, folio. Oxford, Clarendon Press, 1819 (18⅝-11⅞).

'This Bible was laid on the altar at the coronation of his Majesty King George IV. in Westminster Abbey, July 19, 1821, and became the property of James Webber, B.D., as Prebendary of Westminster.'

Presented to the Cathedral Church of Saint Paul, London, to

be used for the daily service, by William Charles Fynes Webber,
M.A., son of the above James Webber, minor canon **and sacrist**
of S. Paul's.   December 25, **1855.**

The volumes were used in **the** Cathedral from Christmas,
1855, **to** Christmas, 1871, when the new Lectionary was introduced, and were then placed by Mr. Webber in the library
They **were** originally bound in blue velvet, now in morocco.
[2 A 1, 2.]

NEW TESTAMENTS.

POLYGLOT.

1568. Novum   Testamentum   Polyglottum, **Hebraica,**
Græca, Latina.   Immanuel TREMELLIUS.   **Heidelbergæ,**
Karl Martias.   Folio (16-11 inches).   1568.

Imperfect, wanting only **the** first title, otherwise a **very fine**
copy.

The Testament is followed **by** 'Grammatica Chaldæa et **Syra**
Imm. Tremellii.'
[2 B 1.]

GREEK TEXTS.

1524. Novi Testamenti [Græci] omnia.   Basileæ, Apud Jo.
Bebelium. Mense Augusto An. 1524.   2 vols. 8vo. (6⅝-4 inches).
[25 G. 18-19.]

** The title **of vol. i. bears** a manuscript note, 'ex Bibliotheca Colbertina.'

1536. Novum Testamentum [Græcum] per Des. Eras. Rotero.
novissime recognitum.   Antverpiæ, apud Martinum Cesarem.
Anno Salutis 1536.   8vo. (5½-3⅜ inches).

Imperfect, wanting K1, and all **after** Vv3 (probably only one
leaf of the index).
[36 G 11.]

1550. Novum Jesu Christi D.N. Testamentum ex Bibliotheca Regia.   Lutetiæ   Parisiorum   Ex   Officina   Roberti
Stephani.   Folio (12½-8½ inches).   **1550.**
[3 C 9.]

1572. Novum Testamentum Græce **cum Vulgata interpre-**
tatione Latina Græci **contextus lineis inserta.**   Ben
Ariæ MONTANI Hispalensis.   Antverpiæ. Chris. Plantinus.   **Folio**
(15¼-14½ inches).   1572.
[2 B 8.]

** This Testament is bound up with the Hebraicorum
Bibliorum Veteris Testamenti Latina interpretatio, etc.   1571.

1576. Novum Testamentum [Græcum].   Obscurorum vocum
et quorundam loquendi generum accuratas partim suas partim
aliorum interpretationes margini adscripsit Henr. STEPHANUS.
Lutetiæ. Henr. Stephanus.   8vo. (4⅝-3 inches).   **1576.**
[38 C 33.]

1582. **Novum Testamentum [Græcum] sive novum fœdus.**
Cuius Græco contextui respondent interpretationes duæ : una
vetus : altera, **nova** Theodori Bezæ, diligenter ab **eo** recognita.
Eiusdem Th. **Bezæ annotationes** quas itidem hac tertia editione
recognovit. [Lutetiæ Parisiorum. Robertus **Stephanus.**] Folio
(13½-8¾ inches). 1582.
[2 C 15.]

1628. **Novum Jesu Christi Domini Nostri Testamentum.**
Textui Græco conjuncta **est** versio Latina Vulgata, summorum
Pontificum Sixti V. and Clementis VIII. autoritate edita et
recognita. **Quæ sunt** hoc tomo præstita, docebit sequens ad
Lectorem **epistola. Tomus** Tertius. Lutetiæ Parisiorum, Apud
Claudium **Sonnium,** 1628. **Folio (14-9** inches.)
[30 A 16.]
⁎ This is the New Testament portion or third volume of
the Bible of this date.

1633. **Novi** Testamenti [Græci] Libri **omnes, recens nunc
editi. Cum** notis et animadversionibus doctissimorum ; præsertim
vero **Roberti** Stephani, Josephi Scaligeri, Isaaci Casauboni.
Variæ item Lectiones ex **antiquissimis** exemplaribus et **celeber-
rimis** Bibliothecis desumptæ. Londini Apud Richardum
Whittakerum Bibliopolam. 8vo. (6⁵⁄₁₆-4 inches). **1633.**
[26 G 34.]
Appended to this volume is The Whole Book of Psalmes,
collected into Eng. Meeter by T. Sternhold, J. Hopkins and
others. London, printed by A. M. for the Companie of
Stationers, 1647.

1633. **Novum Testamentum [Græcum].** Ex Regiis aliisque
optimis editionibus, hac nova **expressum :** cui quid accesserit,
Præfatio **docebit.** Lugd. Bat. **Ex Officina** Elzeviriorum. 8vo.
(4⁵⁄₈-2⅝ inches). 1633.
[38 C 35.]

1642. **Novum Testamentum Græcum, cum variis lectionibus.** R. Stephani. Lutetia Parisiorum, ex. typog. reg.,
3 vols. Folio (16¼-10½ inches). **1642.**
[1 B 5-7.]
⁎ These three volumes comprise two copies of the Testament : the first is interleaved and bound in 2 vols., lettered 1
and 2 ; the second copy is not interleaved, but is uniformly
bound in 1 vol., lettered vol. 3. Both copies are copiously
annotated in MS. by the Rev. Dr. Mangey.

1642. **Novum Testamentum [Græcum] sive novum fœdus.**
Cuius Græco contextui respondent interpretationes duæ : una
veteris : **altera nova** Theodori Bezæ diligenter ab eo recognita.
Eiusdem Th. **Bezæ** annotationes. **Accesset** etiam Joachimi
Camerarii in Novum Fœdus Commentariis. Cantabrigiæ. Roger
Daniel. Folio (13½-8½ inches). 1642.
[2 C 1.]

1652. **Novi Testamenti** [Græci] Libri **Omnes**. Editio nova accurata. Londini, ex officina Rogeri **Danielis**. 1652. 8vo. (5⅞-3¼ inches).
[36 H 17.]
Appended to this copy is The Whole Book of Psalmes, collected into **Eng**. Metre by T. Sternhold, J. Hopkins and others. London, printed by the Companie of Stationers, 1654.

1665. **Novum Testamentum Græcum**. Cantabrigiæ. J. Field. 1665.
A small edition in 8vo. (5¹⁷/₁₆-2⅞ inches), inlaid and mounted to folio size (12⅞-8⅛ inches).
[2 C 2.]

1710. **Novum Testamentum Græcum** cum lectionibus **variantibus** MSS. exemplarium, versionum, editionum, SS. **Patrum et** Scriptorum ecclesiasticorum ; et in easdem notis. **Accedunt** loca Scripturæ Parallela aliaque exegetica. . . . Studio **et labore** Joannis Millii S.T.P. . . . Roterodami, Apud **Casparum** Fritsch et Michaelem Böhm. Folio (14⅞-9¼ inches). **1710**.
[6 C 8.]

1711. **Novum Testamentum** [Græcum] Post priores Steph. Curcellæi, tum et D.D. Oxoniensium labores ; quibus Parallela Scripturæ Loca, **nec non** variantes lectiones ex plus C. MSS. & antiquis versionibus collectæ, exhibentur . . . Cum prolegomenis G.D.T.M. [Gerardus De Trajecto Mosæ] et **notis** in fine adjectis. Amstelædami, **ex** officina Wetsteniana. 1 **vol.** in 2. 8vo. (6½-3⅞ inches). **1711**.
[22 G 12-13.]

1751. **Novum Testamentum Graecum** editionis receptæ cum lectionibus variantibus Codicum MSS., Editionum, Aliarum Versionum et Patrum. Nec **non** commentario pleniore ex Scriptoribus veteribus Hebraeis, **Graecis et** Latinis . . . . Opera et studio Joannis Jacobi Wetstenii. Amstelædami, ex officina Dommeriana. 2 vols. in 3. Folio (13⅜-8½ inches). **1751**.
[31 B 11-13.]
Appended to this copy is **Duæ Epistolæ S.** Clementis Romani, Discipuli Petri Apostoli, Quas **ex** codice manuscripto Novi Testamenti Syriaci nunc primum erutas, cum versione Latina apposita, Edidit Jo. Jacobus Wetstenius. Lugduni Batavorum. Typis Eliæ Luzac Jun. (27 pp.). **1752**.

1763. **Novum Testamentum Græcum, ad** fidem Græcorum solùm Codicum MSS. nunc primùm expressum, adstipulante Joanne Jacobo Wetstenio: Juxta sectiones Jo. Alberti Bengelii divisum ; Et nova Interpunctione sæpius illustratum. Accessere in altero volumine Emendationes Conjecturales. Virorum doctorum undecunque collectæ. Londini. Cura, Typis et sumptibus G.B. 2 vols. 8vo. (6½-3⅞ inches). 1763.
[25 G 3-4.]

1786. **Novum** Testamentum Græcum e **Codice MS. Alex-andrino,** qui Londini in Bibliotheca **Musei Britannici asservatur.** Descriptum a C. G. WOIDE. Londini. Folio (18-11½ inches). 1786.
[1 A 3.]

N.D. **Novum Testamentum Græcum.** Without place, name of printer, or date [probably R. STEPHANUS]. 8vo. (6-3¾ inches).

Imperfect, **wanting title and** all before b1, and all after Kk9, (S. Matthew commences **on** folio 1 (b1), with a space for the initial B five lines deep; Revelation ends **on** folio 397a (HH10); after which follow the Lives of the Evangelists and an Analysis of the several **Epistles,** ending on KK9b).
[38 C 35 *bis.*]

LATIN VERSION.

1540. **Novum** Testamentum Latinum, **ad** antiquissima Græcorum exemplaria, **quam** diligentissime **castigatum : inque** Latinam phrasim transfusum, quicquid **erat** Idiotismi uel Græci uel Hebræi. Quin & scripturarum **concordantiis,** una cum allusionibus, **quam** accuratissime **illustratum.** . . . Estque præfixa præfatio, quæ, præter alia sacrarum literarum cognitu necessaria, argumenta quoque totius noui Instrumenti ex ordine continent. Per B. Galterum Delænum. . . . Excudebat Londini Joannes Mayler. Anno Dñi. 1540. Quarto (9⅛-6½ inches). Imperfect, wanting a2, and all after Nnn4.
[26 E. 34.]

LATIN AND GERMAN VERSION.

1556. Novum Testamentum **Latino** Germanicum, in usus studiosorum, nunc primum **ordinatum** & editum. Das gantz Neüw **Testamēt** Latin unnd Teütsch neüwlich zü gutem **den** studierenden geordnet und aussgangen. Gedruckt zü Basel **bey** Niclaus Brylinger im jar **1556.** 8vo. (6⅛-3⅞ inches).
[36 G. 15.]

GERMAN VERSION.

1591. Das Newe Testament **D.** Mart. Luther. Mit sonder-lichem Fleiss auffs neuw mit Figuren, jeder capitel **summarien,** Concordantzen und Zeiger aller für neiñer Puncten **der H. Schrifft** . . . . Gedruckt zu Franckfurt am Mayn durch **Nicolaum** Bassæum. 1591. 8vo. (6-4 inches).
[56 G. 16.]

DUTCH VERSION.

1553. Her **Nieuwe** Testament **ons Heeren** Jesu Christi. Antwerp, Jan Wijnrijer. 8vo. (15⅛-3 inches). 1553.
[38 C 32.]

2

FRENCH VERSIONS.

1548. Le Nouveau Testament de nostre Seigneur Jesu Christ. [Founded upon COVERDALE.] Anvers, Mathieu Crom. 8vo. ($6\frac{6}{18}$-4 inches). 1548.

[38 C 31.]

*** The cuts in this edition are the same as those used in the 1538 English Coverdale. The volume is quite perfect and in excellent preservation.

1702. Le Nouveau Testament de Notre Seigneur Jesus-Christ. Traduit sur l'ancienne edition latine. Avec des remarques literales et critiques sur les principales difficultez. A Trevoux, De l'Imprimerie S.A.S. Et par les soins d'Estienne Ganeau, Directeur de la dite Imprimerie. 4 parts in 2 vols. 8vo. ($6\frac{6}{18}$-$4\frac{3}{8}$ inches). 1702.

[9 G. 13-14.]

1710. Le Nouveau Testament de Notre Seigneur Jesus Christ. Traduit en François selon l'Edition Vulgate, avec les differences du Grec. Nouvelle edition, revuë. . . . A Mons, chez Gaspard Migeot. 8vo. ($5\frac{7}{8}$-$3\frac{1}{2}$ inches). 1710.

[22 G. 22.]

ITALIAN VERSION.

1576. Il Nuovo Testamento di Giesu Christo Nostro Signore. Della Stampa di Giov. Battista Pineroli. 1576. 8vo. ($6\frac{1}{8}$-4 inches).

[36 G. 14.]

ENGLISH VERSIONS.

[1525?.] New Testament. TYNDALE'S. [Probably printed at Worms by Peter Schoeffer.] 8vo. ($5\frac{7}{8}$-$3\frac{1}{2}$ inches). [1525.]

Imperfect, wanting seventy-one leaves . title, A1-A4, B1, B8, C1, C8, D8, E1, E8, F1, F7, F8, P5, BB1, BB2, BB7, blank leaf BB8, Hh1-Hh8, Pp1, Pp2, Pp3, and all after Pp6 (40 leaves). (These missing leaves have been supplied in facsimile from the Bristol copy by Mr. Francis Fry, and have been bound together in a separate volume.)

[38 C 1.]

*** This is a copy of the first complete English edition of the New Testament, and constitutes the 'gem,' or, using the words of Ames, 'the phœnix of the library;' only one other copy is known to have survived the flames—that in the Baptist College, Bristol, which is almost perfect, wanting only the title-page.

When this copy was first discovered by Dr. Cotton in 1821 it was in half-binding, lettered on the back 'Lant's Testament,' an entirely misleading title.

Dr. Cotton, in describing the volume, says : 'Its former owner, as if afraid of a second Bishop Tonstall, has contrived most ingeniously to disguise and disfigure it by intermixing the leaves of the Gospels and Epistles with each other in the

strangest manner. Surely it well deserves to be carefully taken
to pieces and examined . . .' This ill-advised suggestion has
unfortunately been adopted; the sheets have been arranged in
proper sequence and the volume rebound, thus destroying what
in all probability was a contemporary binding, and, what is even
more to be deplored, the striking evidence that the copy
originally afforded of the methods adopted to disguise and disfigure the interdicted volumes in order to avoid detection in
those early days of the Reformation, when the reading and
possession of any part of the Bible in the vernacular tongue
were strictly prohibited, and the search for copies vigorously
carried out with a view to their destruction.

Although the Testament bears no date, and we have no
evidence that it was dated, certain events in the life of the
translator, which have been brought to light during the present
century, justify us in fixing the date of its production as 'late in
the year 1525.'

That the volume was issued without any mention of the translator's name is evident from Tyndale's own words (in 1528) in
his preface to the 'Wicked Mammon': 'The cause why I set
my name before this little treatise, and have not rather done it
in the New Testament, is . . .' giving us undoubted proof of
the purity of Tyndale's motives in undertaking this work, which
was not intended to secure the fame of the translator. Tyndale
had not laboured for money or applause, but with his character-
istic unselfishness and noble disregard for fame was content that
he himself should be forgotten if only the Word of God might
be permitted to go abroad in the English tongue.

This translation has been referred to, and not inappropriately,
as the 'grand foundation-stone of England's greatness.'

1525. **The New** Testament. TYNDALE'S. Being a verbatim
reprint of the first translation of the Testament published in
[1525] by that eminent Scholar and Martyr, Wm. Tyndale.
With a memoir of his life and writings by George OFFOR.
London: Sam. Bagster. 1836. 8vo. (8¾-6¾ inches).
[38 C 29.]

*** The cuts and initial letters in this reprint are emblazoned
in the same manner as the Bristol copy, and in the exact colours
of it; a title-page has likewise been improvised from the various
cuts ornamentally arranged.

The text is unsatisfactory from a bibliographical point of view.

1525. **The New Testament.** TYNDALE'S. Facsimile texts.
The first printed English New Testament. Translated by
William Tyndale. Supposed to have been printed at Cologne
in the year 1525. Photo-lithographed from the unique fragment now in the Grenville collection, British Museum. Edited
by Edward Arber. Quarto (8¾-6½ inches). **London.** 1871.
[38 C 37.]

*** This fragment is highly interesting as being one of the first sheets of the English **New Testament thrown off by** the press. Tyndale arrived at Cologne early in **the** year 1525, and at once commenced his labours by printing **his** New Testament. But little progress had been made when the work was interdicted, and Tyndale was compelled to fly to Worms for safety, taking with him as many of the printed sheets as he could secure. **There is** no evidence, however, that this edition was ever completed. Before the close of the year, the great object of his life had been accomplished, in the putting forth of the complete New Testament, **a** copy of which has been described in the preceding note.

1534. **The New Testament.** Tyndale's. 'The **Newe** Testament, dylygently corrected and compared with the Greke by Wyllyam Tindale : and fynesshed in the yere of oure Lorde God A.M.D. & xxxiiii., in the moneth of November.' Printed at Antwerp by Marten Emperowr. 8vo. (5⅛-3½ inches).

Imperfect, wanting the last **two** leaves (Ee7 and Ee8).

[38 C 2.]

*** This **is** Tyndale's own second edition.

1536. **The New Testament.** Tyndale's. Name of place **and** printer unknown [but probably printed **at** London by Thomas Berthelet]. Folio (10½-6¹⁵⁄₁₆ inches). 1536.

Imperfect, wanting eight leaves A1 to **A4, Aa4, and** the three last leaves RR1-RR3.

[38 **C 21.**]

1536. **The New Testament.** Tyndale's. Known as the Blank Stone Edition. Name of place and printer unknown [but probably printed at Antwerp by William Vostermann or Symon Cowke]. Quarto (7³⁄₁₆-5⅝ inches). 1536.

Imperfect, wanting title, Wm. T. to the Christian Reader (three leaves), r8, G1-G6, G8, H2, and all after I8. Seven of the missing leaves have been supplied by Mr. George Offor in facsimile, and are inserted—G1-G4, G6, G8 and H2.

[38 C 22.]

*** This edition derives its name, 'The Blank **Stone** Edition,' from the fact that in **the** cut which precedes **his** Epistles the stone **is** blank upon which the Apostle Paul **is** resting his foot ; in **other** copies it has a mole **or** the engraver's initials in the blank space.

Appended to this volume at the commencement **is :** The Book of Common Prayer, wanting the title and some preliminary leaves [probably printed by Barker about 1613]. This is followed by the Psalter after the Great Bible, printed by Robt. Barker, 1613. After the Revelation, 'Here folowe the Epistles taken out of the Old Testament, which are red in the Church after the use of Salysburye upon certayne dayes of the year"; and at the end of the volume, following the New Testament, is the Psalter collected into English meetre by Sternhold, Whittingham, and Hopkins, etc. London, for the Company of Stationers. 1614.

1536. **The New** Testament. TYNDALE'S. Name of place and printer unknown. 8vo. (5⅞-3⅝ inches). [1536.]
Very imperfect, wanting all before D6 (S. Matt. xx.), t8, v4-v8, x2-x7, y1, y2, y5, y7, y8, and all after aa8.
[38 C 24.]

1536. **The New Testament**. TYNDALE'S. Name of place and printer unknown. 8vo. (5-3¼ inches). 1536.
Very imperfect and mutilated, wanting title and any preliminary leaves before *ii, N1-N8, Q5, T1-T8, 26-28, b8, h2-h8, l6, l7, t8, x5, z1.
[38 C 23.]
⁂ This edition is **not identical with the preceding**. In certain points it agrees with the Spencer copy, and in other points it agrees with the Bristol copy; it is quite possible that it is a **made-up copy**.

1536. **The New Testament**. TYNDALE'S. Name of place and printer unknown. A fragment of thirteen leaves, comprising *ii. to *viii. (W. T. to the Reader, An Exhortation by Erasmus Roterodamus, and the second title), A1, A2 to A5, B3 and B4. 8vo. (5⅝-3⅝ inches). [1536.]
[38 C 8.]
⁂ This fragment is bound up at the commencement of the 1539 Testament, printed by M. Crom, and is a portion of the same edition as the Spencer copy, described by Mr. Francis Fry as No. 10.

1538. **The New** Testament. COVERDALE'S Version, with Tyndale's prologues. Printed at Antwerp by Matthew Crom. 8vo. (5⅞-3¾ inches). 1538.
Imperfect, wanting: title and seven following preliminary leaves, A1-Aiii, A7, A8, I1, I2, I7, I8, K1, and K8.
[38 C 3.]
⁂ This edition is illustrated with **some 200 woodcuts**, besides ornamental initials and tailpieces.

1538. **The New** Testament. English and Latin. The English of Myles COVERDALE, with the Latin Vulgate. Printed at Paris by Fraunces Regnault for Richard Grafton and Edward Whitchurch, cytezens of London, in Novembre, 1538. 8vo. (6³⁄₁₆-4³⁄₁₆ inches).
[38 C 4.]

1538. **The New Testament**. English and Latin. The English of TYNDALE, with the Latin of ERASMUS. Printed at London by Robert Redman. Quarto (8⅝-6¾ inches). 1538.
Imperfect, wanting six leaves: the four preliminary leaves comprising title, almanack and kalendar, A1, and the last leaf.
[38 C 5.]
⁂ A facsimile title by Mr. Geo. Offor has been inserted, which is a facsimile of the second title, varying considerably from the first.

1538. **The New Testament.** English and Latin. The English
of COVERDALE with the Latin Vulgate [revised] by Johan
HOLLYBUSHE. Printed at London by James Nicholson. Quarto
(7¼-5⅝ inches). 1538.

Imperfect, wanting **fourteen** leaves : the six preliminary
leaves, comprising title **and** prolegomena, JJ3-JJ6, Vv1, **2, 7,**
and 8.

[38 C 6.]

*** This is usually described as the second edition of the
New Testament in Latin and English, after the Vulgate by
Myles Coverdale, printed by Nicholson   Nothing is known of
Hollybushe, whose name appears on the title-page, and it is now
generally supposed to be a pseudonym adopted by Nicholson in
consequence of the complaints of Coverdale against the in-
accuracies **in** the former edition printed by **him.**

1539. **The New Testament.** COVERDALE'S.   Printed at
Antwerp by Matthew Crom. 8vo. (6-3¾ inches). 1539.

Imperfect, wanting title **and all before** B2, B3, V1-V8, X1-**X3,**
X8, s1 and **2,** and all after **s4.**

[38 C 8.]

*** The illustrations **in this** copy **are the** same as those of the
1538 edition, **but** the type **is** larger.

Appended **to** this copy is a fragment (thirteen leaves) of the
1536 Testament of Tyndale, which will be found described
under that **year.**

1539. **The New Testament.** COVERDALE'S.   Another copy of
the preceding. 8vo. (6-3⅛ inches).

Very imperfect, having only 270 leaves, and wanting all before
sig. C and **many** other leaves.

[38 C 7.]

1539. **The New Testament.** TAVERNER'S.   A Revision of
Matthew's version by Rycharde Taverner. Printed at London
by Thomas Petyt for Thomas Berthelet. Quarto (7¹³⁄₁₆-5⁵⁄₁₆ inches).
1539.

[38 C **9.**]

*** An exceedingly fine **copy in perfect state, which is pro-**
bably unique.

1549. **The New Testament.** English and Latin. **The English**
of TYNDALE with the Latin of ERASMUS. Printed **at London**
by Wyllyam Powell. Quarto (8¾-6½ inches). **1549.**

Imperfect, wanting only the title.

Appended to this volume and preceding the Testament is
The Book of Common Prayer. London, Barker and Bill.
Quarto (much cut down). 1639. And following the Testament is
The Whole Book of Psalmes, by Sternhold, Hopkins, and others
(with music). London, for the Company of Stationers. Quarto.
1639.

[38 C 10.]

1550. **The New Testament.** English and Latin. The English of TYNDALE with the Latin of ERASMUS. Printed at London by Thomas Gaultier, pro I. C. 8vo. (7⅛-4½ inches). 1550.

Imperfect, wanting eleven leaves : title, folios 1 and 6 of the unsigned preliminary leaves, ✠ 3 and 4, A8, Hh6-Hh8, Ii1, Ii2. (The title and A8 have been supplied in facsimile)

[38 C 11.]

*** It has not yet been ascertained to whom the initials I. C. refer ; Lewis suggested John Cawood, others have suggested Sir John **Cheke**, but upon insufficient authority. Sir John Cheke did about this time translate a portion of the New Testament, but it is evident upon comparison that his translation does not agree with the present.

1550. **The New Testament.** CRANMER'S. Printed by Jhon Oswen of Worcester. 8vo. (7⅛-5½ inches). [1550.]

A fragment of eight leaves, commencing on Ss1 ('The notes and expositions of the darke places,' etc.), and ending on Ss8 with the colophon making one complete sheet.

[38 C 34.]

*** This seems to be quite a distinct edition from that described by Lea Wilson.

1551. **The New Testament.** TYNDALE'S. Printed at London by John Daye. Quarto (10½-7 inches). 1551.

[38 C 12.]

*** Although this volume is lettered New Testament, and has the appearance of being a distinct edition, it is in reality the New Testament portion of Daye's Bible of 1551, which is determined from the colophon, ending 'The Ende of the Old and Newe Testament.'

1552. **The New Testament.** TYNDALE'S version revised by Jugge. Printed at **London** by Rychard Jugge. Quarto (7⅜-5⅝ inches). 1552.

Very imperfect, wanting title, and all before Cii, as well as the last leaf with colophon.

[38 C 13.]

*** Although the title and colophon is wanting, we find at the end of 'The Actes of the Apostles' Jugge's large device, with the words 'Imprinted at London by Rychard Jugge,' etc.

Appended to this volume and preceding the Testament is The Psalter or Psalms of David . . . after the translation of the Great Bible. 4to. Printed by Wm. Seres, London [? 1583]; following the Testament is The Whole Boke of Psalmes, by Sternhold, Whittingham, Hopkins, and others. 4to. Printed by Iohn Daye, London, 1580.

Imperfect, wanting all after page 322.

1552. **The New Testament.** TYNDALE'S. Another copy of the preceding, measuring 8₁₆¹-5⅝ inches.

Imperfect, wanting eight leaves : title and first four leaves

of calendar, A1, P5, Q8. A facsimile title in pen and ink has been supplied. Sig. P5 has been made up by a leaf from the 1553 edition.
[38 C 14.]

Appended to this volume, following the Testament, is 'The Whole Boke of Psalmes,' by Sternhold, Hopkins, and others. 4to. Printed by John Daye, London, 1582.

Imperfect, wanting all after H6.

1552? **The New Testament.** TYNDALE'S version revised by **Jugge.** Printed at London by Rychard Jugge. 8vo. (4$\frac{5}{16}$-3 **inches).** Without date [probably 1552].

Imperfect, wanting title and first portion of the Epistle to Edward VI., by R. Jugge, making evidently two leaves. As the preliminary leaves are unsigned, and no perfect copy is known, it is impossible to say with any degree of certainty what is missing.

[38 C 25.]

1566? The **New Testament.** TYNDALE'S version revised by Jugge. Printed at London by Rychard Jugge. Quarto (8$\frac{1}{4}$-6 inches) [1566?].

Imperfect, wanting title and last leaf with colophon. A facsimile title has been supplied by Mr. Geo. Offor.
[38 C 15.]

Appended to this volume is The Psalter [Cranmer's]. Printed by Edw. Whytchurche, London. 4to. [probably 1550].

Imperfect, wanting title and all before A2, also A8, D1, D8.

1566. **The New** Testament. TYNDALE'S version revised by Jugge. Another copy of the preceding, measuring only 7$\frac{1}{2}$-5$\frac{3}{8}$ inches.

Very imperfect and much mutilated.

[38 C 16.]

In this volume, preceding the Testament is 'A Psalter,' printed in a bold black-letter type, probably by Jugge, in the same type as the 1568 Bishops' Bible.

Imperfect, wanting title, colophon, etc.

And following the Testament is The Psalter, preceded by Veni Creator, etc., in metre, with musical notation, and the Song of the Three Children.

Very imperfect, wanting title, colophon, etc.

1575? **The New Testament.** GENEVAN. 8vo. (5$\frac{11}{16}$-3$\frac{1}{4}$ inches). Probably printed abroad in the year 1575.

Imperfect, wanting only the title.

[38 C 28.]

⁂ In this volume at the commencement are eight leaves of the 'Forme of Prayers according to the use of the English Church in Geneva,' bearing the imprint of Johne Ros for Henrie Charteris, 1575.

1582. **The New Testament**. RHEMISH VERSION. Printed at
Rhemes by John Fogny. Quarto ($8\frac{7}{8}$-$6\frac{1}{4}$ inches). 1582.
[38 C 17.]

⁎⁎⁎ This is a translation from the Vulgate by Dr. William
Allyn, being the New Testament translated 'in the English
Colledge of Rhemes,' as the prefatory matter indicates. The
Douay Old Testament portion was not published till 1609-1610.

This copy, with the exception of a small portion of the title,
which is missing, is perfect and in excellent condition.

1583. **The New Testament**. TOMSON'S Revision. Translated
from the Greek into Latin by Beza, and Englished by Laurence
Tomson. Printed at London by Christopher Barker. 8vo.
($4\frac{7}{16}$-$2\frac{7}{8}$ inches). 1583.

Imperfect, wanting title and all after Oo7. The title has been
supplied in facsimile.
[38 C 18.]

⁎⁎⁎ This copy is bound up with the third part of the Genevan
Bible printed by Barker in 1583, which will be found described
under Bibles.

1596. **The New Testament**. TOMSON'S Revision. Printed at
London by the Deputies of Christopher Barker. Quarto
$8\frac{15}{16}$-$6\frac{3}{4}$ inches). 1596.
[38 C 19.]

1605. **The New Testament**. TYNDALE'S, as printed by R.
Jugge. Printed at London by the assignes of Robert Barker.
8vo. ($5\frac{5}{16}$-$3\frac{1}{2}$ inches). 1605.

Imperfect, wanting only one leaf (N2).
[38 C 20.]

Appended to this volume is 'The Whole Booke of Psalmes,'
collected by Sternhold, Hopkins, and others. Printed for the
Company of Stationers. Quarto. 1605.

1608? **The New Testament**. TOMSON'S Revision. Printed at
London by R. Barker. 8vo. ($5\frac{3}{8}$-$3\frac{1}{2}$ inches). [1608?]

Imperfect, wanting title and all before C1 ; other leaves are
slightly defective.
[38 C 26.]

Appended to this volume is 'The Psalms,' by Sternhold,
Hopkins, and others. Printed for the Company of Stationers,
1608.

Imperfect, wanting about nineteen leaves at end.

1616? **The New Testament**. TOMSON'S Revision. Having
the Junius version of the Apocalypse. [Probably printed at
London by R. Barker.] 8vo. ($5\frac{7}{8}$-4 inches). [1616?]

Imperfect, wanting title, and all before the twenty-first chapter
of S. Matthew (C6).
[38 C 27.]

⁎⁎⁎ The text of this copy is made complete by the insertion
of a sheet of a much later edition.

PARTS OF THE BIBLE.

EARLY PRINTED CONCORDANCES AND OTHER RARE THEOLOGICAL TREATISES.

1500. **Fisher** (John), D.D., Bishop of Rochester. 'This treatise, concernynge the fruytfull saynges of Davyd the Kynge and prophete in the seven penytencyall psalmes. Devyded in seven sermons, was made and compyled by the ryght reverente fader in God, Johan Fyssher, docteur of dyvynyte and bysshop of Rochester . . .' Printed at London by Wynkyn de Worde. 8vo. (7 9/16 5 1/8 inches). 1508.
[38 E 20.]
  *** A very fine and perfect copy.

1530 ?. **Tyndale** (William). 'An Exposicion upon the v., vi., vii. chapters of Mathew. Compyled by Wyllyam Tindale. Newly set forth and corrected according to his first copye.' Without place, name of printer, or date [but probably printed abroad about the year 1530]. 8vo. (5 1/16·3 1/2 inches).
[38 E 13.]
  *** This copy is in black letter, whilst the copy described **by** Cotton and Lea Wilson is **in** roman type.

1530-1534. **The Pentateuch.** Translated by William **TYNDALE.** The Books of Genesis, Exodus, Leviticus, and Deuteronomy are in roman type; the Book of Numbers in gothic. Without place or name of printer [but probably printed by Hans Luft, of Marlborowe]. 8vo. (6·3 5/8 inches). **1530-1534.**
[38 E 1.]
  *** A very fine and perfect copy, having the marginal notes intact, which in most copies are cut away, as directed by the Act of Parliament of 1542. Of the Book of Genesis two editions are known, the first edition, in gothic type, was issued in 1530, and the second edition, in roman, was issued in 1534 ; the copy contained in this volume is of the second edition. Of the other books no second edition is known to have been printed, and we may reasonably assume that this copy of the Pentateuch, with the exception of the Book of Genesis, is of the first edition, printed in 1530. This little volume ranks second only **to** Tyndale's Testament in point of interest, and is no less important as a monument of the English language.

1535. **The Concordance of the new testament,** most necessary to be had in yᵉ handes of all soche as in the cōmunycacion of any place contayned in yᵉ new Testament. [By Thomas GYBSON.] Printed **at** London by Thomas Gybson. 8vo. (5 5/8-3 5/8 inches). 1535.
[38 E 31.]
  *** This is a copy of the **first** printed concordance of the English New Testament, and is based upon Tyndale's Version. Bale ascribes it to Coverdale, Barham to Tyndale ; we find,

however, in the Epistle to the Reader, written by Gybson, an intimation of his being the collector or compiler. There is no difficulty in accepting this theory, for he had the reputation of being not only a printer, but a scholar.

1536. **Bible Histories.** Printed at Antwerp by **Symon Cowke.** 8vo. (5$\frac{7}{16}$-3$\frac{3}{8}$ inches). 1536.

Imperfect, wanting about thirty leaves, including title ; (the colophon is intact).

[38 E 15.]

*** This volume is exceedingly rare. The colophon is surmounted by a woodcut representing S. Paul, identical in every way with that contained in the 1536 New Testament, known as the 'Engraver's Mark Edition.'

1537. **The bokes of Salomō,** namely : Proverbia, Ecclesiastes. Sapientia, and Ecclesiasticus, of Jesus, **the sonne** of Sirac, Printed in Southwark **by** James Nicholson. 8vo. (5$\frac{7}{16}$-3$\frac{1}{2}$ inches). **1537.**

[38 E 7.]

*** A very fine and perfect copy. On folio 204 commences the 'Story of Bell,' which is the fourteenth chapter of Daniel, after the Latin, occupying six pages.

1538. [Ridley (Lancelot)]. Exposition of the Epistle of St. Jude. Printed at London by John Gowghe. 8vo. (5$\frac{1}{4}$-3$\frac{3}{4}$ inches). 1538.

[38 E 2.]

*** This is bound up with Tyndale's Exposition of the Epistles of St. John.

1538. **Hierome, of Ferrarye.** 'An Exposicyon upon the Li. Psalme. Made by Hierom. of Ferrarye. Printed in **Parys** [without name of printer]. 8vo. (6$\frac{1}{4}$-4$\frac{1}{4}$ inches). 1538.

Imperfect, wanting only title, which has been supplied in facsimile.

[38 E 21.]

*** The text is in Latin and **English.**

1538. [Sarcerius] Erasmus. 'Cōmon places of Scripture ordrely and after a compendious forme of teachynge set forth with no little labour, to the great profyte and helpe of all suche students in Gods worde as have not had longe exercyse in the same, by the ryght excellent clerke, Erasmus [Sarcerius]. Translated into Englysh by Rychard Taverner.' Printed at London by Johan Byddell. 8vo. (5$\frac{5}{8}$-3$\frac{1}{2}$ inches). 1538.

[38 E 19.]

1539. [Tyndale (William)]. Exposition of the three Epistles of St. John. [Printed at Southwark by James Nicholson.] 8vo. (5$\frac{1}{2}$-3$\frac{3}{8}$ inches). 1539.

Imperfect, wanting only title, otherwise perfect and in excellent state.

[38 E 2.]

1539. **La Vie de nostre Seigneur Jesu Christ,** par figures selon le texte des quattre Évangelistes avec toutes les Évangiles, Epistres et Propheties de toute l'année chantée en l'office de la Messe **avec** aucunes Oraisons. [Par F. Guillaume de Branteghem **de** Alost.] Printed at Antwerp by Adrien Kempe and Matthieu Crome. **8vo.** (6·3⅞ inches). 1539. [38 E 18.]

1540. **Ridley** (Lancelot). A Commentary in Englyshe upon Sayncte Paules Epystle to the Ephesyans. Per Lancelotum Ridleum, Cantabrigensem. Printed at London by Robert Redman. 8vo. (5¹⅜-3½ inches). 1540. [38 E 5.]

1540. **[Luther** (Martin)]. Exposition sur **les** deux Epîtres de **Sainct Pierre** et sur celle de Sainct Jude : **en** laquelle **tout** ce qui touche la doctrine Chrestienne est parfaictement compris. . . . Le tout traduit de Latin en Francoys et nouvellement imprimé. Without place or name of printer. 8vo. (5·3 inches). **1540.** [38 E 26.]

*** Bound up **with** two other treatises of Luther, which **are** described in their proper chronological order (1545 and **1561**).

540. **Here begynneth the Proverbes of Salomon.** Whereunto is added dyvers other Bookes of the Byble. Very good and profytable for every Chrysten man for to knowe. Prynted at London by Robert Redman. 8vo. (5⅛-3½ inches). 1540. Imperfect, wanting twenty-four leaves : title and all before B3, and all after T8. [38 E 8.]

*** This volume contains the **five** books of Solomon.

1542. **Summaire,** c'est une briefve declaration d'aucuns lieux fort necessaires à chascun chrestien, pour mettre sa confiance en Dieu, et à ayder son proclaim. G. Farel. No place. 1542. (5·3 inches). [38 E 26.]

1543. **Melancthon** (Philip). A newe **work** cöcerning both partes **of** the sacrament to be receyved of the lay peple as well under the kind off wine as under the kind off bread, with certen other articles cöcerning the masse and the auctorite off bysshops . . . made by Philip Melanchton and newly translated out off **latyn.** Without place or name of printer. 8vo. (5½-3⅞ inches). **1548.** [38 E 25a.]

1545. **[Luther** (Martin)]. Enseignement très utile **tiré de la** Saincte Ecriture, pour fortifier la personne à voulentiers mourir, & ne craindre point la mort.' Without place or name of printer. 8vo. (5·3 inches). 1545. [38 E 26.]

1546. **Bale** (John). The Actes of Englysh votaryes, comprehendynge their unchast practyces and examples by all ages, from the worldes begynnynge to the present yeare, collected **out**

of their owne legendes and Chronycles. By Johan Bale. Printed
at Wesel, without name of printer. 8vo. (5½-3¾ inches). 1546.
[38 E 25a.]

1548. **Hooper** (John). A Declaration of the ten holy comaunde-
mentes of allmygthye God. Wroten Exo. 20., Deu. 5. Col-
lectyd out of the scripture Canonicall by Joanne **Hopper.**
Without place or name of printer. 8vo. (5¾-3¾ inches). 1548.
[38 E 24.]

1548. Hooper (John). Another **copy of the** preceding, measuring
(6⅛-3¹³⁄₁₆ inches).
Imperfect, wanting **only** the title-page, which has been supplied in facsimile.
[38 E 23.]

N.D. Hooper (John). **Another** copy of the preceding. 'Declaration of the Holie Commandements by John Houper.' Printed
by Robert Waldegrave for Thomas Woodcocke. 8vo. (5⁹⁄₁₆-3¾
inches). Without date.
[38 E 25.]
   ⁎ This is a very much later edition than the two preceding
copies.

1549. Ridley (Lancelot). 'Exposition upon the Epistle of Jude.'
Printed at London by Wyllyam Copland **for Rychard** Kele.
8vo. (5⁷⁄₁₆-3⅝ inches). 1549.
[38 E 3.]
   ⁎ This is not a mere reprint of the 1538 edition, from
which textually it differs considerably.

1549. **Frellon** (Joan). Retratos otablas de las historias del
Testamento Viejo, hechas y dibuxadas por un muy primo y
sotil artifice. Printed at Lyons by Johannes Frellon. 8vo.
(7⅛-5 inches). 1549.
[38 E 16.]
   ⁎ Each page is embellished with a spirited woodcut.

1550. **The Boke of the Prophetes.** (Esaye to Malachi.) This
is undoubtedly the third part of TAVERNER'S Bible, published by J. Daye and W. Seres in five parts; the title-page
bears the date 1530, which is evidently a misprint for 1550.
8vo. (5½-3⅝ inches). [1550.]
Imperfect, wanting all after **FF8 (second chapter** of Malachi).
[38 E 9.]
   ⁎ No perfect copy of this Bible is known.

1550. **A briefe and** compendiouse table, in **a maner of**
a **concordance,** openyng the way to the principall
histories **of the** whole Bible . . . Gathered and set furth
by Henry BULLYNGER, Leo JUDE, Conrade PELLICANE, and by
the other Ministers of the Churche of Tygurie, and **now** first
printed in Englyshe. ['To which is added] the third Boke of
the Machabees, a booke of the Bible also printed unto this
booke, **which** was never **before** translated **or** prynted in any

Englyshe Bible. **Printed at London for Gwalter Lynne.** 8vo. (5⅞-3⅝ inches). **1550.**
[38 E 30.]
  *** This is not the first English edition of the Third Book of Machabees, as set forth in the title-page, for Taverner had already included it in his 1549 Bible, in 5 vols.

1550.   **Marbeck** (John). A Concordance, that is to saie, a worke wherein, by the ordre of the letters of the A B C, ye maie redely finde any worde conteigned in the whole Bible, so often as it is there expressed or mencioned. By Jhon Marbek. Printed at London by Richard Grafton. Quarto (10⅜-7 inches). 1550.
[**38 E** 33.]
  *** This is the first English concordance to the entire Bible. The author's account of the undertaking is worthy of notice. When he had reached the letter 'l,' his papers, including the MSS., were seized and confiscated, and in consequence he had to begin his concordance again. When completed, he showed it to a friend, who promised to assist him in getting it published by the king's authority. Before the work was finally published he found it necessary, by the advice of his publisher, to rewrite his manuscript, going over the same ground for the fourth time. The diligence and labours of such a man deserve to be recorded.
The work refers to the chapters only, and not to the verses.

1550.   **Joye** (George). The Exposiciō of Daniell the Prophete, gathered out of Philip Melancthon, Jhō Ecolampadius, Chonrade Pellicane, and oute of Jhon Draconite, etc. By George Joye. Printed at London by Jhon Daie and Wylliam Seres. 8vo. (5½-3½ inches). 1550.
[38 E 12.]
  *** The title and a **few other leaves are slightly** wormed, otherwise the copy is perfect.

1550.   **Hooper** (John). An oversighte and deliberacion uppon the holy prophet Jonas : made, and uttered before the kinges maiesty and his most honourable councell, by Jhon Hoper in lent last past. Comprehended in seven Sermons. Printed at London by Jhon Tisdale. 8vo. (5-3½ inches). 1550.
[38 E 11.]

1555.   **Fisher** (John), D.D., Bishop of Rochester. This Treatyse, concernynge the fruytfull sayinges of Davyd the Kynge and Prophete in the seven penytencyall psalmes. Devided in vii. sermones, was made and compyled by the righte reverente father in God, John fyssher. Printed at London by Thomas Marshe. 8vo. (5 11/16-3⅝ inches). **1555.**
[38 E 14.]

1560.   **Pilkington** (James), Bishop of Durham. 'Aggeus the Prophete declared by a large commentarye . . .' J. P. L. C.

[James Pilkington, Master of S. John's College, Cambridge, and afterwards Bishop of Durham.] Printed at London by William Seres. 8vo. ($5\frac{11}{16}$ $3\frac{3}{4}$ inches). 1560.
[38 E 10.]

1563. **A briefe and compendyouse table in a maner of a concordance openyng the way** to the principall **histories of the whole Bible** . . . Gathered and set furth by Henry BULLYNGER, Leo JUDE, Conrade PELLICANE, etc. Printed at London by John Tysdale. 8vo. ($5\frac{3}{8}$-$3\frac{5}{8}$ inches). 1563. [38 E 29.]

*** This is an imperfect reprint of the 1550 edition, previously described. Although the title sets forth that the Third Book of Machabees is added, it was not included in the volume.

1569. **Luther** (Martin). Traicte très excellent de la liberté Chrestienne, composé par Martin Luther: auquel est vivement descrite la justification de la Foy, et la fin où se doivent reduire toutes bonnes œuvres. Avec une epistre du dit Luther envoyée au Pape Leo dixieme. Nouvellement traduit de Latin en François. Without place or name of printer. 8vo. (5-3 inches). 1569.
[38 E 26.]

1572. **Fisher** (John). Psalmi seu precationes D. Joan. Fisheri, Episcopi Roffensis. Accessit imploratio divini auxilii contra tentationem ex Psalmis Davidis. Per Th. MORUM. Lugduni: Sebastianum Gryphium. 8vo. ($4\frac{1}{16}$-$2\frac{11}{16}$ inches). 1572.
[38 E 27.]

1580? **Hooper** (John). Certeine Expositions of the constant Martyr of Christ. Master John Hooper, sometime Bishop of Gloucester and Worcester, upon the 23, the 62, the 72 and the 77 Psalmes of the Prophet David. [Printed at London by H. Middleton.] Quarto ($7\frac{9}{16}$-$5\frac{1}{2}$ inches). [1580.]
Imperfect, wanting title and all after folio 127.
[38 E 22.]

1581. **Anderson** (Anthony). The Shield of our Safetie: Set foorth by the Faythfull Preacher of Gods holye Worde, A[nthony] Anderson, upon Symeons sight, in his Nunc dimittis. Printed at London by H. Jackson. Quarto ($7\frac{9}{16}$-$5\frac{1}{2}$ inches). 1581.
[38 E 22.]

1586. **Ridley** (Nicholas), Bishop of London. A breef declaration of the Lordes Supper. Written by the singular learned Man and most constant martyr of Christe: Nicholas Ridley, Bishop of London. Printed at London for Abraham Veale. 8vo. ($5\frac{9}{16}$-$3\frac{3}{8}$ inches). 1586.
[38 E 25.]

1587. **Fenner** (Dudley). The Song of Songs, that is, the most excellent song which was Solomons, translated out of the Hebrue into Englishe meeter with as little libertie in departing

from the wordes . . . By Dudley **Fenner**. Printed at Middelburgh by Richard Schilders. **8vo. (5⅝-3⅞ inches). 1587.**
[38 E 6.]

1590. Chronographia. A Description of time, from the beginning of the world unto the yeare of our Lord 137. . . . Collected out of sundrie authors, but, for the greatest part abridged and translated out of Laurentius Cedomannus, his Annales sacræ Scripturæ. Second edition, corrected and augmented. Printed at London by Richard Field for Robert Dexter. 8vo. (6-4 inches). 1590.
[38 E 17.]

1591. **Turnbull** (Richard). An Exposition upon the Canonicall Epistle of Saint Jude. By Richard Turnbull. Printed at London by John Windet. 8vo. (5⅞-3¾ inches). 1591.
A small portion of the first two leaves is missing, **the** copy is otherwise perfect.
[38 E 4.]

1629. **Saravia** (Hadrian). Vindiciæ Sacræ. A Treatise of the Honor and Maintenance due to Ecclesiastical persons. Done out of the Latin of that famous Divine of Holland, H. Saravia, **sometime** Prebend **of** Canterbury. To which is added : **An** Appendix to Saravia ; Answering foure maine Arguments which Usurpers of the Churches Right usually alledge. Printed at London by T. Coates and R. Coates for **James** Boler. 8vo. (5⁹₁₆-3⅜ inches). 1629.
[38 E 25.]

1657. **Bennet** (Robert), B.D. A Theological concordance of the synonymous terms in the Holy Scripture. By R. Bennet, B.D. Printed at London by **J.** Streater. 8vo. (6½-4¼ inches). 1657.
[38 E 32.]

1665. **The Four Gospels, in Gothic and Anglo-Saxon.** By Francis JUNIUS. With notes, etc., by Thomas MARSHALL. To which is added a Gothic glossary by Francis Junius. Printed at Dordecht by H. and J. Essæi. Quarto (8-6 inches). **1665.**
[38 C 30.]

1777? **A List of various editions of the Bible, and parts thereof, in English, from the year 1526 to 1776.** From a MS. (No. 1,140) in the Archiepiscopal Library at Lambeth, much enlarged and improved. [London.] 8vo. (8⁹₁₆-5½ inches). [1777.]
[38 E 28.]

1872. **Loftie** (William J.). List of a Collection of Bibles, chiefly of the Authorised Version. [By W J. LOFTIE.] 8vo. London. (5⅞-4½ inches.) 1872.
[38 E 57.]

*** Of this list only 50 copies were printed, 25 of which were destroyed by Mr. Loftie's own hands.

LITURGICAL AND OTHER RARE BOOKS,
CHIEFLY THEOLOGICAL,
WITH A FEW IMPORTANT MANUSCRIPTS.

3

CONTENTS.

[1510.] Hore beatissime v'ginis **Marie** ad usum Sarisburiēsis ecclesie accuratissime īpresse cū multis orationib' pulcherrimis et indulgentiis iam ultimo recenter insertis. [Printed at Paris by Thielman Kerver for William Bretton, of London.] 8vo. (6⅝-4½ inches). [1510.]

Imperfect, wanting b7 and 8, l2, q1 and 8, r8, and all after y8. Thirteen leaves (a2 to 8 and b1-6) are misplaced, and will be found following k8 ; of these a2 to 8 are mutilated and partly missing.

[38 D 15.]

_**_* The copy has been badly cropped; the ornamental borders at the head of the pages have been cut into.

1524 **Hore Beate Marie Virginis.** Colophon: Expliciunt Hore diue Virginis Marie, secundum ritum insignis ecclesie Sarū. Anno M.ccccc.xxiiii. . . . [Printed at Paris by Francis Regnault.] Quarto (7¾-5¼ inches). 1524.

Very imperfect, wanting all before F1, M7 and 8, N2, 3, 5 to 8, P3, P6 to 8, and all between P 8 and U4 (except folios 127 and 128), U6, 7 and 8, X1, 2, 4, 5, 6, and 8.

[38 D 12.]

_**_* Printed in the same beautiful type as that used by Regnault in the 1534 Missal.

1525. **Hymnorum cum notis Opusculum** secundum usum insignis ecclesie Sarisburiensis : diurno servitio per totius anni circulum apprime necessarium et ad cōcinnentium confortationē nouissime iā Aṅtwerpie plurimis quidem eliminatis mendis typis exaratum. Impensis honesti viri Francisci brykman ciuis Colonieñ. Quarto (7⅝-5½ inches). 1525.

[38 F 23.]

1528 Processionale ad usum Sar' p reuerendissimū in Christo patrē dñm ñrm dominum episcopū de Wintoñ castigatum ac nouiter impressum. 1528.

Christophor' Ruremūdeñ. Quarto (7⅝-5½ inches).

[38 F 23 b.]

[1533.] **Hore beate** Virginis **Marie** (ad usum **sacrosancte** ecclesie Sarum) iam sequuntur.   Printed at London by Robert Wyer.   8vo. (4¹⅛-3¼ inches).   [**1533.**]
  Imperfect, wanting only the **title-page.**
  [38 D 18.]

1534.   **Missale** ad usum Ecclesie Sarisburiensis.   Parisiis.   **Fran-** ciscus Regnault.   Folio (11⅞-8½ inches).   1534.
  Imperfect, wanting A3 and A4 of part 1, D3, D4, F8, and G1 of part 3; the two leaves G5 of part 2, and A2 of part 3 have been mutilated by cutting out the woodcuts in the text.
  [38 D 4.]
  ** Although slightly wormed in parts, this is on the whole **a** very fine copy of one of the most beautifully printed of the Salisbury Missals.

1538.   [Here after foloweth the **Prymer** in Engysshe and **in** latin sette out alonge : after the use of Sarum.   M.D.xxxviii.] Colophon : Imprynted in Paris be me Fransses regnault, of our Lorde.   mil. d. xxxviij.   8vo. (6½-4 inches).   1538.
  Imperfect, wanting all before B7, C5, D4, E2, F4, **G2 and** 5, H1 and 4, I1, K5, M6.
  [38 D 25.]

1543.   The **Prymer in Englyshe and Laten** after the use of Sarum.   Printed at London by Thomas Petyt.   Quarto (8¼-6¼ inches).   1543.
  Imperfect, wanting all before A7 (probably six leaves).
  At the end of the volume are the two following appendices :
  1° 'An Exposycyon after the maner of a contemplacyon upon the Psalme called "**Miserere Mei Deus**" which Hierom of Fer- rarye made at the latter end of his dayes.' [Having a distinct colophon.]
  2° Here beginneth the **Epystles and Gospels** of every Son- day, and holy day in the yeare.   Printed by T. Petyt, uniform with the Primer, but without date.   [1543.]
  Imperfect, wanting all after G5 (three leaves).
  [38 D 9.]
  ** The appendices were printed separately, and were only occasionally annexed to the Primer.

1554.   **Portiforium seu Breviariû** ad usum ecclesie Saris- buriensis, castigatum suppletû marginalibus quotationibus ador- natum, ac nunc primum ad verissimum ordinalis exemplar in suum ordinem a peritissimis viris redactum.   Parisiis : Per Magdalenam Boursette viduâ Francisci Regnault.   8vo. (5⅞-3⅞ inches).   1554.
  [3ᴷ D 5.]

1554.   **Manuale ad usum** percelebris ecclesie Sarisburiensis. Londini **noviter** Impressum [probably by Richard Grafton]. Quarto (8-5⅞ inches).   1554.

Imperfect, wanting all before a1, h5, and all after r1 (probably only one unnumbered leaf).
[38 D 11.]

*** Although this edition does not bear the printer's name, it has the compartment of Richard Grafton's device.

1554. Horæ [Beatæ Mariæ Virginis in usum Ecclesie Sarisburiensis]. [Probably printed at London by Thomas Petyt.] 8vo. (6⅞-4½ inches). 1554.

Imperfect, wanting all before D5 (folio 29), and all after Y5 (folio 173, missigned 163 roman).
[38 D 10.]

1555. **Missale** ad usūm Ecclesie Sarisburiensis. [Londoni per Joannem Kyngston et Henricum Sutton.] Quarto (8⅝-6¼ inches). 1555.

Imperfect, wanting all before A1 except the last leaf but one (including title, calendar, and part of Benedictio), and the last leaf (r8), probably blank.
[38 D 3.]

[1555.] The **Primer in Latin and English** (after the use of Sarum), with many godlye and devoute prayers. Printed at London by John Wayland. Quarto (7¼-5½ inches). [1555.]

Imperfect, wanting all before *1 ('A right Godly rule'), ¶4, O4. M3 and I1 are partly missing.

Appended to the Primer is :

' A Plaine and godly treatise concernyng the **Masse** and the blessed Sacraments of the aulter, for the instruccyon of the simple and unlearned people.' Beginning on R1.

Imperfect, wanting title (if any), z1, and all after z4 (probably only one leaf).
[38 D 8.]

*** No mention is made in the table of contents of this ' Treatise on the Mass.'

1555. **[Portiforium seu Breviariū** ad usum ecclesie Sarisburiensis, castigatum suppletū marginalibus quotationibus adornatum, ac nunc primum ad verissimum ordinalis exemplar in suum ordinem a peritissimis viris redactum.] Parisiis : Per Magdalenam Boursette viduā Francisci Regnault. 8vo. (5⁷⁄₁₆-3⅝ inches). 1555.

Imperfect, wanting only the title-page.
[38 D 6.]

*** This is a later impression of the 1554 edition, which has already been catalogued in its proper chronological order, and differs only in point of date. This copy bears the date of 1505 in the colophon, which upon close inspection will be found to have been tampered with ; the central figure 5 has been carefully erased and replaced by a cipher, making 1505 in lieu of 1555.

1556. **Portiforium seu Breviarium,** ad insignis Sarisburiensis

ecclesie usum: **accuratissime** castigatum, cum multis annotaciū-
culis **ac litteris Alphabeticis,** Evangeliorum, & Epistolarum
capitulorum originem indicantibus, que nusquam hucusque
addite. Londini, per Joannem Kyngston et Henricum Sutton.
Quarto (8⅞-6½ inches). 1556.
[38 D 2.]

1556. ❦ **Portiforium seu Breuiarium** ad **usum** ecclesie Sarisburiensis castigatum suppletum marginalibus quotationibus adornatum ac nunc primum ad vetustissimum ordinalis exempla in
suum ordinem a peritissimis viris redactum.   Pars Estiualis.
Robert Valentin, Rothomagi. ❦ Apud Robertum Valentinianum
Florentium filium eius.   1556.   Quarto (4⅞-3 **inches).**
[38 F 22.]

RITUALS, INCLUDING PUBLIC AND
PRIVATE DEVOTIONS.

1506. **Missale** Romanum noviter impressum cum quibusdam
missis denovo additis multūque devotis · adjunct. figuris pulcherrimis in capite missarum festivitatum solennium, ut patebit
inspicienti. Venetiis per dominum Bernardinum Stagninum.
8vo. (5⅝-4 inches). **1506.**
[38 H 6.]

1508. **Manipulus** Curatorum per Guidonem de Monte Rocherii.
Printed **at** London by Richard Pynson.   8vo. (5½-3¾ inches).
1508.
[38 D 14.]
    ⁎ A fine and perfect copy of this work, which was very
popular at the close of the fifteenth century, but which is now
scarce, **as** only three or four copies of the early editions are
known to exist.

1536. Prymer in Latin.   Colophon: **Imprinted at** Londō in
Fletestrete at the sygne of the Sonne / ouer agaynst the Condyth /
by me John Byddell, 1536.   8vo. (3⅝-2½ inches).   1536.
    Imperfect, wanting all before b1; part of I1 is also wanting.
[38 D 19.]

[1539.] **Prymer in English.** 8vo. (3⅝-2⁹⁄₁₆ inches).   *Circa* **1539.**
    Imperfect, wanting eleven leaves (including title) **of sigs. A,**
B, and C. F1 and 2, M8, N1 to 8, O1 to 8, P1, X1, **and all**
after X6. (u1 and 3 partly missing.)
[38 D 20.]
    ⁎ The volume begins: **'To serue our** Lorde, with good,'
etc.; and ends on X6ᵇ with: ' have some good thoughtes there of'
(in 'Thoughts to have in the church ').

N.D. **Breviarium** secundum usum et consuetudinem maioris
ecclesie Trajectensis.   Pars Hyemalis.   Sancte Martine, Orate
pro nobis. [Woodcut of S. Martin dividing his cloak.] *Colophon.*

Breuiarii sacre .Traiectēsis ecclesie summis vigiliis de verbo ad
verbum nouissime emēdata deo duce hic suā capit periodū.
Impressa vero. [No date or place.] Quarto (4⅝-3½ inches).
[36 H 57.]

1540. **The Epistles and Gospelles,** with a brief postil upon the
same from after Easter tyll Advent, which is the Somer parte,
set forth for the singuler cōmoditie of all good christē men
and namely of Prestes and Curates . . . [By Richard
Taverner.] Printed at London by Richarde Bankes. Quarto
(7⅝-5½ inches). [1540.]
[38 D 29.]

1540. **The Psalter** or boke of **Psalmes** both in Latyn and
Englyshe wyth a Kalendar, & a **Table** the more easlyer and
lyghtlyer to fynde the psalmes contayned therein. Printed at
London by Richard Grafton. 8vo. (5⅞-3⅝ inches). 1540.
Imperfect, wanting all after q7 (folio 127), probably only one leaf.
[38 D 13.]

1542. **The Prymer in Englyshe and Latyn** wyth the Epystles
and Gospelles : of euerye Sonday, & holye daye in the yere, and
also the exposycion upon Miserere mei deus. wyth many other
prayers +. Printed in London by Wyllyam Bonham. Quarto
(7½-5⅝ inches). 1542.
Imperfect, wanting N4 and 5.
[38 D 7.]
⁂ The Prymer ends on T4ᵃ ; then follow the Epystles and
Gospelles, beginning on A1 and ending on F4.

1548-49. **The forme and maner of makyng and conse-
cratyng of Archebishoppes, Bishoppes, Priestes, and
Deacons.** Printed at London by Richard Grafton. Quarto
(7½-5⅝ inches). 1549.
Quite perfect. B4 is misplaced, and follows A4.
Appended to this volume, and following the 'forme of
Ordinal,' is **The Order of the Communion**, consisting of
nine leaves. Printed at London by R. Grafton. **1548.**
[38 D 30.]

1550. **The Epystles and Gospels** of every Sondaye and holye
daye thorowoute the hole yere, After the use of the Church of
Englande. Printed at **London** by Thomas Raynalde. 8vo.
(5⅛-3½ inches). 1550.
[38 D 34.]

[**1550?**] **The Psalter of David** in english truly translated out of
Latyn, Every Psalme havynge his argument before, declaryng
brefely thentēt and substaunce of the whole Psalme. Whereunto
is annexed in thende certayne godly prayers thoroweout the
whole yere, cōmenly called collettes. Printed at London by
Edwarde Whytchurch. 8vo. (5⅝-3⅝ inches). Without date
[*circa* 1550].
[38 D 41.]

⁎⁎ The volume is slightly wormed in parts. The title **and** a few pages have been mended ; otherwise it is quite perfect.

[1553?] **Book of Common Prayer.**
This is an imperfect copy of the reprint by E. Whitchurch, in quarto, of the Second Prayer Book of Edward the Sixth. No pagination ; printed in long lines ; 37 and 38 lines to a full page.

The Psalter has been separately bound, and the remainder of the book, which is very imperfect, has been bound up with a Bible already described. (See Cranmer's Bible, 1550, *supra*, **p.** 9.) There is wanting all before Bij, B8, M8, and all N.

The Psalter has a separate title :

The Psalter or Psalmes of David, **after the** trāslacion of the great Byble, poynted as it shalbe **sayed or song in** Churches. Quarto (8⅞-5⅞ inches). London. **1553?**
[38 D 38 and 38 A 10.]

A copy of this edition, wanting the title-page, and folios a. j and a. ij, will be found in the British Museum. [C 23, b 26.] In this case also the Psalter has been transposed, though it still forms but one volume.

1556. **Breviarium Romanum** ex Sacra potissimum Scriptura, **et** probatis Sanctorum historiis nuper confectum, ac denuo per eundem auctorem accuratius recognitum. Venetiis in officina ad signum **Agnus** Dei. 8vo. (6-4 inches). **1556.**
[38 H 5.]
⁎⁎ This is one of **the editions of** Cardinal Quignon's recension of the Roman **Breviary.**

1557. **Breviarium Romanum** optime recognitum : in quo Commune sanctorum cum suis psalmis, nōnulle octave, Tabula parisina, Officiūque nominis Jesu, Desponsationis marie, & alia multa, que in ceteris desiderabantur, nuper sunt accomodata. Venetiis in Officina heredum Luce Antonii Junte. 8vo. (5¹¹⁄₁₆-4 inches). **1557.**
[38 D 52a.]
⁎⁎ A very fine and perfect copy. The sides of the original binding, with representations of the Crucifixion and the B.V.M., **have** been ingeniously preserved, and utilised as panels to the modern binding.

1558. **Certaine Godly and devout prayers.** Made in latin by the Reverend father in God, Cuthbert TUNSTALL, Bishop of Durham, and translated into Englishe by Thomas PAYNELL, clerke. Printed **at** London by John Cawoode. 8vo. (5¼-3½ inches). 1558.

Appended to this volume is : '**Psalmes or Prayers** taken oute of holy scripture.' Printed **at** London [probably by Thomas Berthelet], but without printer's **name.** 8vo. (uniform with above). 1556.
[38 D 23.]

1560. Orarium Sev Libellvs Precationum per Regiam maiestatem,

Latine æditus 1560. Londini ex officina Wilhelmi Seres typographi. 8vo. (5⅛-3½ inches). 1560.
[38 D 16.]

1561. **The** Forme of **Prayers** and Ministration of the Sacraméts, &c., sed in the English Church at GENEVA, & approved by the famous & godlie learned man, John CALVIN. Whereunto are also added the prayers which thei use there in the French Church. . . Printed at Geneva by Zacharie Durand. 8vo. (4¼-3 inches). 1561.
[38 D 45.]
*** This and the following two works are bound up in one volume.

1561. **The** Catechisme of Maner to teache children the Christian religion : wherein the Minister demandeth the question, and the Childe maketh answer. Made by the excellent Doctor and Pastor in Christs Church, John CALVIN. Printed at Geneva by Zacharie Durand. 8vo. (uniform with the preceding). 1561.
[38 D 45.]

1561. **Foure Score and seven Psalmes of David** in English Mitre, by Thomas STERNHOLDE and others : conferred with the Hebrewe, and in certeine places corrected, as the sense of the Prophet requireth. Printed at Geneva by Zacharie Durand. 8vo. (uniform with the preceding). 1561.
[38 D 45.]
*** This and the two preceding works are bound up in one volume.

1563. **A** Fourme to be used in Common Prayer twyse aweke, and also an **order of** publique fast, to be used every Wednesday in the weeke, duryng this tyme of mortalitie, and other afflictions, wherewith the Realme at this present is visited. . . Printed at London by Richard **Jugge** and John Cawood. Quarto (7⅝-5⅜ inches). 1563.
Imperfect, wanting, Ai and C4 (both probably blank leaves).
Appended to this volume is **The Seconde Tome of Homelyes** of such matters as were promised and Intituled in the former part of Homelyes, set out by the aucthoritie of the **Queenes Maiestie.** Printed at London by Richard Jugge and Jhon Cawood. Quarto (uniform with the preceding). 1563.
[38 D 28.]

1566. **De Psalmen Davidis,** in Nederlandischer sangs-ryme, door Jan VVtenhoue [UTENHOVE] van Ghentt. Ghedruckt to Londen by Jan Daye. 8vo. (5-3¼ inches). 1566.
Appended to the Psalter are :
1. **Formulier Kerchendienstes.** Londen : Jan Daye. (Uniform with the preceding) 1566.
2. **De** Kleyne **Catechismus,** Kinder of bericht leere der Duytscher Ghemeynte to London. Ghemaeckt door Marten

MICRON. Londen: Jan Daye. (Uniform with the preceding.) 1566.

[38 D 43.]

1568. **Preces priuatæ**, in studiosorum gratiã collectæ, & **Regia** authoritate approbatæ. Math. 26. Vigilate & orate ne **intretis** in tentationem. Londini: Excudebat Gulielmus Seresius. Anno 1568.

Colophon: Londini Per Gulielmium Seresium, sub signo **Herinacei** in cœmiterio Paulino Anno 1668 (*sic*). 8vo. (3¼·2⅝ inches). 1568.

Sheets Kk and Ll are misplaced, and will be found between E and F; the volume is otherwise perfect.

[38 D 22.]

[1569.] **Christian Prayers**. Printed at London **by John** Daye. Quarto (7⅛·4⅞ inches). [1569.]

Imperfect, wanting all before A1, A3 **and 4, B1, C4,** G4, R1 and 4, V1 and 4, X1 and 4, Z1 and 4, **Aa1 to Aa4, Bb1** to Bb4, Cc1 to Cc3.

[38 D 24.]

⁎ This is **a copy of the** extremely rare **first** edition **of** 'Queen Elizabeth's **Prayer Book,'** or, as Dibdin gives it, '**The** Prayer Book of the **Virgin Queen,'** the fourth edition of which he fully describes in the **Decameron**. The pages throughout **are** embellished with a number of very fine and sharp woodcuts, which **are well** worthy of notice. This first edition seems never to have **come under** the notice **of** either Ames, Herbert, **or** Dibdin.

1574. **A briefe and** necessary **Catechisme,** or Instruction Verye needefull **to** bee knowen of **all** Householders, Whereby they maye the better teach and instruct their Families, in such pointes of Christian Religion as is most meete. . . Printed at London **by** John Awdely. 8vo. (5⅞·3⅞ inches). **1574.**

Imperfect, wanting one leaf—B1.

Appended to the Catechism are:

1. **Godlye private Praiers for** Householders to meditate upon and to say in their Families. London: J. Awdely. 1574.

2. A comfortable **Sermon of Faith** in temptations and afflictions. Preached at St. Botulphes 15 Feb., **1573,** by William FULKE, D.D. London: J. Awdely. 1574.

3. **A Lecture or exposition** upon a part **of the V chapter** of **the** Epistle to the Hebrues. Set forth **as it was read in** Paules Church in **London, the** 6 Dec., **1573, by** Edward DERYNG. **London: J. Awdely. 1574.**

[38 D 50.]

1576. **A Brief Fourme of Confession,** instructing all Christian **folke** how to confesse their **sinnes, and** so to dispose themselves, **that they may enjoy** the benefice of true penace, dooing the **woorthy frutes thereof,** according to th' use of Christes Catholique Church. **Newly translated** into English. . . **By John** FOULER.

Printed at Antwerp by John Fouler. 8vo. ($4\frac{7}{16}$-$2\frac{5}{8}$ inches). 1576.
[38 E 49.]

1581. **A godlie** and necessarie Treatise touching the use and abuse of praier, which may verie conveniently be bound with anie praier booke of the like volume. Compiled and made by Thomas KNELL the elder. Printed at London by Henrie Denham. 8vo. ($3\frac{3}{4}$-$2\frac{5}{8}$ inches). 1581.

Appended to this treatise is : The Comentarye or exposition of Wolfegang MUSCULUS upon the LI Psalme. Newlye translated out of Latine into Englishe the xii of Dec., 1565. Printed at London by Richard Serle.

Imperfect, wanting all after L3 (probably 5 leaves).
[38 E 48.]

1585. **The English Creede** consenting with the true auncient catholique, and apostolique Church in al the points and articles of Religion which everie Christian is to knowe and beeleve that would be saved. By Thomas ROGERS. The First Parte. Printed at London by John Windet for Andrew Maunsel. Quarto (11-$7\frac{5}{8}$ inches). 1585.

Imperfect, wanting the first leaf (title). The copy is somewhat mutilated, although only one leaf is actually missing. .
[38 E 32a.]

1586. **A booke of the forme of common prayers,** administration of the Sacraments, etc., agreable to Gods worde, and the use of the reformed Churches. Printed at Middelburgh by Richard Schilders. 8vo. ($5\frac{1}{2}$-$3\frac{5}{8}$ inches). 1586.
[38 D 48.]

1590. **Christianæ** pietatis prima institutio ad usum scholarum latinè scripta. By Alexander NOWELL (Dean of St. Paul's). Printed at London by John Wolff for the Assignes of Richard Day. 8vo. ($5\frac{7}{16}$-$3\frac{5}{8}$ inches). 1590.
[38 D 49.]

*** An abridgment of Nowell's larger Catechism, known as the ' Middle Catechism.'

1592. **Perkins.** Upon the Lords Praier : By order of Catechising, devided into three parts : the first is the Commandements : the second, the Creed : and the third, the doctrine of the Lord's Praier. Printed at London by R. B., and are to be solde by Edward White at the little North doore of Pauls at the signe of the Gun. 8vo. ($5\frac{7}{16}$-$4\frac{1}{8}$ inches). 1592.

Imperfect, wanting J7 and 8 (the two last leaves probably blank).
[38 F. 38.]

[1595?] **Cy cõmence les Heures nostre Dame a lusaige des Sees** toutes au lõg nouvellemẽt imprimees a Rouĕ. A Rouen chez Nicolas Mulot. 8vo. ($5\frac{5}{8}$-$3\frac{3}{4}$ inches).
[1595?]

Appended to the above is 'La Vie ma dame saincte Marguerite vierge & martyre. Avec son Antienne & Oraison.' On les veu a Rouen chez Nicolas Mulot. Uniform with the preceding. [*Circa* 1595.]

[38 D 17.]

＊＊＊ On the *verso* of the last leaf of the ' Life of S. Margaret ' is a wood-cut purporting to represent the exact size of the wound in the side of the Redeemer. A facsimile of the woodcut, with a paper by W. Sparrow Simpson on the ' Devotion to the Sacred Wounds,' will be found in the *Journal of the British Archæological Association*, vol. xxx., pp. 357-374. The tract is rare.

1601. **Alphabet of Praiers.** Dedicated to Lord Robert DUDLEY, Earle of Leicester, by I. C., whose initials appear at the end of the dedication. The volume contains ' Twelve briefe praiers upon the Right Honourable the Earle of Leicester his noble name R. D.' Printed at London by P. **Short.** . . . 8vo. (3⅜-2⅝ inches). 1601.

Imperfect, wanting A1 (the first leaf).

Appended to the Alphabet is: ' This Booke **is** called the **Treasure of Gladness**, and seemeth by the copie, being **a** verie little Manuell, and written in Velam, to be made above **cc. yeeres** past at the least. Whereby it appeareth how God in olde time and **not** of late onely, hath beene truely confessed and honoured. The Copie heereof is for the antiquitie of it preserved, and to bee seene in the Printers' Hall. First Imprinted Anno 1563, and newlie Imprinted 1601.

Imperfect, wanting **A1,** and all after **I6** (probably only two leaves).

[38 D 21.]

1601. Sacerdotale uulgo manuale. seu agenda sacerdotum, ad usum Ecclesiæ et Diœcesis Parisiensis, rationem & modum Sacramenta Ecclesiastica ministrandi continens, Parœchis omnibus, & quibus incumbit animarum cura necessarium. Authoritate Reverendi in Christo Patris D. Domini Henrici de GONDY, Parisiensis Episcopi, restitutum. Parisiis apud Claudium Chapelet. Quarto (9¾·6¾ inches). **1601.**

[38 D 1.]

＊＊＊ A very **fine and perfect copy,** printed in black and **red.**

1616. La Liturgie Angloise ou le livre des Prières Publiques de l'administration des Sacramens & autres Ordres & Ceremonies de l'Eglise d'Angleterre. Nouvellement traduit en Francois par l'ordonnance de **sa** Maiestie d'Angleterre. A Londres, Jehan Bill. Quarto (7⅝-5⅝ inches). 1616.

Appended to the Liturgie is '**Le** Livre des Pseaumes du David.' A Londres, Jehan Bill. Quarto (uniform). 1616.

[38 H 1.]

1621. **Psalms and Hymns** with the Music, in four parts [four voices], by Thomas RAVENSCROFT. 8vo. London ($6\frac{3}{16}$-$4\frac{1}{8}$ inches). 1621.

Imperfect, wanting A1 and ii. (including title), and all after R8.

[38 D 39.]

*** The volume was reprinted in 1633, but this is a copy of the first edition.

1622. **The Psalter or Psalmes of David.** After the Translation of the great Bible, pointed as it shall be sayd or sung in Churches, With the addition of Morning and Evening Prayer. Printed at London for the Company of Stationers. 8vo. ($5\frac{5}{8}$-$3\frac{1}{2}$ inches). **1622.**

Imperfect, wanting A4 and 5, D4 and 5. Some thirty leaves at the beginning are much worn and mended.

Appended to the above is The Whole Booke of Psalmes. Collected into English Meeter by T. STERNHOLD, J. HOPK., and others, conferred with the Hebrew, with apt notes to sing them withall. Printed at London for the Stationers Company. 8vo. (uniform with preceding). 1622.

Imperfect, wanting the last leaf.

[38 D 40.]

1623. **Cantica Sacra,** or The Hymns and Songs of the Church. Being a Collection of those parcells of holy Scripture which either have been or may be as properly sung as the Psalmes. Together with other of the Auncient Songs and Creeds, usually sung in the Church of England. Faithfully and briefely translated into Lyricke verse, fitting the use and capacitie of the Vulgar. And Dedicated to the King's most Excellent Maiestie By G[eorge] W[ITHERS or Wythers]. Without name of printer or place. 8vo. ($5\frac{9}{16}$-$3\frac{1}{8}$ inches). [London, 1623.]

[38 D 42.]

1630. **The Whole Booke of Psalmes.** Collected into English Meeter by Thomas STERNHOLD, John HOPKINS, and others, conferred with the Hebrew, with apt Notes to sing them withall. Printed at London for the Company of Stationers. Quarto ($8\frac{5}{8}$-$6\frac{5}{8}$ inches). **1630.**

[38 D 37.]

*** The title-page bears the 1629 imprint, whilst the colophon has the date 1630.

1643. **The Whole Booke of Davids Psalmes.** Both in Prose and Meeter, with apt notes to sing them withall. Printed at London by R.[ichard] C.[otes] for the Company of Stationers. 8vo. ($4\frac{1}{16}$-3 inches). 1643.

[38 D 44.]

1649. **Formes of Prayer** used in the Court of Her Highnesse The Princesse Royall: at the solemne fast for the Preservation of the King. [London] Anno M.D.CXLIX. 8vo. ($5\frac{7}{8}$-$3\frac{3}{4}$ inches). 1649.

[38 D 33.]

1652. Breviarium **Monasticum** Pauli. V.   Pon. M. auctoritate
recognitum.   Pro omnibus **sub** Regula Sanctissimi Patris
Benedicti militantibus. Denuo multo quam antea accuratius
emendatum et ad limam Breviarii Romani expolitum cum hymnis
novis et offisiis. Parisiis Apud Joannem Billaine.   8vo. (6⅜-4½
inches).   1652.
  Imperfect, wanting Sff8 (one leaf).
  [38 D 52.]

1657. **A Rationale** upon the Book of Common Prayer of the
Church of England. By Anth. SPARROW, B.D.   Printed at
London, and sold by T. G.   8vo. (5⅝-3⅜ inches).   **1657.**
  [38 D 35.]

1662. The Sealed Book of Common Prayer. The Book of
Common Prayer and Administration of the Sacraments and
other Rites and Ceremonies of the Church, according to the
Use of the Church of England. Together with **the** Psalter, or
Psalms of David, Pointed as they **are to** be Sung or Said in
Churches : And the Form or Manner **of** Making, Ordaining,
and Consecrating of Bishops, Priests, and Deacons. London.
Printed by His Maties Printers, Cum Privilegio, MDCLXII.
  The title-page is engraved ' D. Loggan sculpt.' The volume is
bound in rough calf, with the arms of the Cathedral on the side.
The letters patent of exemplification are still attached, together
with portions of the seal in the original box.   It is ruled in red
throughout, and measures 15½-9⅝ inches.
  On the last leaf is the attestation of the hereunder written
Commissioners, certifying the book **to be ' a** true and perfect
copy.'   Their autograph signatures **and seals are** appended :
              JOHN CROFTES, **Dec. Norv.**
              Jos. HENSHAW, **Dec. Cicestr.**
              RICH. CHAWORTH.
              GUILIELM' PAULE, Dec. Lichfield.
              WILL. BRABOURNE.
              MAR. FRANCK, Archd. **S. Alb.**
              GEO. STRADLING.
              JO. PRITCHETT.
  Of **these** signatories
      Joseph Henshaw became Bishop of Peterborough in 1663.
      William Paul became Bishop of Oxford in 1663.
      George Stradling, Dean of Chichester in 1672.
      Mark Frank was also Treasurer of S. Paul's and Prebendary
          of Isledon.
      William Brabourne **was** Prebendary **of** Bromesbury, pro-
          bably also Precentor of Hereford.
  [In archivis.]

1662. **The Book of Common Prayer.** An exceedingly fine
copy of the edition just described, measuring 17⅜-10⅞ inches,
ruled in red throughout.   Folio. London, 1662.

This copy belonged to Bishop **Compton**, and was sumptuously bound in silver, and placed on the altar on great festivals. The cover was stolen in 1810. A description of the binding is given in Malcolm's *Londinium Redivivum*, 144 : 'A most superb silver-gilt and embossed prayer-book, adorned with angels, a glory, pillars, etc., inscribed : *Oculi Domini super istos, et aures ejus in preces eorum ;* and *Fiant orationes pro omnibus hominibus, pro Regibus.'*
[Case B.]

1679. The Book of Common Prayer, and administration of the Sacraments and other Rites and Ceremonies of the Church according to the use of the Church of England : Together with the Psalter or Psalmes of David, Pointed as they are to be Sung or Said in Churches. Printed at Cambridge by John Hayes. Quarto (8¾-6½ inches). 1679.
[38 D 36.]

1684. Garland of Pious and **Godly** Songs. Composed by a devout Man, for the Solace of his Freinds and neighbours in their afflictions. By N. N. Printed at Gant. 8vo. (5¹⁵⁄₁₆-3⅝ inches). 1684.
A small portion of the first leaf is missing, otherwise the volume is perfect.
[38 E 40.]

1687. **Book of Common Prayer.** Folio. London. 1687.
** Bishop GIBSON's copy, with marginal notes in his hand-writing.

1721. **The Orthodox Communicant.** By way of Meditation. Or the Order for the Administration of the Lord's Supper or Holy Communion ; According to the Liturgy of the Church of England. London. Engraven and sold by J. Sturt. 8vo. (6⁹⁄₁₆-4⅛ inches). 1721.
[38 E 52].
** Each page of text is surmounted by an illustration and surrounded by a border, the whole of which, including the text, is printed from engraved copper-plates.

1789. The Book of Common Prayer, and Administration of the Sacraments and other Rites and Ceremonies, as revised and proposed to the use of the Protestant Episcopal Church at a Convention . . . held in Philadelphia from Sept. 27th to Oct. 7th, 1785. Philadelphia printed. London, reprinted for J. Debrett. 8vo. (6¾-4 inches). 1789.
[38 D 51.]

1797. **A Form of** Prayer and Thanksgiving to Almighty God ; to be used on Tuesday the Nineteenth Day of December 1797 being the day appointed by His Majesty's Royal Proclamation for a General Thanksgiving to Almighty God, for the many signal and important Victories . . . vouchsafed to his Majesty's Fleets,

in the Course of the present **war.** Quarto (9¼-7¼ inches). London, 1797.
[38 D 58.]

1872. **A Form of Service** on the occasion of **the** Thanksgiving for the recovery of His Royal Highness the Prince of Wales. To be used at St. Paul's Cathedral 27th February, 1872. Quarto (10¾-8½ inches). London, 1872.
[38 D 57.]

1884. **Psalter** in Malagasy: Ny Salamony Davida Voalahatra **Hohiraina** Isam-Bolana, araka ny fomban'ny Church of England. Printed in Antananarivo, Madagascar. 8vo. (7⅞-5¼ inches). 1884.
[38 D 56.]
*** Psalter used **in the** temporary cathedral **at** Antananarivo **in May,** 1886.

N.D. Latin Psalter in the University Library of Utrecht (formerly Cotton MS. *Claudius* c. vii.), photographed and produced in facsimile. Quarto. London. N.D.

SERMONS, WITH TRACTS AND
TREATISES, CHIEFLY THEOLOGICAL.

1489. **Sermones Dormi Secure** de Tempore et de Sanctis. Quarto. **Basilee.** 1489.

1495. **Quadragesimale** novum editū ac predicatū a quodam fratre minore de observantia in inclita civitate Basilieñ de filio prodigo & de angeli ipius ammonitōne salubri p sermones divisū. Carmina Sebastiani Brant (Doctoris). Basilia per Michaelem Furter. Quarto (6½-4¾ inches). **1495.**
[38 H 3.]
*** A fine and perfect copy. A series of curious **woodcuts** illustrates the parable of the Prodigal Son.

1503. **Centiloquiū Seraphici** doctoris sancti Bonaventure summa diligentia nouiter impressum. Impensis Johannis Parui. 8vo. (5 1/16-3⅞ inches). 1503.
[38 D 53.]
*** A fine and perfect copy.

1523. **Roberti Wakfeldi** Sacrarum literarū professoris **eximij** Oratio de laudibus & utilitate triū linguæ Arabicæ, **Chaldaicæ & Hebraicæ,** atque idiomatibus hebraicis quæ in utroque testamento iueniūtur. Londini apud VVinandum de **Vorde.** Quarto (7⅞-5⅝ inches). [1523].
[38 E 34.]
*** A fine and perfect copy of a rare work. The first book

printed in England in which Hebrew and Arabic characters were used.

1536. **The Confession of** the faythe **of the Garmaynes,** exhibited to the mooste victorious Emperowr Charles the V in the Councell or assemble holden at Augusta the yere of our Lorde 1.5.3.0.

To which is added the Apologie of Melancthon who defended with reasons invincible the aforesayde confessyon. translated by Richarde TAVERNER at the cōmaūdemēt of Lord Thomas CROMWELL . . . [Printed at London by Robert Redman.] 8vo. (6$\frac{5}{16}$-4$\frac{1}{4}$ inches). [1536.]

Part 1 is perfect ; part 2 wants all after BB 5.

[38 D 46.]

1536. Dives and **Pauper.** [By Henry PARKER, D.D.] Colophon : 'That is to say the ryche and the poore, frūctuously treatynge upon the tenne commaundementes, fynysshed . . . In the yere of our Lorde 1536.' Printed at London by Thomas Berthelet. 8vo. (5$\frac{3}{16}$-3$\frac{7}{8}$ inches). 1536.

[38 E 44.]

⁎ The colophon gives 1536 as the date of the book, but the title-page bears the 1534 imprint. As this, however, forms part of the woodcut border surrounding the title, which border Berthelet had already used to embellish the titles of other works, it is quite probable that in utilising it for this work in the year 1536 the printer overlooked the existing date. The first edition of the work was printed by Pynson in 1493.

1537. **Of the auctoritye of the Word of God** agaynst the Bishop of London, wherein are conteyned certen disputacyons had in the Parlement Howse between the Bishops about the things very necessary to be known ; made by **Alexander Alane** [Alesius or HALES] Scot and sent to the Duke of Saxon. Without place or date, but probably printed at Leipzig. 8vo. (5$\frac{11}{16}$-3$\frac{5}{16}$ inches). [1537.]

Imperfect, wanting 17 leaves : A 1 (title); A 7 and 8 ; B 1, 2, 7, and 8 ; C 1 and 8 ; F 1 to 8.

[38 E 42.]

1543. **The Institution of a Christen man,** conteynynge the Exposytion or Interpretation of the commune Crede of the seven Sacramentes, of the X commandementes, and of the Pater noster, and of the Ave Maria, Justyfication & Purgatory. Printed at London by [Thomas Petyt]. Quarto (7$\frac{a}{x}$-5$\frac{1}{2}$ inches). [1543.]

[38 D 27.]

⁎ This is popularly known as the 'Bishops' Book.' The ornamental border surrounding the title-page is the same as that used in Taverner's New Testament of 1539.

1543. **A Necessary Doctrine and Erudition for** any Christen man, set furthe by the Kynges maiestie of Englande,

&c. [Printed at London by Thomas **Berthelet.**] Quarto
(7-5½ inches). 1543.

Imperfect, wanting all after c 2, probably 4 leaves.

[38 D 26.]

*** This is popularly known as the 'King's Book,' and is a
review of the 'Bishops' Book, or Institution of a Christen Man,'
by King Henry VIII. Many writers have erroneously attributed
it to Cranmer.

1545. **A Preservative against Death.** [Probably by ERASMUS.]
Printed at London by Thomas Berthelet. 8vo. (5½-3⅞ inches).
1545.

Imperfect, wanting all before B 1.

[38 E 55.]

1548. **The reckenynge and declaracion of the fayth and
belefe of Huldrike Zwyngly**/ byshoppe of Züryk the chefe
town of Helvitta/ sent to Charles V that nowe is Emproure of
Rome : Holdynge a Parleement or Counsuyll at Ausbrough with
the chefe Lordes and lerned men of Germanye. The yere of
our Lorde M.D.XXX. Translated and Imprynted at Züryk
by Rycharde **Wyer.** 8vo. (5⅜-3¼ inches). 1548.

A poor copy, much cropped, and wanting part **of C 4 and**
parts of E i and E ii.

[38 D 48a.]

1550. **A Sermon** preached the **thyrd** Sonday in Lent before **the**
Kynges Maiestie, **and his** honorable Counsell, by Thomas
LEAVER. Printed at **London by** Jhon Daie. 8vo. (5¼-3 1/16
inches). **1550.**

[38 E 45.]

1550. **The Ymage of both churches** after The moste wonderful **and** heavenly Revelacion of Saincte John the Evangelyst,
contaynyng a very frutefull exposytion or paraphrase upon the
same. Wherin it is cöferred with the other scriptures & most
auctorysed histories. Cöpyled by John BALE, an exyle also in
this lyfe, for the faithfull testimony of Jesu. Printed at London
by John Wyer. **Quarto** (7⅞-5½ inches). 1550.

[38 E 35.]

*** The title is within the same woodcut border as that used
by Petyt in Taverner's Testament of 1539 and the Bishops' Book
of 1543.

1550. **Caelius Rhodoginus.** Lectionum Antiquarum libri xxx
recogniti ab auctore. Basiliæ, per Hier. Frobenium. Folio
(15⅝-7¾ inches). 1550.

[38 B 20.]

*** The binding **is** a restoration **of** an exquisite contemporary binding, **the sides** of which **are** beautifully tooled, and
bear the date 1552.

1551. **Sylvius (Aeneas) Piccolomineus, postea Pius II.**
Opera quæ extant omnia. . . Hisquoque accessit Gnomo-

logia ex omnibus Sylvii operibus collecta & Index rerum
ac verborum omnium copiosissimus. Folio ($12\frac{1}{4}$-$7\frac{1}{2}$ inches).
Basiliæ, 1551.
[38 B 21.]

⁎ The binding of this volume, like that of the preceding,
is a restoration of an exquisite contemporary binding, the sides
of which are beautifully tooled in a Grolieresque style. The
restoration has been most creditably performed.

1555. **Iniunctions** geven in the visitatiō of the Reverend father
in god Edmunde [BONNER], bishop of London, begunne and
continued in his Cathedral churche and dioces of London from
the thyrd day of September, 1554, ontill the viii daye of October
. . . 1555. Printed at London by John Cawood. Consisting
of 9 leaves in Quarto ($7\frac{1}{8}$-$5\frac{3}{8}$ inches). 1555.

Following this is: **A Profitable and necessarye doc-**
trine, with certayne homelyes adioyned thereunto set forth
by the reverend father in God Edumde [BONNER], Byshop of
London, for the instruction and enformation of the people being
within his diocese of London & of hys cure and charge.
London : John Cawood [1555].

Following again is : **Homelies** sette forth by the righte
reverende father in God, Edmunde [BONNER] Byshop of London,
not onely promised before in his booke, intituled, A necessary
doctrine, but also now of late adioyned, and added thereunto
to be read within his diocese of London. . . London : John
Cawood [1555].
[38 D 31.]

1562. **Assertio Septem Sacramentorum Adversus Mart.**
Lutherum, Henrico VIII, Angliæ Rege, auctore.
Parisiis apud Sebastianum Nivellium. 8vo. ($4\frac{7}{8}$-$3\frac{1}{8}$ inches).
1562.

Appended to which is Assertionum Regis Angliæ de Fide
Catholica adversus Lutheri Babylonicam captivitatem defensio.
Authore R. D. Johanne [Fisher] Roffensi Episcopo. Parisiis :
apud Sebastianum Nivellium. 8vo. (uniform), 1562.
[38 E 47.]

1573. **A briefe exposition** of such Chapters of the olde testament as usually are redde in the Church at common praier on
the Sondayes, set forth for the better helpe and instruction of
the unlearned. By Thomas COOPER, Bishop of Lincolne.
Printed at London by Henrie Denham for Rafe Newbery.
Quarto ($7\frac{3}{4}$-$5\frac{1}{2}$ inches). 1573.
[38 D 32.]

1577. **The Staffe of Christian Faith,** profitable to all Christians for to arme themselves agaynst the enimies of the Gospell :
and also for to knowe the antiquitie of the true Churche. . . .
Translated out of French into English by John BROOKE. Printed
at London by John Daye. 8vo. ($5\frac{5}{8}$-$3\frac{5}{8}$ inches). 1577.
[38 E 43.]

1582. A Viewe of a Seditious Bul sent into Englande, from
Pius Quintus, Bishop of Rome, Anno 1569. Taken by the
reverende Father in God, John JEWELL, late Bishop of Salisburie. Whereunto is added a short Treatise of the holie Scriptures. Printed at London by R. Newberie and H. Bynnemann.
8vo. (6·4 inches). 1582.
[38 E 39.]

1582. A Discoverie of the manifold corruptions of the Holy
Scriptures by the Heretikes of our daies, specially the English
Sectaries. . . . By Gregory MARTIN. Printed at Rhemes by
John Fogny. 8vo. (6¼-4 inches). 1582.
[38 E 36.]

1583 A Defense of the sincere and true Translations of
the holie Scriptures into the English tong, against the manifold
cavils, frivolous quarels, and impudent slaunders of Gregorie
Martin one of the readers of Popish divinitie in the trayterous
Seminarie of Rhemes. By William FULKE, D.D. Printed at
London by Henrie Bynneman. 8vo. (6¼-4 inches). 1583.
     Appended to which is: A Briefe confutation of sundry
cavils and quarels, uttered by diverse Papistes in their severall
bookes & pamphlets against the writings of William FULKE.
Printed at London by George Bishop and Henrie Binnemann.
8vo. (uniform with the preceding). 1583.
[38 E 37.]

[1583?]. The Benefite that Christians receyve by Jesus
Christ crucified. Translated out of French into English by
A. G. [probably A. Golding]. Printed at London by H.
Bynneman ; without date. 8vo. (5⅝-3⅞ inches). [Circa 1583.]
[38 E 41.]

1583. Certaine Sermons preached before the Queenes Maiestie
and at Paules crosse, by the reverend father John JEWEL, late
Bishop of Salisburie. Whereunto is added a short Treatise of
the Sacraments gathered out of his sermons. . . . Printed at
London by Christopher Barker. Quarto (6⅞-4½ inches). 1583.
[38 H 4.]

1584. The Confession of Faith, conteining how the troubled
man should seeke refuge at his God, Thereto led by faith with
the declaratiō of the article of iustification at length. The
order of good workes, which are the fruites of faith : And how
the faithful and iustified man should walke and live, in the
perfite, and true Christian religion, according to his vocation.
Compiled by M. Henry BALNAUES, of Halhill. . . . Printed at
Edinburgh by Thomas Vautrollier. 8vo. (5¼-3½ inches). 1584.
[38 D 47.]
     ∗ This Confession was written by Sir Henry Balnaves, a
warm supporter of the Reformation in 1547, whilst an inmate
of the prison in the city of Rouen. The manuscript was afterwards revised by Knox, at the time a prisoner in France, who

divided it into chapters and added a summary. From that time it seems to have been lost sight of until shortly before its publication in 1584, when it was discovered at Ormiston, the seat of the lady to whom the volume is dedicated. The volume is exceedingly rare, only three or four copies being known.

1586. **Foure Bookes of Husbandrie,** collected by M. Conradus HERESBACHIUS, Councellor to the high and mightie Prince, the Duke of Cleve : containing the whole art and trade of Husbandrie, Gardening, Graffing, and planting, with the antiquitie and commendation thereof. Newly Englished and increased by Barnabe GOOGE, Esquire. Printed at London by John Wight. Quarto (7¼-8⅜ inches). **1586.**

With the exception of the title and five leaves at end, which are slightly damaged, the copy is in good condition.
[38 D 31a.]

1602. **The Answere** to the preface of the Rhemish Testament. By T. CARTWRIGHT. Printed at Edinburgh by Robert Waldegrave. 8vo. (5¼-3½ inches). 1602.

Followed by : (1) **An Apologicall Epistle :** Directed to the right honourable Lords and others of her Maiesties privie Counsell. Serving as well for a præface to a Booke entituled A Resolution of Religion. . . . By R. B. [*i.e.*, Robert Parsons]. Printed at Antwerp by Arnold Coninx. 1601.—(2) **An Antiquodlibet,** or an advertisement to beware of secular Priests [anon.]. Printed at Middleburgh by Richard Schilders. 1602.—(3) **Humble Motives for association** to maintaine Religion established. Published as an antidote against the pestilent treatises of secular Priests. Virtus unita valet. [Probably printed at Middleburgh by Rich. Schilders.] 1602.
[38 E 46.]

1602. **Uxore dimissa** propter fornicationem aliam non licet superinducere. Tertia Thesis Joannis HOUSONI, Inceptoris in S. Theologia, proposita & disputata in Vesperiis Oxonii. **Oxon. :** Josephus Barnesius. 8vo. (5¼-3⅜ inches). 1602.
[38 H 7.]

** This is bound together with a number of Sermons of various years.

1602. **Five Godlie Sermons.** Preached by RT. BD. : (1) The Charge of the Cleargie. (2) The Crowne of Christians. (3) The annointment of Christ, or Christian Ointment. (4) A Festivall Sermon upon the Nativite of Christ. (5) The Fruits of hypocrisie. London : J H[arrison]. 8vo. (5¼-3⅜ inches). 1602.
[38 H 7.]

1606. **The Black-Smith.** A Sermon preached at White Hall before the Kings most excellent Majestie on Low Sunday, 1606. By W. S., D.D. [*i.e.*, William Smith]. Printed at London by Ed. Allde. 8vo. (5¼-3⅜ inches). 1606.
[38 H 7.]

1607. Epigrammatum Joannis OWEN, Cambro-Britanni, Libri tres, Editio tertia. 8vo., Lond. (4⅝-2⅝ inches). 1607.
[38 G 1.]

1612. Epigrammatum Joannis OWEN, Oxoniensis Cambro-Britanni, Editio quarta. 8vo., Lond. (5-2⅝ inches). 1602.

Appended to which is: A copy of the 1618 edition, uniform in size, etc. 8vo., Lond. 1618.
[38 G 2.]

1612. A Learned and comfortable Sermon of the certaintie and perpetuitie of faith in the Elect; especially of the Prophet Habakuk's faith. By Richard HOOKER, sometime fellow of Corpus Christi College, in Oxford. Printed at Oxford by Joseph Barnes. Quarto (7⅛-5½ inches). 1612.

In the same volume are: (1) A Remedie against Sorrow & Feare, delivered in a Funerall Sermon. [By R. HOOKER.] 1612. (2) A Learned Sermon of the Nature of Pride. [By R. HOOKER.] 1612. (3) The Answere of Mr. Richard HOOKER to a supplication preferred by Mr. Walter TRAVERS to the H.H. Lords of the Privie Counsell. 1612. Printed at Oxford by Joseph Barnes.
[38 H 2.]

1612. Liturgia Inglesa O Libro del Rezado publico, de la administracion de los Sacramentos, y otros Ritos y ceremonias de la Yglesia de Ingalaterra. Augustæ Trinobantum. Quarto (8¼-5⅞ inches). CIↃ. IↃI. IXIIV. 1612.
[38 D 55.]

1613. A Learned discourse of Justification, workes, and how the foundation of faith is overthrowne. [By R. HOOKER.] 2nd edition, corrected and amended. Printed at Oxford by Joseph Barnes. Quarto (7⅛-5½ inches). 1613.
[38 H 2.]

1614. Two Sermons upon Part of St. Jude's Epistle. [By R. HOOKER.] Printed at Oxford by Joseph Barnes. Quarto (7⅛-5½ inches). 1614.
[38 H 2.]

1625. The Watering of Apollos. Delivered in a Sermon at St. Maries in Oxford the 8 of August, 1624. By John WALL, D.D. Printed at Oxford by John Lichfield and Wm. Turner. 8vo. (5¼-3⅜ inches). 1625.
[38 H 7.]

1628. The Lion in the Lambe, or Strength in Weakness. Delivered in a Sermon at Shelford. . . . By John WALL, D.D. Printed at Oxford by J. Lichfield. 8vo. (5¼-3⅜ inches). 1628.
[38 H 7.]

1641. Canterburies Potion: Wherein Is shewed the great Art of his Doctor in finding out the nature of his Disease: Together With the Medicines hee applied, and the strange effects they wrought in him, To the great ease of his surcharged Body, Collected from the Doctors owne hand. Printed in the yeare 1641, without place or printer. Quarto (7⅛-5¼ inches). Consisting of four leaves.

[38 E 56.]

*** A tract against Archbishop LAUD, satirising in detail the articles for which he was accused of high treason, etc. A woodcut on the first page is evidently intended as a portrait of the Archbishop.

1649. **Jodoci Sinceri Itinerarium Galliæ** Ac iconibus urbium præcipuarum illustratum. Amstelodami: apud Jodocum Jansonium. 8vo. (5¼-3 inches). 1649.
[38 D 54.]

1670. **The Lives of Dr. John Donne, Sir Henry Wotton, Mr. Richard Hooker, Mr. George Herbert.** Written by Izaak WALTON. To which is added some Letters written by Mr. George Herbert . . . . with others to his Mother, Lady Margaret Herbert, written by John Donne, afterwards Dean of St. Pauls. Printed at London by Thos. Newcomb. 8vo. (7½-4½ inches). 1670.
[38 E 50.]

*** The autograph of Izaak Walton is over the portrait of Donne, which faces the first title: 'ffor Mr. Smithwick.— Jz. WA.'

1694. **Epistolæ et Evangelia Dominicorum et Festorum Dierum Suetice,** Latine, et Germanice. 8vo., Stockholm, 1694.
Sumpt Herr Joh. Heermans Exercitium Pietatis tillagdt.
[39 H. 28.]

1718. **An History of the Mitred Parliamentary Abbies** and Conventual Cathedral Churches. By Browne WILLIS, Esq. 2 vols., 8vo. (7⅝-4⅞ inches). Lond., 1718-19.
[38 E 53 and 54.]

*** This copy was originally bequeathed by Thomas BAKER to his honoured friend, Browne Willis, Esq. The second volume contains a great many manuscript additions to the text by the said Thomas Baker, Coll. J., Socius ejectus.

1832. **The Statutes of the most** distinguished order of Saint Michael and Saint George. Printed at London by Chas. Whittingham. Quarto (9½-7¾ inches). 1832.
[38 D 59.]

INDEX EXPURGATORIUS.

This important series was, with a few exceptions, presented to the Library in 1871 by the Rev. Charles Marshall, one of the Prebendaries of the Cathedral.

Edition.		*Press Mark.*
4to., Antwerp, 1571	- - - -	38 F 14
4to., Madrid, 1583	- - - -	38 F 18
4to., Madrid, 1584	- - - -	38 F 18, No. 2
4to., Salmuri, 1601	- - - -	1 G 11
8vo., Rome, 1607	- - - -	38 H 11
4to., Madrid, 1612	- - - -	38 F 5 and 1 D 2
4to., Hispali, 1632	- - - -	38 F 4
4to., Madrid, 1640	One volume, in 2 parts.	38 F 8, 9
4to., Rome, 1665	- - - -	47 F 5
4to., Madrid, 1667	- - - -	40 B
4to., Rome, 1667	- - - -	1 B 3
8vo., Rome, 1704	- - - -	38 H 9
4to., Madrid, 1707	Two volumes.	38 F 2, 3
8vo., Prague, 1726	With appendix.	38 H 8
4to., Madrid, 1747	Two volumes.	38 F 6, 7
4to., Rome, 1758	- - - -	38 F 10
8vo., Parma, 1783	- - - -	38 H 10
8vo., Rome, 1787	- - - -	38 F 21
4to., Madrid, 1790	With supplement, 1805.	38 F 13
8vo., Rome, 1819	- - - -	38 F 20
8vo., Paris, 1826	Second edition.	38 H 12
4to., London, 1835	Edited by J. Mendham.	38 F 11
8vo., Dublin, 1837	Edited by R. Gibbings.	38 H 13
8vo., Rome, 1841	- - - -	38 F 17

Jacobi Gretseri, Soc. Jesu Theologi, De Jure et More Prohibendi, Expurgandi, et Abolendi libros hæreticos et noxios adversus Junium et G. Pappam. 4to., Ingolstadii, 1603. 38 F 19, **No. 2.**

Danielis Franci Disquisitio Academica de Papistarum Indicibus librorum prohibitorum et expurgandorum. 4to., Lipsiæ, **1684.** 38 F 15.

Storia Polemica delle Prohibizioni **de' Libri,** scritta de Francesc Antonio Zaccaria. 4to., Rome, **1777.** 38 F 12.

The Literary Policy of the Church of **Rome,** exhibited in an account of her Damnatory Catalogues or Indices both Prohibitory and Expurgatory. By Joseph Mendham. Second edition. 8vo., London, 1830. 38 H 14.

LITURGICAL BOOKS.

Roman Missals.

Vade Mecum. **Missale** Itinerantium. 4to., Nuremberg, 1507.
Missale Romanum. 8vo., Rothomagi, 1525.
Missale Trajectense. Folio, Antwerp, 1540.
Missale Romanum. 8vo., Paris, Ex Officina Jacobi Keruer, 1577.
Missale Romanum. 4to., Antwerp, 1598.
Missale Ratisbonense. Folio, Ingolstadt, 1624.
Missæ approbatæ per summos Pontifices: de

> S. Philippo Nerio Confess.
> S. Maria de Monte Carmelo.
> S. Angelo Custode.
> Impressione Sacrorum Stigmatum.
> 4to., Venice, 1628.

[This volume contains the Missal, and two Appendices, Mediolani, 1707, and Taurini, 1701, with other special offices.]

Missale Fratrum Ordinis **B.V.M.** de **Monte Carmelo**.
4to., Paris, 1661.
Missale Fratrum **Ordinis B. V. |M. de Monte Carmelo.**
Folio, Paris, 1665.
Missale Romanum. 4to., Antwerp, 1673.
Missale Romanum. Folio, Lugduni, 1682.
Antiqui Libri Missarum Rom. Ecclesiæ. 4to., Rome, 1691.
Missale S. Barbaræ. Folio, Venice, 1693.
Missale Romanum. 4to., Ex ducali Campidonensi typographeo, 1720.
Missale Sacri Ordinis Prædicatorum. Folio, Rome, 1726.
Missale Sacri Ordinis Cartusiensis. Folio, Gratianopoli, 1771.
Missale Romanum in quo Missæ Sanctorum Ordinum, S. P. FRANCISCI, suo ordine inseruntur ad **usum** Fratrum et Sororum eorundem Ordinum. Folio, Avenione, 1776.
The Divine Office for the Use of the Laity. 8vo., N. P., 1780. Two vols.
Missale **Bajocense.** 8vo., Lugduni, 1790.
Missale **Romanum.** 4to., Madrid, 1791.
Missale **Romanum.** 4to., Venice, 1803.
Missale **Romanum.** 8vo., Dublin, 1804.
Missal for **the Use of the Laity.** 8vo., Manchester, 1806. Two volumes.
Missale Ambrosianum. Folio, Milan, 1831.
Missale Romanum. 4to., Venice, 1840.
Missale Sacri Ordinis Prædicatorum. 8vo., Rome, 1855
Missale Romanum. Folio, Mechlin, 1858.
Missale Romanum. Folio, Vindebonæ, 1861.

BREVIARIES.

Breviarium Romanum. 4to., Lugduni, 1556.
Brev. Fratrum Prædicatorum juxta decreta Salmanticensis capituli reformatum. 8vo., Venice, **1572**.
Brev. Romanum. 8vo., Paris, 1577. **Apud Jacobum** Keruer.
Brev. Romanum. 8vo., Antwerp, 1613.
Brev. Monasticum. 8vo., Paris, 1632.
Officia Nova in Breviario Romano. 8vo., Antwerp, 1671.
Brev. Romanum. 4to., Antwerp, 1674. Two volumes.
Breviarium Novissimum Monasticum. 4to., Campoduni, 1677
Brev. Romanum. 8vo., Antwerp, **1752**. Four volumes.
Brev. Leodiense. 4to., Leodii., **1766**. Four volumes.
Brev. Aurelianense. 8vo., Aurelianis, **1771**. Pars Hyemalis.
Brev. Parisiense. 8vo., Paris, **1778**. Four volumes.
Brev. Romanum. 4to., Olisipone, **1786**. Four volumes.
Brev. Romanum. 8vo., Venice, **1793**.
Brev. Romanum. 4to., Venice, 1803.
Breviarium Sanctæ Lugdunensis **Ecclesiæ primæ Gallia-rum** sedis. 8vo., Lugduni, 1815.
Brev. Romanum. 8vo., Norwich, 1830. Four volumes.
Brev. Romanum cum Officio trium Ordinum S. Francisci. 8vo., Mechlin, 1848.
Brev. Monasticum. **8vo.**, Rome, 1858. **Two volumes.**
Breviarium Romanum ad usum Carmelitarum **Discalcea-**torum. 8vo., Mechlin, 1861. Four volumes.
Breviarium juxta ritum sacri Ordinis Prædicatorum. 8vo., Mechlin, 1865. Two volumes.
Breviare des Religieuses Ursulines. 8vo., Malines, 1866.
Breviarium Romano-Seraphicum. **8vo.**, Mechlin, 1868.
The Roman Breviary translated by **John,** Marquis of Bute. 4to., London, 1879. Two volumes.
Breviarium Romanum a Francisco Cardinali Quignonio. Curante J. W Legg. **8vo.**, Cambridge, 1888.

RITUALS.

Rituum Ecclesiasticorum sive Sacrarum Cæremoniarum SS. Romanæ Ecclesiæ libri **tres non ante** impressi. Folio, Venice, 1516.
Sacra **Institutio** Baptizandi juxta ritum sanctæ Romanæ Ecclesiæ. 8vo., Paris, 1575.
Rituale Sacramentorum Romanum. 4to., Rome, **1584.**
Rituale Romanum. 4to., Antwerp, 1625.
Rituale Romanum. 8vo., Paris, 1665.
Rituel de la Province de Reims. 4to., **Paris,** 1677.
Rituel du Diocèse d'Alet. 8vo., Paris, 1678.
Rituel du Diocèse de Quebec. 8vo., Paris, 1703.
Rituale Atrebatense. 4to., Atrebati, 1757.
Rituale Augustanum. 4to., Augustæ Vindelicorum. 1764.

Rituale Romanum. 4to., Madrid, 1766.
Rituale Romanum. 8vo., Paris, *circa* 1857.

PONTIFICALS.

Pontificale Romanum. Folio, Rome, 1645.
Pontificale Romanum. 12mo., Paris, 1664.

SACERDOTALE.

Obsequiale sive Sacerdotale Ecclesiæ et Diocoesis Constantiensis.
4to., Constantiæ, 1597.

PROCESSIONALS.

Processionale Romanum. 8vo., Paris, 1663.
Processionale Monasticum Benedictinum. 8vo., Paris, 1719.
Processional de Fréjus. 8vo., Paris, 1787.

ANTIPHONALS.

Antiphonale Romanum. Folio, Paris, 1623. Two volumes.
Antiphonale Romanum. Folio, Paris, *circa* 1854.
Organum comitans ad Graduale Romanum et ad Vesperale
Romanum. Fr. X. Haberl et Jos. Hanisch. 4to., Ratis-
bonæ, Neo Eboracæ, et Cincinnatii, 1875-1877. Two volumes.

MANUAL.

Manuale ad Sacramenta Ecclesiæ Ministranda, reformatum ex
Romano et iis quibus Galliæ Ecclesiæ passim utuntur. 8vo.,
Burdigalæ, 1596.

PSALTERIUM.

Psalterium Romanum. Folio, Lugduni, 1764.

OTHER ROMAN OFFICES.

Directorium Benedictinum perpetuum. 8vo., Rorschachii,
1621.
Octavarium Romanum. 8vo., Antwerp, 1628.
Officium B. Mariæ Virginis. 4to., Antwerp, 1677.
Nouveau Livre de l'Eglise à l'usage de Rome. 8vo., Paris,
1719.
L'Ordre des Dames de la Croix de l'Estoile. 8vo., Linz,
1726.
The Office of the Holy Week. 6th edition. 8vo., London,
1766.
Sanctorale Macloviense. 8vo., Maclovii, 1768.
L'Office de la glorieuse Vierge Marie, à l'usage des Religieux
de S. Dominique avec les Roubriques Françaises. 8vo., Toulouse,
1773.
Officia Sanctorum Franciscanorum. 8vo., N.P. or D.
Office de S. Omer, précédé de sa vie. 8vo., S. Omer, 1822.
Liber Evangeliorum, Epistolarum, et Lectionum Prophe-
tiarum juxta ritum Sanctæ Lugdunensis Ecclesiæ, primæ
Galliarum sedis. 4to., Lugduni, 1842.

RITUAL BOOKS OF THE CISTERCIANS.

Missale. 4to., Antwerp, 1762.
Rituale. 8vo., Paris, 1689.
Kalendarium. 8vo., Paris, 1726.
Processionale. 8vo., Paris, 1737.
Psalterium. Folio, Paris, 1747.
Breviarium Cisterciense juxta Romanum. 8vo., Paris, 1659.
Breviarium. Pars Hyemalis. 8vo., Brussels, 1794.
    Pars Vernalis. 8vo., Westmalle, 1854.
    Aestivalis et Autumnalis. 8vo., Brussels, 1794.
Officia Nova in Breviario Cisterciensi. 8vo., Westmalle, 1871.

GREEK CHURCH.

ΜΗΝΑΙΟΝ. Twelve volumes. Folio, Venice, 1872.
ΕΥΑΓΓΕΛΙΟΝ ΘΕΙΟΝ ΚΑΙ ΙΕΡΟΝ. Folio, Venice, 1872.
ΤΑ ΤΕΣΣΑΡΑ ΘΕΙΑ ΚΑΙ ΙΕΡΑ ΕΥΑΓΓΕΛΙΑ ΜΕΤΑ ΤΗΣ **ΙΕΡΑΣ**
 ΑΠΟΚΑΛΥΨΕΩΣ ΤΟΥ ΕΥΑΓΓΕΛΙΣΤΟΥ ΙΩΑΝΝΟΥ. **8vo.,**
 Venice, 1868.
ΤΡΙΩΔΙΟΝ. Folio, Venice, 1869.
ΠΑΡΑΚΛΗΤΙΚΗ ΗΤΟΙ ΟΚΤΩΗΧΟΣ **Η ΜΕΓΑΛΗ.** Folio, Venice,
 1872.
ΟΚΤΩΗΧΟΣ . . . ΙΩΑΝΝΟΥ ΤΟΥ ΔΑΜΑΣΚΗΝΟΥ. **8vo., Venice,**
 1877.
ΠΕΝΤΗΚΟΣΤΑΡΙΟΝ. Folio, Venice, 1860.
ΕΥΧΟΛΟΓΙΟΝ ΤΟ ΜΕΓΑ. 4to., Venice, 1869.
ΩΡΟΛΟΓΙΟΝ **ΤΟ** ΜΕΓΑ. 4to., Venice, 1876.
ΣΥΜΕΩΝ ΑΡΧΙΕΠΙΣΚΟΠΟΥ ΘΕΣΣΑΛΟΝΙΚΗΣ ΤΑ ΑΠΑΝΤΑ
 ΕΙΣ ΕΞ ΜΕΡΗ ΔΙΑΙΡΕΘΕΝΤΑ. 4to., Venice, 1863.
ΠΗΔΑΛΙΟΝ ΤΗΣ . . . ΕΚΚΛΗΣΙΑΣ. 4to., Athens, 1841.
ΤΥΠΙΚΟΝ ΕΚΚΛΗΣΙΑΣΤΙΚΟΝ. 8vo., Venice, 1869.
ΑΙ ΘΕΙΑΙ **ΛΕΙΤΟΥΡΓΙΑΙ** ΧΡΥΣΟΣΤΟΜΟΥ ΚΑΙ ΒΑΣΙΛΕΙΟΥ.
 8vo, Venice, 1876.
ΑΓΙΑΣΤΑΡΙΟΝ ΤΟ ΜΕΓΑ. 8vo., **Venice, 1873.**
ΚΑΤΑΧΗΣΙΣ. 8vo., Venice, 1837.
ΨΑΛΤΗΡΙΟΝ. 8vo., Venice, 1842.
ΨΑΛΤΗΡΙΟΝ . . . ΕΚΔΟΣΙΣ ΠΕΜΠΤΗ 8vo., Venice, 1868.
ΕΙΡΜΟΛΟΓΙΟΝ. **8vo., Venice,** 1837
ΕΙΡΜΟΛΟΓΙΟΝ. 8vo., **Venice,** 1866.
ΕΙΡΜΟΛΟΓΙΟΝ. In Slavonic.
ΣΥΝΤΑΓΜΑ ΤΩΝ ΚΑΝΟΝΩΝ **ΤΩΝ ΑΠΟΣΤΟΛΩΝ. ΤΟΜΟΣ**
 ΕΚΤΟΣ. **8vo,** Athens, 1859.
ΑΚΟΛΟΥΘΙΑ . . . ΤΕΡΑΣΙΜΟΥ. 8vo., Venice, 1861.
ΑΚΟΛΟΥΘΙΑ ΤΟΥ ΑΝΑΓΝΩΣΤΟΥ κ.τ.λ. 8vo., Venice, 1861.
ΑΚΟΛΟΥΘΙΑ ΤΟΥ ΑΓΙΟΥ ΙΕΡΟΜΑΡΤΥΡΟΣ ΧΑΡΑΛΑΜΠΟΥΣ.
 8vo., Athens, 1817.
ΙΕΡΟΔΙΑΚΟΝΙΚΟΝ. 8vo., Venice, 1860.
ΑΠΟΣΤΟΛΟΣ ΗΤΟΙ ΠΡΑΞΕΙΣ ΚΑΙ ΕΠΙΣΤΟΛΑΙ ΤΩΝ ΑΓΙΩΝ
 ΑΠΟΣΤΟΛΩΝ. 8vo., Venice, 1868 ; 8vo., Venice, 1842 ; 8vo.,
 Venice, 1879.

ΕΞΟΜΟΛΟΓΗΤΑΡΙΟΝ ΗΤΟΙ ΒΙΒΛΙΟΝ ΨΥΧΩΦΙΛΕΣΤΑΤΟΝ
8vo., Venice, 1868.

GREEK CHURCH AND ORIENTAL.

Liber Pontificalis **Ecclesiæ Græcæ.** Folio, Paris, 1643.
Rituale Græcorum. Folio, Paris, 1647.
J. Goar. Versio et Notæ ad **Euchologion** sive Rituale Græcorum. Folio, Paris, 1647.
Renaudot. Liturgiarum Orientalium Collectio. 4to., Paris, 1716.
Tetralogia Liturgica : sive Chrysostomi, S. Jacobi, S. Marci, divinæ missæ : quibus accedit Ordo Mozarabicus. Edited by J. M. NEALE. 8vo., London, 1849.
Michael Rajewsky. Euchologion der Orthodox-Catholischen Kirche. 3 parts. 8vo., Wien, 1861-62.
Offices from the Service Books **of the Holy Eastern** Church. By R. F. LITTLEDALE. 8vo., London, 1863.

ARMENIAN.

An Armenian Liturgy. 8vo., 1702.
[36 C. 62.]

MOZARABIC.

Liturgia Mozarabica in duobus tomis divisa-quorum prior continet Missale Mixtum, posterior Missale Gothicum. (Migne *Patrologiæ Cursus completus.*) Two volumes. 8vo., Paris, 1862.

RITUAL BOOKS.

ENGLAND, IRELAND, SCOTLAND.

SARUM.

Missale ad usum insignis et præclaræ Ecclesiæ Sarum. Edited by F. H. Dickinson. 8vo., Burntisland, 1861-83.
Processionale ad usum insignis et præclaræ Ecclesiæ Sarum. Edited by Dr. Henderson. 8vo., London, 1882.
Manuale ad usum insignis Ecclesiæ Sarum.
[An abbreviated reprint in Dr. Henderson's edition of the York *Manual.*]
The Psalter or Seven ordinary Hours of Prayer according to the Use of the Illustrious and Excellent Church of Sarum, etc. Edited by J. D. C[hambers]. 4to., London, 1852.
The Church of our Fathers, as seen in S. Osmond's Rite for the Cathedral of Salisbury, with dissertations on the Belief and Ritual in England before and after the coming of the Normans. By Daniel Rock. Three volumes (in four). 8vo., London, 1849-53.

YORK.

Missale ad usum insignis Ecclesiæ Eboracensis. Edited by Dr. Henderson. Two volumes. 8vo., Leeds, 1874.

Breviarium ad usum **insignis** Ecclesiæ Eboracensis. Edited by the Hon. and Rev. **Stephen** Lawley. 8vo., London, 1880-83.

Manuale et **Processionale ad** usum insignis Ecclesiæ Eboracensis. Edited by Dr. Henderson. 8vo., Leeds, 1875.

Liber Pontificalis **Chr.** Bainbridge, Archiepiscopi Eboracensis. Edited by Dr. Henderson. **8vo.**, Burntisland, 1875.

Pontifical of **Egbert,** Archbishop of **York, A.D.** 732-767. Edited by W. **Greenwell.** 8vo., London, **1853.**

HEREFORD.

Missale ad usum percelebris Ecclesiæ Herfordensis. Edited by Dr. **Henderson. 8vo., Leeds, 1874.**

Manual Offices from the **Hereford Missal.**
[See Dr. Henderson's **edition of the York** *Manual.*]

WESTMINSTER.

Missale ad usum Ecclesiæ Westmonasteriensis. Edited **by Dr. J.** W. Legg. *Fascic.* 1   8vo., London, 1891.

The Manner of the Coronation of King Charles the first of England at Westminster, 2 Feb., 1626. Edited by Chr. Wordsworth). 8vo., **London,** 1892.

EXETER.

The Leofric Missal, as used in the **Cathedral of** Exeter during the Episcopate of **the first** Bishop, A.D. **1050-1072.** Together with some Account of **the Missal of** Robert **de** Jumièges. Edited by F. E. Warren   4to., Oxford, 1883.

Legenda Sanctorum, compiled by John de Grandison, Bishop of Exeter, **1**327. Edited by H. E. Reynolds. 4to., London, 1880.

Ordinale secundum usum Exon. Edited **by H.** E. Reynolds. 4to., **London.**

LINCOLN.

Consuetudinarium Ecclesiæ Lincolniensis tempori Richardi **de** Gravesend Episcopi (1258-1279) redactum. Edited by H. **E.** Reynolds. 4to., London, 1880.

Consuetudinarium, **etc.,** with introductory notes by Christopher Wordsworth, Rector **of Glaston. 4to.,** London, 1885.

IRELAND.

The Manuscript Irish **Missal** belonging to the President and Fellows of Corpus Christi College, Oxford.   Edited by F. E. Warren. **8vo.,** London, 1870.

Missale Drummondiense : the Ancient Irish Missal in the possession of **the** Baroness Willoughby de Eresby, Drummond **Castle,** Perthshire. Edited by G. H. Forbes. 8vo., Burnt-island, 1882.

SCOTLAND.

Breviarium Aberdonense. Pars Æstiva. Pars Hyemalis. 4to., London, 1854.

Kalendar of Scottish Saints, with personal notices of those of Alba, Landonia and Strathclyde. By A. P. Forbes, Bishop of Brechin. 4to., Edinburgh, 1872.

BOOK OF COMMON PRAYER.

Book of Common Prayer. Bound up with the Greek Testament of 1633, and the Psalms of Sternhold and Hopkins of 1641. 8vo., London, 1641.
[36 G. 13.]

Book of Common Prayer. The frontispiece presents a view of the western façade of S. Paul's Cathedral. Folio, London, 1766.
[43 A. 10.]

Prayers of Intercession for their Use who Mourn in Secret for the Publique Calamities of this Nation, with an Anniversary Prayer for the 30th of January. 8vo., London, 1659.
[36 G. 43.]

The Booke of Common Prayer and Administration of the Sacraments, and other parts of Divine Service for the Use of the Church of Scotland. 4to. (10½-7½ inches), Edinburgh, 1637.
[18 D. 5.]

The Book of Common Prayer . . . for the Use of the Church of Scotland. With a Paraphrase of the Psalms in Metre by King James the VI. 8vo., Edinburgh, 1712.
[From the copy printed at Edinburgh in the year 1637.]

Book of Common Prayer for the Church of Ireland. Folio, Dublin, 1750.
This volume contains, in addition to the Book of Common Prayer, the following special offices, etc. :
Form of Prayer for the Visitation of Prisoners. 1711.
Act for keeping and celebrating Oct. 23 as an Anniversary Thanksgiving in this Kingdom.
Act for the more effectual suppressing of popular Cursing and Swearing. ·
Form for receiving lapsed Protestants.
Form of Consecration or Dedication of Churches.
Office for the Restauration of a Church.
A short Office for Expiation and Illustration of a Church Desecrated or Prophan'd.
The New Version of the Psalms of David (Tate and Brady), 1751.

The Book of Common Prayer for Ireland. Printed from the manuscript originally annexed to Stat. 17 & 18, Car. II.

c. 6 (Ir.), and now preserved in the Rolls Office, Dublin. Edited by A. J. Stephens. Three volumes. 8vo., London, 1849-50.

Mr. Pickering's Black Letter Reprints of Editions of **the** Prayer-Book. Seven volumes. Folio, London, 1844.

> First Prayer-Book of Edward VI. 1549.
> Second   „   „   1552.
> Prayer-Book of Elizabeth. 1559.
>   „   James I   1604.
>   „   Charles I. (Laud's).   1627.
>   „   Charles II.   1662.
>   „   Victoria.   1844.

Facsimile of the Black-letter Prayer-Book of 1636, showing the Manuscript alterations made in 1661, and authorised by the Act of Uniformity. Folio, London, 1870.

Facsimile of the Original Manuscript of the Book of Common Prayer, signed by Convocation, December 20th, 1661, and attached to the Act of Uniformity, 1662. Folio, London, 1891.

The Book of Common Prayer, with notes, legal and historical. By Archibald John Stephens. Three volumes. 8vo., London, 1849-54.

> [This edition exhibits the text of the Sealed Books with the variations of several copies.]

The Book of Common Prayer. Reprinted from the Sealed Copy in the Tower of London. 8vo., London, 1853.

TRANSLATIONS.

ARABIC.

Liturgiæ Ecclesiæ Anglicanæ partes precipuæ : viz. Preces matutinæ et vespertinæ, Ordo administrandi Coenam Domini, Ordo Baptismi Publici . . . in Linguam Arabicam traductæ. Opera Edvardi Pocock. 8vo., Oxoniæ, 1674.
[**36 F.** 11.]

LATIN.

1574. **Liturgia Anglicana.** Title **lost** : colophon, Londini : Excudebat Thomas Vautrollerius. **4to.,** London, 1574.
[36 G. 19.]

1670, 8vo., London. J. D., editor.
> [This is the first edition of Dr John **Durel's** translation.]

1696. **8vo. London.**
1703. **8vo. London.** Tho. Parsel.
1713.   „   „   „   Editio altera.
1727.   „   „   „   Editio quarta.
1744.   „   „   „   Editio sexta.
1759.   „   „   Preface not signed. Editio septima.

GREEK.

1665. 8vo. Cambridge. Duport's translation.
1818. 8vo. London.

FRENCH.

1616. 4to. London. See *supra*, p. 44.
1616. 8vo. London.
1717. ,, ,,
1788. ,, ,,
1853. ,, ,,

ENGLISH AND LOW DUTCH.

1748. 8vo. Amsterdam. Fourth Edition.

ITALIAN.

1685. 8vo. London. First edition.
1796. 8vo. London. Translated by A. Montucci and L. Valetti, Professori di lingua Italiana.

SPANISH.

1612. 4to. Augustæ Trinobantum. See *supra*, p. 54.

INDO-PORTUGUESE.

1826. **O Livro de Oraçao Commum** . . . Traducido em Lingo de Indo-Portugueza. 8vo., London, 1826.

BOOKS UPON LITURGICAL SUBJECTS.

Hierurgia : or the Holy Sacrifice of the Mass. By DANIEL ROCK. Two volumes. 8vo., London, 1833.

Monumenta Ritualia Ecclesiæ Anglicanæ. By WILLIAM MASKELL.

First edition. Three volumes. 8vo. London. 1846.
Second ,, Three volumes. 8vo. London. 1882.

The Ancient Liturgy of the Church of England, according to the Uses of Sarum, York, Hereford and Bangor. By WILLIAM MASKELL.

Second edition. 8vo. London. 1846.
Third edition. 8vo. London. 1882.

Hierurgia Anglicana. 8vo., London, 1848.

Liturgiæ Britannicæ. By W. KEELING. 8vo., London, 1851.

Essays on Liturgiology and Church History. By J. M. NEALE. 8vo., London, 1863.

Divine Worship in England in the 13th and 14th Centuries, contrasted with and adapted to that in the 19th. By J. D. CHAMBERS. 4to., London, 1877.

Bibliographia Liturgica. **Catalogus Missalium** Ritus Latini ab Anno MCCCCLXXV impressorum. Collegit W. H. Jacobus Weale. 8vo., London, 1886.

The Offices of the **Old Catholic** Prayer-Book, done into English, **and compared with the** Offices of the Roman and **Old** German Missals. 8vo., Oxford, 1876.

A FEW IMPORTANT MANUSCRIPTS.

Deed relating to the Obits and Services in Henry the Seventh's Chapel, Westminster Abbey.

A manuscript very-sumptuously bound in velvet, lined with damask, with green silk tassels at the corners. On each side are five silver-gilt bosses ; those at the four corners bear a portcullis, on a ground party per pale argent and vert : that in the centre bears the royal arms, with supporters, surmounted by a crown. Three clasps of enamelled silver, bearing Tudor roses, close the book. Pendant from it are four silver boxes (one box is imperfect) containing fragments of seals : the boxes are inscribed—

SI . ARCHI . CANT.   S . CAPI . WINTON
SI . CAPITOL . CANTO.

whilst the fourth box bears on one side the arms, Gules, two keys in saltire or, impaling the arms of the Confessor. And on the other side, these two coats of arms impaling each other in chief ; and below, Azure, on a chief indented or a pastoral staff paleways and a mitre gules, for Westminster Abbey. The velvet cover extends nearly a foot below the volume, and covers the seal-boxes. The initial letter represents King Henry VII. seated, giving this very volume to Abbot Islip, who kneels before him : behind the Abbot are four kneeling monks. The document commences

'This indenture Septipartite made betwene the moost xp̃en King Henry the vij^th by the grace of God King of Englande and of ffraunce and lord of Ireland the sixtene day of July the xix yere of his moost noble reigne of the oon partie, And the moost Reu'ende ffadre in God William Archebisshop of Caunterbury of the seconde partie, And the right Reu'ende fadre in God Richard Bisshop of Winchest'r of the thirde partye, and John Islipp Abbot of the Monast'ie of sainct Petre of Westm̃ and the Priour and Convent of the same place of the fourth partie, And the Dean and Chanons of the Kinges free Chapell of our ladie and Saincte Stephen the furst martir w'in the Kinges palois of Westm̃ of the fithe partie, And the Dean and Chapitre of the Cathedral Churche of sainte Paule in the Citie of London of the sixte partie, And the Maire and Coialtie of the citie of London of the seventh partie.'

The Deed itself is a Deed of Penalties. A similar Deed in the British Museum enumerates the

'Grete Penalties and Sommes of Money to be forfaited and

paied as often as the said Abbot, Priour and Convent, or their successours shall make Default in observyng and perfourmyng of any of the Covenantes or Graunts conteigned and specified in the original Indenture conteyninge the Fundacion of the holie and devout Wille of the said Kyng.'

Marginal references throughout the deed direct attention to the minute details comprised within its purview : such as, 'the daily Collects at high masse, the daily Collects at the Chapitre Masse, the houres of the saieng of the thre Chauntrie Masses, the knolling of the bell bifor the saienge of the thre Chauntrie Masses, the ringing of the bell to the Sermones, the distribucion of Almesse, the hundreth Tapers to stand continuelly about the herse and tombe and thretie of theym to brenne at the said obites, the twenty and foure Torches, the thre monks scolars, the thretene poor men, the thre poor women, the wodde and cole for the poor men, a monke for the ou'sight of the said poor men,' etc., etc. These details give a very complete view of the services in Henry the Seventh's Chapel.

The exact date of the Indenture is 1504. The Prelates named are William **Warham**, Archbishop of Canterbury, and Richard Fox, Bishop of Winchester.

[A volume corresponding with the above, but containing four indentures, is preserved in the British Museum. Harleian MS., No. 1498.]

Manuscript, in English, about the middle of the Fifteenth Century, on vellum, relating to the Monastery of Sion in Isleworth. The Rule of the House was that of S. Austin with the additions of S. Bridget. The volume contains :

    1. The Additions to the Rule, in fifty-eight chapters.
    2. A Ceremonial Calendar.
    3. A Table of Signs to be used during the hours of silence by the Brethren.
    4. The Reule of our Savyour.
    5. The Reule of S. Austyne.

In the British Museum (Arundel MS., No. 146) is a similar but imperfect volume, containing the rules and constitutions for the Sisters of this Order. The Cathedral volume contains the Rules of the Brethren. The British Museum MS., including the very curious Table of Signs, has been printed by Aungier in his *History and Antiquities of Syon Monastery, the Parish of Isleworth*, etc. (8vo., London, 1840), pp. 405-409. The deficiencies of the original have been supplied from the Cathedral MS.

Treatises of Avicenna. Fourteenth century, in Latin. This volume certainly belonged to Old S. Paul's in 1458.*

Psalterium. Probably one of the service books of the ancient

---

* See Dugdale's *History*, edition 1818, p. 393.

Cathedral. **The obits in** the calendar **enumerate many names** familiar **in the history of** S. Paul's. Thirteenth century.

Sermones discipuli de Tempore et de Sanctis. 4to., Argentorati, 1495. This is **a** printed book ; **on the** title-page **is the** following manuscript note :

'Orate charitative pro [anima] Johis Tyndalle qui dedit hunc librum Conventui de Grenwych fratrum minorum de observancia die professionis sui filii fratris Willielmi Anno domini 1508.'*

Psalterium. Fourteenth century.

Processionale. 1497. On the **covers** are **some** fragments of early musical notation in *neumes*.

Breviarum. Fifteenth century.

Horæ. French. Fifteenth century.

Sermones. Two volumes. Fifteenth century.

Myrrour or Glasse of Christes Passion, with a translation by John **Fewterer.** (A collection of Meditations **on** Passages from the **Psalms.**) 1533.

(Townely arms, dated 1603, **on side.**)

Officia Propria Festivitatum et Sanctorum totius Ordinis S.S. Trinitatis Redemptionis captivorum. Augustæ Taurinorum. 1712.

Manuscript Collections relating to S. Paul's Cathedral. By the Rev. John Pridden, formerly Minor Canon ; inducted **in 1782** ; died in 1825. Four volumes.

Four volumes of Miss Hackett's Manuscript Collections relating to S. Paul's Cathedral and the Choir School.

---

* Of this inscription I have given some brief **account in my** *Gleanings from Old S. Paul's.*

CONTENTS.

1539? ❡ The enquirie and verdite of the quest panneld of the death of Richard Hune, wich was founde hanged in Lolars tower.

[Imperfect : only four leaves, title, and *To the Reader*. B.L., 8vo. The British Museum copy, to which the date above given is assigned, is cropped and imperfect, wanting all after c. iii.]

1539? Transcript by the Librarian of such portions of the above tract as exist in the British Museum copy, but are wanting in the Cathedral copy.

1561. Brief discovrs de la tempeste et fouldre aduenue en la cité de Londres en Angleterre, sur le grand temple & clocher, nômé de Sainct Paul, le quatriesme Iuin, M.D.LXI. À Paris, Par Guillaume Nyuerd, Imprimeur & Libraire, tenant sa boutique ioignant le pont aux Muniers, vers le chastellet : au bon Pasteur. Avec privilege. 4to., Paris, 1561.*

1561. 1885. Reprint by G. Blacker Morgan of The Trve Report of the burnyng of the Steple and Church of Poules in London, IVth June, 1561. Privately printed by Hazell, Watson, and Viney. London, 1885.

1563. The burnynge of Paules Church in London in the yeare of oure Lord 1561, and the IIII. day of June by lyghtnynge, at three of the clocke, at after noone, which continued terrible and helplesse vnto nyght. Printed by Willyam Seres. 8vo., London, 1563.

To this is added :

* The English and Latin versions of this Tract are not in the Cathedral Library.

1561. The True Report of the Burnyng of the Steple and Churche of Poules in London. B.L. W. Seres, London, 1561, 8vo. Eight leaves, without pagination. In the British Museum.

1561. Exemplum literarum amici cviusdam ad amicum quendam suum, de vera origine conflagrationis pyramidis & Templi Paulini Londinensis. Excusum Londini, in Officina Johannis Day, 1561. [Four leaves, 4to., printed in italics with the exception of the title-page. A copy in the Public Record Office.]

The English tract is reprinted in my *Documents illustrating the History of S. Paul's Cathedral*. (Camden Society.) Pp. 113-125, and pp. 202-206.

1563. **A Confutacion of an Addition,** wyth an Appologye written and cast in the stretes of VVest Chester, agaynst the causes of burnyng Paules Church in London whych causes the reuerend Byshop of Duresme [James PILKINGTON] declared at Paules Crosse 8 Junii, 1561. Imprynted at London by Wyllyam Seres dwellinge at the West end of Paules, at the signe of the Hedgehogge. ❡ the tenth of March, Anno **1563.**

1563. **Here folowe also** certain questions propounded **by him** [*i.e.*, the Author of the ' Addicion '] which are fullye . . . aunswered. [The 'Confutacion' and what follows probably written by Bishop Pilkington himself.] B.L. W. Seres, London, 1563.
Without pagination.

1579. 1872. **Newes out of Powles Churchyarde,** written in English Satyrs. By Edward HAKE, M.P. for New Windsor. Edited by Charles Edmonds. L.P. Originally printed in 1579. Reprinted, 8vo., London, 1872.

1614. **H. H[olland].** Monvmenta Sepvlchraria Sancti Pavli. The Monuments, Inscriptions, and Epitaphs of Kings, **Nobles, Bishops,** and others, buried in the Cathedrall Church of St. Pavl, London. Together with the foundation of the Church : **and a** catalogue of all the Bishops of London, etc., Vntil this present yeere of Grace, 1614. Printed for M. Law and H. Holland. 4to., London.
[This is the first edition. The second was published in 1633.]

1616. **The Complaint of Pavles to all Christian Sovles :**

> Or an humble supplication,
> To our good King and Nation,
> For Her newe Reparation.

Written by Henrie FARLEY. Amore, Veritate, & Reverentia. C. Legge [London], 1616, 4to.

1618. **Valens Arithmæus.** Mausoléa Regum, Reginarum, Dynastarum, nobilium, sumtuossima, artificiosissima, magnificentissima, LONDINI Anglorum in Occidentali Urbis angulo structa . . . cura Valentis Arithmæi. 12mo., Francof., Marchion, 1618.
[Pp. 123-144 relate to S. Paul's. To this is added *Aræ Exequiales.*]

1633. **Ecclesia** Sancti Pavli Illvstrata . . . together with a copy of the Pope's Pardon buried with Sʳ Gerard Braybroke, 1390. Together with a Preface, touching the Decayes and for the Repayring of this famous Church. By H[enry] H[OLLAND]. J. Norton. Sold by H. Seyle. 4to., London, 1633.

1621. **St. Pavles** Chvrch her Bill **for the Parliament,** As it **was** presented to the Kings Maᵗⁱᵉ on Midlent-Sunday last, and intended for the view of that most **high and** Honorable Court, and generally for all such as beare **good will to** the reflourishing estate of the said Chvrch. Partly in **Verse,** partly in Prose.

Penned and published for her good by Hen. FARLEY, Author of her Complaint. Anno Dom. M.DC.XXI. [London], 4to.
(Without pagination.)

On the title and on the last leaf but one is a woodcut of the Cathedral, showing Paul's Cross in sermon time.

1633. **Charles I.**, King. His Maiestie's Commission, and further declaration: concerning the reparation of Saint Pauls Church. 20 Dec., 1633. R. Barker . . . and the assigns of J. Bill. 4to., London, 1633.

1641. **The arraignement of Svperstition**, or a Discovrse betweene a Protestant, A Glasier, and a Separatist. Concerning the pulling downe of Church-Windowes. Shewing, the good mind of the Protestant, the indifference of the Glasier, and the puritie and zeale of the Seperatist. 4to., London, 1641.

[This scarce tract is reprinted in my *Gleanings from Old S. Paul's*, pp. 70-75. It is in verse.]

1641. **Saint Paul's Potion prescribed by Doctor Commons**, being very sicke of a dangerous Fulnesse, with the great effects it wrought. 4to., 'N.P., 1641.

1642. **Newes from Paules**: containing a Relation of the angry Disputation betwixt the two Church Quarrellers, Orange-Tawnie and Purple: being a Contention about the Lawfulnesse or Vnlawfulnesse of Organs and other Ceremonies. 4to., London. Printed in the year of Discord, 1642.

[Bound up with *Saint Paul's Potion*.]

1647? **Paul's Churchyard**, Libri Theologici, Politici, Historici, Nundinis Paulinis (una cum Templo) prostant venales juxta seriem Alphabeti Democratici. Done into English for the Assembly of Divines. (Two Centuryes.) [Sir John BIRKENHEAD.] 4to., N.P.

1647? **Two Centuries of Pauls Churchyard**: una cum Indice Expurgatorio in Bibliothecam Parliamenti, sive Librorum, qui prostant venales in Vico Vulgo Vocato Little Brittain. Done into English for the benefit of the Assembly of Divines, and the two Vniversities. [Sir John BIRKENHEAD.] Small 4to., N.P., *circa* 1647.

[British Museum Sale Duplicate, 1787.]

1649. **Newes from Powles**, or the new Reformation of the Army: with a true Relation of a Coult that was foaled in the Cathedrall Church of St. Paul in London, and how it was Publiquely Baptized by Paul Hobsons souldiers, one of them p . . g in his Helmet, and sprinkling it in the Name of the Father, Son, and holy Ghost ; and the Name (because a bald Coult) was called Baal-Rex. With a Catalogue of the Blasphemies, Murders. Cheats, Lies and Juglings of some of the Independent Party. Printed in the year 1649.

1649. **The Army's Martyr**: or a faithful Relation of the barbarous and illegall Proceedings of the Court-Martiall at White-Hall upon Mr. Robert LOCKIER . . . who was shot to death in Paul's Church-yard upon the 27 of April 1649. With a Petition of divers well-affected persons presented to the General in his behalf. 4to., London, 1649.

1649. **An Act of the Commons of England in Parliament assembled** ; For the Abolishing of Deans, Deans and Chapters, Canons, Prebends, and other Offices and Titles, of or belonging to any Cathedral, or Collegiate Church or Chappel within England and Wales. Together with several Ordinances of Parliament for the Sale of Bishops-Lands, unto which the said Act hath relation. 4to., London, 1649.

1659. **Bibliotheca Militum** : or The Souldiers Publick Library. Lately Erected for the Benefit of all that love the Good Old Cause, at Wallingford-House : and already furnished with diverse excellent Treatises, herein mentioned. 4to., London, 1659.
[Bound up with Two Centuries of Pauls Churchyard, etc.]

1659. **The Acts and Monuments of our late** Parliament : or, A Collection of the Acts, Orders, Votes, and Resolves that hath passed in the House. By J. CANNE, Intelligencer Generall. 4to., London, 1659.
[Bound up with Two Centuries, etc.]

1658. The History of **St.** Paul's Cathedral in **London.** By William DUGDALE. 4to., London, 1658.
[Later editions were issued in 1716 and 1818.]

1660. **A Dialogue between a living** Cobler and the Ghost **of a dead Shoomaker,** not long since slain, with others wilfully murdered near the Royall Exchange in London, as may be seen in these following lines . . . also a strange and Wonderfull Relation of a Voyce mightily heard in Pauls, Admired of all that heard it. 4to., London, 1660.
[Bound up with S. Pauls Potion.]

1661-18 . . . **A Short** Direction for the performance of **Cathedrall Service.** Published for the Information of such Persons, as are ignorant of it, And shall be call'd to officiate in Cathedrall, or Collegiate Churches, where it hath formerly been in use. By E. L. 4to., Oxford, 1661. Reprinted 18 . . .

1662. A brief relation of the Persecutions and Cruelties that have been acted upon the people called Quakers in and about the City of London, since the beginning of the 7th Month last, til this present time. With a general Relation of Affairs, signifying the state of the People through the Land. 4to., London, 1662.
[At p. 5, a remarkable incident in the Cathedral is recorded.]

1667. Pyrotechnica Loyolana, Ignatian, Fire-works, or, the Fiery Jesuits Temper and Behaviour. Being an Historical Compendium of the Rise, Increase, Doctrines, and Deeds of the Jesuits. Exposed to Publick view for the sake of London. By a Catholick-Christian. 4to., London, 1667.

[Opposite the title is a plate with the burning of S. Paul's, depicted in the upper dexter corner.]

1684? **Payne Fisher.** The Tombes, Monumentes, and Sepulchral Inscriptions, Lately Visible in St. Paul's Cathedral, and St. Faith's under it, etc. (Pp. 168, with three unnumbered leaves.) 4to., London.

1684? **Payne Fisher.** The Tombes, Monumentes, and Sepulchral Inscriptions Lately Visible in St. Paul's Cathedral Compleatly Rendred in Latin & English, with Several Historical Discourses, on Sundry Persons Intombed therein. A Work never yet Performed by any Author Old or New. Pp. 168.

.*. The author's Animadversion to the Reader (six leaves) is dated, from the Fleet, under the generous jurisdiction of Richard Manlove, Esq., the Worthy Warden thereof.

1684-1885. Major **Payne Fisher.** The Tombs, Monuments, &c., visible in S. Paul's Cathedral (and S. Faith's beneath it) previous to its destruction by Fire AD. 1666. Edited by G. Blacker Morgan. 4to., London, 1684; privately reprinted, 4to., London, 1885.

1695. Henry **Wharton.** Historia de Episcopis et Decanis Londinensibus : necnon de Episcopis et Decanis Assavensibus, a prima utriusque sedis fundatione ad annum 1540. 8vo., London, 1695.

1710. **The London**-Puppies Memorial, complaining of the Great Hardships they have lately suffer'd by the Unmerciful Hands of S. Paul's Dog-whippers. 8vo., N.P., 1710.

After 1710. **A Proposal** (by Renatus HARRIS, Organ-builder) for the Erecting of an Organ in S. Paul's Cathedral, over the West Door, at the Entrance into the Body of that Church (three pages). 4to., N.P., N.D.

[Reprinted in my *Documents illustrating the History of S. Paul's Cathedral.*]

1716. The History of **St. Paul's Cathedral in London** from its Foundation . . . whereunto is added a continuation thereof, setting forth what was done in the Structure of the New Church to the year 1685. Likewise an Historical Account of the Northern Cathedrals, and Chief Collegiate Churches in the Province of York. By Sir William DUGDALE. The Second Edition corrected and enlarged by the Author's own Hand. To which is prefixed his Life, written by himself. Publish'd by Edward Maynard, D.D., Rector of Boddington in Northamptonshire. Folio, London, 1716.

Also a large paper copy of the same edition.

1716. **St. Paul's Church**; or the Protestant Ambulators. A Burlesque Poem. 8vo., London, 1716.

1717. ΠΕΡΙ ΑΡΧΩΝ **Libri** Septem. Accedunt Liturgica.
Auctore **Gulielmo** NICOLS, A.M. Ecclesiæ **Stockportensis**
Rectore. 12mo., London, 1717.
[Frontispiece : View of the interior of S. Paul's.]

1717. **The** Inquisition, A Farce. As it was Acted at Child's
Coffee-House, and the King's-Arms Tavern, in St. Paul's Churchyard. Wherein the Controversy between the Bishop of Bangor
[*i.e.*, Benjamin Hoadly] and Dr. Snape is fairly Stated, and set
in a true Light. By Mr. J. PHILIPS. 8vo., London, 1717.

1750. Order of Proceedings for the Installation of Thomas
[SECKER], Lord Bishop of Oxford, as Dean of S. Paul's. **1750.**
Manuscript.

1761. Account of S. Paul's Cathedral (from *London and its
Environs Described*). 8vo., London, 1761.

1765. An Historical Description of S. **Paul's Cathedral.**
8vo., London, 1765. Printed for J. Newbery.

In the same volume is **An** Historical Description of
the Tower of London. 8vo., London, 1767. Printed for
J. Newbery.

1776. R. **Keach.** War with the Devil : or the Young Man's Con-
flict with the Powers of Darkness. Twenty-second Edition.
8vo., London, 1776.
[On page 131 is a rude cut, ' London in Flames.']

c. 1783. A Catalogue of the Library of the late Rev. Mr. John
Mangey, late Prebendary of St. Paul's, and Vicar of Dunmow
in Essex, including the valuable Library of his Father, the
learned Dr. Thos. Mangey, formerly Prebendary of Durham,
etc. (**1,511** vols.) MS., quarto.
Catalogue of Humfrey Wanley's **Books.**

1784. **An** Historical Description of St. Paul's Cathedral :
To which are added, A Description of the Monument, also
some Conjectures concerning London Stone and other Roman
remains, etc. 8vo., London, 1784.

1787. A **Form of** Prayer to be used Yearly on the Second
of September, for the dreadful Fire of London. 4to.,
London, 1787.

⁎ The Form of Prayer for September 2 will be found in
the Latin Prayer-Books :
8vo., London, 1727. Thos. Parsel, or Parsell.
8vo., London, 1744.   „   „
8vo., London, 1759.
but not in the Latin Prayer-Books of 1698 and 1703.
It is also in the French Prayer-Book :
8vo., London, 1788.
Copies of these Latin and French Prayer-Books are in the
Cathedral Library.
⁎ The use of this Form of Prayer in S. Paul's Cathedral
was discontinued in 1859.

1789. **Plan of S. Paul's** Cathedral and of the manner of fitting it up for Divine Service on the General Thanksgiving April 23, 1789, for the Accommodation of their Majesties, the Royal Family, and Court, and of both Houses of Parliament. By Order and under the Direction of Earl Salisbury, **Lord Chamberlain** of the Household, to R. MYLNE, Surveyor to the Fabric.

[With an autograph letter from Mr. Mylne, dated October 15, 1789, presenting the plan to the Dean and Chapter. This original plan shows the arrangements for seating all the more distinguished persons, whose names appear upon the margin.]

1789. **The Order of Procession of the King, Queen, etc.,** to St. Paul's Church on Thursday the 23d of April, 1789, being the Day appointed for a General Thanksgiving on Account of His Majesty's Recovery. To which is prefixed, An Account of the Processions into the City of London by different Kings and Queens, from Edward III. to the present Time. 8vo., London [1789].

1789. **An Authentic Account of the** Order of the Grand Procession, as it will be arranged, on their Majesties going to S. Paul's Cathedral on the 23d of April: together with the Names of all the Great Officers of State who will attend His Majesty, and those of the Ladies who will accompany the Queen. 8vo., London [1789].

1789. **A Fragment dropped** from the pocket of **a certain Lord**, on Thursday, the 23rd April, 1789, on his way to St. Paul's with the Grand Procession, with Notes by the Finder. 8vo., London, 1789.

1793. **Select Fables of Æsop,** and other Fabulists, in three books, collected by Mr. Dodsley. For the use of Schools. 12mo., Dublin, 1793.

[At p. 134, The Fly in S. Paul's Cupola.]

1796? Hints respecting the Monument erected to John **Howard** in Saint Paul's Cathedral.

18— James **Sykes,** Virger. Historical Sketch of S. Paul's Cathedral. 8vo., London, N.D.

1811. **Earle, J.** (successively Bishop of Worcester and Salisbury). Microcosmography, or a piece of the world discovered, in essays and characters.* With notes and an appendix by Dr. Philip Bliss. 8vo., London, 1811.

[Pp. 116-119 relate to Paul's Walk.]

1813. Plans, Elevation, Section, and View of the Cathedral Church of St. Paul, London; engraved by J. Le Keux, from drawings

---

* In the British Museum are several early editions, in 12mo.:

1628.
1629. The fifth.
1630. The sixth.
1633. Also called the sixth, but different from the last.
1638. The seventh.

by James Elmes, architect. With an Historical and Descriptive Account by Edmund Aikin, architect.   4to, London, 1813.

1814. **Thanksgiving Day**, 7 July, 1814. **Report** from Committee appointed to consider of the Manner of The House going to St. Paul's Church, on Thursday the 7th day of this instant July.

[House of Commons Report (four leaves), with Plan of the Choir of the Cathedral as arranged for the Service.]

1814. **Correspondence and Evidences respecting the ancient Collegiate School attached to Saint Paul's Cathedral.** Maria Hackett. The Fourth Edition, considerably enlarged. 4to, London, 1814.

Also the editions published in 1816 and 1832, together with Miss Hackett's Manuscript Collections.

1817. **Registrum Eleemosynariæ D. Pauli Londoniensis**, now first printed from a manuscript in the British Museum, with corroborative and explanatory Notes. Maria Hackett. 4to, London, **1817.**

Also the edition published in **1827**.

1816. [Miss Hackett.] **A Popular Account of S.** Paul's Cathedral. 8vo., London.

1816.	**1825.** Another edition.
1816. Another edition.	**1826.** 15th edition.
1818. A new edition.	**1829.** 18th **edition.**
1823. 10th edition.	**1833.** 19th edition.
1824. 12th edition.	**1835.** 21st edition.
1825. 13th edition.	**1837.**

1818. **The** History of Saint Paul's Cathedral in London, from its foundation. . . By Sir William DUGDALE. Knt., Garter Principal King at Arms. With a continuation and addition, including the Republication of **Sir** William Dugdale's Life from his own Manuscript: by Henry ELLIS, F.R.S., Keeper of the MSS. in the British Museum. Folio, London, 1818.

· **Also** a large paper copy of the same edition.

1820. **The Asses' Skin Memorandum Book lost in S. Paul's.** To which is added, A Condolence with **the Ultras.** (In verse.) 8vo., London, 1820.

1823. **The Historical, Descriptive, and Critical Account of the Cathedral Church of St. Paul, London. By** JOSEPH GWILT, architect. (Not published.) 8vo., London, 1823.

[One of **25** copies. This copy was presented to the Library by the Rev. R. H. Barham, librarian.]

1826. **The** New Testament, with explanatory Notes by J. WESLEY. 12mo., London, 1826.

(**The** binding is stamped with a representation of the west front of S. Paul's Cathedral.)

1828. **Camberwelliana**: or a Narrative, containing among other interesting subjects, a few gentle hints to . . . the Dean and Chapter of St. Paul's Cathedral. By Joseph SPARROW. 8vo., London, 1828.

1836. **Souvenirs relatif a Saint Paul de Londres**, suivis de quelques détails sur un autre monument de la même ville, La Tour de Londres. Par Gabriel PEIGNOT. 8vo., Paris, 1836.

1836. **A History and Description of S. Paul's Cathedral ;** containing a concise account both of the old and new Cathedrals. [Anon.] Dedicated to F. W. Blomberg, D.D., Canon Residentiary. 8vo., London, 1836.

1837. **George Godwin, jun., architect.** A History and Description of S. Paul's Cathedral. Plates from original drawings by R. W. **Billings, engraved by Lekeux,** Challis, and Turnbull. 8vo., London, 1837.

1838. **Manuscript Reports on the Library of S. Paul's Cathedral,** March 21, 1838, March 19, 1839, March 21, 1840, March 21, 1843, in the handwriting of the Rev. R. H. BARHAM, Librarian. 4to., MS., 1838.

1839. **Plan for a more extensive application to Divine Service of the hitherto unoccupied portions of the Cathedrals of England,** but more especially of S. Paul's Cathedral, in a letter to the Dean, etc. By a Clergyman. 8vo., London, 1839.

1839. **R. C. Packman, Minor Canon.** Spiritualities and Temporalities of S. Paul's Cathedral. First edition, 8vo., London [1839]. Second edition, 8vo., London, 1839.

1851. **The Children in S. Paul's.** An account of the anniversary of the assembled Charity Schools of London and Westminster in the Cathedral Church of S. Paul. By T. B. MURRAY, M.A., Prebendary, etc. 8vo., London, 1851.
　　[Frontispiece, 4,000 charity children witnessing a royal procession to S. Paul's, September 20, 1714.]

1854. **Remarks on a Danish Runic Stone** from the eleventh century found in the central part of London. [S. Paul's Churchyard.] By Charles Christian RAFN. 8vo. Copenhagen. 1854.
　　[The original stone is now in the Guildhall Museum ; a cast from it was presented by Dr. Sedgwick Saunders to the Cathedral Library in 1890.]

"**Scandinavian**" or "**Danish**" sculptured Stones found in London : and their bearing on the supposed "Scandinavian" or "Danish" origin of other English sculptured stones. By the Rev. G. F. BROWNE.
　　Paper from the *Archæological Journal*, xlii., pp. 251-259, with plate of the stone discovered in S. Paul's Churchyard.

1855. **The** Companion to S. Paul's Cathedral. By E. M.
CUMMINGS [Dean's Virger]. Nineteenth edition. 8vo., London,
1855.

1857. Pavements from Chertsey **Abbey, Surrey.** By Henry
SHAW, F.S.A. **4to.,** London.
Ten plates.

1857. **Order of** opening the Convocation of the Clergy of the
Province of Canterbury on Friday, the 1st Day of May, 1857 [at
S. Paul's Cathedral]. 4to., London, 1857.
Also other editions of the *Order.*

1858. The Domesday of S. Paul's of the year 1222, with an
Introduction, Notes, and Illustrations by William Hale HALE,
Archdeacon of London. (Camden Soc.) 4to., London, 1858.

186—. S. **Paul's Cathedral Guide,** with 'Arnott Brothers &
Co.' on the title.
[Messrs. Arnott were drapers in S. Paul's Churchyard.]

1861. Forma Precum in utraque Domo Convocationis, sive
synodi Prælatorum et cæteri cleri, seu Provincialis seu Nationalis,
in ipso statim cujuslibet sessionis initio solenniter recitanda.
4to., London, 1861, and other editions.

1862. **A Guide** over S. Paul's **Cathedral.** By D. LEEF
[Virger]. 8vo., London, 1862.
A new edition, 8vo., London, N.D.

1864. **The Companion** to S. Paul's Cathedral. By E. M.
CUMMINGS. [Dean's Virger.] Twenty-eighth edition. 8vo.,
London, 1864.

1864-1878. **Service Books at Festivals of Societies.**
Sons of the Clergy, 1864, 1866, 1869, 1870, 1873, 1875-8.
Infant Orphan Asylum, Jubilee, 1877.
Officers' Daughters' School, 1878.
London Gregorian Association, **1873, 1875.**
Guild of S. Luke, 1878.
Tonic Sol-Fa Association, Jubilee, 1891.

1868. **Remarks on a Visitation Mandate of Archbishop
Boniface to the Dean** and Canons of S. Paul's, A.D.
1253. By Thomas HUGO, M.A., etc. (Large paper.) **8vo.,**
London, 1868.

1869. Annals of S. Paul's Cathedral. By Henry Hart
MILMAN, D.D., late Dean of S. Paul's. Second edition. 8vo.,
London, 1869.

1869. The Companion to S. Paul's Cathedral. By E. M.
CUMMINGS. [Dean's Virger.] Thirty-fifth edition. 8vo., London,
1869.

1871. The Charter and Statutes of the College of the
Minor Canons in S. Paul's Cathedral. Communicated

to the Society of Antiquaries by W. Sparrow SIMPSON, D.D. 4to., Westminster, 1871.

1871. **Report of the** Committee appointed to consider the arrangement of the Musical Services in S. Paul's Cathedral. 4to., London, 1871.

1872. **The old Cheque-Book,** or Book of Remembrance, of the Chapel Royal from 1561 to 1744. Edited by Edward F. RIMBAULT, LL.D. (Camden Soc.) 4to., London, 1872.
[Contains many particulars relating to musicians who have held office in the Cathedral.]

1872. **Prince of Wales.** Thanksgiving Service. February 27, 1872. Collection of Papers and Letters relating to the Ceremony.

1872. A Form of Service on the occasion of the Thanksgiving for the Recovery of His Royal Highness the **Prince of Wales.** To be used at Saint Paul's Cathedral 27th February, 1872. By authority. 4to., London, 1872, and also large paper.

1872. **S. Paul's Commutation.** Order in Council. *London Gazette,* August 13, 1872.

1873. **William** Longman. A History of the Three Cathedrals dedicated to S. Paul in London. 8vo., London, 1873.

1873. **S. Paul's Cathedral.** Service for the Admission of **Choristers.**

c. 1873. **S. Paul's Cathedral.** Order of the late Evening Service.

1873. Registrum Statutorum et Consuetudinum Ecclesiæ Cathedralis Sancti Pauli Londinensis. Edited by W. Sparrow SIMPSON 4to., London, 1873.
[Privately printed.]

1873-1892. **The** Weekly Music Bills **of S. Paul's Cathedral,** under three successive Succentors
Rev. W. C. F. Webber, January, 1873—April, 1876.
Rev. W. Sparrow Simpson, Easter, 1876—Easter, 1885.
Rev. W. Russell, Easter, 1885—present time.

1874. **W. C. Fynes Webber.** Letter to the Dean on the Ritual arrangements of the Cathedral, together with a plan. (Three pages.) June, 1874.

1874. Account of the Executors of Richard [de **Gravesend**], Bishop of London, 1303, and of the Executors of Thomas [de **Bitton**], Bishop of Exeter, 1310. Edited by the late Venerable W. Hale HALE, M.A., Archdeacon of London, and the Rev. H. T. ELLACOMBE, M.A. (Camden Soc.) 4to., London, 1874.

1874. A **Guide to** S. Paul's **Cathedral.** Anon. 8vo., London, 1874.

1875. **Minor Canons' Act,** June 29, 1875, 38 & 39 Victoria, c. 74.

1876. **Minor Canons' Scheme.** Order in Council. *London Gazette,* July 21. 1876.

1876. A Calendar of the Ecclesiastical Dignitaries of S. Paul's Cathedral from the year 1800 to the present time, 1876. 8vo. Compiled by W. Sparrow SIMPSON, Librarian.
[Communicated to the London and Middlesex Archæological Society.]

1876-1885. Reports on **the Music of the Cathedral** by the Succentor, W. Sparrow SIMPSON.
First Report. Easter, 1876—Easter, 1877. 4to., London, 1877.
Second Report. Easter, 1878—Easter, 1879. 4to., London, 1879.
Third Report. Easter, 1880—Easter, 1881. 4to., London, 1881.
Fourth Report. Easter, 1882—Easter, 1883. 4to., London, 1883.
Fifth Report. Easter, 1883—Easter, 1885. 4to., London, 1885.

1877. **Order** of Service for the Marriage of the Lady Mayoress (**Ada Louisa** White) with **Mr.** Cecil Herbert Thornton Price in S. Paul's Cathedral, 9 Aug., 1877. 8vo., London.

1877. The **Abbey Church of Saint** Albans, Hertfordshire. Illustrated by James NEALE, F.S.A., architect. Folio, London, 1877.

1878. Agreement (relating to the Opening of S. Paul's Churchyard) between the Dean and Chapter, and the Mayor and Commonalty and Citizens. July 11, 1878 (Corn, Coal, and Finance Committee) 4to., London.

1878. Conference of Bishops of the Anglican Communion holden at Lambeth Palace, July, 1878. Letter from the Bishops, including the Reports adopted by the Conference. **Service** at S. Paul's. Order of Ceremonial. 8vo., London, 1878.

1878. Service used at the Dedication of the Peal of Twelve **Bells** in S. Paul's Cathedral, All Saints Day, 1878.

1879. Enthronement of Bishop **Lightfoot** to the See of Durham. 8vo., Durham, 1879.

1879. Handbook to the Cathedrals of England. Saint Paul's. With illustrations. 8vo., John Murray, 1879.
['This **Handbook** is essentially an abridged edition of Dean Milman's *Annals of S. Paul's,*' with additional matter. Edited by Arthur MILMAN, Esq.]

1880. **Documents Illustrating the History of S.** Paul's

Cathedral. Edited by W. Sparrow SIMPSON. (Camden Soc.) 4to., London, 1880.

1881. Chapters in the History of Old S. Paul's. W. Sparrow SIMPSON. 8vo., London, 1881.

1882. **On the Recent Discoveries of Portions of Old S. Paul's Cathedral.** Communicated to the Society of Antiquaries by Francis Cranmer PENROSE, Esq., F.R.I.B.A., Surveyor to the Fabric of S. Paul's. 4to., Westminster, 1882.

188 . . Notes on S. Paul's Cathedral. By Francis C. PENROSE ; with discussion at the Institute of British Architects. (Twelve pages.)
[A plan of the newly-discovered cloisters, and a plan of Old S. Paul's accompanies the paper.)

1882. Great Paul from its Casting to its Dedication. By S. J. MACKIE, C.E. With a Preface on Bells, by John STAINER, M.A., Doc.Mus., Organist of S. Paul's. 8vo., London, 1882.

1882. F. C. Penrose. On the recent discoveries of portions of Old S. Paul's Cathedral. (Society of Antiquaries.) 4to., London, 1882.

1883. **Ninth Report of the Royal Commission on Historical Manuscripts.** 4to., London, 1883.
[Contains Mr. Maxwell LYTE's Report on the Records of the Dean and Chapter.]

1884. **A List of the Lenten Services in S.** Paul's Cathedral **1884**, with the Names of the Preachers, the Subjects of their Discourses, etc. (Griffith and Farran.) 4to., London, 1884. A similar list for 1885.

1884. Manuscript Catalogue of Music in S. Paul's Cathedral. Compiled by Henry KING, Assistant Vicar Choral. 1884. 4to.

1884. Commemoration of the Consecration of Bishop Seabury. 14 November, 1784. Being the Order of Service in St. Paul's Cathedral, 14 November, 1884. 8vo., London, 1884.

1885. **Tiles from Chertsey Abbey, Surrey,** representing Early Romance Subjects. By Manwaring SHURLOCK, F.R.C.S. Folio, London, 1885.

1885-1892. Report on the Music of the Cathedral. By the Succentor, the Rev. William RUSSELL, M.A., Mus. Bac.
First Report. Easter, 1885—Easter, 1887. 4to, London, 1887.
Second Report. Easter, 1889—Easter, 1890. 4to., London, 1890.

1887. Two Inventories of the Cathedral Church of S. Paul, London, dated respectively 1245 and 1402. Edited by W. Sparrow SIMPSON, etc. 4to., Westminster, 1887.
[Communicated to the Society of Antiquaries.]

1889. W. Sparrow Simpson. Gleanings from Old S. Paul's. 8vo., London, 1889.

1890. W. Sparrow **Simpson.** On the Statutes of Dean **COLET** for the Government of Chantry Priests and other Clergy of S. Paul's Cathedral. (Society of Antiquaries.) 4to., London, 1890.

1890. Papers relating to the Funeral of Lord Napier of Magdala, 21 January, 1890.

1891. **The Organists and Composers of S. Paul's Cathedral.** by John S. BUMPUS. 8vo., London, 1891.

1891. **The Palaces or Town Houses of the Bishops of London.** By W. Sparrow SIMPSON.
[Communicated to the *Transactions* of the London and Middlesex Archæological Society.]

1892. **Mandate of Bishop Clifford** superseding the ancient Use of S. Paul's by the Use of Sarum. Edited by W. Sparrow SIMPSON
[Communicated to the *Proceedings* of the Society of Antiquaries.]

1892. **The Greeting of the Ward of Castle Baynard** to its Alderman, the Rt. Hon. David **Evans,** F.R.G.S., Lord Mayor of London, 9th November, 1891. Privately printed for the reception committee of Castle Baynard Ward. 4to., London, 1892. (Only sixty **copies** printed.)

Photograph of the Model of Baynard's Castle, erected in S. Paul's Churchyard 9 Nov., 1891, from which was presented the Address of the Inhabitants of Castle Baynard Ward to their Alderman, the Rt. Hon. David EVANS, F.R.G.S., Lord Mayor.

1892. **John B. Marsh. S. Paul's Cross :** the most famous spot in London. 8vo., London, 1892.

1892. Memoir concerning the **Seabury** Commemoration held at S. Paul's Cathedral, London, the 14th day of November, 1884. By George SHEA. 8vo., Cambridge [America], 1892.

Collections relating to S. Paul's Cathedral. **Gathered by** W. Sparrow SIMPSON, D.D.
A series of quarto volumes.

Three volumes of Collections, printed and manuscript, relating especially to the Decoration of the Cathedral, the Bells, and the Wellington Monument. Compiled by Thomas CHIPPERFIELD.

The Misfortunes of S. Paul's Cathedral. (In verse. **Four** leaves. No title.) 4to.

Papers relating to the Election **and** Installation of a Bishop.

Collection **of** Newspaper Cuttings relating to the Cathedral.

The Manuscript Collections relating to S. **Paul's Cathedral**
of the Rev. John **Pridden** : admitted a Minor Canon in 1782.
Five vols.

PAUL'S CROSS SERMONS.

1550. ❡ A Sermon preached at Pauls Crosse the XIIII day of
December, by Thomas **Leuer**. Anno. M.D.L. Imprynted at
London by Jhon Day dwellyng ouer Aldersgate. 8vo., London,
1550.

B.L., without pagination.

1555. A notable and very fruictefull Sermon made at Paules Crosse
the XXV. day of August, by maister Hughe **Glasier**, Chapleyn
to the Quenes most excellent maiestie, Perused by the reuerende
father in god Edmond bishop of London, and by him approued,
commended, and greatly liked : and therefore nowe set furth in
print, by his auctoritie and commaundement.

Read, and iudge.
Loke, and lyke.

Imprinted at London by Robert Caly, within the precinct of
the late dissolued house of the graye Freers, nowe conuerted to
an hospital, called Christes hospitall. The XII. day of October,
1555. 8vo., London, 1555.

1560. ✠ The copie of a Sermon [on 1 Cor. xi. 23] pronounced by
the Byshop of Salisburie [John **Jewel**] at Paules Crosse the
second Sondaye before Ester in the Yere of our Lord, 1560.
Whervpon D. **Cole** first sought occasion to encounter, shortly
set forthe as nere as the authour could call it to remembraunce,
without any alteration or addition. 8vo., John Daye [c. 1560].

B.L., without pagination.

c. 1571. John Brigges [**Bridges**, Bishop of Oxford]. ❡ A Sermon
preached at Paules Crosse on the Monday in Whitson weeke,
Anno Domini 1571. Entreating on this sentence, Sic Deus
dilexit, etc. [S. John iii. 16]. At London, printed by Henry
Binneman for Humfrey Toy. N.D. 4to.

1572. **Wimbledon**, R. ❡ A Sermon, etc. ❡ Imprinted at
London by John Awdely. (*See the next article.*)

1575. **Wimbledon**, R. ❡ A Sermon [on S. Luke xvi. 2] no
lesse fruitful then famous. Made in the yeare of our Lord God,
m.ccclxxxviij. and founde out hyd in a wall. Which Sermon is
here set forth by the old copy, without adding or diminishing
saue the old & rude English here and there amended.
❡ Imprinted at London by John Awdely. 1575, 8vo.

B.L., without pagination.

1582. R. **Wimbeldon**. A sermon no lesse fruitfull then famous.
Preached at Paules Crosse on the Sunday of Quinquagesima,

by R. Wimbeldon, in the raigne of King Henry the fourth, in the yeare of our Lorde 1388, And found out hid in a Wall, etc.
¶ Imprinted at London by John Charlewood, 1582.

B.L., forty-four leaves, without pagination.

Other editions of this sermon :

1584. By John Charlewood. London. B.L.

1603. By James Roberts. London.

1617. By W. Jaggard. London. B.L. Eleventh edition.

1634. By T. Cotes. London. B.L. Fourteenth edition.

See also, *infra*, 1738.

The British Museum has also the thirteenth edition, printed in 1629 by T. and R. Cotes; and the fifteenth by T. Cotes, printed in 1635, etc.

1578. **White, Thomas.** A Sermon [on Zeph. iii. 1-3] Preached at Pawles Crosse on Sunday the ninth of December, 1576, by T. W[hite]. 8vo., Imprinted at London by Francis Coldock, 1578.

B.L. [See *Athenæ Oxonienses*, i. 413.]

1578. A Sermon preached at Pavls Crosse by John **Walsal**, one of the Preachers of Christ his Church in Canterburie, 5 October, 1578. And published at the earnest request of certein godlie Londoners and others. 8vo., London, G. Byshop, *c.* 1578.

1579. **Knewstub, J.** A Confutation of Monstrous & Horrible heresies, taught by HN, and embraced of a number who call themselves the Familie of Loue. ✠ A Sermon preached at Paules Crosse the Fryday before Easter, commonly called good Fryday, in the yeere of our Lorde, 1576. By John KNEWSTUB. 8vo., London, 1579.

1580. Two **Sermons** preached, the one at Paules Crosse the eight of Januarie, 1580; the other at Christes Church in London, the same day in the after-noone; by James BISSE, Maister of Arte, and Fellowe of Magdalene Colledge in Oxenford. 8vo., at London; Printed by Robert Waldegraue, etc.

On the title, in red ink, the date of publication has been added with a pen—1585.

1583. **Certaine Sermons** preached before the Queenes Maiestie and at Paules Crosse. By John JEWEL, Bishop of Salisbury. C. Barker. 8vo., London, 1583. Without pagination.

1584. Two Sermons preached by the reuerend father in God Richard [Curteis] Bishop of Chichester, the first [on Rev. xii. 1-9] at Paules Crosse. The second [on Acts xx. 28-31] at Westminster before the Queenes Maiestie. At London. Printed by T. Man, and W. Brome. Anno. 1584, 8vo., B.L.

[Paul's Cross Sermon preached March 4, 1576 ; Westminster Sermon preached third Sunday in Lent, 1576.]

✱✱✱ An earlier edition, 8vo., London, 1576, B.L.

[1585.] ¶ A couvnter-poyson, modestly written for the time, to make aunswere to the objections and reproches, wherewith the aunswerer to the Abstract would disgrace the holy Discipline of Christ. At London, Printed by Robert Waldegrave. 4to.

1586. **A Defence of the** reasons of the **Counter-poyson,** for maintenance of the Eldership, against an aunsvvere made to them by Doctor Copequot, in a publike Sermon at Pawles Crosse, vpon Psal. 84. 1584. 8vo., N.P., 1586.

The **Counter-poyson** was a reply to the **Answer**— probably by WHITGIFT — to a book called an **Abstract** of certain Acts and Canons.

[Note by W. MASKELL.]

1588. **Bancroft,** Richard [successively Bishop of London and Archbishop of Canterbury]. A Sermon [on S. John iv. 1] preached at Paules Crosse the 9. of Februarie, being the first Sunday in the Parleament, Anno. 1588, by Richard Bancroft D. of Diuinitie, and Chaplain to the Right Honorable Sir Christopher Hatton Knight, L. Chancelor of England. Wherein some things are now added, which then were omitted, either through want of time, or default in memorie. London, by E. B. for Gregorie Seton, 1588. 8vo.

[In the British Museum is another edition. J. Norton. Sold by G. Emerson, London, 1637, 4to.]

1590. **A Sermon** preached at Pavles Crosse the ix. of November, 1589. By William JAMES D. of Diuinitie, and Deane of Christes-church in Oxford. Imprinted at London by George Bishop and Ralph Newberie, 1590. 4to.

1591. **A Sermon** Preached at Paules Crosse the second Sunday in Mychaelmas tearme last. 1590. By Geruase BABINGTON D. of Diuinitie. Not printed before this 23. of August, 1591. ¶ Imprinted at London by Thomas Este, dwelling in Aldersgate Streete, etc.

(See a later edition, *infra,* 1599.)

1591. **A Sermon** preached at Pauls Crosse on the 17. day of Nouember 1590, being the first day of the 33. yeare of the Queenes Maiesties raigne, commonly called, the Queenes day. By John DUPORT Doctour of Diuinitie. 8vo., London. Printed by John Wolfe for Edward Aggas. 1591.

1592. **A Sermon** [on 1 Cor. xiv. 1] teaching discretion in matters of religion, and touching certayne abuses nowe in the Churche: Preached at Paules Crosse the 21. of Nouember by Robert TEMPLE Bachelor in Diuinitie sometimes of Magdalene Collegge in Oxford. London : by R. B. for Edward Aggas, 1592. 8vo.

1593. **Hearts Delight.** A Sermon preached at Pauls Crosse in London in Easter terme. 1593. By Thomas PLAYFERE Professour of Diuinitie for the Lady Margaret in Cambridge. 8vo., Cambridge, 1603.

(In the same volume, a sermon by Playfere in Exeter Cathedral, 1596.) 8vo., London. 1633.

1597. John Howson [successively Bishop of Oxford and of Durham].
A Sermon [on S. Matt. xxi. 12, 13] preached at Paules Crosse
the 4. of December, 1597. Wherein is discoursed that all buy-
ing and selling of spirituall promotion is unlawfull. By John
Howson, student of Christes Church in Oxford. A. Hatfield
for T. Adams. 4to., London, 1597.

1598. The Trumpet of Warre. A Sermon [on 2 Chron. xx.
20] preached at Paules Crosse the seuenth of Maie 1598. By
M. Steph. Gosson Parson of Great Wigborow in Essex.
Printed at London by V. S. for I. O. dwelling in Paules churchyard at the signe of the Parot [1598 ?]. 8vo.

1598. A Second Sermon, preached at Paules Crosse, the 21. of
May, 1598. vpon the 21. of Math. the 12. and 13. verses.
Concluding a former Sermon Preached the 4. of December
1597. vpon the same Text. By John Howson Student of
Christes-church in Oxford. A. Hatfield for T. Adams. 4to.,
London, 1598.

1599. A Sermon Preached at Paules Crosse the second Sunday in
Mychaelmas tearme last 1590. By Geruase Babington D. of
Diuinitie. Not printed before this 23. of August 1591. 8vo.,
London, Thomas Este, 1599.

1599. The effect of Certaine Sermons touching the full
redemption of mankind by the death and bloud of
Christ Jesus . . preached at Paules Crosse and elsewhere in
London, by the right Reuerend Father Thomas Bilson, Bishop
of Winchester. 4to., London, 1599.

1601. A Sermon [on S. Matt. xxi. 22] preached at Paules Crosse,
on the first Sunday in Lent Martii 1, 1600. With a short discourse of the late Earl of Essex his confession, and penitence,
before and at the time of his death. By William Barlow
Doctor of Diuinitie. Whereunto is annexed a true copie, in
substance, of the behaviour, speache and prayer of the said Earle
at the time of his execution. 8vo., London, Mathew Law,
1601, B.L.

1602. A Sermon of the Steward's Danger : Preached at
Paules Crosse the 15. of August by John Hayward. 8vo.,
London, Humfrey Lownes, 1602.

1602. A Sermon [on Gen. ix. 27] preached at Paules Crosse the
13. of June, 1602. By M. Francis Marburie. 8vo., London,
Peter Short, 1602. Without pagination.

1605. A Sermon preached at Paules Crosse the 9. of June, 1605,
upon the 20. of the Reuelation the 12. vers. . . . By Samuell
Gardnier, Doct. of Diuinitie. 4to., London, Edward White,
1605.

1606. Jonahs Sermon, and Ninivehs repentance. A Sermon
preached at Pauls Crosse Jun. 20. 1602, and now thought fit to
be published for our meditations in these times. By Ro.

WAKEMAN Master of Arts and fellow of Balioll Colledge in Oxford. The second impression. 8vo., Oxford, 1606.

1606. Barlow, William [successively Bishop of Rochester and of Lincoln]. The Sermon [on Psal. xviii. 50] preached at Paules Crosse, the tenth day of November, being the next Sunday after the Discouerie of this late Horrible Treason [the Gunpowder Plot]. Preached by the right Reverend Father in God William, Lord Bishop of Rochester. G. W. for Mathew Lawe, London, 1606. 4to.

1608. A Sermon preached at Paules Crosse, vpon the 1. of November, being All-Saints Day, Anno 1607. By Sa. COLLINS. Batchelour in Diuinitie, and fellow of the Kings Colledge in Cambridge. 4to., London, 1608. By Humfrey Lownes for Richard Bonian.

1608. Foure Sermons lately preached by Martin Fotherby, Doctor in Diuinity, and Chaplain vnto the Kings Maiestie. . . . The Third at Paules Crosse, vpon the day of our deliuerance from the gun-powder treason. Nouemb. 5, Anno. 1607. London, Henry Ballard for C. K. and W. C., 1608. 4to.

1608. The Sermon [on Jer. li. 9] preached at the Crosse, Feb. xiiii., 1607. By W. CRASHAWE, Batchelour of Diuinitie, and preacher at the Temple : justified by the Authour, both against Papist, and Brownist, to be the truth, &c. Imprinted by H. L. for E. Weaver. 4to., London, 1608.
[In the British Museum is the second impression, reviewed by the author.—Imprinted by H. L. for M. Lownes. 4to., London, 1609.]

1609. Gods mercies and Jerusalems miseries. A Sermon Preached at Pauls Crosse the 25. of June, 1609. By Lancelot DAWES, Master of Arts and Fellow of Queenes Colledge in Oxford. 8vo., printed for Cle. Knight, 1609. No place.

1609. Davids Teacher, or The Trve Teacher of the Right-Way to Heaven. Discovering erroneous Teachers and Seditious Sectuaries. Preached at Paules-Crosse the 3. of September, 1609. By Ro: JOHNSON, M. of Arts, chaplaine to the Right Reuerend Father in God, the L. Bishop of Lincolne. London : T. Haueland for Mathew Law, and are to be solde at his shop in Pauls-Church-yard, neere S. Austins-gate, at the Signe of the Fox, 1609. 4to.

1609. Loves complaint, for Want of Entertainment. A Sermon [on 1 Cor. xiii. 6, 7] preached at Pavles Crosse, the third of December, 1609. By William HOLBROOKE. 4to., London, Nathaniel Butter. N.D. Without pagination.

1609. Sauls prohibition staide. Or the apprehension, and examination of Saule. And the Inditement of all that perse-cute Christ. With a reproofe of those that traduce the Honour-able Plantation of Virginia. Preached in a Sermon, Commaunded **at Pauls** Crosse, vpon Rogation Sunday, being the 28. of May, 1609. By Daniel PRICE, chapleine in **ordinarie** to the Prince, and Master of Artes of Exeter Colledge **in Oxford.** 4to., London, 1609.

1609. **A** Sermon at **the** solemnizing **of the** Happie Inauguration of our most gracious and Religious Soueraigne King James. . . Preached at Paules Crosse, the **24.** of March last, 1608. By Richard CRAKANTHORPE, Doctor **of** Diuinitie. **4to.,** London, Tho. Adams, **1609.**

1609. J. H. [Joseph **Hall,** successively Bishop of **Exeter** and **of** Norwich]. The Passion Sermon [on S. John **xix. 30**] preached at Paules Crosse, on **Good-Friday** Apr. 14, 1609, **by** I. H. Printed by W. S. for E. Edgar. **8vo.,** London, 1609.
[In the British Museum is **another** edition. **Printed by** W. S. for E. Edgar. 16mo., London, 1609.]

1609. **A Sermon** preached [on Hosea vii. 7-12] at Pavles Crosse the seauenth of May, M.DC.IX. By George BENSON, Doctor **of Diuinitie,** sometimes fellowe of Queenes Colledge in Oxford. Imprinted by H. L. for R. Moore. 4to., London, 1609.

1609. **Cheaste,** Thomas. The Way to Life. Delivered in a Sermon [on Amos v. 6] preached at Paules Crosse . . . 1608. N. O[kes] for W. Jones, London, 1609. 4to.

1611. **A** Sermon preached at Pauls Crosse the third of March 1610. By Theophilus HIGGONS. In testimony of his heartie reunion with the Church of England, and humble submission **thereunto.** Published by Command. **4to.,** London, 1611.

1611. The Sinne against the Holy Ghost plainly described . . in a Sermon preached at Pavles Cross, April 14, 1611. By **Iohn** DENISON, Bachelor of Diuinitie. 4to., London, 1611.

1612. The Gallants Burden. **A Sermon** [on Isaiah xxi. 11, 12] preached at Pavles Crosse, **the twentie** nine of March, being the first Sunday in Lent **1612.** By **Tho.** ADAMS, Preacher of Gods Word at Willington in Bedford-shire. 4to., London, **1612.**
[The British Museum **has an edition.** 4to., London, 1616.]

1612. Repentance not to be repented of. A Sermon preached at Pauls Crosse October **18,** 1612 . . . since reuiewed and enlarged by William HULL. **Doctor in** Diuinitie. **4to.,** London, 1612.

1613. The Christian Pathway. Deliuered **in a Sermon** [on Ephes. v. 1] preached at Paules Crosse the last of June, **1611.** By Mr. Thomas CHEASTE, Minister **and** Preacher of **Gods** Word. N. Okes. **4to.,** London, 1613.

1613. **Englands Svmmons.** A Sermon preached at Pauls Crosse the third of January, 1612. By Thomas SUTTON, Master of Arts and fellow of Queenes Colledge in Oxford. 4to., London, 1613.

1613. **The** White Devil, or the Hypocrite Vncased. In a Sermon [on S. John xii. 6] preached at Pavls Crosse, March 7, **1612.** By Thomas ADAMS, minister of the Gospell at Willington, in Bedford-shire. The second edition. **T. Snodham for** R. Mab. 4to., London, 1613.

> The British Museum possesses also 'a fourth impression.'

1613. **The** Earnest of our Inheritance : together with a description of the new Heaven and of the New Earth . . . Preached at Pauls Crosse the second day of August, 1612. By Thomas DRAXE, Bachelour of Diuinity. 4to., London, 1613.

1613. **The** Cryer. A Sermon preached at Pavls Crosse the fifth of Februarie. By Nathanaell CANNON, Preacher of Gods word at Wokeingham. Felix Kingston. 8vo., London, 1613.

1613. London's Warning by Laodicea's Luke-Warme-nesse, or a sermon preached at Paules-Crosse, the 10 of October, 1613, being the first Sunday in Tearme. By Sampson PRICE, M^r of Arts, of Exeter-Colledge ; and Preacher to the Cittie of Oxford. 4to., London, 1613.

1613. **The** godly Merchant, or the greate gaine. A Sermon preached at Paules Crosse Octob. 17, **1613.** By William PEM-BERTON, Bachelour of Diuinity, and Minister of Gods Word at High Onger in Essex. 4to., London, 1613.

1614. Ivstifying and saving Faith distingvished from the Faith of the Deuils. In a Sermon [on S. James ii. 19] preached at Pauls Crosse in London, May 9, 1613. By Miles MOSSE, Pastor of the Church of God at Combes in Suffolke, and Doctor of Diuinitie. C. Legge, Printer to the Vniversitie of Cambridge. 4to., 1614.

1615. **Sermons** preached at Pavls Crosse and else-where, by Iohn HOSKINS, sometimes Fellow of New-Colledge in Oxford, minister and Doctor of Law. (The volume contains two sermons, one 'preached at Saint Maries in Oxford' [on S. Luke xii. 48]; the other 'preached at Pavls Crosse '). 4to., London, 1615.

1615. Two Sermons preached : the one at Hereford, the other at Pavls Crosse. By Iohn HOSKINS, minister and Doctor of the Law. 4to., London, 1615.

1615. Two Sermons preached : the one at Saint Maries in Oxford [on Hosea viii. 12], the other being the conclvsion of the Re-hearsall Sermon at Pauls Crosse, 1614. By Iohn HOSKINS, Minister and Doctor of the Law. 4to., London, 1615.

1615. A Learned and Graciovs Sermon Preached at Paules Crosse, by that famovs and Iudicious Diuine, Iohn SPENSER, D. of Diuinity, and late President of Corpus Chr. Coll. in Oxford. Published for the benefite of Christs Vineyard, by H. M. 4to., London, 1615.

1615. Two Sermons ; the former delivered at Pavles Crosse the

fovre and twentieth of March, 1615, being the anniuersarie
commemoration of the Kings most happie succession in the
Crowne of England. The latter at the Spittle on Monday in
Easter Weeke, 1613. By Iohn WHITE, D.D. 4to, London,
1615.

1615. A Divine Enthymeme of trve Obedience : or a Taske
for a Christian. Preached at Pauls Crosse the tenth of September, 1615, by Anthonie HUGGET, Maister of Arts, and
Parson of the Cliffe neare Lewis in Sussex. 4to, London,
1615.

1615. A Sermon against oppression and fraudulent
dealing : preached at Pavles Crosse, the eleuenth of December,
by Charles RICHARDSON, Preacher at Saint Katherines neare the
Tower of London. 4to., London, 1615.

1616. The Patterne of an Invincible Faith. A Sermon
preached at Paules Crosse, the first Sunday afrer Trinity, being
the 2d of June, 1616. By William WORSHIP, Doctor of
Diuinitie. 4to., London, 1616.

1616. Gods Plentie, feeding trve Pietie. In a Sermon [on
Psa. lxxxi. 10] preached at Pavls Crosse, on the 18 day of June,
1615. To warne the Oppressor, whose trust is in the World ;
and to ease the Oppressed, who trusteth in the Lord. By Iohn
WHALY. W. Stansby. 4to., London, 1616.

1616. The laver of the heart ; or Bath of sanctification [on
Jerem. iv. 14]. Preached at Pauls Crosse the first of September
last, 1615. By Gabriel PRICE, Minister and Preacher of Gods
Word. F. Kyngston, for T. Man. 4to., London, 1616.

1616. A Sermon [on Psal. ci. 8] concerning the punishing of
Malefactors. Preached at Paules Crosse, the first of October,
by Charles RICHARDSON, Preacher at Saint Katharines neere the
Tower of London. Printed for W. Butler. 4to., London,
1616.

1617. Balme from Gilead to recouer Conscience. In a
Sermon Preached at Pauls-Crosse, Octob. 20, 1616. By Samvel
WARD, Bach. of Diuinitie, and Preacher of Ipswich. 4to.,
London, 1617.

1617. The Evnvches Conversion. A Sermon preached at
Paules Crosse, the second of February, 1617, by Charles
SONNIBANK, Doctor of Diuinitie, and Canon of Windsor.
Printed by H. L. for Richard Fleming ; and are to be Sould at
his Shop at the great South doore of Paules, on the right hand
going vp the steps, 1617. 4to., London, 1617.

1617. The Rainebow, or, a Sermon [on Genesis ix. 13] preached at
Pavls Crosse the tenth day of Iune, 1617. By Immanvel BOVRNE
Master of Artes and Preacher of Gods Word. Printed for T.
Adams. 4to., London, 1617.

1618. Antichrist arraigned : in a Sermon at Pauls Crosse, the third Sunday after Epiphanie. With the Tryall of Guides, on the fourth Sunday after Trinitie. By Thomas THOMPSON, Bachelour in Diuinitie, and Preacher of Gods Word. 4to., London, 1618.

1618. **Balme from Gilead to recouer Conscience.** In a Sermon [on Heb. xiii. 18] preached at Pauls Crosse, Octob. 20, 1616. By Samuel WARD, Bach. of Diuinitie, and Preacher of Ipswich. Printed by T. S., for R. Jackson and W. Blades. 8vo., London, 1618.

1619. **A Sermon** [on Isaiah xxxviii. 17] of Pvblicke Thanks-giving for the happy recouery of his Maiesty from his late dangerous sicknesse : Preached at Pavls-Crosse the 11 of Aprill, 1619, by the B. of **London.** [John KING.] Published by commandement. Printed for T. Adams. 4to., London, 1619.

1619. Londons **Warning by Jervsalem.** A Sermon [on Micah vi. 9] preached at Pavls Crosse on Mid-Lent Sunday last. By Francis WHITE, Mr of Arts, and sometime of Magdalene Colledge in Oxford. Printed by George Purslowe, for Richard Flemming : and are to be sold at his Shop at the signe of the three Flower-de-Luces, in Saint Pauls Alley, neere Saint Gregories Church, 1619. 4to, London, 1619.

1620. **A Sermon** [on Psal. cii. 13, 14] at Paules Crosse on behalfe of Paules Church, March 26, 1620. By the B. of London. [John KING.] Both preached and published by his Majesties commandement. E. Griffin for E. Adams. 4to., London, 1620.

1620. **Rabboni** ; Mary Magdalens Teares, of Sorrow, Solace. The one for her Lord being lost. The other for Him being found [on S. John xx. 16]. . . Preached at S. Pauls Crosse, after the Rehearsall, and newly reuised and enlarged : By Thomas WALKINGTON, Doctor in Diuinity, and Minister of the Word at Fulham. E. Griffin, for R. Whitakers. 8vo., London, 1620.

1621. **The sinne vnto death,** or an ample Discovery of that fearefull sinne, The Sinne against the Holy Ghost, together with the signes, degrees, and preseruatiues thereof. In a Sermon preached at Pauls Crosse, August 26, 1621. By Tho. BEDFORD, Mr of Arts in Queenes Colledge in Cambridge. 4to., London, 1621.

1621. **A Sermon** [on S. John xv. 20] preached at Pavls Crosse the 25 of November 1621. Upon occasion of that false and scandalous Report (lately Printed) touching the supposed Apostasie of the right Reuerend Father in God John King, late Lord Bp of London. By Henry KING, his eldest Sonne. Whereunto is annexed the Examination, and Answere of Thomas Preston, P. taken before my Lords Grace of Canterbury touching this scandal. Published by Authority. F. Kyngston for W. Barret. 4to., London, 1621.

The 'Examination' of Preston is without pagination.

1621. **The Brazen Serpent**: or the Copie of a Sermon Preached at Pavls Crosse, Decemb. 31, 1620. By John ANDREWES, Priest and Preacher of the Word of God at Saint Iames Clerkenwell in Middlesex. 4to., London, 1621.

1622. The Trve VVay of a Christian to the New Iervsalem .. Delivered first in Briefe, in a Sermon preached at Paules-Crosse the first Sunday in the New Yeere 1617, and newly reuised and enlarged by Immanvel BOVRNE, Master of Artes, and now Parson of Ashouer in the County of Derby. 4to., London, 1622.

1622. Gods Goodnes **and** Mercy, layd open in a Sermon, preached at Pavls-Crosse on the last of Iune, 1622. By Mr. Robert HARRIS, Pastour of the Church of God at Hanvvell in Oxfordshire. 4to., London, 1622.

1623. A Sermon preached at Paules-Crosse the second day of June, being the last Sunday in Easter Terme 1622. By Thomas AILESBVRY Student in Diuinitie. 4to., London, 1623.

1623. A Svb-Poena from the Star Chamber of Heaven. A Sermon [on S. Luke iii. 9] preached at Pauls Crosse the 4. of August, 1622. With some particular Enlargements which the limited time would not then allow. By Dan. DONNE, Master of Arts, and Minister of the Word. (Dedicated to Dean Donne and others.) A. Mathewes for I. Grismand. 8vo., London, 1623.
[Pp. 115-118 wanting.]

1623. **The** Kings **Towre** and Trivmphant Arch of London. A Sermon preached at Pavls Crosse, August 5, 1622. By Samvel PVRCHAS, Bacheler of Diuinitie, and Parson of Saint Martins Ludgate, in London. 8vo., London, 1623.

1623. **The** Royal Receipt: or, Hezekiahs Physicke. A Sermon [on Isa. xxxviii. 2, 3, and 2 Kings xx. 2, 3] delivered at Pavls-Crosse, on Michaelmas Day, 1622. By Elias PETLEY. [Dedicated to Dean Donne.] Printed by B. A. for E. Blackmore. 4to., London, 1623.

1624. **The Temple.** A Sermon preached at Pavls Crosse the fifth of August, 1624. By Tho. ADAMS. 4to., London, 1624.

1624. Hold fast. A Sermon preached at Pavls Crosse vpon Sunday being the xxxi. of October, Anno Domini 1624. By Iohn GEE, Master of Arts, late of Exon Colledge in Oxford. 4to., London, 1624.

1625. The Watchman Warning. A Sermon preached at Pavls Crosse the 26. of September, 1624. By William PROCTER, Master of Arts, and Minister of Gods Word. 4to., London, 1625.

1625. A Sermon preached at Pavls Crosse the 24. of October,

1624. By Robert BEDINGFIELD, Master of Arts, and Student of Christ Church in Oxford. 4to., Oxford, 1625.

1625. **A Sermon** preached at Pavles Crosse : laying open the Beast, and his Marks. Vpon the 14. of the Reuelations, vers. 9, 10, 11. By Richard SHELDON, a Conuert from out of Babylon, Doctor in Diuinitie, His Maiesties Chaplaine. 4to., London, 1625.

1626. **A Sermon** [on Ezek. xxxvii. 22] preached at Pauls Crosse March the 24. 1624, by Barten HOLYDAY, Archdeacon of Oxford. W. Stansby for N. Butter. London, 1626, 4to.

1627. **The White Wolfe** ; or, a Sermon [on S. Matthew vii. 15] preached at Pavls Crosse, Feb. 11, . . . anno 1627. . . wherein Faction is vnmasked, especially the Hetheringtonian Faction. By Stephen DENISON, minister of Katherine Cree-church, London. G. Miller, 4to., London, 1627.

The British Museum possesses also a copy with a slightly different title.

1627. **The Arraignment of the Arrian**, His Beginning, Height, Fall. In a Sermon preached at Pauls Crosse, June 4, 1624, being the first Sunday in Trinitie Terme. By Humphry SYDENHAM, M^r of Arts, and Fellow of Wadham Colledge in Oxford. 4to., London, 1627.

1628. **Tormenting Tophet**, or a Terrible description of Hell, able to breake the hardest heart, and cause it quake and tremble. Preached at Pavls Crosse the 14 of June, 1624. By Henry GREENWOOD. (Hempsted in Essex.) 8vo., London, 1628.

1628. **Two Sermons** preached at Pavles-Crosse, London, The one Nouemb. 21, the other Aprill 15, 1627, being the Fifth and Sixth *ad Populum*. By Robert SAVNDERSON, Bachelour in Diuinitie, and sometimes Fellow of Lincolne Colledge in Oxford. 4to., London, 1628.

1629. **A Sermon** [on S. Luke xxi. 34] preached at Pavls Crosse on Sunday the eight and twentieth day of Iune, 1629, by Richard FARMER, sometimes of Pembroke-Hall in Cambridge, now Parson of Charwelton in the County of Northampton Printed for J. Bowler. 4to., London, 1629.

1631. **Gods Goodnes** and mercie laid open in a Sermon preached at Pavls Crosse on the last of June, 1622. By M. Robert HARRIS, Pastor of the Church of God at Hanwell in Oxfordshire. The fourth Edition, corrected, amended, and much enlarged by the same Authour. 4to., London, 1631.

1634. **The way to prosper.** A Sermon preached at S. Pavls Crosse on Sunday the 27. day of May, being Trinity Sunday. By John GORE, Rector of Wenden-lofts in Essex. The second Edition. 4to., London, 1634.

1635. **Two Sermons** [on 1 Cor. i. 10 and 1 S. John iv. 1-3]

the first, preached at Canterbury, April 14, **1635**. The second
at Saint Paul's Crosse, the eighteenth of Aprill, 1630. By
Edward BOUGHEN, Parson of Wood-Church in Kent. Printed
by R. B. 4to., London, 1635.

1635. **Two Sermons :** the former concerning the right use of
Christian Liberty, preached at S. Pauls Crosse, London, May 6 :
the latter, concerning the perswasion of Conscience, preached
at a Metropoliticall visitation at Grantham, Lincoln : Aug. 22,
1634. By Robert SAUNDERSON, Chaplaine to his Maiestie.
4to., London, 1635.

1636. **Certain Sermons** preached upon severall occasions. By
John GORE, Rector of Wenden-lofts in Essex.
     The way to prosper. Paul's Crosse. Trinity Sunday, 1632.
     The way to be content. Cathedral. 26 May, 1634.
     A summer **Sermon.** Cathedral. 1635, printed.
     A Winter Sermon. Cathedral. Shrove Tuesday, **1634**.
     Unknowne kindnesse. Cathedral. **1635.**
     The Oracle of God. Cathedral. **20 Dec.,** 1635.
     The Poore Mans Hope. Place not **stated.**
     T. Cotes for T. Alchorn. 4to., London, **1636.**

1638. **A Discovrse abovt the state of trve happinesse,**
delivered in certaine sermons in Oxford, and at S. Pauls
Crosse. By Robert BOLTON, Batchelour in Divinitie and
Minister of God's Word at Broughton in Northampton Shire.
The seventh edition. **4to., London,** 1638.

1640. **The Love-sicke Spouse.** A Sermon preached at St.
Pauls Crosse. [By **Dr. John** STOUGHTON.] Printed for J.
Bellamie, **etc.** 4to., **London, 1640.**
     [No. **2 of** XV. **Choice Sermons** preached upon several
occasions.]

1641. **Ten Sermons** vpon severall occasions preached at Saint
Paul's Crosse, and Elsewhere, by the Right Reverend Father in
God, Arthur LAKE, late Lord Bishop of Bath and Wells. 4to.,
London, 1641.
     (The British Museum has an edition, 4to., London, **1640.**)

1642. **A Sermon** appointed for Saint Pauls Crosse, but **Preached
in** Saint Pauls Church, on the day of His Majesties Happy
Inauguration, March **27,** 1642. By Richard GARDYNER, D.D.,
and Canon of Christ Church, Oxon. 4to., London, 1642.

1653. **A Sermon preached** at St. Paul's Cross **on Good** Friday,
April 16, 1625. **By a late** Reverend Bishop **of the** Church of
England. 4to., **London,** 1653.

1658-18 .. **The Saints Ark,** or, **City of** Refuge in the Day of
his Distress : discovered in two **sermons** ; one of which was
preached at Paul's Cross, the other **in** St. Mary's Church, Cambridge ; upon special Occasions. By Richard SIBES, D.D., late
Master of Catharine Hall, Cambridge, and Preacher at Gray's
Inn, London. 8vo., London, reprint, 18 . .

1676. A **Caveat for the** Covetous, in a Sermon preached at
Pauls Crosse the fourth of December, 1669. By William
WHEATLIE, Preacher of the VVord of God in Banburie. 8vo.,
London, 1676.

1738. The Regal, Clerical, and Laical Bayliffs, Cited by
three Som'ners, to give a Reckoning of their Bayliwicks. A
Sermon in two parts, no less Fruitful than Famous : preach'd at
Paul's Cross . . . 1388, and found out hid in a Wall By
Richard WIMBLEDON. The Fourteenth Edition. 8vo., London,
1738.
[See *supra*, 1575, etc.]

SERMONS PREACHED FOR THE MOST PART IN S. PAUL'S CATHEDRAL.

c. 1511. The Sermō of doctor **Colete,** made to the Conuocacion
of Paules. The Colophon is : Thomas Berthelet regius im-
pressor excudebat. Cum priuilegio.
[A perfect copy of this rare book is in the Archiepiscopal
Library at Lambeth. See Maitland, *Early printed Books in the
Lambeth Library,* p. 239.] Sheets A and B only : sheet C, six
leaves, is wanting.

1550. A fruitfull Sermon made in Poules churche at London in
the Shroudes the seconde daye of Februari, by Thomas LEUER.
Anno M.D. & fiftie. Small 8vo., London, Day and Seres,
1550.

1555. A Notable Sermon made within S. Paules Church in
Lōdon, in the presence of certen of the Kinges and Quenes
moost honorable priuie coūsell at the celebration of the exequies
of the righte excellent and famous **princesse, lady** Jone, Quene
of Spayne, Sicilie & Nauarre, etc., the xviij of June, Anno
1555. By Maister John FECKENAM, **Deane of the** sayd Churche
of Paules.

    ❧ Set forth at the request of some in auctoritie whose request
    could not be denayed. Excusum Londini in ædibus Roberti
    Caly, Typographi, Mense Augusti, Anno 1555. Cum priuilegio.
    8vo., London, 1555.

1574. A Lecture or Exposition upon a part of the V chapter
of the Epistle to the Hebrues. Set forth as it was read in
Paules Church in London the 6 Dec., 1573, by Edward
DERYNG. J. Awdely, 8vo., London, 1574.

1599. Christs **Checke** to S. Peter for his curious question,
out of these words in Saint Iohn : Quid ad te ? Begun in Paules
Church on S. Iohns day the Euangelist, 1597, out of part of
the Gospel appointed for that day, and prosecuted the same day

this yeare 1598, in the same place, and else where at other times in sixe seueral Sermons. [By Lavrence BARKER.] 8vo., London, 1599.

16 .. Nine select Sermons preached upon special occasions in the Parish Church of St. Gregories by St. Pauls. By the late Reverend John HEWYTT, D.D. Together with his publick Prayers before and after Sermon. 8vo., London, N.D.

Dr. Hewytt was beheaded on Tower Hill 8 June, 1658. An ardent Royalist.

1601. A Sermon preached at Pauls in London on the 17 of November, Ann. Dom. 1599, the one and fortieth yeare of her Maiesties raigne, and augmented in those places wherein, for the shortnes of the time, it could not there be then delivered. By Thomas HOLLAND, Doctor of Divinity, & her Highnes Professor thereof in her Vniversity of Oxford. 4to., Oxford, 1601.

1608. A Sermon preached at Whitehall the 5 Day of November, Ann. 1608, by John KING, Doctor of Divinity, Deane of Christ-Church in Oxon and Vicechauncellor of the Vniversity. 4to., Oxford, 1608.

1614. A Summons to Ivdgement. Or a Sermon appointed for the Crosse, bvt delivered vpon occasion in the Cathedrall church of S. Paul, London : the 6. day of Iune, 1613, beeing the first Sunday of Midsommer Terme. By Thomas BAVGHE, student of Christ-Church in Oxford. 4to., London, 1614.

1617. Maries Memoriall. A Sermon preached at St. Maries Spittle on Munday in Easter Weeke, being Aprill 1, 1616. By Daniel PRICE, Doctor in Diuinitie, and Chaplaine vnto the Kings Maiestie. 4to., London, 1617.

1621. Ad Reverendissimos Patres & Presbyteros Totius Prouinciæ Cantuariensis in Synodo Londini Congregatos : habita in Ecclesia Cathedrali S. Pavli, Anno Dom. 1620, Ian. 31. Per Johannem BOWLE, Decanum Sarisburiensem. 4to., London, 1621.

1622. ΠΟΛΕΩΣ-ΝΑΩ-ΔΑΦΝΗ. Londons Lawrell : or a Branch of the Graft of Gratitvde, first budded in the Temple and now begun to blossom, vpon Davids Thankfvlnes to the Lord for a Cities kindnesse. By Edw. DALTON, one of the Lecturers in the Cathedrall Church of S. Pauls, London. 4to., London, 1622.

1623. Two godly and profitable Sermons earnestly inueighing against the sins of this Land in generall, and in particular against the sinnes of this Citie of London. Preached in the Citie of London, by Thomas HOPKINS, minister at Yeardley in the county of Worcester. 4to., London, 1623.

1623. The Bishop of London [John King] his Legacy, or, certaine motiues of D. KING, late Bishop of London, for his change of Religion, and dying in the Catholike and Roman

Church. With a Conclusion to his Brethren, the LL. Bishops of England. 4to., Permissu Superiorum, 1623. No place.

1624. Columba Noæ Olivam adferens iactatissimæ Christi Arcæ. Concio Synodica . . . in Aede Pavlina Londinensi Feb. 20, 1623, a Ios. HALLO, S.T.D., Decano Wigorniensi. 4to., London, 1624.

1625. **The Spirituall Spring.** A Sermon preached at Pavls, wherein is declared the necessity of growing in grace and the goodly gaine that comes thereby. By Richard LEE, Preacher of the word of God at Woluerhampton in Staffordshire. 4to., London, 1625.

1635. **Labour** forbidden and Commanded. A Sermon preached at St. Pavls Church, September 28, 1634. By Edward RAINBOWE, Fellow of Magdalen Colledge in Cambridge. 4to., London, 1635.

1637. **Three Sermons:** two of them appointed for the Spittle, preached in St. Paul's Church, by John SQUIER, Vicar of St. Leonards, Shoredich in Middlesex: and John LYNCH, Parson of Herietsham in Kent. 4to., London, 1637.

1637. Mortification Apostolicall. Delivered in a Sermon in Saint Pauls Church, upon Summons received for the Crosse: on the last Sunday in Easter Terme, May 21, 1637. By William WATS, Rector of St. Albans Woodstreet, London. 4to., London, 1637.

1637. **A Plea for Peace:** or, a Sermon preached in St. Pavls Church in London, July 9, 1637. By Henry VERTUE, Parson of the Parish Church of Alhallowes, Honey-Lane in London. 4to., London, 1637.

1639. **God save the King.** A Sermon preached in St. Pauls Church the 27th of March, 1639, being the day of His Maiesties most happy Inauguration, and of His Northerne Expedition. By Henry VALENTINE, D.D. 4to., London, 1639.

1640. **The Peace of Enmity.** A Sermon Preached in Paules Church the 12 day of February, in the yeere of our Lord God, 1639, by Augustine HILL, Rector of Dengey in the County of Essex. 4to., London, 1640.

1640. **A Sermon** preached at St. Pavls March 27, 1640. Being the Anniversary of His Maiesties happy Inauguration to his Crowne. By Henry KING, Deane of Rochester, and Residentiary of St. Pauls: One of His Majesties Chaplaines in Ordinary. 4to., London, 1640.

1641. **A Trve Copy of that Sermon** which was preached at Saint Pavls the tenth day of October last, by Thomas CHESHIRE, minister of Gods holy Word and Sacraments. 4to., London, 1641.

1641. **A Sermon** preached in the Cathedrall Church of S. Paul.

On the fourteenth day of November, **1641**. In the Evening. By Doctor WESTFEILD, one of the Prebendaries of the said Church. 4to., London, 1641.

[Dr. Westfield was consecrated Bishop of Bristol in 1642.]

1642. **The Presentment of a Schismaticke**, **by** the Right Reverend Father in God, Thomas [MORTON], Lord Bishop of Durham, in his Sermon preached at the Cathedrall Church of Saint Pauls the 19 of June, 1642. **4to.**, London, 1642.

1642. **The Good of Peace, and ill of VVarre**, Set forth in a Sermon preached in the Cathedrall Church of S. Paul, the last day of July, 1642. By Ephraim VDALL, Rector of S. Austins, London. **4to.**, London, 1642.

1642. **Christophilo**, the true Christian subject decyphered, in **a** Sermon preached **at** Saint Pauls, London, on the seventh **of** August, Anno 1642. By Benjamin SPENCER, minister of S[t] Thomas Parish in Southwarke. 4to., London, 1642.

1642. A Patheticall Perswasion to pray for Publick **Peace**, propounded in a Sermon preached in **the** Cathedrall **Church** of Saint Paul, Octob. 2, **1642**. By Matthew GRIFFITH, **Rector of S.** Mary Magdalens, **neer** Old-Fish-Street, **London.** 4to., **London, 1642.**

1645. Reall Thankfulnesse : or, a Sermon preached in Pauls Church, London, vpon the second **day of November**, 1645, at a Publike Thanksgiving for the taking **in of the Towns** and Castles of Caermarthen and Mounmouth in Wales, **it** being the first Lords-Day after the Inauguration **of** the Right Honourable Thomas Adams, now Lord Major **of that famous** City. By Simeon ASH, preacher at Basingshaw, **London, and** one of the **assembly** of Divines. **4to.**, London, **1645.**

1646. **Hæreseo-machia :** or, the mischiefe which Heresies doe, and the means to prevent it. Delivered in a Sermon in Pauls. [Before Lord Mayor, etc., Feb. 1, 1645.] By James CRAN-FORD, Pastour of Christopher Le Stocks, London. **4to.**, London, 1646.

1646. The Dvty of such as would walke worthy of the Gospel to Endeavour Union, not Division nor Tolera-tion. Opened in **a** Sermon at Pauls upon the Lords **Day**, Feb. 8, 1646. By Matthew NEWCOMEN, Preacher of the **Gospel** at Dedham in Essex. **4to.**, London, 1646.

1646. ΨΕΥΔΕΛΕΥΘΕΡΙΑ. Or, Lawlesse Liberty, set **forth in a** Sermon preached before **the** Right Honourable the Lord Major of London, etc., in Paul's, Aug. 16, 1646. By Edvvard TERRY, Minister of the Word, and Pastor of the Church at Great Green-ford, in the **County** of Middlesex. Sept. **11**, 1646. Imprimatur, John Downame. **4to.**, London, **1646.**

1646. The Present Duty and Endeavour of the Saints, opened in a Sermon at Pauls upon the Lords Day, December

14, 1645, by Joseph CARYL, minister of the Gospell at Magnus, neere London Bridge. 4to., London, 1646.

1648. **Good Counsel for evil times.** Or, a plain Sermon preached at Pauls in London, April 16, 1648. By Edw. BOWLES, M.A., of Katherin-Hall, Cambridge. Printed by the desire and Order of the Lord Maior and Aldermen of that famous City. 4to., London, 1648.

1648 ?. ΙΠΠΟΣ ΠΥΡΡΟΣ. The Red Horse, or the Bloodines of War, Represented in a Sermon (to perswade to Peace) preached at Pauls, July 16, at five of the clocke in the afternoone. By Jo. GEREE, M.A., and Pastor of S. Faiths under Pauls. And now published to cleare the Preacher from Malignancy imputed to him by some left-eared Auditors. 4to., London [1648?].

1648. **A Thanksgiving Sermon:** preached to . . . the Lord Mayor . . . upon occasion of the many late and signall Victories and Deliverances vouchsafed to the Parliament forces, in Pauls Church, London, July 27, 1648. By Stephen MARSHALL, B.D., Minister of Gods Word at Finchingfield in Essex. 4to., London, 1648.

1649. **A motive to Peace and Love.** Delivered in a Sermon at Pauls the first Lords Day in June, Anno Dom. 1648. By Humfry CHAMBERS, D.D., and Pastor of Pewsy in the County of Wilts. 4to., London, 1649.

1651 ?. **The Oppressor Destroyed.** As it was delivered in a Sermon at Pauls, Septem. 21, 1651. Preached before the Right Honourable the Lord Mayor. . . It being a Sermon in commemoration of the 3^d of Sept., on which day it pleased the Lord to vouchsafe a wonderfull Victorie to the Parliament Forces before Worcester, in the total defeat of the Enemie. By Joseph CARRYL, Minister of the Gospel at Magnus, neer London-Bridge. 4to., London, c. 1651.

1651. Matthew **Barker,** Preacher of the Gospel at Leonards, Eastcheap, London. Sermon. S. Pauls, before the Lord Mayor. Jesus Christ the Great Wonder. Discovered for the amazement of Saints. 4to., London, 1651.

1652. **Jesus Christ the Mysticall or Gospell Sun,** sometimes seemingly eclipsed, yet never going down from His people : or Eclipses spiritualised. Opened in a Sermon at Pauls before the Right Honourable the Lord Mayor, Aldermen, etc., March 28, 1652. The day before the late Solar ECLIPSE. By Fulk BELLERS, Master of Arts, and Preacher of the Gospel in the City of London. 4to., London, 1652.

1654. **A Voice from Heaven,** calling the People of God to a Perfect Separation from Mystical Babylon. As it was delivered in a Sermon at Pauls before the Right Honorable the Lord Major and Aldermen of the City of London, on Novem. 5,

1653. By William STRONG, Preacher of the Gospel at the Abby, Westminster.   4to., London, 1654.

1654.   **The Magistrates Dignity and Duty.**   Being a Sermon preached on Octob. 30, 1653, at Pauls Church, before the Right Honourable Thomas Viner, Lord Major, and the Aldermen of the City of London.   Being the first Sermon after his entrance into his Majoralty.   By William SPURSTOWE, D.D., minister of Gods Word at Hackney, neere London.   4to., London, 1654.

1655.   The Saints longings after their Heavenly Country.   A Sermon preached at St. Pauls Church on Tuesday, the sixth of June, 1654.   At a Solemn Anniversary meeting of the Cheshire Gentlemen, and Freemen of the City of London born in the same County.   By that faithfull and painfull Servant of Jesus Christ, Mr. Ralph ROBINSON, late Minister of Mary Wolnoth, London.   4to., London, 1655.

1655.   Communion with God.   In Two Sermons preach'd at Pauls : The first, Sept. 3, 1654.   The second, March 25, 1655. By Samuel ANNESLEY, LL.D., minister of the Gospel at John Evangel, London.   4to., London, 1655.

1655.   **Joy in the Lord** : opened in a Sermon preached at Pauls, May 6.   By Edward REYNOLDS, D.D.   4to., London, 1655.

1655.   **The Corruption of Minde.**   Described in a Sermon preached at Pauls the 24 day of June, 1655.   By Richard VINES, Preacher of Gods Word at Lawrence-Jury, London. 4to., London [1655].

1655.   The Pillar and Pattern of Englands Deliverances. Presented in a Sermon to the Right Honourable the Lord Mayor and Aldermen, with the several Companies of the City of London, in their solemn Meeting at Pauls on the Lords Day, Novem. 5, 1654.   Being also the First Sabbath after his Lordships entrance upon his Majoralty.   By Thomas HORTON, Doctor in Divinity, and Professor thereof in Gresham Colledge, London.   4to., London, 1655.

1655.   **God's** appearing for the Tribe of **Levi** : Improved in a Sermon preached at St. Pauls, Nov. 8, to the Sons of Ministers, then solemnly assembled.   By Geo. HALL, minister of St. Botolph, Aldersgate.   4to., London, 1655.

1655.   **Upon the Meeting of the Sons of the Clergy,** at a Sermon preached before them in Saint Pauls Church, the eighth of November, 1655, specifying their several capacities, as they stood in the time of the Law, and now under the Gospel.   By E. G. [In Verse.]   4to., London, 1655.

1655.   **The Monster of Sinful Self-seeking anatomized.** Together with a description of the Heavenly and Blessed Selfeseeking.   In a Sermon preached at Pauls the 10 of December,

1654. By Edm. CALAMY, B.D., and Pastor of Aldermanbury, London. 4to., London, 1655.

1656. Zion's Birth-Register, unfolded in a Sermon to the Native-Citizens of London. In their Solemn Assembly at Pauls on Thursday, the viii. of May, A.D. M.DC.LVI. By Thomas HORTON, D.D. 4to., London, 1656.

1656. **The One Thing Necessary.** Preached in a Sermon at Pauls before the Right Honourable the Lord Major . . . Aug. 31, 1656. By Thomas WATSON, Minister of Stephens Walbrook, LOND. 8vo., London, 1656.

1656. **Justice Triumphing**: or, the Spoylers Spoyled. Laid forth in a Gratulatory Sermon for the Miraculous Discovery of, and our Glorious Delivery from, the Barbarous Powder-Plot : preached at Pauls, November the 5th, 1646 [sic]. By Nath. HARDY, M.A., Preacher to the Parish of St. Dionis, Backchurch, London. 4to., London, 1656.

1657. The City **Remembrancer,** or a Sermon preached to the Native Citizens of London at their solemn Assembly in Pauls on Tuesday, the 23 of June, A.D. MDCLVII. By Edm. CALAMY, B.D., and Pastor of the Church at Aldermanbury. 8vo., London, 1657.

1657. **A State of Glory for Spirits of just men upon Dissolution demonstrated.** A Sermon preached in Pauls Church, Aug. 30, 1657, before the R^t Honourable the Lord Mayor and Aldermen of the City of London. By Tho. GOODWIN, D.D., President of Magd. Coll., Oxon. 4to., London, 1657.

1657. **The Active and Publick Spirit,** Handled in a Sermon, preached at Pauls, October 26th, 1656. By Thomas JACOMB, Minister at Martins-Ludgate, London. 4to., London, 1657.

1657. **Mercies Memorial**: or, Israel's thankful Remembrance of God in their high estate, for his mercifull remembring of them in their low estate. In a Sermon before . . the Lord Mayor [at Pauls] on the 5th of November 1656. By Ralph VENNING. 4to., John Rothwell, London, 1657.

1658. **The Heavenly Vision**: or, a Discovery of what is truly Good. Held forth in a Sermon preached at Pauls, Febr. 21, 1657. Before the Right Honourable the Lord Maior and Aldermen of the City of London. By John WELLS, B.D., late Fellow of Queens Colledge in Cambridge, and Preacher of the Word (at present) at Christ-Church, London. 4to., London, 1658.

1658. **The Olive-Branch** presented to the Native Citizens of London, in a Sermon preached at S. Paul's Church, May 27, being the day of their Yearly Feast. By Nath. HARDY, Preacher to the Parish of S. Dyonis Back-Church. 4to., London, 1658.

1658. Judgement to come : or, Christ on the Throne of his Finall Judgement. In a Sermon preached before the Right Honourable Sr Richard Chiverton Knight, Lord Maior of the City of London and the Right Worshipfull the Aldermen at

St. Pauls, Sept. 12, **1658.**   By Thomas **RUTTON,** Pastor of
M. le Bow, London.   **4to.,** London, 1658.

1658.   ΦΙΛΑΛΗΛΙΑ.   Or, the Grand Characteristick whereby a
Man may be Known to be Christ's Disciple.   Delivered in a
Sermon at St. Paul's, before the Gentlemen of Wilts, Nov. 10,
1658. It being the day of their Yearly Feast.   By Thomas
PIERCE, Rector of Brington.   4to., London, 1658.

1659.   **True Gain,** opened in a Sermon preached at Pauls, Nov. 9,
1656.   By Edward REYNOLDS, D.D.   4to., London, 1659.

1659.   **God's arraignment of Adam:** declared in a Sermon
preached at St. Pauls, Septemb. 5, 1658, before the right
Honorable the Lord Major, Aldermen, and Common-Council.
By Thomas CARTWRIGHT, M.A. of Queens Coll. Oxon, and **now**
Vicar of Walthamstow in Essex.   4to., London, 1659.

1659.   ΤΗΣ   ΠΙΣΤΕΩΣ   ΕΛΕΓΧΟΣ: or the Reason of Faith:
briefly discuss'd in a Sermon preach'd at Pauls before the
Right **Honourable** the Lord Mayor &c., the third of October,
1658 . . . **By** Peter VINKE, B.D., sometimes fellow of Pembroke-Hall in Cambridge and now Minister of M. Corn-hil,
London.   **4to.,** London, 1659.

1659.   **The Saints Duty in Contending for the Faith delivered to them.** A Sermon preached at Pauls Church before
the Right Honourable the Lord Major, **and Aldermen of the**
City of London, July 17, 1659.   By John TEMPLER, B.D.,
late Fellow of Trinity Colledge in Cambridge, and now Minister
of the Gospel at Balsham in Cambridgeshire.   4to., London, 1659.

1659.   **The misery** of a deserted People. Opened in a Sermon
preached at Pauls before the Lord Major, Aldermen, and
Common-Counsel, **Decemb. 2,** 1659.   Being a day of solemn
Humiliation by them **appointed.**   By Edward REYNOLDS, D.D.
4to., London, **1659.**

1660.   Κακουργοι sive Medicastri: slight Healings for Publique
Hurts.   Set forth in a Sermon preached in St. Pauls Church,
London, before the Right Honourable the Lord Mayor, Lord
General, Aldermen, Common Council, and Companies of the
Honourable City of London, February 28, 1659.   Being a day
of Solemn Thanksgiving unto God for Restoring the Secluded
Members of Parliament to the House of Commons: (And for
preserving the City) as a Door of Hope thereby opened to the
fulness and freedom of future Parliaments: The most probable
means under God for healing the hurts, and recovering the
health of these three Brittish Kingdomes.   By John GAUDEN,
D.D. [112 pages.] 4to., London, **1660.**

1660.   **The Wall and Glory of Jerusalem** in a Sermon preached
in St. Pauls Church, London, before the Right Honorable the
Lord Mayor, Lord General, Aldermen, Common Council, and
Companies of the Honorable City of London, February 28,

1659, being a Day of Solemn Thanksgiving unto God, for restoring the Parliament and Common Council, and for preserving the City. By Edward REYNOLDS, D.D. 4to., London, 1660.

1660. **Englands Season for Reformation of Life.** A Sermon delivered in St. Paul's Church, London : on the Sunday next following His Sacred Majesties Restauration, M.DC.LX. By Tho. PIERCE, Rector of Brington. 4to., London, 1660.

Another Edition, without author's name. 4to., no place or date.

1660. **Right Rejoycing** : or, the Nature and Order of Rational and Warrantable Ioy. Discovered in a Sermon preached at St. Pauls before the Lord Maior and Aldermen, and the several Companies of the City of London, on May 10, 1660. Appointed by both Houses of Parliament to be a day of solemn Thanksgiving for God's raising up and succeeding his Excellency, and other Instruments, in order to his Majestie's Restoration and the settlement of these Nations. By Richard BAXTER. 4to., London, 1660.

1660. **Evangelical Politie** : or, a Gospel Conversation. A Sermon preached at St. Paul's, London, May 20, 1660. Being the Sunday next (but one) before his Majesties happy return to his said Citie. By James DUPORT, (now) D.D., one of his Majesties Chaplains in Ordinary. 4to., Cambridge, 1660.

1660. **Evangelical Worship is Spiritual Worship**, as it was Discussed in a Sermon preached before the Right Honourable the Lord Maior, at Pauls Church, Aug. 26, 1660. By Matthew POOLE, Minister of the Gospel at Michael Quern in London. 4to., London, 1660.

Also the second edition. 4to., London, 1660.

1661. **Christian Concord** : or, S. Pauls Parallel between the Body Natural and Mystical. Exemplified in a Sermon preacht in the Cathedral Church of S. Paul, on Sunday, the 13th of January, 1660. By Matthew GRIFFITH, D.D. 4to., London, 1661.

1661. **Concio Synodica ad clerum Anglicanum**, ex Provincia praesertim Cantuariensi, in Æde Paulinâ Londinensi habita viii. Idus Maias MDCLXI. Per Thomam PIERCE, S.T.D., Prebendarium Cantuariensem. 4to., London, 1661.

(Two editions.)

1661. **Regina Dierum** : or, The Joyful Day : in a Sermon preached at S. Pauls before the Right Honourable the Lord Mayor, etc., on Wednesday, May 29, 1661. The Anniversary Thanksgiving for His Majesties most wonderful, glorious, peaceable and joyful Restauration to the actual possession of His undoubted, hereditary, Soveraign and Regal authority. Being also His most memorable Birth-Day. By Henry HIBBERT, minister of the Word. 4to., London, 1661.

1661. **Deceivers Deceiv'd:** or, The Mistakes **of Wickedness in** Sundry Erroneous and Deceitful Principles, practised in our late fatal Times, and suspected still in the Reasonings of unquiet Spirits. Delivered in a Sermon at S. Paul's, October 20th, 1661. Before the Right Honorable Sir Richard Browne, Knight and Baronet, Lord Maior of the City of London ; and the Aldermen his Brethren. Being the Initial also of the Reverend D[r] John BARWICK, Dean of the said Church : at the first Celebrity of Divine Service with the Organ and Choristers, which the Lord Maior himself Solemniz'd with his Personal presence from the very beginning. By Sam. STONE, etc.   4to., London, 1661.

1661. **A Sermon of** Conforming **and** Reforming, **made to the** Convocation at **S.** Pauls Church in London **by** John COLET, D.D., Dean of the said Church : upon Rom. xii. 2, Be ye reformed, etc. Writ an hundred and fiftie years since. To which is now added an Appendix of B[p] Andrews, and D[r] Hammond's solemn petition and advice to the Convocation, with his directions **to** the Laity **how to** prolong their **happiness.** 4to., Cambridge, 1661.

1663. **A Sermon** preached at the Cathedral Church of St. **Paul,** Novemb. 9, 1662. By Robert SOUTH, M.A., Publick Oratour to the University **of** Oxford, and Chaplain **to** the Lord high Chancellour.   **4to.,** London, 1663.

1663. **Cor Humiliatum et Contritum. A Sermon** preached at S. Pauls Church, London, Nov 29, 1663. By Richard LEE, D.D., chaplain to the most Renowned George Duke of Albemarle his Grace, and Rector of Kings-Hatfield in Hartfordshire. Wherein was delivered the profession of his judgement against **the** Solemn **League** and Covenant, the late King's Death, **etc.**   **4to., London, 1663.**

1663. Η ΗΜΕΡΑ ΕΚΕΙΝΗ. An Advent Sermon delivered at the Cathedral of St. Paul's Church, December vii. Being the Second Sunday **in** Advent, **1662. By J. GOAD, B.D.   4to.,** London, **1663.**

1664. ΠΑΝΤΑ ΔΟΚΙΜΑΖΕΤΕ. A Sermon treating of **the** Tryall of all Things by the Holy Scripture . . . with an Attempt touching the Examen of Ceremonies. Delivered in St. Paul's Cathedral, November 8 [by **J.** GOAD].   4to., London, 1664.

1664. **The Wisdon of being religious.** A Sermon preached at St. Pauls. By John TILLOTSON, preacher to the Honourable Society of Lincolns-Inn.   4to., London, **1664.**

1697-8. **The Advantage of a Learned Education.** Being a Sermon preached at the Cathedral Church of St. Paul, on St. Paul's Day, 169$\frac{7}{8}$. Before the Gentlemen Educated at That School, upon the Reviving their Antient Anniversary Meeting. By W. NICHOLLS, D.D.   4to., London, 169$\frac{7}{8}$.

1698. **Sermon** before the Lord **Mayor,** Judges, **and** Aldermen.

S. Pauls, 30. January, 1697-8. By Sampson Estwick, B.D., and Chaplain of Christ Church, Oxon. 4to., London, 1698.

1698. Sermon before the Lord Mayor at S. Pauls. 23. Oct. 1698. By Edward Oliver, M.A., Fellow of Corpus Christi College, Cambridge; and Chaplain to the Right Honourable George Earl of Northampton. 4to., London, 1698.

1698. A Reverse to Mr. Oliver's Sermon of Spiritual Worship. A Sermon on the same Subject. Preached before the Lord Mayor at St Paul's Church, August 26th, 1660. By Matthew Poole, minister at St Michael Quern, London. Now Reprinted, and may serve as an Answer to the aforesaid Sermon. 4to., London, 1698.

1698. **A False Faith not justified by Care for the Poor.** Prov'd in a Sermon preach'd at St Paul's Church, August 28th, 1698. By Luke Milbourne, a Presbyter of the Church of England. 4to., London, 1698.

1699. **A Rowland for an Oliver:** or, a Sharp Rebuke to a Sawcy Levite. In Answer to a Sermon preach'd by Edward Oliver, M.A., before Sir Humphrey Edwin, late Lord Mayor of London, at St. Paul's Cathedral, on Sunday, October 22, 1698. The Second Edition. 4to., London, 1699.

1699. A Sermon preach'd at the Anniversary Meeting of the Gentlemen Educated at St. Paul's School, at St. Paul's Church, January 25, 169⅞. By John Pulleyn, A.M., and Prebendary of St. Paul's. 4to., London, 1699.

1699. **Sermon.** S. Pauls. 29. May, 1699, before the Lord Mayor, etc. By Tho. Morer, Rector of St. Anne, etc., Aldersgate. 4to., London, 1699.

1699. Sermon before the Lord Mayor at S. Pauls. 2. Sept. 1699. Being the Fast for the Fire of London. By William Sherlock, D.D., Dean of S. Paul's, etc. 4to., London, 1699.

1699. **Sermon.** S. Pauls. 5. Nov. 1699, before the Lord Mayor. By Tho. Morer, Rector of St. Anne's, etc., Aldersgate. 4to., London, 1699.

1699. A Sermon preach'd at St. Paul's Cathedral, November 22, 1699, being the Anniversary Meeting of the Lovers of Music. By W. Sherlock, D.D., Dean of St Paul's, etc. 4to., London, 1699.

1700. **The Trinity Asserted.** Sermon before the Lord Mayor, preached at S. Paul's upon Trinity-Sunday, Anno Dom. 1700. By John Howard, M.A., Rector of Marston-Trussel in Northamptonshire. 4to., London, 1700.

1701. Concio ad Synodum .. habita in Æde Paulina Londinensi x. die Februarii, A.D. MDCC. Per Guilielmum Hayleium, S.T.P., Decanum Cicestrensem. 4to., London, 1701.

1702. **Sermon** before the Lord Mayor. S. Paul's. 5 November,

1702. By Tho. KNAGGS, M.A., and Chaplain to the Right Honourable Fulk, Lord Brook. 4to., London. 1702.

1702. **A Sermon** preach'd before the Queen and **both Houses of** Parliament, at the Cathedral Church of St. Pauls, **Nov. 12,** 1702, being **the** Day of Thanksgiving for the Signal Successes Vouchsafed to Her Majesties Forces by Sea and Land : Under the Command of the Earl of Marlborough in the Low Countries ; And James Duke of Ormond, General, and **Sir** George Rook, Admiral, at Vigo, **etc.** And likewise, for the Recovery of His Royal Highness the Prince of Denmark. By Jonathan [TRE-LAWNEY], Bishop of Exeter. 4to., London, 1702.

1702. **A Sermon** preach'd at St. Paul's Cathedral, the 8th of December, 1702, before the Gentlemen educated at **Eton** College. By J. ADAMS, Rector of St. Alban VVood-Street, **and** Chaplain in **Ordinary to** Her Majesty. 4to., London, 1702.

1703. **Sermon.** S. Pauls, Sunday, 28 Feb., 170⅔, before the Lord Mayor. By Edward LAKE, D.D., Rector of the United Parishes of St. Mary at hill and St. Andrew Hobart. Text. Revelat. xxi. 8. 4to., London, 1703.

1704. **Sermon** before the Lord Mayor, S. Pauls, 19 January, 1703-4, being the Fast-Day appointed by Her Majesty's Proclamation, upon occasion of the late Dreadful Storm and Tempest, and to implore the Blessing of God, upon Her Majesty, and Her **Allies, in the present** War. By Ofspring BLACKALL, D.D., Chaplain in Ordinary to Her Majesty. 4to., London, 1704.

1704. **Sermon** before the Lord Mayor. S. Pauls. 31 January, 1703-4, being the Anniversary of **the** Martyrdom of King Charles I. By Jo. CLIFTON, Chaplain to **the** Right Honourable the Lord Mayor. 4to., London, 1704.

1704. **A Sermon** preach'd **before the Queen, at the** Cathedral Church of St. Paul, London. On the seventh of September, **1704.** Being the Thanksgiving-Day for the late Glorious Victory **obtain'd** over the French and Bavarians **at** Bleinheim near Hochstet, on Wednesday the second of **August,** by the Forces of Her Majesty and **Her** Allies, under **the command** of the Duke of Marlborough. By William SHERLOCK, D.D., Dean of St. Pauls, etc. 4to., London, 1704.

1705 ?. **A Sermon** preach'd before the **Most Reverend the Arch-**bishop . . and the **clergy** of the **Province of Canterbury,** assembled in Synod at the **Cathedral Church of St. Paul, London,** October the **25, 1705. Done from the Latin. By George** STANHOPE, D.D., **Dean of Canterbury, etc.** 8vo., **London.** No date.

1705. **A Sermon** preached before the Queen at the Cathedral Church of St. Paul, London, on the 23d of August, 1705, being the Thanksgiving-Day for the late Glorious Success in Forcing the Enemies Lines in the Spanish Netherlands, **by** the Arms of her Majesty and her Allies, under the Command of the Duke of Marlborough. By Richard WILLIS, D.D., Dean of Lincoln, etc. 4to., London, 1705, and 8vo., London. [1705.]

1705. **A Review of the Case of** Judah and Ephraim, and its application to the Church of England and the Dissenters. . . . In a Letter to the Reverend Dr. WILLIS, Dean of Lincoln, occasion'd by his Thanksgiving-Sermon, on the 23d of August, 1705, before Her Majesty at St. Pauls. 4to., London, 1705.

1706. **A Sermon** preach'd before the Queen at the Cathedral Church of S. Paul, London, the xxvii[th]. Day of June, 1706. Being the Day appointed for a General Thanksgiving to Almighty God for the success of Her Majesty's Arms in Flanders and Spain, etc. By George STANHOPE, D.D., Dean of Canterbury, etc. 4to., London, 1706.
The Fourth Edition. 8vo., London, 1706.

1706. **Sermon** before the Lord Mayor, S. Pauls, 5 Nov., 1705. By Giles POOLEY, D.D. 4to., London, 1706.

1707. **A Sermon** preach'd before the Queen at the Cathedral-Church of St. Paul, on May the First, 1707. Being the Day appointed by Her Majesty for a General Thanksgiving for the Happy Union of the Two Kingdoms of England and Scotland. By the Right Reverend Father in God, William [TALBOT], Lord Bishop of Oxford. 4to., London, 1707.
Another Edition, 8vo., London, 1707.

1707. **The Eternity of Hell Torments** asserted and vindicated. Sermon before the Lord Mayor, S. Paul's, 15 June, 1707. By Richard JENKS, M.A., and Lecturer of the United Parishes of St. Mary at Hill, and St. Andrew Hobart. 8vo., London, 1707.

1707. **Sermon** in S. Paul's, at the Funeral of Mr. Tho. Bennet. 30 Aug., 1706. By Francis ATTERBURY, D.D., Dean of Carlisle. 8vo., London, 1707.

1707. A Letter to the Reverend Dr. Francis Atterbury : occasion'd by the Doctrine lately deliver'd by him in a Funeral Sermon on 1 Cor. xv. 19, August 30, 1706. 8vo., London, 1707.

1707. **A Large** Vindication of the Doctrine contained in the Sermon preach'd at the Funeral of Mr. Thomas Bennet. In answer to a Pamphlet, intituled, A Letter to the Reverend Dr. Francis Atterbury, etc. By Francis ATTERBURY, D.D., etc. 8vo., London, 1707.

1707. **A Sermon** preach'd before the Queen, and the Two Houses of Parliament, at St. Paul's, on the 31st of December, 1706, the Day of Thanksgiving for the Wonderful Successes of this Year. By Gilbert [BURNET], Bishop of Sarum. 4to., London, 1707.
Another Edition, 8vo., London, 1707.

1707-1766 **Sermons.** At the Anniversary Meeting of the Children educated in the Charity Schools.

Francis **GASTRELL**, D.D., S. Sepulchre's. **1707.** The Second
  Edition.
Samuel BRADFORD, D.D., S. **Sepulchre's.** **1709.**
John ROBINSON, Bp. of London, S. Sepulchre's. **1714.**
Edmund GIBSON, Bp. of Lincoln, S. Sepulchre's. **1716.**
Thomas SECKER, Bp. of Oxford, Christ Church. **1743.**
  A **New** Edition. 1766.

1708. A Second Letter to the Reverend Dr. Francis **Atterbury** in
  answer to his Vindication **of the** Doctrine preach'd by Him **at
  the** Funeral of Mr. Bennet. The Second Edition. **8vo.,**
  London, 1708.

1708. **A Sermon** preach'd . . at the Cathedral Church of S. Paul,
  January the 19th, 1703-4. Being **the** Fast-Day, appointed by
  Her Majesty's Proclamation upon the occasion of the Late
  Dreadful Storm **and** Tempest ; and to implore **the** Blessing of
  God upon Her Majesty and Her Allies, in the present War. By
  Ofspring **BLACKALL**, D.D., Now Lord Bishop of Exeter. 8vo.,
  London, **1708.**

1708. A Sermon **preached before the** Queen at St. Pauls, August
  the **19th, 1708.** **The** Day of Thanksgiving for our Deliverance
  from the late Invasion, and for the Victory obtain'd **near
  Audenard. By** William [FLEETWOOD], Lord Bishop **of St.
  Asaph. 8vo., London,** 1708.

1709. **Sermon** before the Lord Mayor **at** S. Paul's, **31 January,**
  1708-9. By Geo. SMALRIDGE, D.D. **8vo.,** London, **1709.**

1709. **Sermon** before the Lord Mayor at **S. Paul's.** 22. Nov., 1709,
  Being the Day appointed by Her **Majesty's** Royal Proclamation
  for a Public Thanksgiving. **By J.** ADAMS, D.D., Rector of
  S. Alban, Woodstreet, and **Chaplain in** Ordinary **to** Her
  Majesty. **8vo., London, 1709.**

1710. **Sermon** before the **Lord Mayor at** S. Pauls. **29 January,**
  1709-10. By Geo. SMALRIDGE, D.D. 8vo., London, **1710.**

1710. **Sermon** before the Lord Mayor at S. **Paul's.** **30 January,**
  1709-10. By Andrew SNAPE, D.D., Chaplain to **his Grace the**
  Duke of **Somerset, and** Rector of St. Mary at Hill. 8vo.,
  London, 1710.

1711. **Sermon.** S. Paul's. Convocation. Translated from the
  Latin. By White KENNET, D.D., Dean of Peterborough,
  Chaplain in Ordinary to Her Majesty. 8vo., **London, 1711.**

1711. **The Excellency and Usefulness of a Publick Spirit.**
  A Sermon preached in the Cathedral Church of St. Pauls **at**
  the Anniversary Meeting of the Gentlemen educated at St Paul's
  School, January the 25th, 17$\frac{10}{11}$. By Edward TENISON, LL.B.,
  Arch-Deacon of Carmarthen. 4to., London, 1711.
  [With a view of **the** School as frontispiece.]

1711. **The Dissolution** of the World by Fire. Sermon
  before the Lord Mayor. S. Pauls. 3 Sept., 1711. The Day

of Humiliation for the dreadful Fire in the Year 1666. By Benjamin IBBOT, M.A., Rector of the United Parishes of S. Vedast, etc. 8vo., London, 1711.

1713. **Of Original Sin.** Sermon before the Lord Mayor. S. Paul's. 22. Feb., 17$\frac{12}{13}$. By William DELAUNE, D.D., and President of S. John Baptist College, Oxon. 4to., London, 1713.
The Second Edition. 8vo., London, 1713.

1713. **A Sermon** preach'd before Both Houses of Parliament, in the Cathedral Church of St Paul, on Tuesday, July 7, 1713. Being the Day appointed by His Majesty for a General Thanksgiving for the Peace. By George [HOOPER], Lord Bishop of Bath and Wells. 4to., London, 1713; 8vo., London, 1713.

1713. Sermon before the Lord Mayor at St Paul's, July 26, 1713. On Occasion of the much-lamented Death of the Right Honourable and Right Reverend Henry [Compton], late Lord Bp. of London. By Thomas GOOCH, D.D., Fellow of Gonville and Caius College in Cambridge, and lately one of his Lordship's Domestick Chaplains. 4to., London, 1713.

1714. **Sermon** before the Lord Mayor. S. Paul's. 8. March, 1713. Ascension Day. By Benjamin IBBOT, Rector of the United Parishes of St Vedast alias Foster's, and St Michael Quern, and Chaplain to His Grace the Archbishop of Canterbury. 8vo., London, 1714.

1715. **The Way to Stable and Quiet Times.** A Sermon before the King at the Cathedral Church of St. Paul, London, on the 20th of January, 1714. Being the Day of Thanksgiving to Almighty God for Bringing His Majesty to a Peaceable and Quiet Possession of the Throne, and thereby Disappointing the Designs of the Pretender, and all his Adherents. By Richard [WILLIS], Lord Bishop of GLOCESTER. 4to., London, 1715.

1715. **Christian Love and Charity.** Sermon before the Lord Mayor at S. Pauls. The First Sunday in March, 17$\frac{14}{15}$. By Henry TOPPING, A.M., Lecturer of Covent Garden, and Chaplain to the Bishop of London. 8vo., London, 1715.

1715. **A Seasonable Discourse of the Rise, Progress, Discovery, and Utter Disappointment of the Gun-Powder Treason.** Sermon. S. Pauls. Before the Lord Mayor. By White KENNETT, D.D., Dean of Peterborough. 4to., London, 1715.

1716. **The Subject's Duty to the Higher Powers.** Sermon before the Lord Mayor at S. Pauls, Jan. 30, 1715. By R. SKERRET, M.A., Lecturer of St Peter's, Cornhill, etc. 8vo., London, 1716.

1716. **The Church of England, under God, an impregnable Bulwark against Popery.** A Sermon preached at St Paul's Cathedral, with several other Churches in London and

at the Royal Hospital, Greenwich ; on Occasion of the Many
Deliverances vouchsafed this Church and Nation from Popish
Conspiracies ; commemorated usually November 5. By Philip
STUBBS, M.A., Rector of S' James, Garlick-Hythe, First Chaplain
of the Royal Hospital for Seamen at Greenwich ; and Arch-
Deacon of S' Albans. The second edition. 8vo., London,
1716.

1718. **A Sermon** preach'd at the anniversary meeting of the
Gentlemen educated at S. Paul's School, at the Cathedral-
Church of S' Paul, on Saturday, January 25, 17$\frac{17}{18}$, being the
Feast of S' Paul's Conversion. By S. KNIGHT, D.D., Prebendary
of Ely, and Chaplain to the R' Hon. Edward E. of Orford.
4to., London, 1718.

1721. Sermon before the Lord Mayor, at S. Pauls. 30 January,
1720. By Francis HASLEWOOD, M.A., Rector of Chinkford in
Essex, etc. The third edition. 8vo., London, 1721.

1722. **The Signs of the Times.** Sermon before the Lord
Mayor at S. Paul's, Dec. 8, 1721. Being the Day appointed
for a General Fast for the Prevention of the Plague. By
Edmund MASSEY, M.A., Lecturer of S' Alban Woodstreet. **The
fifth edition.** 8vo., London, 1722.

1723. **Sermon** before the Lord Mayor at S. Pauls, May 29, **1723**
(Restoration Day). By Daniel WATERLAND, D.D., Chaplain in
Ordinary to His Majesty. 4to., London, **1723.**

1723. **Sermon.** S. Paul's. Sons of the Clergy. 13 Dec., 1722.
By Pawlet ST. JOHN, D.D., Rector of Yelden in Bedfordshire.
8vo., London, 1723.

1725. Sermon. Sons of the Clergy. S. Pauls, December 9,
1725. By Joseph ROPER, B.D., Rector of the United Parishes
of St. Nicholas, Cole Abbey, and St. Nicholas Olaves. 4to.,
London, 1725.

1727, Sermon before the Lord Mayor at S. Pauls, 29 May, 1727
(Restoration). By Ross LEY, Rector of St. Matthew's, Friday-
street, and Chaplain to His Majesty's **Fourth Troop** of Horse-
Guards. 4to., London, **1727.**

1728-9. **The Expediency of a Divine Revelation Represented.** Sermon before the Lord Mayor at S. Pauls, Feb. 16,
172$\frac{8}{9}$. By John CONYBEARE, D.D., Fellow of Exeter College
in Oxford. 8vo., London, 1728-9.

1728. **The Happiness and Advantages of a Liberal and
Virtuous Education.** A Sermon preached in the Cathedral
Church of St. Paul on January the 25th, 1728, at the anni-
versary Meeting of the Gentlemen educated at St. Paul's School.
By **Thomas** HOUGH, M.A., Fellow of Trinity College in Cam-
bridge. **4to.,** Cambridge, **1728.**

1730. **The Expediency of a Divine Revelation Represented.** Sermon before the Lord Mayor. By John CONV-

BEARE, D.D. S. Pauls, 16. Feb., 1728-9. The Second
Edition. 8vo., London, 1730.
[Bound with Dr. Snape's Sermon dated 1710.]

1733. **An Excellent Sermon in Defence of Passive-Obedience and Non-Resistance**: preach'd on Sunday the 7th of October, 1733, at St. P - - L'S Cathedral; by the Reverend Mr. SC - RL - CK, from these Words, Speak not Evil of Dignities, etc. 4to., London, 1733.

1733. Remarks upon Mr. Chambres's Sermon on the Restoration, preached at St. Paul's, May 29th, 1733. 8vo., London, MDCCXXXXIII. (*sic.*).

1741. **A Sermon** preached before the Sons of the Clergy at their Anniversary Meeting in the Cathedral Church of St. Paul's, April 16, 1741. By Edward YARDLEY, B.D., Archdeacon of Cardigan. 4to., London, 1741.

1741. **Concio ad Synodum** . . habita in Ecclesia Cathedrali S. Pauli, London, Die 2. Decemb. A.D. 1741. A Zacharia PEARCE, S.T.P., Eccles. Cathedr. Winton. Decano. 4to., London, 1741.

1748. **Sermon** before the Lord Mayor at S. Pauls, 2. Sept. 1748. Being the anniversary Fast appointed for the dreadful Fire in London in the Year 1666. By William PARKER, M.A., Fellow of Balliol College in Oxford. 8vo., Oxford, 1748.

1750. **The Devout Laugh**; Or Half an Hour's Amusement to a Citizen of London, from Dr. PICKERING's Sermon at St. Pauls, January 30, 1749-50 . . . A Letter from Rusticus to Civis. 8vo., London, 1750.

1755. **A Sermon** preached at the Cathedral Church of St. Paul on January 25, 1755, at the Anniversary Meeting of the Gentlemen Educated at St. Paul's School. By Joseph FEARON, M.A., Fellow of Sidney-Sussex College in Cambridge, and Chaplain to the Rt. Hon. Anne Viscountess Dowager Irwin. 4to., London, 1755.

1757. **The Benefits** of a Liberal and Religious Education. A Sermon preached in the Cathedral Church of St. Paul, on Wednesday, June 29, 1757. Being the Anniversary Meeting of the Gentlemen educated at St. Paul's School. By the Rev. Thomas FAIRCHILD, of Chigwell, Essex. 4to., London, 1757.

1789. **A Sermon** preached at the Cathedral Church of St. Paul, London, before His Majesty and both Houses of Parliament, on Thursday, April 23, 1789. Being the Day appointed for a General Thanksgiving. By Beilby [PORTEUS], Lord Bishop of London. The Third Edition. 4to., London, 1789.

1789. **Examination of a Sermon** preached in **St. P. C.**, before the Lord Mayor, 25. May, 1788, by the Rev. Richard HARRISON, Chaplain to his Lordship. 8vo., London, 1789.

8

1790. **The Surprise of Death.** **Sermon before** the Lord Mayor at S. Pauls. Good Friday, **1790. By C. E.** DE COETLOGON, Chaplain **to the** Mayoralty. **4to., London, 1790.**

1807. **Concio apud Synodum Cantuariensem æde Paulina habita** XVI die Decembris MDCCCVI., **a** Joanne LUXMORE, S.T.P., Decano Glocestriensi. 4to., London, **1807.**

1837. **The New Reign.** The Duties of Queen Victoria: a Sermon preached at the Cathedral Church of St. Paul's, by the Rev. SYDNEY SMITH. 8vo., London, 1837.

1851. [**1710.**] The Measures of Christian Charity and their rewards, as stated by Bishop **Sherlock,** in **a** Sermon preached before the Sons of the Clergy at S. Paul's Cathedral, A.D. 1710. [With autograph letter from the Editor, Joshua WATSON.] 8vo., Daventry, 1851.

---

*CLERGY OF S. PAUL'S CATHEDRAL :**

SEPARATE SERMONS, BOOKS, OR TRACTS OF OR RELATING TO.

BISHOP ANDREWES.

1627. A Sermon preached at Jesus Chappell, **neere** Southampton. **At the** Consecration thereof, by the Right Reuerend Father **in** God, Dr. **Andrewes,** late Lord Bishop of Winchester. Deliuered by James ROULANSON, **B.** of Diuinitie, and Chaplaine to the Kings most Excellent Majesty. **4to.,** London, 1627.

DEAN BARWICK.

1721. Vita Johannis **Barwick,** S.T.P., Ecclesiæ Christi & **S. Mariæ** Dunelmensis primum, S. Pauli postea Londinensis Decani, **a** Petro BARWICK, M.D. 8vo., London, **1721.**

1724. **The** Life of the Rev. Dr. John **Barwick, D.D.,** successively Dean of Durham and S. Pauls, written in **Latin** by his Brother Dr. Peter BARWICK, translated into English **by** the Editor **of the Latin Life. 8vo.,** London, 1724.

DR. BURGES.

1641. **The First Sermon preached before the Honourable House of Commons now assembled in Parliament at their Publique Fast.** Novemb. **17, 1640. By** Cornelius BURGES, Doctor of Divinitie. **4to., London, 1641.**

DR. CHURCH, Prebendary.

1752. **A Sermon** preached before the Royal College of Physicians, **London, in the Parish-Church of St.** Mary-le-Bow, on Wednes-

---

* Arranged in the alphabetical **order of the names** of the clergy.

day, Sept. 20, 1752, being one of the Anniversary Sermons, appointed by the Will of the late Lady Sadleir, pursuant to the Design of her first Husband, William Croune, M.D. By Thomas CHURCH, D.D., Vicar of Battersea, and Prebendary of St. Paul's. 4to., London, **1752.**

DEAN COLET.

1513 ?. O Felix Colonia. Absolutissimus de octo orationis partium constructione libellus, emendatus per D. ERASMUM Roterodamum [prefatory letter from Dean COLET to Will. LILY dated 1513]. 4to., Cologne, **1513 ?.**

1674. **Daily Devotions.** Or, The Christians Morning and Evening Sacrifice... By John COLET, D.D., Dean of St. Pauls, London, and Founder of that Famous School near adjoyning. The last edition, with a brief Account of the Authors Life, by Dr. FULLER. 12mo., London, **1674.**

1724. The Life of Dr. John Colet, Dean of S. Paul's. By Samuel KNIGHT, D.D., Prebendary of Ely. 8vo., London, **1724.**
A new edition, 8vo., Oxford, 1823.

1886. **Dean Colet, the Founder of S. Paul's School.** A Lecture delivered in the Schoolroom of S. Vedast's, Foster Lane, April 16, 1886, by Rev. J. H. LUPTON, Surmaster of S. Paul's School. 8vo., London, **1886.**

1887. A Life of John Colet, D.D., Dean of S. Paul's, and Founder of S. Paul's School. By J. H. LUPTON, M.A., Surmaster of S. Paul's School, etc. 8vo., London, **1887.**

BISHOP COMPTON.

1688. An exact account of the Whole Proceedings against the Right Reverend Father in God, Henry **[Compton]**, Lord Bishop of London, before the Lord Chancellor and the other Ecclesiastical Commissioners. 4to., London, **1688.**

1754. Christ's Hospital. Prayers appointed by the Right Reverend Father in God Henry Compton, late Lord Bishop of London : for the Use of the children of Christ-Hospital. 4to., London, 1754.

DR. CURREY, Prebendary.

1870. **Old Times and New Learning.** A Sermon preached in the Chapel of St. John's College, Cambridge, at the annual commemoration of Benefactors, on May 6, 1870. By the Rev. G. CURREY, D.D., Preacher of the Charterhouse, formerly Fellow and Tutor of the College. 4to., Cambridge, **1870.**

DEAN DONNE.

1622. **A Sermon vpon the XX Verse of the V Chapter of the Booke of Ivdges.** Wherein occasion was iustly taken for

the Publication of some Reasons, which his Sacred Maiestie had
been pleased to giue, of those Directions for Preachers, which
hee had formerly set foorth. Preached at the Crosse the 15th
of September, 1622, by Iohn DONNE, Doctor of Diuinitie, and
Deane of Saint Pavls, London. And now by commandement of
his Maiestie published, as it was then preached. 4to., London,
1622.

[This is the first edition. This copy has the dedication to
George Marquesse of Buckingham.]

**1622. A Sermon vpon the XV. Verse of the XX. Chapter
of the Booke of Ivdges...** By John DONNE. . . **Another**
edition. 4to., London, 1622.

[The text is really Judges v. 20.]

1625. **The First Sermon preached to King Charles at
Saint James:** 3° April, 1625. By Iohn DONNE, Dean of
Saint Pauls, London. **4to.,** London, **1625.**

1625. Manuscript. Sermons made by **I. Donne**, doctor of deuinty
& Deane of Pauls, An° Domini 1625. Knightley CHETWODE.
[Apparently the writer of the volume.]

Sermons contained in this MS. :
>   Psalm cxliv. 15.
>   1 Tim. iii. 16.
>   Psalm lxviii. i.   Before the King.
>   Hosea ii. **19.**   At S. Clements, **at Mr.** Washington's
>   marriage.
>   2 Cor. iv. 6.   The Spittle. Easter Monday, 1622.

[At the end of the volume, 'A Common Place Book, 1696.'
In the middle of the volume are some verses dated 1696, with
this note : 'The reason why I wrote severall of these following
verses was not that I thought them **all** good, but the subjects
were what I had **occasion** to make use of.']

1626. A Sermon, preached to the Kings Mᵗⁱᵉ at Whitehall, **24.**
Febr. 1625. By Iohn DONNE, Deane of Saint Pauls, London.
And now by his Maiestes commandment Published. 4to.,
London, 1626.

1632. Deaths Dvell, or a Consolation to the Soule, against the
dying Life, and liuing Death of the Body. Delivered in a
Sermon at White Hall, before the Kings Maiesty, in the begin-
ning of Lent, 1630. By that late learned and Reuerend Diuine
Iohn DONNE, Dʳ in Diuinity, & Deane of S. Pauls, London.
Being his last Sermon, and called by his Maiesties houshold The
Doctors owne Fvnerall Sermon. 4to., London, 1632.

[Opposite the title is a portrait, half-length, of Dr. Donne in
his shroud. 'Martin B. scup.']

1634. **A Sermon upon the xliiii Verse of the xxi Chapter
of Matthew.** By Dr. DONNE, Dean of Pauls. 4to., Cambridge,
1634.

1634. A Sermon upon the xix verse of the ii chapter of Hosea. By Dr. DONNE, Dean of Pauls. 4to., Cambridge, 1634.

1634. Two Sermons preached before King Charles, upon the xxvi verse of the first chapter of Genesis. By Dr. DONNE, Dean of Pauls. 4to., Cambridge, 1634.

1839. The Works of John Donne, Dean of St. Paul's 1621-1631, with a Memoir of his Life. By Henry ALFORD, M.A. Six volumes. 8vo., London, 1839.

ARCHDEACON HALE.

1868. An Essay on the Union between the Church and the State, and the Establishment by Law of the Protestant Reformed Religion in England, Scotland, and Ireland. W. H. HALE, M.A., Archdeacon of London. 8vo., London, 1868.
[The Cathedral possesses a large collection of the Charges and Pamphlets of Archdeacon Hale.]

THEOPHILUS LANE, Minor Canon.

1844. Extracts from the Letters of a beloved Brother [Rev. Theophilus Lane, Minor Canon of S. Paul's] written during the last six months of his life, etc. 12mo., London. No date. (Not published.)

DEAN MILMAN.

1837. Address delivered at the Opening of the City of Westminster Literary, Scientific, and Mechanics Institute. By the Rev. H. H. MILMAN, Prebendary, and Minister of St. Margaret's, Westminster. 8vo., London, 1837.

Catalogue of the Books of Richard de Gravesend, Bishop of London, 1303. Ten pages. H. H. MILMAN, Dean.
[The Library possesses a set of the works of Dean Milman. These pamphlets are specially enumerated, because such short tracts may easily escape the notice of a bibliographer.]

DEAN NOWELL.

1560-1601. 'Scripture Text Book of Rev. Alexander Nowell, D.D. (Dean of S. Pauls, Prebendary of Canterbury),' etc.
[The volume is lettered 'Dean Nowell—Scripture Common Place Book,' and is probably in the Dean's autograph.]

1583. A true report of the Disputation or rather priuate Conference had in the Tower of London with Ed. Campion Iesuite, the last of August, 1581. Set downe by the Reuerend learned men them selues that dealt therein. 4to., London, Christopher Barker, 1583.
[The 'Reuerend learned men' were 'the Deane of Paules,' that is Alexander NOWELL, and others.]

1638. Christianæ Pietatis prima **institutio ad** usum Scholarum Græcè & Latinè **scripta.** 12mo., London, 1638.
[The Greek translation of Nowell's Catechism was by Dr. Whitaker, a nephew of Dr. Nowell's. (*MS. note by* Dr. Thos. Turton, Bishop of Ely.)]

1795. **Catechismus,** sive prima institutio disciplinaque pietatis Christianæ, Latinè explicata : authore Alexandro Nowello. 8vo., Oxon., 1795.

1809. The Life of Alexander Nowell, Dean of S. Paul's. By Ralph Churton, M.A., Archdeacon ⸰of S. Davids, etc. 8vo., Oxford, 1809.

PREBENDARY Row.

1850. **Letter to the Rt. Hon. Lord John Russell, M.P.,** on the Constitutional Defects of the University and Colleges of Oxford, with suggestions for a Royal Commission of inquiry into the Universities. By a member of the Oxford Convocation. [Rev. C. A. Row, Prebendary.] 8vo., London, 1850.

DEAN SHERLOCK.

1693. A Sermon preached at the Funeral of the Reverend Richard Meggot, D.D., and late Dean of Winchester, Decemb. 10th, 1692, at Twickenham. By William **Sherlock,** D.D., Dean of St. Paul's. 4to., London, 1693.

1695. **Remarks** upon a book lately published by Dr Will. Sherlock, Dean of St. Paul's, etc., entituled a Modest Examination of the Oxford Decree. 4to., Oxford, 1695.

1696. The Master of the Temple as bad a Lawyer, as the Dean of Paul's **[Sherlock]** is a Divine. In a Letter from a Gentleman of the Temple to his (quondam) Tutor in Oxford. About the Law-Part in Dr Sherlock's modest Examination of the Oxford Decree. 4to., London, 1696.
[Imperfect.]

1697. The nature and measure of Charity. Sermon before the Lord Mayor at the Parish Church of St. Bridget, on Tuesday in Easter-Week, April 6, MDCXCVII. By William Sherlock, D.D., Dean of St. Paul's, etc. 4to., London, 1697.

1697. The Danger of Corrupting the Faith by Philosophy. A Sermon preach'd before the Right Honble the Lord-Mayor and Court of Aldermen, at Guildhall-Chappel, on Sunday, April 25, 1697. By William Sherlock, D.D., Dean of St. Paul's, Master of the Temple, and Chaplain in Ordinary to His Majesty. 4to., London, 1697.

1697. A Vindication of Dr. Sherlock's Sermon concerning *The Danger of* **Corrupting the** *Faith by Philosophy,* in answer to some Socinian Remarks. By William SHERLOCK, D.D., etc. 4to., London, 1697.

DR. STUART, 'Dean of S. Paul's.'

[There is no extant evidence known to me that Dr. Stuart was ever installed as Dean of S. Paul's.]

1657. **Catholique Divinity**: or, the most solid and sententious Expressions of the Primitive Doctors of the Church, &c. By Dr. STUART, Dean of St. Pauls, afterwards Dean of Westminster, and Clerk of the Closet to the late K. Charles. 8vo., London, 1657.

1658. **Three Sermons** preached by the Reverend and Learned Dr Richard **Stuart**, Dean of St. Pauls, afterwards Dean of Westminster, and Clerk of the Closet to the late King Charles. To which is added a fourth Sermon, preached by the Right Reverend Father in God Samuel Harsnett, Lord Archbishop of York. The second edition Corrected and Amended. 8vo., London, 1658.

DEAN STILLINGFLEET.

1667. **A Sermon** preached before the King, March 13, 166$\frac{6}{7}$, by Edward STILLINGFLEET, B.D., Chaplain in Ordinary to his Majesty. (Prov. xiv. 9.) 4to., London, 1667.

1674. **The Reformation Justify'd**: in a Sermon preached at Guildhall Chappell, Septemb. 21, 1673, before the Lord Major and Aldermen, etc. By Edw. STILLINGFLEET, D.D., etc. (Acts xxiv. 14.) 4to., London, 1674.

1674. **A Sermon** preached November V., 1673, at St. Margaret's, Westminster. By Edward STILLINGFLEET, D.D., etc. (S. Matt. vii. 16, 17.) The second edition. 4to., London, 1674.

1678. **A Sermon** preached on the Fast-Day, November 13, 1678, at St. Margarets, Westminster, before the Honourable House of Commons. By Edward STILLINGFLEET, D.D., Dean of St. Paul's, and Chaplain in Ordinary to His Majesty. The third edition. 4to., London, 1678.

1679. **A Sermon** preached before the King at White-Hall, March 7, 167$\frac{8}{9}$. By Edward STILLINGFLEET, D.D., Dean of St. Pauls, and Chaplain in Ordinary to His Majesty. (S. Matt. x. 16.) 4to., London, 1679.

1680. **The Rector of Sutton** committed with the Dean of St. Paul's. Or, a Defence of Dr Stillingfleet's *Irenicum*, his Discourses of *Excommunication, Idolatry,* and other Writings ; against his late Sermon, entituled, *The Mischief of Separation.* By the author of the Christian Temple [*i.e.*, Vincent Alsop]. 4to., London, 1680.

1687. **A letter** to Mr. G[odden], giving a True Account of a Late Conference at the D. of P. [By Edward STILLINGFLEET, Dean.] 4to., London, 1687.

1687. A Second Letter to **Mr.** G[odden], in Answer to **Two**
Letters Lately Published concerning The Conference at the
D. of P. [By Edward STILLINGFLEET, Dean.] 4to., London,
1687.

BISHOP TERRICK.

1772. A Letter to the Bishop of London [Richard **Terrick**] on his
Public Conduct, Pointing out, among other particulars, his
Lordship's inattention to Public Ordinations, & Hireling
Preachers, In which is delineated the Character of a late Ex-
amining Chaplain. By a Curate. 4to., London, 1772.

PLAYS ACTED BY THE CHILDREN OF
S. PAUL'S.

1601. **Love's Metamorphosis, a** Witty **and** Courtly Pastorall,
written by **Mr.** John **Lilly.** First plaid by the children of Paules,
and now by the children of the Chapell. **4to.,** London, 1601.
[Title lost.]

1606-1877. **Nobody and Somebody.** With the true Chronicle
Historie of Elydure, who was fortunately three seuerall times
crowned King of England. The true copy thereof, as it hath
beene acted by the Queens Maiesties Seruants.
[Reprint edited by Alexander Smith. Originally printed in
1606, privately reprinted in 1877 (only fifty copies).]

1607. Thomas **Decker and** John **Webster.** Northward Hoe :
Sundry times **acted by the** Children of Paules. 4to., London,
1607.

1607. **Tho.** Decker and Iohn **Webster.** West-Ward Hoe.
it hath beene diuers times Acted by the Children of Paules.
4to., London, 1607.

1616. Iacke Drvms Entertainement, or The Comedie of
Pasquil and Katherine, As it hath beene sundry times plaid by
the Children of Powles. Newly **corrected.** W. Stansby for
C. Knight. 4to., London, 1616.

1616. Thomas **Midleton.** A Tricke to catch the Old One : as it
hath beene often in Action, both at Paules, the Blacke Fryers,
and before his Maiestie. 4to., London, 1616.

1630. Thomas **Middleton.** The Phoenix, as it hath beene sundrie
times acted by the Children of Paules. **4to.,** London, 1630.

1630. Thomas **Middleton.** Michaelmas Terme, as it hath beene
sundry times acted by the Children of Paules. 4to., London,
1630.

1632. John **Lilly.** Six Court Comedies, often presented and acted
before Queene Elizabeth by the Children of her Majesties

Chappell, and the Children of Paules. Small 8vo., London,
1632.

[The six Comedies are 'Gallathea,' 'Endimion,' 'Campaspe,'
'Sapho and Phao,' 'Mydas,' 'Mother Bombie.']

1640. Thomas **Middleton.** A Mad World my Masters : A Comedy.
As it hath bin often Acted at the Private House in Salisbury
Court, by her Majesties **Servants.** Composed by T. M. Gent.
4to., London, 1640.

1877. Henry Carey **Shuttleworth, M.A., Minor** Canon, and
William **Russell.** M.A., Mus. Bac., **Minor** Canon. King
Marigold : a Musical Madness. Written for **and** dedicated **to**
the boys of the Choir School of S. Paul's Cathedral. 8vo.,
London, 1877.

SIR CHRISTOPHER WREN.

1651. **Newes** from the Dead, or a True and exact Narration of the
miraculous deliverance of **Anne Greene,** who being executed at
Oxford, Decemb. 14. 1650, afterwards revived ; and by the care
of certain Physitians there is now **perfectly recovered. . . .**
Written by a Scholler in Oxford. . . **The second impression.**
[Verses by **Christopher** WREN will be found at pages 13 and 14.]
4to., Oxford, 1651.

1712. **Frauds and Abuses at St. Paul's.** In a Letter to a
Member of Parliament. (By Dr. HARE, Residentiary of S.
Pauls.) 8vo., London, 1712.

1713. An **Answer** to a Pamphlet entitul'd *Frauds and Abuses at
St. Paul's.* With an **Appendix** relating to the Revenues and
Repairs of the Cathedral. 8vo., London, 1713.

1713. An **Abstract** of an Answer lately publish'd to a Pamphlet
intitled *Frauds and Abuses at St. Paul's.* 8vo., London, 1713.

1713. Fact against **Scandal,** or, a Collection of Testimonials,
Affidavits, and other **Authentick Proofs** in vindication of Mr.
Richard Jennings Carpenter, Langley Bradley Clockmaker, and
Richard Phelps Bell-Founder : to be referr'd to in an Answer
which will speedily be publish'd to a late false and malicious
Libel, Entituled, *Frauds and Abuses at St. Paul's.* To which is
added, an Appendix relating to Mr. Jones and Mr. Spencer ; and
the Copy of a Certain Agreement between the Minor Canons,
etc., of the said Cathedral. 8vo., London, 1713.

1713. A Continuation of **Frauds and Abuses at St.** Paul's,
wherein is considered at large, the Attorney General's Report,
in relation to a Prosecution of Mr. Jennings the Carpenter, in
Answer to *Fact against Scandal,* etc. 8vo., London, 1713.

1713. The Second **Part** of Fact against Scandal; in Answer to a Pamphlet intitled *A Continuation of Frauds and Abuses at St. Paul's.* 8vo., London, 1713.

1713. An Account of **some** Roman Urns, and other antiquities, lately Digg'd up near Bishops-Gate. With brief Reflections upon the Antient and Present State of London. In a Letter to Sir Christopher Wren, Kt., Surveyor-General of Her Majesty's Works. [By J. WOODWARD, Gresham College, 23 June, 1707.] 8vo., London, 1713.

1750. Parentalia : or, Memoirs of the Family of the Wrens ; **viz. :** of Mathew Bishop of Ely, Christopher Dean of Windsor, etc., but chiefly of Sir Christopher **Wren** . . . Compiled by his son, Christopher; now published by his Grandson, Stephen WREN, Esq., with the care of Joseph Ames, F.R.S. Folio, London, 1750.

1823. Memoirs of the Life and Works of Sir Christopher Wren : with a brief view of the progress of Architecture in England. By James ELMES, M.R.I.A., Architect. 4to., London, 1823.

1848-49. The Works of Sir Christopher Wren. The Dimensions, Plans, Elevations, and Sections of the Parochial Churches of Sir Christopher Wren, erected in the cities of London and Westminster. By John CLAYTON, Architect. Folio, London, 1848-49.

1852. Sir Christopher Wren and his Times, with illustrative sketches and anecdotes of the most distinguished Personages of the seventeenth century. By James ELMES. 8vo., London, 1852.

1871. William Calvert Shone. Gleanings about Sir Christopher Wren and S. Paul's Cathedral, to which is added, An appeal for Funds for the proposed Completion of the Interior of St. Paul's. 8vo., London, 1871.

1881. Sir Christopher Wren, his Family and his Times, with original letters, and a Discourse on Architecture hitherto unpublished. 1585-1723. By Lucy PHILLIMORE. 8vo., London, 1881

1881. The Towers and Steeples designed by Sir Christopher Wren: a descriptive, historical, and critical Essay by Andrew T. TAYLOR. 8vo., London, 1881.

Elevations, Plans, and Sections of Fifty Churches designed and built under the direction of Sir C. Wren. From the Crace Collection.

SACHEVERELL CONTROVERSY.

(ONE OF THE SERMONS WHICH GAVE RISE TO THE CONTROVERSY WAS PREACHED IN S. PAUL'S CATHEDRAL.)

1672. Eutropius et Aur. Victor ex Recensione, et cum notulis T. Fabri. Autograph of H. Sacheverell on title. 'Ex libris

H. Sacheverell e Coll. Mag. Oxoñ 1683.' 12mo., Salmurii, 1672.

1708. **The Nature, Guilt,** and **Danger of Presumptuous** Sins. Sermon before the University of Oxford. 14. Sept., 1707. By Henry SACHEVERELL, M.A., etc. 8vo., Oxford 1708.

1709. **The Communication of Sin.** A Sermon preach'd at the Assizes held at Derby 15. Aug., 1709. By Henry SACHEVERELL, D.D., etc. 8vo., London, 1709.

1709. **The Perils of False Brethren, both in Church, and** State: set forth in a Sermon preached before the Right Honourable the Lord Mayor, Aldermen, and Citizens of London at the Cathedral-Church of St Paul, on the 5th of November, 1709. By Henry SACHEVERELL, D.D., Fellow of Magdalen College, Oxon, and Chaplain of St Saviour's, Southwark. 4to., London, 1709; and 8vo., London, 1709. The second edition. 8vo., London, 1709.

1709. **The Bull-Baiting:** or SACH – – LL dress'd up in Fire-Works, lately brought over from the Bear-Garden in Southwark; and expos'd for the diversion of the Citizens of London, at Six Pence a piece. By John DUNTON. Being Remarks on a scandalous Sermon Bellow'd out at S. Pauls on the Fifth of November last before the . . . Lord Mayor and Court of Aldermen by Dr. Sach – – ll. 4to., London, 1709.

1709. The Cherubim with a Flaming Sword, that appear'd on the Fifth of November last, in the Cathedral of St. Paul, to the Lord Mayor, Aldermen, and Sheriffs, and many Hundreds of People, etc. Being a Letter to my Lord M——, with remarks upon Dr. **Sa** – – ll's Sermon. 8vo., London, 1709.

1710. The Mischief of Prejudice; or some Impartial Thoughts upon Dr. Sacheverell's Sermon preach'd at St. Paul's, Nov. 5, 1709. 8vo., London, 1710.

1710. A Defence of **Her** Majesty's Title **to the Crown,** and a justification of Her entring into a War with France and Spain: as it was deliv'd in a Sermon preached before the University of Oxford on the 10th Day of June, 1702. Being the Fast appointed for Imploring a Blessing on Her Majesty and Allies engag'd in the present War. By Henry SACHEVERELL, M.A., etc. Being the Discourse referr'd to in the Doctor's Answer to the Articles of Impeachment against him. The second edition. 8vo., London, 1710.

1710. The Speech of Henry **Sacheverell**, D.D., upon his Impeachment at the Bar of the House of Lords in Westminster-Hall, March 7, 170$\frac{9}{10}$. 8vo., London, 1710.

1710. **An** Alphabetical List of the Right Honourable the Lords and also of those Members of the Honourable House of Commons in England and Wales, that were for Dr. **Henry**

Sacheverell. London Printed in the Year 1710. Price Two
Pence. Broadside, with Portrait of Henry **Sacheverell**, D.D.

1710. **Collection** of Passages referr'd to by Dr. Henry **Sacheverell**
in his Answer to the Articles of his impeachment. The second
edition. 8vo., London, 1710.

1710. A visit to St Saviour's, Southwark, with **Advice to Dr.**
Sacheverell's Preachers there. By a Divine **of the Church**
of England. **8vo.**, London, 1710.

1710. Submission to Governours considered, in a letter to a Friend
and Admirer of Dr. **Sacheverell**, occasion'd by the late reviv'd
Doctrine of Unlimited Passive Obedience. 8vo., London,
1710.

1710. **The Character of a true Ch. of England-man**,
exclusive of Dr. West, Mr. Hoadly, and their Adherents,
however Dignify'd **or** Distinguish'd. 8vo., London, 1710.

1710. **A** letter to the Rev. Dr. Henry **Sacheverell**, on occasion
of his Sermon, and late Sentence pass'd on him by the Honourable House **of Lords**, by a Cambridge Gentleman, A.B. **8vo.,**
London, 1710.

1710. **The High Church Mask pull'd off,** or modern addresses
anatomized. 8vo., London, 1710.

1710. **Undone Again,** or the Plot discover'd. 8vo., London,
1710.

1710. **The Voice of the People, no Voice of God.** By
F. A., D.D. 8vo. No place. 1710.

1710. **The** Answer of Henry **Sacheverell,** D.D., to the Articles
of Impeachment, exhibited against Him by the Honourable
House of Commons, etc., for Preaching Two Sermons. I. At
the Assizes held **at** Derby, August the 15th. II. **At the**
Cathedral Church of St. Paul, Novemb. 5th, **1709.** 8vo.,
London, 1710.

1710. **A Speech without doors.** 8vo., London, 1710.

1710. A Collection of Poems, etc., for and against Dr. **Sacheverell.**
The Third Part. 8vo., London, 1710.

1710. The Bishop of Salisbury [Gilbert **Burnet**]. His speech in
the House of Lords on the first article of **the** Impeachment of
Dr. Henry Sacheverell. 8vo., London, **1710.**

1710. **The Limehouse Dream,** or, **The** Churches Prop. [With
curious woodcut opposite Title, representing Fanatics endeavour-
ing **to pull down** the **Dome** of S. Pauls, etc.] 8vo., London,
1710.

1710?. **An Appeal to** Honest People against Wicked Priests.
8vo., London, c. **1710.**

1710. **The Modern Fanatick,** with a large and true account of the Life, Actions, Endowments, etc., of the Famous Dr. S . . . . . l. By William BISSET, Eldest Brother of the Collegiate Church of St. Katherine, and Rector of Whiston, in Northamptonshire. 8vo., London, 1710.

1713. **False Notions of Liberty** in Religion and Government destructive of both. A Sermon preached before the Honourable House of Commons at S. Margaret's, Westminster, on Friday, May 29, 1713. By Henry SACHEVERELL, D.D., Rector of St. Andrew's, Holborn. 8vo., London, 1713.

1713. **The Christian Triumph :** or, The Duty of praying for our Enemies. In a Sermon preach'd at S. Saviour's in Southwark. **On Palm-Sunday,** 1713. By Henry SACHEVERELL, D.D. 8vo., London, 1713.

1714. **A Sermon** preach'd before the Sons of the Clergy, at their Anniversary Meeting in the Cathedral Church of St. Paul, December 10, 1713. By Henry SACHEVERELL, D.D., Rector of St. Andrew's, Holborn. 8vo., London, 1714.

FUNERALS OF NELSON AND WELLINGTON.

FUNERAL OF NELSON, 9 JANUARY, 1806.

1806. Services and Anthems to be used upon Thursday the 9th Day of January, 1806, being the Day appointed for the Public Funeral of the Lord Viscount **Nelson,** K.B., . . . in the Cathedral Church of St. Paul, London. By Authority of the Dean of St. Paul's. 4to., London, 1806.

1806. Account of Lord Nelson's Funeral reprinted from the Naval Chronicle of 1806 and from the London Gazette. To which is added, a copy of Lord Nelson's Will and Codicils. (Sir Chas. Young's copy.) 8vo., London, 1806.

1806. Fairburn's Edition of the Funeral of Admiral Lord **Nelson** . . at S. Paul's, 9 January, 1806. (Plate of the Procession and Car.) 8vo., London [1806?].

1806. A correct account of the Funeral of Horatio Lord Viscount **Nelson,** etc. 8vo., Liverpool, 1806.

1806. **Funeral of Lord Nelson.** A collection of Papers relating to the ceremony.

[See also amongst the Engravings a series relating to the Funeral.]

FUNERAL OF WELLINGTON, 18 NOVEMBER, 1852.

The Order of Proceeding in the **Public** Funeral of the late Field Marshal Arthur, **Duke** of Wellington,

K.G., to be solemnized in St. Paul's Cathedral, on Thursday, the xviii day of November, 1852.

> 1st impression, not dated, 6 leaves.
> 2nd   „   „   6   „
> 3rd   „   „   7   „
> 4th   „   „   7   „
> 5th   „   dated Nov. 17, 7 leaves
> 6th   „   „   9   „

Funeral Regulations to be observed.   2 leaves.   Richard Mayne, Commissioner of Police, 13 Nov., 1852.

Service and Anthems to be used upon Thursday the 18th Day of November, 1852, being the Day appointed for the Public Funeral of His Grace Field Marshal the Duke of Wellington, K.G., in the Cathedral **Church** of St. Paul, London. By **Authority** of the Dean of St. Paul's.   4to., London, 1852.

1852. Service at the Duke of Wellington's Funeral, with manuscript notes as to the time occupied in the recitation of parts of the Service.

Proclamation of the Titles of the Duke.

Plan of the arrangements for the Funeral.

Ticket of Admission, signed by Dean Milman.

The Order of the Proceeding and Ceremonies observed in the Public Funeral of the late Field Marshal Arthur, Duke of Wellington, K.G., solemnized in St. Paul's Cathedral on Thursday the xviii day of November, 1852. Folio, **42 pages.**

This Account of the Solemnity of the Funeral of the late **Field Marshal Arthur, Duke of Wellington, K.G.,** is printed for the purpose of Presentation to the Foreign Ministers, Distinguished Visitors, and Officers present upon that mournful occasion.   Charles Geo. Young, Garter.   College of Arms, 15th December, 1852.

1852.   **Funeral of the Duke of Wellington :** a collection of Papers relating to the Ceremony, together with Views of the Procession and the Funeral.

1852.   **Funeral** Car of the late Duke **of Wellington :** a series of illustrations.   Large **folio.**

1852.   1. Complete Guide to the Funeral of the Duke **of Welling-** ton . . .   By Charles Maybury ARCHER.   8vo., London, 1852.
   2. Explanatory Programme of the Personnel of the Funeral Procession.
   3. Guide to the Funeral Service of the Duke of Wellington **in** St. Paul's Cathedral with a Plan of the Interior.

1852-3   **A Voice from the Tomb. A** Dialogue between Nelson and Wellington overheard at S. Pauls (in 42 parts).   [By John Spencer WILSON.]   8vo., London, 1852-3.
   [See also among the Engravings a Series relating to the Funeral.]

THE DECORATION OF S. PAUL'S CATHEDRAL.

1852. **A Few** Remarks **on S. Paul's and its appropriate** Decorations. By Francis Cranmer PENROSE (Royal Institute of British Architects). (12 pages.)
[Discussion on this paper. 10 pages.]

1861. **S. Paul's Cathedral Fund.** Speeches delivered at a Meeting in the Egyptian Hall, Mansion House, on Friday, the 8th February, 1861. 8vo., London, 1861.

1870. **Fund for the Completion of S. Pauls.** Appeal presented at the Public Meeting held at the Mansion House on Wednesday, the 13th of July, 1870. 8vo., London, 1870.

1871. **Remarks and Suggestions on the Scheme for the Completion of St. Paul's Cathedral.** By George Edmund STREET, A.R.A. 8vo., London, 1871.

1871. **A Letter to the Very Rev. the Dean of St. Paul's,** printed at the request of the Executive Committee for the completion of S. Paul's Cathedral. By Frederick Heathcote SUTTON. 8vo., London, 1871.

1871. **S. Paul's Cathedral.** Report of Executive Committee, March, 1871. 8vo., London, 1871.

1871. Letter from G. E. Street, A.R.A., to George Richmond, R.A., 29 Feb. 1871, on the Restoration of S. Paul's. (7 pages.) 4to., London, 1871.

1871. **Report** on Decoration. S. Paul's Cathedral. W. BURGES, Architect. (Lithograph.) 4to., London, 1871.

1872. The Completion of S. Paul's. Article from the *Quarterly Review*, No. 266.

1872. **Description of a Scheme for the Internal Embellishment of S. Paul's, to** be submitted to the Committee for the Completion of the interior of the Cathedral. By F. C. PENROSE, Surveyor to the Fabric. (3 pages.) July, 1872.

1872. **A Book of Subscriptions for the Completion of the Cathedral Church of St. Paul, 1872.** Autograph signatures of the Queen, Prince and Princess of Wales, the Duke of Edinburgh, Archbishop Tait, Bishop Jackson, and others.

1873. **S. Paul's Cathedral Fund.** Statement of Account, with list of Subscriptions to 1873.

1874. **What shall be done with S. Paul's.** Remarks and Suggestions as to the Alterations made and proposed to be made. With a Plan. By J. T. MICKLETHWAITE, F.S.A., and Somers CLARK, jun^r. 8vo., London, 1874.

1874. Proposal for the Completion of St. **Paul's Cathedral.** By James FERGUSSON, F.R.S., etc. 4to., London, 1874.

1874. **S. Paul's Cathedral.** Article in the *Contemporary Review*, October, 1874, by Jas. FERGUSSON.

1874. **The Completion of S. Paul's.** A Letter to the Very Rev. the Dean of S. Paul's, Chairman of the executive Committee. **23** Nov., 1874. By George CAVENDISH BENTINCK, M.P. **8vo.**, London, 1874.

1874. A Description of Mr. **Burges'** Model for the Adornment of St. Paul's now Exhibited at the Royal Academy. 8vo., London, 1874.

1874, etc. Portfolio of original **Sketches and** Tracings **for** the Decoration of S. Paul's. By W. BURGES.

1874. Article on the Decoration **of S. Paul's,** by Edw. W. GODWIN. August, 1874.

1876. S. Peter's and S. Paul's. Notes on the Decoration of a few Churches in Italy, including S. Peter's on the Vatican at Rome, with suggestions for proceeding with the completion of S. Paul's in a letter to the Very Rev. R. W. Church, D.C.L., Dean of S. **Paul's.** By Edmund OLDFIELD, M.A., F.S.A. 8vo., London, 1876.

1876. S. Paul's Cathedral. The Impression and the Remedy. By the Author of the **Art** Impressions of Dresden. 8vo., London, 1876.

1877. S.P.C. Memorandum on Figure-Subjects for the Dome and some other parts of the Building. By Edmund OLDFIELD. Printed by the Sub-Committee. (16 pages.)

1878. **Further Memorandum on Figure-Subjects for the Dome.** Submitted to the Sub-Committee on 18 February, 1878. Third Memorandum submitted **5** March, **1878.** By Edmund OLDFIELD.

1878. S. Paul's Cathedral. Report of the Sub-Committee appointed June, 1877. (10 pages.)

1879. A Suggestive Design for the Decoration of the Cupola of S. Paul's Cathedral, London, by Richard Popplewell PULLAN and Charles Heath WILSON. (8 pages.) 4to., London, 1879.

1883. **The Decoration of the Dome of S. Paul's Cathedral.** By R. Popplewell PULLAN. (From the *Transactions* of the Royal Institute of British Architects.) 4to., London, 1883.

1884. An unfinished Drawing of the Dome of S. Paul's, by the late Mr. R. W. BILLINGS, architect, presented to the Dean and Chapter of S. Pauls by the Executors of his Widow **through** Drayton WYATT, **Esq.** May, **1884.**

9

CONTENTS.

1633. **The Survey of** London: . . Begunne first by the paines and industry of Iohn Stow in the yeere 1598. Afterwards inlarged by the care and diligence of A[nthony] M[unday] in the yeere 1618, and now completely finished by the study and labour of A[nthony] M[unday], H[enry] D[yson], and others. 4to., London, 1633.

1676. **Camera Regis**, or, A Short View of London. By John BRYDALL, Esq. 8vo., London, 1676.

1708. **Repertorium Ecclesiasticum Parochiale Londinense**: An Ecclesiastical Parochial History of the Diocese of London . . By Ric: NEWCOURT, Notary Publick. (Two volumes.) 4to., London, 1708.

   [This copy belonged successively to Dr. Cresswell, Archdeacon Hale, and Dean Mansel.]

   Another copy. Large paper.

1720. **John Stow.** A Survey of the Cities of London and Westminster . . written at first in the year 1598 . . since reprinted and augmented by the author; now lastly corrected . . By John Strype, M.A. (Two volumes.) Folio, London, 1720.

1732. **New Remarks of London:** or a Survey of the Cities of London and Westminster, of Southwark, and part of Middlesex and Surrey within the circumference of the Bills of Mortality. Collected by the Company of PARISH-CLERKS. 12mo., London, 1732.

1736. **Robert Seymour.** An Accurate Survey of the Cities of London and Westminster . . . with a compleat History of S. Paul's Cathedral and Westminster-Abbey. Small 4to., London, 1736.

1754-55. **Survey of London.** John Stow, by Strype. The sixth edition. (Two volumes.) Folio, London, 1754-55.

1756. **The History and Survey of London from its Foundation to the Present Time.** By William MAITLAND, F.R.S., and others. (Two volumes). Folio, London, 1756.

1766. London **and Westminster improved,** illustrated by
Plans. To which is prefixed, A Discourse on Publick Magnifi-
cence. . . . By John GWYNN. Quarto, London, 1766.

1775. Walter Harrison. A New and Universal Description and
Survey of the Cities of London and Westminster. Folio, London,
1775.
Another issue. Folio, London, 1776.

1788. Londres et ses environs; ou Guide des Voyageurs,
curieux et amateurs dans cette partie de l'Angleterre. . . .
Ouvrage fait à Londres, par M.D.S.D.L. Two volumes, 12mo.,
Paris, **1788.**

1792-96. Daniel Lysons. The Environs of London : being an
Historical Account of the Towns, Villages, and Hamlets within
Twelve miles of that Capital. (Four volumes.) **4to.,** London,
1792-6.

1794 ?. **The New, Complete, and Universal History,**
Description and Survey of the Cities of London and Westminster . . . Written and compiled . . **by** a Society of Gentlemen, the whole revised, **corrected and** improved. By William
Thornton, Esq., etc. 4to., London, c. 1794.
[List of Lord Mayors brought down to the 'present year,'
1794.]

1796?. A new and complete History and Description of
the Cities of London, Westminster. . . By Richard
SKINNER, Esquire. Folio, London, c. 1796.
[List of Lord Mayors ends in 1796.]

1802-7. James Peller Malcolm. Londinium Redivivum : or **an**
Antient History, and modern **description** of London. (Four
volumes.) 4to., London, **1802-7.**

1810. Richard Burton. Historical Remarks on the Ancient and
Present State of the Cities of London and Westminster. A New
edition. Small 4to., Westminster, **1810.**

1811. The History of London and its Environs . . . like-
wise an Account of all the Towns, Villages, and Country within
Twenty-Five miles of London. **By** the late Rev. Henry
HUNTER, **D.D., and other Gentlemen.** (Two volumes.) 4to.,
London, **1811.**

1818. London Interiors, a grand national exhibition **of** the
religious, regal, and civil solemnities, scientific meetings and
commercial scenes of the British Capital, beautifully engraved on
steel. (Two volumes.) 4to., London, 1818.

1819. **Londina Illustrata.** Graphic and Historical Memorials of
Monasteries, Churches, Chapels, Schools, Charitable Founda-
tions, **Palaces,** Halls, Courts, Processions, Places of Early
Amusement, and Modern and Present Theatres in the Cities
and Suburbs of London and Westminster. (Two volumes.)
Published by Robert WILKINSON. **4to.,** London, 181**9.**

1819. **Wilkinson's Londina Illustrata.** A Large Paper copy of the whole of the Plates.

*** Lowndes says that only twelve copies were printed upon Large Paper.

1824. **A Description of London** : Embellished with Engravings. Published by W. Darton, 58, Holborn Hill. 8vo., London, 1824.

1834. **C. F. Partington.** National History and Views of London and its Environs: embracing their Antiquities, modern improvements . . . from original drawings by eminent artists. (Two volumes.) 8vo., London, 1834.

1842. **1598.** A Survey of London, written in the year 1598 by John **Stow.** A new edition, edited by William J. Thoms, F.S.A. 8vo., London, 1842.

[1873-8.] **Old and New London,** a narrative of its History, its People, and its Places. Vols. 1 and 2, by Walter Thornbury. Vols. 3 to 6, by Edward Walford. Together with a volume of maps. 4to., London [1873-8].

1883. **W. J. Loftie.** A History of London. (Two volumes.) 8vo., London, 1883.

Supplement to the first edition. 8vo., London, 1884.

BOOKS RELATING TO LONDON GENERALLY.

1588. 1879. **The** Particular Description of England, **1588.** With views of some of the Chief Towns and Armorial Bearings of Nobles and Bishops, by William Smith, Rouge Dragon. Edited from the original MS. by Henry B. Wheatley, F.S.A., and Edmund W. Ashbee, F.S.A. [Contains an early view of S. Paul's Cathedral.] 4to., London, 1879.

1623. Something written by occasion of that fatall and memorable accident in the **Blacke Friers** on Sunday, being the 26. of October, **1623,** *stilo antiquo,* and the 5. of November, *stilo novo,* or Romano. Printed M.DC.XXIII. 4to., No place, 1623.

1623. The dolefvll Euen-Song, or a Trve Particvlar and Impartiall narration of that fearefull and sudden calamity, which befell the Preacher, Mr Drvry, a Iesuite, and the greater part of his Auditory, by the downefail of the floore at an Assembly in the **Black-Friers** on Sunday, the 26. of Octob. last, in the afternoone. Together with the Rehearsall of Master Drvrie his Text, and the diuision thereof, as also an exact Catalogue of the names of such as perished by the lamentable accident: And a briefe Application thereupon. 4to., London, 1623.

1630. **Orders and Directions,** together with a Commission for the better administration of Justice, and more perfect informa-

tion of His Maiestie. How and by whom the Lawes and
Statutes tending to the relief of the Poore, the well ordering and
training vp of youth in Trades, and the Reformation of Dis-
orders and disordered persons, are executed throughout the
Kingdom. 4to., London, 1630.

1632. London and the Countrey **Carbonadoed and
Quartred** into seuerall characters. By D. LUPTON.
8vo., London, 1632.

1640. Articles to be enquired of within the Diocese of
London in the third Trienniall Visitation of the Right
Honourable and Right Reverend Father in God, William
[Juxon], Lord Bishop of London . holden in the yeare of
our Lord God, **1640.** 4to., London, 1640.

1641. The Sermon and Prophecie of Mr. James **Hvnt** of the
County of Kent. Who professeth himselfe a Prophet, which
hee hath endeavoured to deliver in most churches in and about
London, but since delivered in the Old-Baily and in Wood
Street Counter, Octob. 9, **1641.** Written with his owne hand.
4to., No place, **1641.**
   [Curious woodcut of Prophet Hunt preaching in a tub.]

1641. A Discoverie of Six Women Preachers in Middlesex,
Kent, Cambridgeshire, and Salisbury. With a relation of their
names, manners, life, and doctrine, pleasant to be read, but
horrid to be judged of. Their names are these, Anne Hemp-
stall, Mary Bilbrow, Ioane Bauford, Susan May, Elizab. Bancroft.
Arabella Thomas. 4to., No place, **1641.**

1642. **A Collection of Sundry Petitions** presented to the
Kings most excellent Majestie in behalfe of Episcopacie,
Liturgie, and supportation of Church-Revenues, and Suppres-
sion of Schismaticks. 4to., No place, **1642.**

1642. **A letter** intercepted at a Court Guard of the City of
London, wherein is discovered a most desperate and bloody
Act to be performed on divers good ministers and their congre-
gations on the Fifth of March next : which by Gods great
mercie may now happily be prevented. 4to., London, 28 Feb.,
1642.

1643. Three Looks over London, or Plain Dealing is a Jewell.
4to., London, 1643.
   [Woodcut on title : Preaching at Paul's Cross. Autograph on
title of W. H. IRELAND.]

1647. Strange Newes from New-Gate : Or, a true Relation of the
false Prophet that appeared in Butolphs Church near Bishops-
Gate upon Sunday last in Sermon-time, professing himself to be
Christ. With his Examination before the Lord Mayor and his
Confession. Also his Examination at the Sessions in the Old-
Bayly before the Judges.

Printed in the year,
When false Prophets did appear,
1647.
[Curious woodcut on title.]

1657. 1817. **The Fatal Vespers:** a True and **Full** Narrative of that signal judgement of God upon the Papists by the Fall **of** the House in Black Friars, London, upon their fifth of November, 1623. Collected for the information and profit of each Family, by Samuel CLARK, Pastor of Bennet Fink. Originally printed London, 1657 ; reprinted, **4to., London, 1817.**

1661-1871. Paradise Transplanted **and** Restored, in **a** most artfull and Lively Representation of **the** Several Creatures, Plants, **Flowers, and** other Vegetables, **in their** full growth, shape, and **colour,** shown at Christopher **Whiteheads** at the two wreathed Posts in Shooe-Lane, London. Written by I. H., Gent. 4to., London, 1661 ; reprinted [on vellum] 1871.

1668. **A true Copie** of a **Speech** spoken to His Sacred Majesty, Charles II. In S. Paul's Church-yard, **as His Majesty passed from the Tower of** London to White-hall the Day before **His Royal Coronation,** April **22, 1661.** By James **HEWLETT, one of the Children** then harboured in CHRIST'S HOSPITAL. 4to., London, 1668.

1668-1885. Major Payne **Fisher.** Catalogue of the Tombs in the Churches in the City of London A.D. 1666. Edited by G. Blacker Morgan. 4to., London, 1668 ; privately reprinted, 4to., London, 1885.

1672. **Proposals** moderately **offered** for the full peopleing and inhabiting the City of London, and to restore the same to her **antient** flourishing Trade, which will sute **with** her splendid Structure. 4to., London, 1672.

1682. **The London Cuckolds.** A Comedy ; As it is Acted at the Duke's Theatre. By Edward RAVENSCROFT, Gent. 4to., London, 1682.

1683. **His Majesties Declaration** to All His Loving Subjects, concerning the Treasonable Conspiracy against His Sacred Person and Government, lately discovered. Appointed **to be** Read in all Churches and Chappels within this Kingdom. 4to., London, 1683.
[The Rye-House Plot.]

1683. **Parish Churches no Conventicles,** from the Ministers reading in the Desk when there is no Communion. For the Vindication of the Practice of Parochial Ministers. In answer to **a** late Pamphlet, **stil'd** Parish-Churches turn'd into Conventicles, pretended **to be** written by Rich. HART, but really penn'd by Mr. T. A., Barrister at Law . . . By O. U. in a letter to his Friend N. D. 4to., London, 1683.

1683. London's Remembrancer. A Call and Pattern for True and Speedy Repentance. Being an abridgment of those many severe Sermons by Thomas REEVE, B. in Divinity, intituled God's Plea for Nineveh. The only seasonable Work that can be done in this day. 4to., London, 1683.

1698. A Journey to London in the Year 1698. After the Ingenuous Method of that made by Dr. Martin Lyster to Paris in the same Year. Written originally in French by Monsieur SORBIERE, and Newly Translated into English. 8vo., London, 1698.

1698. Ecclesia et Factio. A dialogue between Bow-Steeple Dragon and the Exchange Grasshopper. 8vo., London, 1698. [In verse.]

1698. An Answer to the Dragon & Grashopper, in a Dialogue between an Old Monkey and a Young Weasel at the Three-Crane-Tavern in the Poultry, where they are daily to be seen. As also, Some Remarks upon the Amsterdam and London Æsop's. 8vo., London, 1698. [Bound up with *Ecclesia et Factio.*]

1702. The Oration, Anthems, and Poems, Spoken and Sung at the Performance of Divine Musick, for the Entertainment of the Lords Spiritual and Temporal, and the Honourable House of Commons. At *Stationers' Hall*, January the 31st, 1701. Undertaken by Cavendish WEEDON, Esq. 4to., London, 1702.

1734. A Critical Review of the Public Buildings, Statues and Ornaments in, and about London and Westminster. To which is prefix'd the Dimensions of St. Peter's Church at Rome, and St. Paul's Cathedral at London. 8vo., London, 1734.

1740. News from the Dead, or a faithful and Genuine Narrative of an extraordinary Combat between Life and Death, exemplified in the case of William DUELL, one of the Malefactors who was Executed at Tyburn on Monday the 24th of this Instant November, for a Rape, Robbery, and Murder, and who soon after return'd to Life at Barber-Surgeons-Hall, where he had been brought too from the Place of Execution, in Order to be Anatomis'd, &c. 8vo., London, 1740. [With curious frontispiece.]

1740. Lives of the Professors of Gresham College : to which is prefixed the Life of the Founder, Sir Thomas Gresham . . by John WARD, Professor of Rhetoric in Gresham College, and F.R.S. 4to., London, 1740.

1751. Observations on the Past Growth and Present State of the City of London. To which are annexed, a complete Table of the Christenings and Burials within this city from 1601 to 1750, etc. By Corbyn MORRIS. Folio, London, 1751.

1751. **The Morning** Walk ; or City encompass'd, a Poem in Blank Verse. By W. H. DRAPER. 8vo., London, 1751.

1759. An Historical Account of the Curiosities of **London** and Westminster, in Three Parts. 1. The Tower; 2. Westminster Abbey ; 3. S. Paul's Cathedral, etc. 12mo., London, 1759. Another Edition. 12mo., London, 1765.

1761. The Form of the Proceeding to the Royal Coronation of their most excellent Majesties King George III. and Queen **Charlotte.** Tuesday. 22. Sept. 1761. 4to., London, 1761.

1769. **The** City Remembrancer : being Historical Narratives of the **Great** Plague at London 1665, Great Fire 1666, and Great Storm 1703, etc. (Two volumes.) 8vo., London, 1769.

1772. **Fitz-Stephen's** Description of the City of London, newly translated from the Latin Original . . By an Antiquary. 4to., London, 1772.

1783. An Historical Account of the Origin, Progress, and Present State of **Bethlem Hospital,** founded by Henry VIII. for the Cure of Lunatics, and enlarged by subsequent Benefactors for the Reception and Maintenance of Incurables. By Thomas BOWEN. 4to., London, 1783.

1778. City Petitions, Addresses, and Remonstrances . . commencing in the year 1769, and including the Last Petition for the Burial of the Right Honble. the Earl of Chatham in S. Paul's Cathedral. With His Majesty's Answers. Also Mr. Alderman Beckford's Speech to the King on the Twenty-Third of May, 1770. 12mo., London, 1778.

1783. London's Gratitude: or an Account of such pieces of Sculpture and Painting as have been placed in the Guildhall at the expense of the City of London. To which is added, a List of those distinguished persons to whom the Freedom of the City has been presented for Public Services since the year 1758. 8vo., London, 1783.

1788. **The Wreck of Westminster Abbey,** being a selection from the Monumental Records of the most conspicuous Persons who flourished towards the latter end of the 18th century. By the **Author of** Kilkhampton Abbey [Sir Herbert CROFT, Bart.]. Sixth edition. 4to., London, MMI.

1793. **John Luffman.** The Charters of London complete : also Magna Charta, and the Bill of Rights. 8vo., London, 1793.

1802. **Case Respecting the Maintenance of the** London-Clergy . . . By John MOORE, Ll.B., Rector of St. Michael's, Bassishaw, and Minor Canon of St. Paul's. 8vo., London, 1802. And also the Third Edition. 8vo., London, 1812.

1803?. Spiritual Characteristics represented in an Account of a most curious Sale of Curates by Public Auction, who were to be disposed of in consequence of the **Clergy** Residence Act. By an Old Observer. London, c. 1803.

1804. Mark **Noble**. **A** History of the **College of Arms** and the lives of all the Kings, Heralds, and Pursuivants from **the** Reign of Richard III., Founder of the College, until the present time 4to., London, 1804.

1806. The Order to be observed in the Publick Funeral Procession of the late Honourable William **Pitt** . . . in Westminster Abbey. **22.** Feb., 1806. 4to., London, 1806.

1812. **London**: a Descriptive Poem, in Four Parts. Adorned with eight Copper Plates. By a Well Known Cockney. Small 4to., London, 1812.   .

1814. H. B. **Wilson**, B.D., Second Under Master. The History **of Merchant Taylors' School**: in Two Parts. 1. Of its founders, patrons, benefactors, and masters. **2.** Of its principal **scholars. 4to.**, London, 1814.

1817. J. **Bruce**. **The** History of the Ancient Savoy Palace (built by the Duke de Savoy, A.D. 1245) now the Scite of the Waterloo Bridge. **8vo.**, London, 1817

1817. **A** Description of the Royal Hospital for Seamen, at **Green-wich**: with a Short Account of the Establishment of the Royal **Naval Asylum.** 8vo., London, 1817.

1821. The **Ceremonies to be** observed at the Royal Coronation of **His most excellent Majesty** King **George** the **Fourth.**   19. **July, 1821. 4to.**, London, 1821

1822. **Prospectus. View** of London and **the** surrounding **Country,** taken with Mathematical Accuracy from an Observatory purposely erected over the Cross of S. Paul's Cathedral: to be published in Four Engravings. By Thomas HORNOR. First Edition, 8vo., London, **1822.** Second Edition, 8vo., London, **1823.**

1824. London, or Interesting Memorials of its Rise, Progress, and present State by Sholto and Reuben **Percy,** Brothers of the Benedictine Monastery, Mount Benger. [*i.e.*, Thomas Byerley **and Joseph** Clinton Robertson.] (Three volumes.) 12mo., **London, 1824.**

1825   Lithographic Sketch of the North Bank of the Thames, from Westminster Bridge to London Bridge, showing the proposed Quay and some other improvements suggested by Lieut.-Colonel **Trench,** etc. London, **1825.**

1825. **Historical Notices of the Collegiate Church or Royal Free Chapel and Sanctuary of S. Martin-le-Grand, London,** formerly occupying the site now appropriated to the New General Post Office . . with observations **on the different** kinds of Sanctuary **formerly** recognized by the **Common Law.** By Alfred John KEMPE. 8vo., London, 1825.

1825. **The Public Edifices of the British Metropolis**; with Historical and Descriptive Accounts of the Different Buildings. 4to., London, 1825.

1825. **Illustrations of the Public Buildings of London,** with Historical and Descriptive Accounts of each Edifice. By J. BRITTON, F.S.A., and A. PUGIN, Architect. (Two volumes.) 4to., London, 1825.

1827. **The Citizen's Pocket Chronicle.** 12mo., London, 1827.

1827. **A Chronicle of London from** 1089 to 1483 ; written in the fifteenth century . . To which are added numerous contemporary Illustrations. [Only two hundred and fifty copies printed.] 4to., London, 1827.

1839 ?. **Tallis's** London Street Views, exhibiting upwards of one hundred Buildings in each number, elegantly engraved on steel . . to which is added an Index map of the streets, etc. Long 4to., London, *c.* 1839.

1842. Frederick **Prickett.** The History and Antiquities of Highgate, Middlesex. 8vo., London, 1842.

1844. The **Architectural Antiquities of the Collegiate Chapel of St. Stephen, Westminster:** the late House of Commons. By Frederick MACKENZIE. Folio, London, 1844.

1848. The Diary of Henry **Machyn,** Citizen and Merchant-Taylor of London from 1550 to 1563. Edited by John Gough NICHOLS (Camden Soc.). 4to., London, 1848.

1849. Ceremonial for the **Private** Interment of Her late most Excellent Majesty **Adelaide** the Queen Dowager in the Royal Chapel of S. George at Windsor. 13. December, 1849. 4to., London, 1849.

1851. **Vestiges of Old** London. A Series of Etchings from Original Drawings . . by John Wykeham ARCHER. 4to., London, 1851.

1851. **Guide** illustré **du** Voyageur à Londres **et aux Environs.** 8vo., Paris et Londres [1851].

1852. **Notes in reference to the Plan of the Lord Mayor in proceedings through or within the City of London.**

1852. Chronicle of the **Grey Friars of** London, edited by John Gough NICHOLS. (Camden Soc.) 4to., London, 1852.

1853. William **Robins.** Paddington: Past and Present. 8vo., London, 1853.

1855. Jacob Henry **Burn.** A descriptive Catalogue of the London Traders, Tavern, and Coffee House Tokens current in the seventeenth century presented to the Corporation Library by Henry Benjamin Hanbury Beaufoy. Second edition. 8vo., London, 1855.

1855. **London in the Olden Time** . . . with a Pictorial Map of the City and its Suburbs as they existed in the reign of Henry VIII. . . . by William NEWTON. Folio, London, 1855

1859. Sion **College**: founded by Thomas White D.D. (This Account was compiled by Dr. RUSSELL, President in **1845**; and continued by William SCOTT, President in 1858.) 8vo., London, 1859.

1860, etc. London **and Middlesex Archæological Society.** Transactions, from the commencement in 1860. 8vo., London, 1860, etc.

1861. William **Munk**, M.D. The Roll of the Royal College of Physicians of London.

Vol. i. **1518—1700.**

Vol. ii. **.701—1800.**

8vo. London, 1861.

1861. **Liber Albus**: the White Book of the City of London, compiled in 1419 by John CARPENTER, Common Clerk, and Richard WHITTINGTON, Mayor. Translated by Henry Thomas RILEY, M.A. (Camden Soc.) 4to., London, 1861.

1861. Henry **Mayhew**. London Labour and the London Poor. (Four volumes.) 8vo., London, 1861.

[The fourth volume has Answers to Correspondents bound up with it.]

1862. The **Criminal Prisons** of London, and Scenes of Prison Life. By Henry MAYHEW and John BINNY. 8vo., London, 1862.

1863. 1677. The Little London **Directory** of 1677. The oldest printed **list** of the Merchants and Bankers of London. Reprinted, 8vo., London, **1863.**

1864. Ceremonials to be observed by the Lord Mayor, Aldermen, Sheriffs, and **Officers of the** City of London : together with certain of their **Rights and** Privileges necessary to be remembered. [Proof.] 8vo., London, 1864.

1865 to the present time. **London Diocese Book from** its commencement in **1865.** 8vo., London, 1865, etc.

1865. The last **Ten Years** of the Priory of S. Helen Bishopsgate **in the City** of London ; with a Topography of that House. By Thomas HUGO, M.A., etc. **8vo.,** London, 1865. Large **paper.**

1867. Old London. Papers **read at the** London **Congress of the** Archæological Institute, July, 1866. 8vo., London, **1867.**

1868. Henry Thomas **Riley.** Memorials of London and London Life in the Thirteenth, Fourteenth, **and** Fifteenth Centuries : **being a series of extracts,** local, social, **and** political, from the **early archives of the City of** London, A.D. 1276-1419. 8vo., London, 1868.

1869. Report **to the Common Council** from the Improvement Committee, with Report **from** William **Haywood,** Esq., C.E.

Engineer to the Commissioners of Sewers, in relation to the Traffic of the City. Presented 22 July, 1869. 4to., London. 1869.

1870. **Analytical Indexes** to Volumes II. and VIII. of the series of Records known as the Remembrancia, preserved among the archives of the City of London. 1580-1664. (W. H. and H. C. Overall.) 8vo., London, 1870.

1871. **Kelly's Post-Office Guide to London in 1871**, Visitor's Handbook to the Metropolis, and companion to the Directory. 8vo., London, 1871.

1873. **John E. Price.** Roman Antiquities illustrated by remains recently discovered on the site of the National Safe Deposit Company's Premises, Mansion House, London. 4to., London, 1873.

1874. **Alexander Wood.** Ecclesiastical Antiquities of London and its Suburbs. 8vo., London, 1874.

1874. **On Recent Discoveries in Newgate Street.** By John Edward PRICE. (From Transactions of London and Middlesex Archæological Society, vol. v.) 4to., London, 1874.

1875-77. **A Chronicle of England** during the Reigns of the Tudors, from 1485 to 1559, by Charles WRIOTHESLEY, Windsor Herald. (Two volumes.) Edited by William Douglas HAMILTON. (Camden Soc.) 4to., London, 1875-77.

1876. **The Annals of St. Helen's, Bishopsgate, London.** By the Rev. John Edmund Cox, D.D., Vicar. 8vo., London, 1876.

1876. Joseph F. B. **Firth.** Municipal Government: or London Government as it is, and London under a Municipal Council. 8vo., London, 1876.

1876. **The Marriage, Baptismal, and Burial Registers of the** Collegiate Church or Abbey of St. Peter, Westminster. Edited and annotated by Joseph Lemuel CHESTER. 8vo., London, 1876.
[Private edition.]

1877. **Return of the present Income of the Parochial Charities of the Cities of London and Westminster,** 13 February, 1877. (House of Commons.) 4to., London, 1877

1877. **Temple Bar.** By E. W. GODWIN, F.S.A., illustrated. (From the *British Architect and Northern Engineer*, Oct. 19 and 26, 1877.) 4to., Manchester and London, 1877.

1878. **W. H. and H. C. Overall.** Analytical Index to the Series of Records known as the Remembrancia preserved among the archives of the City of London, 1579-1664. 8vo., London, 1878.

1879. **Catalogue of Maps, Plans, and Views of London**

and **Westminster** collected and arranged by Frederick Crace. Edited by his son, John Gregory CRACE. 8vo., London, 1879.

1879. Also, **a** smaller **Catalogue**, compiled for use when the Collection **was** lent for Exhibition in the South Kensington Museum. 8vo., London, 1879.

1879. **A Lecture on Pre-Adamite London**, given in the Theatre of Merchant Taylors' School . . . 13 February, 1879. By Edwin NASH, F.R.I.A., Master of the Merchant Taylors' Company, 1878-79. 8vo., London, 1879.

1880. **Some Account of Sion College**, by W. H. MILMAN, M.A., Librarian. 8vo., London, 1880.

1880. **Three Fifteenth Century Chronicles**, with Historical Memoranda by John STOWE, the Antiquary, and contemporary notes **of** occurrences written by him in the reign of Queen Elizabeth, edited by James GAIRDNER. (Camden Soc.) 4to., London, 1880.

1880. London in 1880: illustrated with Bird's-eye views of the principal Streets. By Herbert FRY. 8vo., London, **1880**.

1881-82. **The Cripplegate.** [Newspaper.] **31. Dec.**, 1881, **to 30. Dec.**, 1882. Folio, London, 1881-82

1882-83. Charles J. **Robinson**. A Register of the **Scholars** admitted into **Merchant Taylor's School** from 1562 to **1874**. (Two volumes.) 8vo., London, 1882-83.

1884. William John Charles **Moens**. The Marriage, Baptismal, and Burial Registers, 1571 to 1874, and Monumental Inscriptions, of **the** Dutch Reformed Church, Austin Friars. With a short account of **the** Strangers **and their** Churches. 4to., Lymington, 1884.

1884. **Surrey Bells and London Bell-Founders.** A Contribution to the Comparative Study of Bell Inscriptions. By J. C. L. STAHLSCHMIDT. **8vo, London, 1884.**

1884. **London's Roll** of Fame : being Complimentary Votes **and Addresses from** the City of London, on Presentation of the Honorary Freedom of that City and on other Occasions, to Royal Personages, Statesmen, etc. . . . with their Replies and Acknowledgments. From 1757 to 1884. With a critical and historical Introduction [by Benjamin Scott, Chamberlain of London]. **4to., London,** 1884.

1884. **The Historical Charters and Constitutional Documents** of the City of London. With an Introduction and Notes by an Antiquary. [*i.e*, Walter de **Gray** Birch.] **4to., London, 1884.**

1884. **Robert** Barlow **Gardiner**. The Admission Registers of **S. Paul's** School from 1748 to 1876, edited with Biographical **Notices, and** Notes on the Earlier Masters and Scholars from the **time of its** foundation. 8vo., London, 1884.

1885. Reginald R. **Sharpe**, D.C.L. Calendar of Letters from the Mayor and Corporation of London *circa* A.D. 1350-1370, enrolled and preserved among the archives of the Corporation at the Guildhall. 8vo., London, 1885,

1885. Edwin de Lisle. The Majesty of London. 8vo., London, 1885.

1886. Essays on the Street Alignment, Reconstruction, and Sanitation of Central London, and on the Re-housing of the Poorer Classes, to which prizes offered by William **Westgarth** were awarded by the Society of Arts, 1885. 8vo., London, 1886.

1886 to present time. The London Diocesan Magazine. First number is dated May, 1886. Vols. I.—IV. 8vo., London, 1886, etc.

1886. A Descriptive Account of the Guildhall of the City of London : its History and Associations. By John Edward PRICE, F.S.A., F.R.S.L. 4to., London, 1886.

1887. London **City Churches Destroyed since 1800** or now Threatened. By W. NIVEN. Folio, London, 1887.

1887. London Marriage Licences, 1521-1869. From Excerpts by the late Colonel CHESTER, D.C.L. With Memoir and Portrait. Edited by Joseph FOSTER. 8vo., London, 1887.

1887. **A Discourse** on some **Unpublished Records** of the City of London. By Edwin FRESHFIELD, etc. 4to., London, 1887.

1889-91. **Labour and Life of the People** : edited by Charles BOOTH. (Two volumes, with Appendix and Maps.) 8vo., London, 1889-91. Contributors :

Jesse Argyle.	Octavia Hill.
Geo. E. Arkell.	James Macdonald.
Ernest Aves.	Beatrice Potter.
Graham Balfour.	David F. Schloss.
Charles Booth.	H. Llewellyn Smith.
Clara E Collet.	Mary C. Tabor.
Stephen N. Fox.	Margaret A. Tilland.
E. C. Grey.	E. A. Valpy.

1889. **Notable Churches** of the City of London. (*Church Bells'* Album, No. 4.) 4to., London, 1889.

1889. **Hampstead Hill** : its Structure, Materials, and Sculpturing. by J. Logan LOBLEY. The Flora, by H. T Wharton ; Insect Fauna, F. A. Walker ; the Birds, J E. Harting. 8vo., London, 1889.

1889. Catalogue of the Guildhall Library of the City of London. With additions to June, 1889. [Charles Welch, F.S.A., Librarian.] 8vo., London, 1889.

1889-90. Calendar of **Wills** proved and enrolled in the Court of Husting, London, A.D. 1258-1688. Edited by Reginald R. SHARPE, D C.L., Record Clerk. (Two **volumes.**) 8vo., London, 1889-90.

1890. The Post-Office **London Directory** for 1890. 4to., London, 1890.

1890 (?). Charles W. **Bardsley**. Romance of the London Directory. **8vo.,** London [1890 ?].

1890. Herbert **Fry**. London in **1890,** illustrated with Bird's-eye Views of the Principal Streets, **also** its Chief Suburbs and Environs. 8vo., London, 1890.

1890. George **Clinch**. Marylebone and S. Pancras : their History, Celebrities, Buildings, and Institutions. 8vo., London, 1890.

[1890]. William **Booth** [called 'General' Booth]. In Darkest England, and the Way **Out.** 8vo., London [1890].

1890? In **Darkest London.** A new and popular edition of *Captain Lobe.* A Story of the Salvation Army. By John LAW, with an Introduction by 'General' Booth. 8vo., London.

1890?. My Salvation **Army** Experience. By Rev. Wyndham S. HEATHCOTE, B.A. (four years an Officer in the Salvation Army). 8vo., London, *c.* 1890.

1891. Life **in Darkest London** : a Hint to 'General' Booth. By the Rev. A. Osborne JAY, M.A. 8vo., London, 1891.

1891. **'General' Booth's** 'Submerged Tenth '; or, The Wrong Way to do the Right Thing. By the Rev. Philip DWYER, A.M. 8vo., London, 1891.

1891. **General** Booth and **his Critics.** By H. GREENWOOD, M.A., LL.D. 8vo., London, 1891.

1891. **Social** Diseases and Worse **Remedies** : Letters to the *Times* on Mr. Booth's Scheme. By T. H. HUXLEY, F.R.S. 8vo., London, 1891.

1891. **London City.** Its History, Streets, Traffic, Buildings, People. By W. J. LOFTIE, B.A. Illustrated by W. Luker. Engraved by Ch. Guillaume et Cie., Paris. 4to., London, 1891.

18.. **Topographical Memoranda** of the Ward of Farringdon Without. By an Antiquary [Mr. Underhill.] 4to., **no** place **or date.**

    [Only fifty copies **printed.** Unpublished.]

1892. A Biographical History of **Guy's Hospital**. By Samuel WILKS, M.D., and G. T BETTANY, M.A. Large **paper.** London, 1892.

PARISHES IN AND NEAR THE CITY.

List of the City Parishes, tracts relating to which will be found in the following pages.

All Hallows, Barking.
S. Andrew, Holborn.
S. Bartholomew, Exchange.
S. Bartholomew the Great.
Blackfriars.
S. Botolph, Bishopsgate.
Christ Church, Newgate Street.
S. Christopher-le-Stocks.
S. Clement, Eastcheap.
S. Dionis Backchurch.
S. Faith.
S. Giles, Cripplegate.
S. Gregory-by-S. Paul's.
S. John Evangelist, Westminster.
Guildhall Chapel.
S. Katherine's Hospital.
S. Laurence Pountney.
S. Leonard, Shoreditch.

S. Margaret, Lothbury.
S. Margaret, Westminster.
S. Martin-in-the-Fields.
S. Mary, Islington.
S. Mary Woolnoth.
S. Mary Aldermary.
S. Mary-le-Bow.
S. Mary Overy.
S. Mary Woolchurch Haw.
S. Matthew, Friday Street.
Mercers' Chapel.
S. Mildred, Bread Street.
S. Mildred, Poultry.
S. Peter, Cornhill.
S. Sepulchre.
S. Stephen, Coleman Street.
S. Swithin.
S. Thomas Apostle.

ALL HALLOWS, BARKING.

1681. **The Birth and Burning of the Image** called S. Michael, containing the substance of a narrative lately given into the Vestry of All Saints, Barkin, London, etc., etc., etc. Small folio, London, 1681.

1864. Collections in illustration of the Parochial History and Antiquities of the Ancient Parish of All Hallows, Barking. By Joseph MASKELL. 4to., London, 1864.

S. ANDREW, HOLBORN.

1704. A Sermon preach'd in the Parish-Church of St. Andrew's, Holborn, June 8, 1704 being Thursday in Whitson-Week, at the first Meeting of the Gentlemen concern'd in Promoting the Charity-Schools in and about the Cities of London and Westminster. At which time and place, the several Masters and Mistresses of the said Schools appear'd, with the Poor Children under their Care: in Number about Two Thousand. By Richard WILLIS, D.D., Dean of Lincoln. 4to., London, 1704.

S. BARTHOLOMEW, EXCHANGE.

1890. **The Vestry** Minute Books of the Parish of St. Bartholomew, Exchange, in the City of London. 1567-1676. By Edwin FRESHFIELD. 4to., London, 1890.
[Privately printed.]

S. Bartholomew the Great.

1888. Norman **Moore**, M.D. The Church of S. Bartholomew the Great. West Smithfield: its foundation, present **condition, and Funeral Monuments.** 8vo., London, 1888.

Blackfriars.

1625. **The Trivmph of the Chvrch over Water and Fire.** Or, a Thankfull Gratulation for that Miraculous Deliverance of the Church and State of Great Britaine, from the Romish Tophet : or, that barbarous and savage Powder-plot. As it was delivered (for substance) in a **Sermon** at Blacke Fryers in London on the fifth of November, **1625.** By Theodor Hering, Minister of the Word of God.   4to., London, 1625.

  *** See also the Pamphlets catalogued, *supra*, p. 133 and p. 135.

S. Botolph, Bishopsgate.

188-. **The Parochial Registers** of S. Botolph, Bishopsgate. A. W. C. Hallen.   8vo., London, 188-.

Christ Church, Newgate Street.

1641. **An Order from the High Court of Parliament** which was read on Sunday last in every church, being the 19 Day of December, **1641.** Subscribed by Alderman Soames, and Captain **Ven**, Burgesses in the honourable City of London. Also The **True** Coppie of a **Seditious** Paper, delivered in the Pulpit to the minister of Christ **Church** upon Sunday, being the 19. of December, and afterwards presented to the Lord Mayor by Mr. Mamsbridge, Reader of Christ Church, **and** Petti-Canon of Saint Paul's, London.   4to., **London, 1641.**

1646. **Gods Doings and Mans Duty,** Opened in a Sermon preached before both Houses of Parliament, the Lord Major and Aldermen of **the** City of London, and the Assembly of Divines, [at Christ Church] **at the** last Thanksgiving Day, April 2, for the Recovering of the West, and disbanding 5000 of the King's Horse, &c., 1645. By Hugh Peters, Preacher of the Gospel. The second edition, corrected **by the** Author. 4to., London, 1646.

S. Christopher-le-Stocks.

1886. **Minutes of the Vestry Meetings** and other **Records of** the Parish of St. Christopher-le-Stocks, in the City **of London.** Edited by Edwin Freshfield, etc.   4to., London, **1886.**
  [Privately printed.]

1885. **Accomptes of the Churchwardens** of the Paryshe of St. Christofer's in London.   1575 to 1662.   Edited by Edwin Freshfield, Doctor of Laws, Vice-President of the Society of

Antiquaries of London, and one of the Churchwardens of the Parish. 4to., London, 1885.
[Privately printed.]

1882. **The Register Book** of the Parish of St. Christopher-le-Stocks, in the City of London. Edited by Edwin FRESHFIELD, etc. Three volumes. 4to., London, 1882.

S. CLEMENT, EASTCHEAP.

1878. **Three Worthies of London.** Pearson, Fuller, Walton. Sermon at the Unveiling of a Window at S. Clement, Eastcheap. By Jas. Augustus HESSEY, Archdeacon of Middlesex. 8vo., London, 1878.

S. DIONIS BACKCHURCH.

1878. **Correspondence and Proceedings** under the Union of Benefices Act, resulting in the . . . removal of the Parish Church of S. Dionis Backchurch. By W. H. LYALL, Rector. 8vo., London, 1878.

S. FAITH.

1649. ΚΑΤΑΔΥΝΑΣΤΗΣ : Might overcoming Right, or a cleer answer to M. John Goodwin's Might and Right well met. . . . By John GEREE, M.A., and Pastour of Faith's under Pauls in London. 4to., London, 1649.

S. GILES, CRIPPLEGATE.

1727. **Act, 6 Geo. II.,** for providing a maintenance for the Rector of the new Church near Old Street in the Parish of Saint Giles, Cripplegate, etc. 4to., London, 1733.

1826. **Act, 7 Geo. IV., cap. 54,** for extinguishing Tithes and customary payments in lieu of Tithes and Easter Offerings within the parish of S. Giles, Cripplegate.

1883. William Denton. Records of S. Giles', Cripplegate. 8vo., London, 1883.

1888. **An Account of the Church and Parish of St. Giles** without **Cripplegate,** in the City of London. By John James BADDELEY, Churchwarden. 8vo., London, 1888.

    ** See also *supra*, p. 142.

S. GREGORY BY S. PAUL'S.

After 1658. **Nine select Sermons** preached upon special occasions in the Parish Church of St. Gregories by St. Pauls. By the late Reverend John HEWYTT, D.D. 8vo., London, N.D.
[Dr. Hewytt was beheaded on Tower Hill June 8, 1658.]

GUILDHALL CHAPEL.

1679. **A Sermon** preached to those who had been Scholars of S. Paul's School, in Guild-hall Chapel, London, at their Anni-

versary Meeting on St. Pauls Day, 167⅞. **By** W. WYATT, M.A.
and Student of Christs-Church in Oxford. 4to., London, **1679.**

S. JOHN EVANGELIST, WESTMINSTER.

1892. S. John the Evangelist, Westminster: **Parochial Memorials.** By J. E. SMITH, Vestry Clerk of S. Margaret **and** S.
John the Evangelist, Westminster. **8vo.,** Westminster, **1892.**

S. KATHERINE'S HOSPITAL.

1711. A **Letter** to the Eldest Brother of the Collegiate Church of
St. Katherine, in Answer to his Scurrilous Pamphlet entitul'd
the Modern Fanatick, etc. 8vo., London, 1711.

S. LAURENCE POUNTNEY.

1831. H. B. **Wilson,** D.D., Rector. A History of **the** Parish of
S. Laurence Pountney, London : including . . . an account
of Corpus Christi (or Pountney) College in the said Parish.
4to., London, **1831.**

S. LEONARD, SHOREDITCH.

1637. A Thanksgiving for the Decreasing . . . of the Plague. By
John **Squier,** Priest, Vicar of S. Leonard's, Shordich, &c. The
second edition, revised. **4to.,** London, 1637.

S. MARGARET, LOTHBURY.

1876. On the Parish Books of **S.** Margaret, Lothbury,
S. Christopher le Stocks, and S. Bartholomew by the Exchange
in the City of London. Communicated to the Society of Antiquaries by Edwin FRESHFIELD, Esq., M.A., F.S.A. 4to.,
London, 1876.

1887. The **Vestry Minute Book** of the Parish of St. Margaret,
Lothbury, in the City of London, 1571-1677. Edited by Edwin
FRESHFIELD, etc. 4to., London, 1887.
[Privately Printed.]

S. MARGARET, WESTMINSTER.

1648. **England's Spirituall Languishing,** with the causes and
cure. By Thomas MANTON, Minister of Stoke Newington.
[**Sermon** before Ho. of Commons, Fast, S. Margaret's, West-
minster, 28 June, **1648.**] 4to., London, 1648.

S. MARTIN-IN-THE-FIELDS.

1684. A **Sermon** preached at the Anniversary Meeting **of the**
Natives of S. Martins in the Fields, at their own Parochial
Church, on May 29, 1684. By Richard BURD, A.M., Chaplain
to the Right Honourable the Lord President, and Lecturer of
St. Mary, Aldermanbury. 4to., London, 1684.
    (Opposite the title **a** plate of S. Martin dividing his cloak
with a beggar. The Royal Arms above.)

S. Martin-le-Grand.

1767. **A full and plain account** of the Christian Practices observed by the Church in S. Martins-le-grand, London, and other Churches in Fellowship with them. Second edition. 8vo., London, 1767.

    * See also *supra*, p. 138.

S. Mary Aldermary.

1835. **Letter to the Parishioners** of the United Parishes of St. Mary Aldermary, and St. Thomas the Apostle in the City of London, on the Non-payment of their Tithes. By the Rev. H. B. Wilson, D.D., Rector. 4to., London, 10 Nov., 1835.

S. Mary, Islington.

1811. **The History, Topography, and Antiquities** of the Parish of St. Mary, Islington, in the County of Middlesex. By John Nelson. 4to., London, 1811.

S. Mary-le-Bow.

1681. **A Sermon** preached before the Right Honourable the Lord-Mayor and Aldermen of the City of London, at Bow-Church, September 2, 1680. Being the Anniversary Fast for the Burning of London. By Gilbert Burnet. The second edition. 4to., London, 1681.

1828. **Observations on the Church of St. Mary le Bow,** chiefly relating to its original Structure. By George Gwilt, Esq., F.S.A., in a Letter to Henry Ellis, Esq., F.R.S., Secretary [of the Society of Antiquaries]. 4to., London, 10 June, 1828.

S. Mary Woolnoth.

1660. **Divine Arithmetick,** or the Right Art of numbering our Dayes. Being a Sermon preached June 17, 1659, at the Funeral of Mr. Samuel Jacomb, B.D., Minister of the Gospel at S. Mary Woolnoth in Lombard Street, London, and lately Fellow of Queens Colledge in Cambridge. By Symon Patrick, B.D., Minister of the Gospel at Batersea in Surrey. 4to., London, 1660.

1886. **The Transcript of the Registers** of the United Parishes of S. Mary Woolnoth and S. Mary Woolchurch Haw, in the City of London, 1538-1760. To which is prefixed a short account of both Parishes, etc. By J. M. S. Brooke, M.A., Rector, and A. W. C. Hallen, M.A. 8vo., London, 1886.

S. Mary Overy.

1833. **Annals of St. Mary Overy;** an Historical and Descriptive Account of St. Saviour's Church and Parish. By W. Taylor. 4to., London, 1833.

S. MATTHEW, FRIDAY STREET.

1627. Henry **Burton**. The Baiting of the Pope's Bull, or an unmasking of the Mystery of Iniquity folded up in a most pernitious Breeue or Bull sent from the Pope lately into England, to cause a rent therein for his Re-entry. With an advertisement to the Kings seduced subiects. 4to., London, 1627.

1628. Henry Burton. Israels Fast, or a Meditation vpon the Seuenth Chapter of Joshuah ; a faire Precedent for these Times. By H[enry] B[urton], Rector of S. Mathewes, Fryday-street. 4to., London, 1628.

1636. For God and the King. The summe of two Sermons preached on the Fifth of November last in St Matthewes, Friday Streete, **1636.** By Henry BVRTON, Minister of GODS Word there and then. **4to.**, no place, 1636.

1636. **An Apology of an Appeale.** Also an Epistle to the true-hearted Nobility. By Henry BURTON, Pastor of St. Matthevves, Friday-Street. **4to.**, **no place**, 1636.

1637. A Briefe **and moderate** answer to **the** Seditious **and** Scandalous Challenges **of** Henry **Burton, late** of Friday Street, **in the** two Sermons, by **him** preached on the Fifth of November, **1636.** And **in** the Apologie prefixt before them. By Peter **HEYLYN.** 4to., London, 1637.

1637. The answer of John **Bastwick,** Doctor of Phisicke, to the exceptions made against his Letany **by** a learned Gentleman, which is annexed to the Letany it selfe, as Articles super-additionall against **the** Prelats. 4to., **no place**, 1637.

1637. A Speech delivered in the Starr Chamber on Wednesday, the xivth of June, 1637, at the Censvre of John **Bastwick,** Henry **Burton,** and William **Prinn,** concerning pretended Innovations in the Church. By the most Reverend Father in God, William [LAUD], **L.** Archbishop of Canterbury his Grace. 4to., **London,** 1637.

1638. A breife relation of certaine speciall and **most** materiall passages, and speeches in the Starre-Chamber, occasioned and delivered Iune the 14th 1637, at the Censure of those three Worthy Gentlemen, Dr. **Bastvvicke,** Mr. **Burton, and** Mr. **Prynne. 4to., no place,** 1638.

1641. **England's Bondage and Hope of Deliverance.** A Sermon before the Honourable House of Parliament at **St.** Margarets in Westminster by Mr. Henry BURTON, late Rector **of St.** Mathewes Friday-street, **in** London, Iune 20, 1641. **4to., London, 1641.**

1641. **Jesv-worship confvted : or,** Certaine Arguments against Bowing at the Name Jesvs. With objections to the contrary, Fully Answered. By that worthy Divine Henry BURTON, Minister of Gods Word. 4to., London, 1641.
[With Portrait, "ætatis suæ 63" on title.]

1643. A Narration of the Life of Mr. Henry **Burton** . . . according to a Copy written with his owne hand. 4to., London, 1643.

1644. Henry **Burton.** A vindication of Churches commonly called Independent.
The first edition, 4to., London, 1644.
The second edition, 4to., London, 1644.

1645. **Vindiciæ Veritatis.** Truth vindicated against calumny: in a Briefe Answer to Dr. Bastwick's two late books, entituled, Independency not God's Ordinance, etc. By Henry BURTON, one of his quondam-fellow-sufferers. 4to., London, 1645.

1645. **Truth shut out of doores** : or, A briefe and true Narrative of the occasion and manner of proceeding of some of Aldermanbury Parish, in shutting their Church-doores against me . . . By me, Henry BURTON. 4to., London, 1645.

1645. **Truth still Truth, though shut out of doores** : or, a Reply to a late Pamphlet, entituled, The Doore of Truth Opened : published in the name and with the consent of the Whole Church of Aldermanbury. By Henry BURTON. 4to., London, 1645.

1645. **Innocency cleared, True worth Predicated, against false Aspertions** : in a Letter sent to Mr. Henry **Burton** from a Christian Friend; In Defence of Dr. **Bastwick**, one of his Quondam Fellow-sufferers. Signed B. S. 4to., London, 1645.

1645. **Flagellum Flagelli,** or Dr. Bastwick's quarters beaten up in two or three pomeridian exercises, by way of animadversion upon his first Booke, intituled, Independency not God's Ordinance. By G. S. [SALTMARSH]. 4to., London, 1645.

1869. **Notes on the History and Antiquities** of the United Parishes of S. Matthew, Friday Street, and S. Peter, Cheap, in the City of London. By W. Sparrow SIMPSON, Rector. 8vo., London.
(Only 100 copies struck off on large paper.)

MERCERS' CHAPEL.

1658. **A Sermon** touching the Use of Humane Learning. Preached in Mercers-Chappel, at the Funeral of that Learned Gentleman Mr. John **Langley,** late School-Master of Pauls School in London, on the 21 day of September, 1657. By Ed. REYNOLDS, D.D. 4to., London, 1658.

1708. Philip's Memento Mori : or, The Passing Bell. A Sermon preach'd in Mercers Chappel at the Funeral of Mr. **Bennet** merchant. By Daniel FEATLEY, D.D. 8vo., London, 1708.

S. MILDRED, BREAD STREET.

1881. Drawing of the Interior, by R. **Payne,** architect.

S. Mildred, Poultry.

1872. **The History of the** Church of St. Mildred the Virgin, Poultry, in the City of London: with some particulars of the Church of St. Mary, Colechurch. By Thomas MILBOURN. **8vo.,** London, 1872.

S. Peter, Cornhill.

1684. **A Sermon** concerning the Excellency and Usefulness of the Common Prayer. Preached by William BEVERIDGE, D.D., Rector of St Peters, Cornhill, London: at the Opening of the said Parish Church, 27th of November, **1681.** The seventh edition. **4to.,** London, **1684.**

1870?. **The Church of S. Peter upon Cornhill**: its History. Rev. R. WHITTINGTON, Rector. 8vo., London, N.D.

1877-9. **A Register** of the Christninges, Burialles and Weddinges within the Parish of Saint Peeters vpon Cornhill, beginning at the raigne of our most Soueraigne ladie Queen Elizabeth. Edited by Granville W. G. LEVESON-GOWER, F.S.A. **8vo.,** London, 1877-9.
(Two **volumes.**)

S. Sepulchre.

1708. **Sermon** at S. Sepulchre's at **the meeting of** the Charity Schools, **27** May, 1708. By Robert **Moss, D.D.,** Chaplain in Ordinary to Her Majesty, and Preacher **to the** Honourable Society of Grays-Inn. 8vo., London, **1708.**

S. Stephen, Coleman Street.

1887. Some Remarks upon the Book of Records and History of the Parish of St. Stephen, Coleman Street, in the City of London. Communicated to the Society of Antiquaries by Edwin FRESH-FIELD, LL.D., V.P. **4to.,** Westminster, 1887.

S. Swithin.

1629. **A White Sheete,** or a Warning for Whoremongers, **a Sermon** preached in the Parish Church of St. Swithins by **London** Stone, the 19 of July, Anno Domi: **1629, the** day appointed by Honourable Authoritie for penance **to be done** by an inhabitant there for fornication, continued more **than** two yeares, with **his** Maide-Servant. By Richard **COOKE, B.** of D. and Parson there. **4to.,** London, 1629.

1684. A Discourse on my **Lord** Arch-Bishop of Canterbury's **and** my Lord Bishop of London's Letters to the Clergy, touching Catechising and the Sacrament of the Supper; with what is required of Churchwardens and Ministers in reference to Obstinate Recusants. Also **a** Defence of Excommunication . . . By William BASSET, Rector **of** St. Swithin . . London. 4to., London, 1684.

S. Thomas Apostle.

1829. **A Second Letter** to the Parishioners of St. Thomas the Apostle in the City of **London**. To which is prefixed the Report of **His** M. Commissioners for Inquiry concerning Charities, so far as relates to Charitable Devises, etc., in the Parish of St. Thomas the Apostle. By the Rev. H. B. **Wilson**, D.D., Rector. 4to., London, 1829.

LIVERY COMPANIES OF THE CITY OF LONDON.

The Companies generally.
The Twelve Great **Companies**.
Barber Surgeons.
Carpenters.
Grocers.
Ironmongers.

Leather Sellers.
Mercers.
Merchant Taylors.
Saddlers.
Skinners.
Stationers.

The Companies Generally.

1836-7. **The History** of the Twelve Great Livery Companies of London . . by William **Herbert**, Librarian to the Corporation of London. (Two volumes.) 8vo., London, 1836-37.

1884. **City of London** Livery Companies' **Commission**. Reports and Appendices. (Five volumes.) 4to., London, 1884.

Barber Surgeons.

1890. **The Annals** of the Barber Surgeons of **London**, compiled from their records and other sources by Sidney **Young**, one of the Court of Assistants of the Worshipful Company of Barber Surgeons of London, with illustrations by Austin **Young**. 4to., London, 1890.

Carpenters.

1848. Edward **Basil Jupp**. An Historical **Account** of the Worshipful Company of Carpenters in the City of London. 8vo., London, 1848.

Grocers.

1869. Baron **Heath**. Some account of the Worshipful Company of Grocers in the City of London. Third edition. 8vo., London, 1869.

1883. **Grocers' Company**. Copies in Facsimile of Manuscript Records, A.D. 1345 to 1428. Transcribed and Translated.
   [Presented by the Worshipful **Company** of Grocers, 27 **Dec.**, 1883.]

Ironmongers.

1851. John **Nicholl**. Some Account of the Worshipful Company of Ironmongers. 8vo., **London**, 1851.

1869. **A Catalogue** of the Antiquities and Works of Art exhibited at Ironmongers' Hall, London, in the month of May, 1861. Compiled by a Committee of the Council of the London and Middlesex Archæological Society. 4to., London, 1869. (Two volumes.)

LEATHER-SELLERS.

1871. **History and Antiquities** of the Worshipful Company of Leather-sellers of the City of London ; with Fac-similes of Charters, and other Illustrations. By William Henry BLACK, F.S.A. 4to., London, 1871.

MERCERS.

1884. **The Admission Register** of **St.** Paul's School from 1748 to 1876. By the Rev. Robert Barlow GARDINER, M.A., Fourth Master. 8vo., London, **1884.**

MERCHANT TAYLORS.

1826. **Librorum Impressorum** qui in Bibliotheca **Scholæ Mer**catorum Scissorum adservantur Catalogus. 8vo., London, **1826.**

1875. **Memorials of the Guild of Merchant Taylors** of **the** Fraternity of St. John the Baptist in the City **of** London ; **and** of its Associated Charities and Institutions. Compiled **and** selected by the Master of **the** Company for the Year 1873-74 [Charles Matthew CLODE], (being the 574th Master in Succession). 8vo., **London,** 1875. [Printed **for private circulation.** Presented by the Company.]

1888. Charles Mathew Clode. The Early History of the Guild **of Merchant Taylors . . . with Notices** of the Lives of some **of its eminent members.** Two volumes. 8vo., London, 1888. [Printed for private circulation. Presented by the Company.]

1882-83. **A Register of the** Scholars admitted into Merchant Taylors' School from A.D. 1562 to 1874. By the Rev. Charles J. ROBINSON, M.A., Rector of West Hackney. 8vo., London, 1882-83.

SADDLERS.

1889. **John W. Sherwell. A** descriptive and Historical Account **of the Guild of Saddlers of** the City of London. **8vo.,** London, **1889.** **[For private** circulation. **Presented by the Company.]**

SKINNERS.

1876. James Foster **Wadmore.** Some Account of the **History** and Antiquity of the Worshipful Company of Skinners, **London.** 8vo., London, 1876.

STATIONERS.

1875. **A Transcript of the Registers of** the Company of Stationers of London, 1554-1640 A.D. Edited by Edward ARBER, F.S.A. Vols. i.-iv. (all **at** present issued). 4to., London, 1875. [Privately printed.]

1890. Edward **Arber.** A **List** founded on the **Registers of the** Stationers' Company of 837 London Publishers (who were by Trade Printers, Engravers, Booksellers, **Book Binders, etc.)** between 1553 and 1640. 4to., London, **1890.**

S. PAUL'S SCHOOL.

1718. **Preces, Catechismus, et Hymni,** in **usum** antiquæ et Celebris Scholæ juxta D. Pauli Templum **apud** Londinates. 8vo., London, 1718.

1777. The **London Vocabulary,** English and Latin . . . adorned with Twenty-Six Pictures. For the Use of Schools. The seventeenth edition, corrected. By James GREENWOOD, Author **of the** English Grammar, and late Sur-Master of St. Paul's School. 12mo., London, **1777.**
   [Imperfect.]

1818. **Erasmus.** Concio de Puero Jesu olim pronunciata a **puero in Schola** Joannis **Coleti** Londini instituta in qua praesidebat Imago Pueri Jesu docentis specie. [Edited by Samuel BENTLEY.] 8vo., London, 1818.

1836. **A Catalogue of the Library** of St. Paul's School. 8vo., London, 1836.
   [Not published.]

A Miscellaneous Collection of Apposition Papers. Various dates.
   See also *supra*, p. **154.** The Admission Registers of the School, edited by the Rev. R. B. Gardiner.

See also **Sermons** preached at S. Paul's Cathedral **before the** Gentlemen educated at S. Paul's School. See

1678-79.	Wyatt, p. **147.**	**1728.**	Hough, p. **112.**
1699.	Pulleyn, p. **107.**	**1755.**	Fearon, p. **113.**
1711.	Tenison, p. **110.**	**1757.**	Fairchild, p. **113.**
1718.	Knight, p. **112.**		

   Sermon on death of **Mr.** Langley, see *Mercer's Chapel*, p. **151.**

CHEAPSIDE CROSS.

1641. **The Resolvtion of those Contemners** that will have no Crosses, being ingeniously expressed in exhortation to those, that will admit of no Crosse, unlesse it be their crosse-Wayes ; or some Crosse Street where their conventicles are . . . . 4to., London, **1641.**

1641. **Cheap-side Crosse censured and condemned** by a Letter sent from the Vicechancellour **and** other Learned Men of the famous Vniversitie of Oxford, in answer to a question propounded by the Citizens of London, concerning the said Crosse, at the yeere **1600, in which** yeere it was beautified. 4to., London, 1641.

1641. The Pope's Proclamation, together With the Lawes and Ordinances established by him and his Shavelings, concerning his adherents and rights which hee claimeth in England, whereunto is added Six Articles exhibited against Cheapside Crosse, whereby it stands guilty of high Treason, and ought to be beheaded. 4to., 1641.

1641. The Doleful Lamentation of **Cheapside Crosse :** or old England sick of the Staggers. 4to., London, 1641.

1642. The Resolution of the **Roundheads** to pull down Cheapside Crosse. 4to., 1642.
   [Bound up with 'The Pope's Proclamation.']

1642. **Articles of High Treason** Exhibited against Cheap-side Crosse, with The Last Will and Testament of the said Crosse, and certaine Epitaphs upon her Tombe by R. OVERTON. Newly Printed, and newly come forth with his Holinesse Priviledge to prevent False Copies. 4to., London, **1642.**

1643. The **Downe-fall of** Dagon, or the taking downe of Cheap-side **Crosse this** second of May, **1643. . . .** 4to., London. **No date.**
   [Woodcut on title representing the taking down of the cross.]

THE FIRE OF 1666, AND PLAGUE OF 1604, 1636, AND 1665.

1518. Transcript by R. Clark. On Visiting a House supposed to have been infested with the Plague. Hagenoæ in ædibus Thomæ Anshelmi Badensis. Anno M.D.XVIII. Mense Februario. With some verses by Chatterton, adapted by Richard Clark to Music by Henricus Loritus (died 1563).

1604. James **Godskall.** The Arke of Noah, for the Londoners that remaine in the Cittie to enter in, with their families, to be preserued from the deluge of the Plague. Item, An Exercise for the Londoners that are departed out of the Citie into the Countrey, to spend their time till they return. Whereunto is annexed an Epistle sent out of the Countrey, to the afflicted Citie of London. Made and written by Iames Godskall the yonger, Preacher of the Word. 4to., London, **1604.** Thos. Creede.

1630. **London looke backe,** at that yeare of yeares 1625, and looke forward, vpon this yeare, 1630. Written, not to Terrifie, But to Comfort. 4to., London, 1630.
   [On the title a woodcut of a skull, **wreathed.]**

1637. **A Thanksgiving for the** decreasing, and hope of the

---

* In the British Museum is the following : 1630. London. Lookebacke. A description of the . . . mortality An. 1625 in heroicke . . . lines. By A. H., of Tr. College, in Cambridge. [With an 'Epistle to the Christian Reader,' by H. D.] Printed for T. Harper and H. Holland, London. 1630. 4to.

removing of the Plagve. Being a Sermon preached at St. Pauls
in London, vpon the i. of Ianuary, 1636. By Iohn SQVIER,
Priest, Vicar of St. Leonards Shordich, sometime Fellow of
Iesus Colledge in Cambridge. 4to., London, 1637.

1665. Pillulæ Pestilentiales : Or a Spiritual Receipt for Cure
of The Plague, delivered in a Sermon preach'd in St. Paul's
Church, London, in the midst of our late Sore Visitation. By
Rich. KINGSTON M.A. and Preacher at St. James Clerken-well.
8vo., London, 1665.

1665. Certain necessary directions as well for the Cure of
the Plague, as for preventing the Infection : with many easie
Medicines of small Charge, very profitable to His Majesties Subjects. Set down by the Colledge of Physicians. 4to., London,
1665.

c. 1665. The Orders and Directions of the Right Honourable
the Lord Mayor, and Court of Aldermen, to be diligently
observed and kept by the Citizens of London, during the time
of the present Visitation of the Plague . . . 4to., London,
c. 1665.

1666. Lex Ignea : or, The School of Righteousness. A Sermon
preach'd before the King, Octob. 10, 1666, at the Solemn Fast
for the late Fire in London. By William SHERLOCK, D.D.,
Dean of St. Pauls. 4to., London, 1666.
[On the title, Hollar's view of the burning of S. Paul's.]

1666. A Sermon [on Amos iv. 11] preached before the Honourable House of Commons, at St. Margarets, Westminster, Octob.
10, 1666, being the Fast-day appointed for the late dreadfull
Fire in the City of London. By Edward STILLINGFLEET, B.D.
Rector of St. Andrews, Holborn, and one of His Majesties
Chaplains in Ordinary. The fourth edition. 4to., London,
1666.

1666. London's Calamity by Fire bewailed and Improved, in a
Sermon preached at St. James Dukes-Place. . . By Robert
ELBOROUGH, Minister of the Parish that was lately St. Laurence
Pountney, London. 4to., London, 1666.

1667. Seasonable Thoughts in Sad Times, being some
Reflections on the Warre, the Pestilence, and the Burning of
London. Considered in the Calamity, Cause, Cure. By Joh.
TABOR, M.A. (In verse.) 8vo., London, 1667.

1667. A True and Faithful Account of the Several Informa-
tions exhibited to the Honourable Committee appointed by the
Parliament to inquire into the Late Dreadful Burning of the
City of London. Together with other Information touching the
Insolency of Popish Priests, and the Increase of Popery, etc.
4to., London, 1667.
Another edition, 4to., no place, 1667.

1667. A Short and Serious Narrative of London's Fatal

Fire, with its Diurnal and Nocturnal **Progression, from Sunday**
Morning (being) the Second of September, **Anno Mirabili 1666.**
Until Wednesday Night following. **A Poem, as also** Londons
Lamentation **to** her Regardless Passengers. **4to.,** London,
1667.

1667.   Poemata Londinensia. [Simon **Ford,** D.D.] Conflagratio
Londinensis Pœtice Depicta. The Conflagration of London :
Poetically described, both in Latin and English. 1667.
Londini quod reliquum. Or, Londons Remains : in Latin and
English. 1667.   Actio in Londini Incendiarios.   Londini
renascentis imago poetica.   Ad Serenissimum Britanniarum
Monarcham Carolum. II.   **1668.**   4to., London, 1667, 1668.

1668.   **Description exacte** de tout ce qui s'est passé dans les
Guerres entre le Roy d'*Angleterre*, le Roy de *France*, les *Estats*
des Provinces Unies de Pay Bas, et l'Evesque de *Munster*.
Commençant de l'An **1664,** & finissant **avec** la conclusion de
Paix, **faite** à Bredà **en** l'An 1667.   **Avec** une Introduction pre-
liminaire, contenant **l'Exile** & la Restitution **du present** Roy
d'Angleterre, etc.   **4to.,** Amsterdam, 1668.

(At p. 169 is a **plate of** the Great Fire **of 1666.**)

1670.   **Trap ad Crucem ;** or the Papist's Watch-word. **Being an**
Impartial Account **of** some late Informations **taken before**
several of his Majesties Justices of the Peace in and about the
City of London.   Also a Relation of the several Fires that of
late have hapened in and about the said City.   4to., London,
1670.

1720-21   **An Account of the Burning of the City of**
London as it was publish'd by the special Authority of King
and Council in the year 1666 . . .   Also the whole Service
appointed for the Day, which for many Years has been left out
of the Book of Common-Prayer.   From all which it plainly
appears, that the Papists had no hand in that dreadful conflagration.   Very useful for all those **who** keep the Annual Solemn
Fast on that Occasion.   8vo., **London,** 1720.

The third edition, 8vo., London, **1721.**

1721.   **A Collection** of very valuable and Scarce Pieces relating to
the last **Plague in the year 1665.**   The second edition.   8vo.,
London, **1721.**

1769.   **The City Remembrancer :** being Historical Narratives
of the Great Plague at London, 1665 ; Great Fire, 1666 ; and
Great Storm, 1703 . .   Collected from curious and authentic
Papers, originally compiled by the late learned Dr. **HARVEY,**
his Majesty's Physician to the Tower, and enlarged with **Autho-**
rities of a more recent Date.   (Two volumes.)   8vo., London,
1769.

MAPS, PLANS, AND VIEWS OF LONDON, AND
ESPECIALLY OF S. PAUL'S CATHEDRAL.

CONTENTS.

Londinium Augusta. A Plan of Roman London. STUKELEY, delin., 1722. From the *Itinerarium Curiosum.* (6¾-11 inches.)

Roman London. With tables of remains found in London. A woodcut. (10-7 inches.)

Londinum Feracissimi Angliæ Regni Metropolis. Plan of London, before the destruction of the steeple of S. Paul's, from the *Civitates Orbis Terrarum*, by BRAUN and HOGENBERGIUS. The title on a centre tablet at top. The arms of Queen Elizabeth on left, those of the City on right. Four figures at bottom, and tablets of description on right and left. (19½-13½ inches.)

Civitas Londinum, circiter MDLX. 'This plan shows the ancient extent of the famous Cities of London and Westminster as it was near the beginning of the reign of Queen Elizabeth ; these plates, for their great scarcity, are re-engraved to oblidge the Curious, and to hand to Posterity this old Prospect.' The above is a copy (engraved by G. VERTUE) of the Ancient Map of Ralph AGGAS, engraved about 1560, but not published till 1603. (75-28 inches.)

Civitas Londinum. A Fac-simile (Reduced) of the Map by AGGAS, 1560, by Edward Weller, F.R.G.S. (49-18½ inches.)

A View of London about the Year 1558. Reduced from the Aggas Map. From Maitland's London. (18½-12 inches.)

London and Westminster in the Reign of Queen Elizabeth. Anno Dom. 1563. NEELE, sculpt. (22-8½ inches.)

London and Westminster in the Reign of Queen Elizabeth. Anno Dom. 1563. J. COOK, sc., 1847. (22-9 inches.)

London and Westminster in the Reign of Queen Elizabeth. Anno Dom. 1563. Surrounded by 20 views. A lithograph, published by Wm. DARTON. (28-16½ inches.)

A Plan of London as in Q. Elizabeth's days. Sold by John Bowles. At the bottom of the map are 5 views of buildings, and

11

underneath them : 'The South Prospect of London as it appeared when it lay in ruins after that dreadful fire in 1666.' Thos. Bowles, sculpsit. (22-14½ inches.)

Plan of the City of London in the Time of Queen Elizabeth. Engraved for Lambert's *History of London*, 1805. (8-5 inches.)

Typus Parochiæ Divi Martini, vulgo St. Martins, Outwich, una cum Parte Parochiæ Divi Petri in Cornehill in Civitate Londini, inventus et sælus, per Gulielmum Goodman, 1ᵐᵒ Januarii, An. 1599. T. A., fecit. (6¾-4½ inches.)

Middle-sex described with the most famous Cities of London and Westminster. 'Jacobus Hondius, cælavit. Cum Privilegio, Anno 1610. Described by John Norden. Augmēted by J. Speed.' With plans of London and Westminster, and views of Saint Peter's, Westminster, and Saint Paul's.

Middle sex described. Reprinted by Kelly and Co. (17-13 inches.)

A Plan of the City and Suburbs of London, as fortified by order of Parliament in the Years 1642 and 1643. G. Vertue, sc., 1738. (14-8½ inches.)

An exact delineation of the Cities of London & Westminster, and the Suburbs thereof, together wᵗʰ yᵉ Burrough of Southwark, and all yᵉ Throughfares, Highwaies, Streets, Lanes, and Common Allies within yᵉ same, composed by a Scale, and Ichnographically described by Richard Newcourt, of Somerton, in the Countie of Somersett, gentleman. With views of Westminster Abbey and S. Paul's Cathedral. Engraved by William Faithorne, 1658. Copied and engraved by Geo. Jarman, and published by Evans and Sons, on 5 sheets. (75-39 inches.)

An exact delineation of the Cities of London & Westminster. (Faithorne's plan. Republished by Stanford, 1878, on 4 sheets.) (75-39 inches.)

An exact Surveigh of the Streets, Lanes, and Churches comprehended within the Ruins of the City of London. 'First described in six Plats, 10 Decembʳ, Aᵒ Domⁱ, 1666, by the order and directions of the Lord Mayor, Aldermen, and Common Councell of the said City. John Leake, John Jennings, Willᵐ Marr, Willᵐ Leybourn, Thomas Streete, Richard Shortgrave, surveyors, and reduced into one entire Plat by John Leake for the use of the Commissioners. For the regulation of streets, lanes, etc. Re-engraved by G. Vertue, 1723, with 7 views of buildings. On 2 sheets. (Each 25-21 inches.)

Proposals of a New Model for Rebuilding the City of London, with Houses, Streets, and Wharfs, to be forthwith set out by His Majesty's and the City Surveyors. By Val. Knight, 20 Sept., 1666. With description. (14-22 inches.)

The Same, without the description. (14-11 inches.)

London Restored, or Sir John **Evelyn's** Plan for Rebuilding that antient Metropolis after the Fire in 1666. B. COLE, sculp. (13½-8 inches.)

Sir John **Evelyn's** Plan for Rebuilding the City of London after the Great Fire in 1666. (11½-6½ inches.)

Sir Christopher **Wren's** Plan for Rebuilding the City of London after the Great Fire in 1666. (12-7 inches.)

A Plan of the City of London after the Great Fire, 1666, according to the design and proposal of Sir Christopher WREN for rebuilding it. Showing the Situation of the Great Streets, S. Paul's Cathedral, the Exchange, Guildhall, Custom House, etc. (11½-7½ inches.)

A Plan of London, containing 25 Churches only, reserved on their old Foundations, with all the principal Streets almost in the same part they formerly were, and Spaces for all the rest of the Houses, Lanes, and Alleys of note. Underneath is Sir C. WREN's Plan, as described in preceding article. Sumptibus *Societat. Antiquar.*, 1748. (19-14 inches.)

Sir Christopher **Wren's** Design for rebuilding the City of London. From a *Report* (1800) *upon the Improvements of the Port of London.* (27-15½ inches.)

Grundtrik der Statt London, wie solche vor, und nach dem Brand anzuschern, sampt dem Newen Model, wie selbige widrum Auffgebauwet werden solle. Model, wie die Abbgebrante Statt London, widrum Auffgebauwet werden solle. (15½-12 inches.)

Londres, Ville Capitalle del' Angleterre. (6½-4¾ inches.)

Plan des Villes de Londres et de Westminster et leurs Faubourgs avec le Bourg de Southwark. Par Pierre MORTIER à Amsterdam. (13-9½ inches.)

Londinium celeberrima **Metropolis**, splendidissima Regia et opulentissimum Angliæ Emporium, accuratissime delineata, per Matthæum SEUTTER. Map, with inscription in Latin and German. Beneath, a prospect of London, with 63 references to places of interest. Coloured. J. T. KRAUS, delin. (23-20 inches.)

London. A map from BEEVERELL's *Delices de la Grande Bretagne.* (6¼-5¼ inches.)

London, etc. Accurately Survey'd by Rob. MORDEN and Philip LEA (about 1705). Portraits of William and Mary and 11 views at the top, also long view of London at the bottom, mounted on 13 sheets together. (7 ft. 11 in. by 5 ft. 10 in.)

Plan des Villes de Londres et de Westminster, et leurs Faubourgs, avec le Bourg de Southwark. Par de Fer. 1705. C. INSELIN, sculpt. (13½-9 inches.)

Londen, Westmunster, u. Soudwark. G. BODENEHR excudit Augustæ Vindelicoru. (28-6½ inches.)

A New Mapp of the City of London, etc. Anno 1716. Printed and sold by T. BAKEWELL, **next y^e Horn in Fleet S^t.** $(11\frac{1}{4} \cdot 8\frac{1}{2}$ inches.)

A Plan of the City's of London, Westminster, and Borough **of** Southwark, with the new Additional Buildings, anno 1720. Revised by J. SENEX ; S. PARKER del. et sculp. The arms of the City and dedication at top on left, and references to Parishes and Buildings at bottom. $(23\frac{1}{2} \cdot 20$ inches.)

London about 1720. The sheet containing S. Paul's from a large **map** of London. $(23\frac{1}{2} \cdot 20\frac{1}{2}$ inches.)

Regionis quæ est circa Londinum, specialis representatio geographica, ex autographo majori Londinensi desumta, curantibus HOMANIANIS Heredibus, 1741. With a **view** of London beneath. $(22\frac{1}{2} \cdot 20$ inches.)

A Plan of the **Cities of London** and Westminster **and** Borough of Southwark, with **the** contiguous Buildings. From an Actual Survey taken by John ROCQUE and engraved by John PINE. Scale about 9 inches to a mile. In **24** sheets and Index Plan. (Each $27 \cdot 19\frac{1}{2}$ inches.)
     'This work was begun 1737, and published 1746 by John Pine, at the Golden Head, against Burlington House, Piccadilly, and John Tinney, at the Golden Lion, Fleet Street.'

An Exact Survey of the Citys **of** London, Westminster, y^e Borough of Southwark, and the Country near Ten Miles round, begun in 1741 and ended in **1745** by John ROCQUE and engrav'd by Richard PARR.

Faringdon within and Baynard's Castle, with its Divisions into Parishes, taken from the last Survey, with Corrections. With elevations of S. Paul's. From STOW'S *Survey* (1754). **(14-12** inches.)

A Pocket Map of London, Westminster, and Southwark, with y^e New Buildings to y^e Year 1755. R. W. SEALE, sculp. $(20 \cdot 10\frac{1}{4}$ **inches.)**

Baynards Castle Ward and Faringdon Ward within, with their Divisions into Parishes, according to a new Survey. With elevations of S. Paul's and other buildings. B. COLE, sculpt., **1755.** $(19 \cdot 14\frac{1}{2}$ inches.)

The City Guide, or a Pocket Map of London, **Westminster, and** Southwark, with y^e new Buildings to y^e Year 1758. **Printed by** Thos. BOWLES in St. Paul's Church Yard, and John **BOWLES** & Son, at the Black Horse in Cornhil. **(20-10** inches.)

A Correct Plan of the Cities of London & **Westminster** & Borough **of** Southwark, including the Bills of Mortality, with the additional Buildings, etc. From the *London Magazine*, 1761. **(16-** 9 inches.)

A New and Correct Plan of London, Westminster, and Southwark, with the additional Buildings to the Year 1770. From CHAMBERLAIN'S *History of London.* (20-11¾ inches.)

A New and Complete Plan of London, Westminster, and Southwark, with the additional Buildings to the Year 1777. Engraved for HARRISON'S *History of London.* (19¾-11½ inches.)

Bowles's New Pocket Plan of the Cities of London and Westminster, with the Borough of Southwark, comprehending the New Buildings and other Alterations to the Year 1780. Printed for Carington BOWLES. (35¼-17½ inches.)

A Plan of the Cities of London and Westminster, with the Borough of Southwark. Engrav'd by W. FADEN, succ' to the late T. Jeffreys, 1788. (22-12¾ inches.)

A New Pocket Plan of the Cities of London and Westminster, with the Borough of Southwark, comprehending the New Buildings and other Alterations to the Year 1790. Printed for Wm. FADEN, Charing Cross. (35½-17½ inches.)

Plan of the Cities of London and Westminster, the Borough of Southwark, and parts adjoining, showing every House. By R. HORWOOD. Published 1794, in 32 sheets (each 20-21½ inches).

Plan of the proposed Docks, etc., on the Surrey Side of the River Thames. From a *Report* (1796) *on providing Accommodation for the Trade and Shipping of the Port of London.* J. BASIRE, sculp. (19½-15 inches.)

A New Pocket Plan of the Cities of London and Westminster, with the Borough of Southwark, comprehending the New Buildings and other Alterations to the Year 1798. (19½-9¾ inches.)

A Topographical Map of the Country twenty Miles round London, planned from a scale of two Miles to an Inch. By Wm. FADEN, Charing Cross, Sept. 1st, 1800. (Circular, 22¾ inches.)

Plan showing the Position of the Double Bridge and the proposed Avenues. Geo. DANCE, Arch'. From a *Report* (1800) *upon the Improvement of the Port of London.* J. BASIRE, sculp (20-12 inches.)

A General Plan of the E. & N.E. Parts of London and Places adjacent that may receive a supply of Thames Water from the intended East London Water Works, as proposed and surveyed by R. DODD, engineer, 1805. (17½-23 inches.)

London, extending from the Head of the Paddington Canal West, to the West India Docks East, with the proposed Improvements between the Royal Exchange and Finsbury Square. Publish'd Oct' 6, 1806, by J. STRATFORD. (21¼-13 inches.)

Langley and Belch's Map of London, 1812. With 24 small views of buildings. (30½-20½ inches.) !

An entire New Plan of the Cities of London and Westminster, with the Borough of Southwark. Published by E. Mogg, 1815. (35¼-18 inches.)

Langley and **Belch's** Map of London, 1818. With 24 small views of buildings. (30¼-20½ inches.)

An entire New Plan of the Cities of London and Westminster, with the Borough of Southwark. Published by E. Mogg, 1819. (35¼-18 inches.)

Map of the County of Middlesex from an Actual Survey made in the Years 1819 and 1820, by C. & J. Greenwood. With views of S. Paul's & Westminster Abbey. Corrected to the year 1829. (26-21 inches.)

A Plan of London and Westminster, with the Borough of Southwark. Published by W. Faden, 1820. (35¾-18 inches.)

The Stranger's Guide to London and Westminster. Published by E. Mogg (circa 1820). (22½-16 inches.)

Smith's New Plan of London, Westminster, & Southwark, with 350 References to the Principal Streets. Printed for C. Smith, Mapseller, 1822. (25-16½ inches.)

Map of **London, from an Actual Survey made in** the Years **1824,** 1825, and 1826, **by C. and J. Greenwood.** On 6 sheets. (Each 25½-25 inches.)

Cruchley's New Plan of London. Engraved and published by Cruchley, Mapseller (1829). (33-16½ inches.)

Middlesex. With view of St. Paul's in upper right hand corner. Engraved on steel by Picot and Son, Manchester. (13¾-8¾ inches.)

London in Miniature, with the Surrounding Villages. Published by E. Mogg, 1838. (37½-20 inches.)

Cross's New Plan of London. Published by J. Cross, 1838. (38½-25¼ inches.)

Plan of London, from Actual Survey, 1838. With 33 small views of buildings. Published by O Hodgson. (32½-21½ inches.)

Bauerkeller's New Embossed Plan of London, 1841. Published by Ackermann & Co. (45-26½ inches.)

Wallis's Guide for Strangers through London, 1843. Published by E. Wallis, 42, Skinner St. (28½-22 inches.)

The Railway Bell and Illustrated London Advertiser Map of London, 1845. Surrounded with views of buildings. (37-29½ inches.)

Davies's Map of the British Metropolis, containing the Boundaries of the Boroughs, etc. Published by B. R. Davies, 1848. (35½-26 inches.)

Ordnance Map of London, 12-inch **scale,** 43 sheets and Index, 1848; and 5-feet scale sheets 471, 617, 643, 644, 669, and 670, with **Index,** 1850.

Davies's New Map of London and its Environs, showing the New Railways, etc. Published by E. STANFORD, 1871. (40½-27 inches.)

London. Drawn and engraved expressly for the Post Office Directory, 1874, by B. R. DAVIES. (35¾-26½ inches.)

Photo Relief Map of North London, by H. F. BRION and Rev. Edmund McCLURE. (16½-13½ inches.)

Photo Relief Map of South London, by the same. (16½-13½ inches.)

London in 1892. A B C Pictorial Plan. Published by C. BAKER and Co. (27½-14½ inches.)

British Museum. Catalogue of Maps: London. Quarto. London. 1884.

VIEWS OF LONDON TO 1666.

London in the Time of Henry VIII. H. W. BREWER inv¹ et del¹, 1887. Reprinted from the *Builder*, with Key. (43-12 inches.)

The Procession of King Edward VI. from the Tower of London to Westminster, Feb. xix. MDXLVII., previous to his Coronation. Drawn from a coeval painting at Cowdray in Sussex, by S. H. GRIMM ; engraved by J. BASIRE. *Soc. Antiq.*, 1787. (51½-25½ inches.)

The Procession of King Edward VI. Lithograph by H. DUDLEY, 1836. (24½-12½ inches.)

Van den Wyngaerde's View of London, *circa* 1550. *Topogaphical Society of London*, 1881-2. In 7 sheets. (Each 17¾-21¾ inches.)
 The same case contains **Braun's Map** of London, and **Visscher's View.**

A South-East View of London, before the Destruction of S. Paul's Steeple, A.D. 1560. From a painting in the possession of Mr. J. GROVE, of Richmond. Engraved by B. HOWLETT, 1818. (12½-9¾ inches.)

Ancient London, from the Picture at the Surrey Zoological Gardens. A woodcut. (8½-4½ inches.)

Picture Model of Old London, at the Surrey Zoological Gardens. A woodcut, 1844. (8-6 inches.)

London. A long View from S. Catherine's in the East to the Palace at Westminster. Two tablets of description. J. C. VISSCHER delineavit (1616). (86-18 inches.)
 The plates of this view are still in existence.

London, by VISSCHER. The sheet of the copy showing S. Paul's. (22-18 inches.)

London in 1616 and 1890. Supplement to the *Graphic*, **Nov. 1st.,** 1890. (41-15 inches.)

Carolus D. G. Magnae Britanniae, Franciae, Scotiae et Hyberniae Rex, Anno. 1626. A portrait of CHARLES I. on horseback, the background being **a** view of London with old S. Paul's, etc. (10-13¼ inches.)

Fortifications of the City of London, 1641-2. A series of **20** plates from drawings supposed to have been executed for the Parliament by Col. EYRE.

View of London from the Top of Arundel House. From *Views of Arundel House,* after HOLLAR, 1646, published by J. THANE, **1792.** (7¼-10¼ inches.)

London. A long View of the whole of London, Westminster, and Southwark. W. HOLLAR delineavit et fecit, 1647. Published by Cornelius Danckers. Lithographic copy by R. MARTIN, 1832. (87-18 inches.)
This View, like that **of Visscher,** shows **all the** principal buildings of the **City. At the top and** base are various emblematic figures.

View of London as it was in the Year 1647. Reduced copy from HOLLAR by R. BENNING, 1756. In **2** sheets. (Each 19-12 inches.)

View of London, as it was in the Year **1647.** Similar to the above, but coloured. In **2** sheets.

London in **1657. From** BRAYLEY's *Londiniana.* (13½-5¼ inches.)

London before **the Fire.** Cut from **an** old Map (?). (6-2¾ inches.)

Londinum, Urbs praecipua Regni Angliae. Before the Fire. A **foreign print.** (20-15½ inches.)

Londres, Ville Capital (*sic*) du Royaume d'Angleterre. **A reduced copy of** the preceding. (12½-8½ inches.)

Londres, Ville Capitale du Royaume d'Angleterre. The foreground is similar to the preceding, but S. Paul's **is** altered, as rebuilt after the Fire. (20½-13¼ inches.)

A True and exact Prospect of the Famous Citty **of** London. From Sᵗ Marie Overs Steeple in Southwarke, in its flourishing Condition before the Fire. Another Prospect of the sayd Citty, taken from the same place, as it appeareth now after the sad calamatie and destruction by Fire in Yeare MDCLXVI. Winceslaus HOLLAR, delin. et sculp. 1666. **Cum** Privilegio. (26¾-8¾ inches.)

A True and exact Prospect, etc. **A** later impression of the above, without the words 'cum privilegio.' (26¾-8¾ inches.)

Tootehill Fields. With S. Paul's in the distance. Engraved by W. HOLLAR. (6½-3¾ inches.)

Islington, a series of 6 views taken near the New River Head. W. HOLLAR delin. et sculpsit, 1665. (Each 5-3½ inches.) Three of the above show Old S. Paul's in the distance.

London. London the glory of Great Britaines Ile. Behold her Landschip here and tru pourfile. Copy of the original by HOLLAR, in HOWELL's *Londinopolis,* 1657. (12½-8½ inches.)

A Book of the Prospects of **the** Remarkable Places in and about the City of London, by John SELLER (about 1680). Containing 28 views, with engraved title, including 'The Cathedral Church of S' Paul before ye fire,' and 'S' Pauls,' **being a** variation from Wren's design.

VIEWS OF LONDON 1666—1799.

London. Showing the City in flames. J. DANCKERTS excu. (10¾-8½ inches.)

Londres, Capitale de l'Angleterre. Before the Fire. By DANCKERTS. (Same foreground as in above.) (10¾-8½ inches.)

De so vermaerde Kerk van S. Paul tot London. Pet. Schenk ex. Amstel. (Showing that part of London before the Fire, coloured.) (10½-8½ inches.)

The Great Fire of London, 1666, engraved from an original picture in the possession of Mrs. Lawrence. J. STOW, sculp. From WILKINSON's *Londina Illustrata.* (16¾-12 inches.)

A View of Part of London as it appeared in the Great Fire of 1666, from an original painting in Painter Stainers' Hall. Peter MAZELL del. et sculp. From PENNANT's *London.* (12½-5¾ inches.)

The Great Fire of London. P. J. de LOUTHERBOURG, pinx.; A. SMITH, sculp., 1805. (12-9½ inches.)

The Great Fire of London in the Year 1666. Engraved by W. BIRCH from an original Picture in the Possession of R. GOLDEN, Esq. Painted by Old GRIFFIER at the time of the Fire; coloured. From the *Antiq. Repertory.* (15-11¾ inches.)

Abbildung der Statt London, sambt dem erschröcklichen brandt daselten, so 4 tagen lange gewehrt hatt, A° 1666 im 7 bris. (13½-8½ inches.)

London. Showing the City rebuilt. A similar foreground to that in Danckerts' view, but with some variations. (11-8¼ inches.)

London. The same print as above, but coloured.

London and Westminster, 1669. Published by J. MAWMAN, January 1st, 1821, an aquatint from COSMO's *Travels.* (33½-8¼ inches.)

A Catalogue of the Churches of the City of London, Royal Palaces, Hospitals, and Public Edifices, built by Sir C. WREN from 1668 to 1718. The names on labels, arranged as a pyramid. H. HULSBERGH, sculp. $(1:\frac{3}{4}-17\frac{1}{4}$ inches.)

A Vision of the City of London, constructed on the Plan left by Sir Christopher WREN. Woodcut, drawn and engraved by Worthington G. SMITH, under the direction of Mr. GODWIN. $(10\frac{1}{4}-14\frac{3}{4}$ inches.)

Lambeth Marsh, as it appeared about the Year 1670. Etched by J. BARNETT, 1820. From a series of views illustrating Old London (never completed). $(11\frac{1}{4}-9\frac{1}{4}$ inches.)

The Prospect of London and Westminster, taken from Lambeth, by W. HOLLAR. Showing Lambeth Palace in the foreground, and extending from Peterborough House to Limehouse. Date, 1674. Mounted on 2 sheets. $(63\frac{1}{2}-12\frac{1}{2}$ inches.)

A Prospect of London and Westminster, taken at several Stations to the Southward thereof. Wil. MORGAN, Robt. MORDEN, & Phil. LEA (? 1680). In 3 sheets. (Together, 95-11$\frac{1}{4}$ inches.)

Lambeth, His Grace the Lord Archbishop of Canterbury's Pallace, 1697. L. KNYFF, del., J. KIP, sculp. (S. Paul's, etc., seen in the distance.) $(19\frac{1}{2}-14$ inches.)

A Prospect of the City of London, Westminster, and St. James's Park. Dedicated to Her Royal Highness Wilhelmina Carolina Princess of Wales, by John Kip. John KIP, delineavit et sculpsit (1710). 12 sheets. Mounted on 8. (80-53 inches.)

A New Prospect of ye North side of ye City of London, with New Bedlam and Moorefields (pubd 1710). Jos. NUTTING. sculp. Printed and sold by Jas. WALKER, at ye Star in Py-corner, near West Smithfield, in 3 sheets. (Together, 58-27 inches.)

The South Prospect of London and Westminster (*circa* 1720). With long descriptions in English and French on scrolls in two upper corners, and 118 references to places of interest. Printed and sold by J. BOWLES. (47-19$\frac{1}{2}$ inches.)

London, from Somerset House to the Tower (1720). **(44-15** inches.)

The South Prospect of the City of London, **1732.** Printed and sold by John BOWLES. $(59\frac{1}{2}-24\frac{1}{2}$ inches.)

London, 1739. From the *London Magazine.* $(4\frac{1}{2}-3\frac{1}{2}$ inches.)

Gesigt langs de Rivier de Theems op de Brug van Londen, u. van Westminster. Two views on one plate. C. PHILIPS, Jac. fil. fec., 1754. $(9-6\frac{3}{4}$ inches.)

London. A view looking up the River, about 1740. $(9-5\frac{1}{4}$ inches.)

A Perspective View of ye Royal Palace of Somerset next ye River. J. MAURER, delin. et sculp., 1742. $(16\frac{1}{2}-10$ inches.)

A Perspective View of y^e Royal Palace of Somerset, next y^e River. (Same plate as the preceding, but coloured.)

The South-East Prospect of London. MAURER, del.; T. BOWLES, sculp., 1746. (16-10¾ inches.)

View of the City of London, taken through one of the Centres of the Arches of the New Bridge at Westminster. Canaletti pinx.; S. WALE, delin.; R. PARR, sculp., 1747. (23-17 inches.)

The Cause of Eclipses and the Motion of the Earth delineated. With a view of London, taken from the New River Head. From the *Universal Magazine*, 1748. (9¼-8 inches.)

A long View of London and Westminster, taken from Mr. Scheve's Sugar House, opposite to York House; from Mr. Watson's Summer House, opposite to Somerset House; from Mr. Everard's Summer House, opposite to St. Bride's Church; and from St. Mary Overy's Church, Southwark. Engraved by S. & N. BUCK, 1749, in 5 sheets. (Together, 156-12 inches.)

A View of London taken off Lambeth Church. J. BOYDELL, delin. et sculp., 1752. (17-10½ inches.)

A View of London taken off Lambeth Church. (Similar to the above, but coloured.)

A Perspective View of the North West Front of ye Parish Church of St. Bride's. S. Paul's in the distance. J. DONOWELL, delin.; T. BOWLES, sculp. (15½-10¼ inches.)

Charterhouse Square. S. Paul's in the distance. Sutton NICHOLLS, delin. et sculp., from STOW's *Survey*, 1755. (18¼-13½ inches.

Gesigt van den Tuin van Somerset's Paleis, Langs den Theems tot op de Brug van Londen. Is. TIRION, excudit; C. PHILLIPS junior fecit, 1753. (17-7 inches.)

A View of Westminster Bridge. S. Paul's, etc., in the distance. Beneath is a description in five lines in English and French. Tho. BOYDELL, delin. et sculp., 1753. (16½-10¼ inches.)

A View of the Tower, with the Bridge, and part of the City of London from the River. J. MAURER, delin.; MÜLLER, Junr sculp^t, 1753. Coloured. (15¼-10¼ inches.)

A View of London and Westminster, etc., from One Tree Hill, in Greenwich Park. TILLEMANS, pinxt.; STEVENS, delin. et sculp., 1752. Coloured. (15¾-10¼ inches.)

A View of London, from One-Tree-Hill in Greenwich Park. *Gentleman's Magazine*, 1754. (9¾-8 inches.)

View of London, etc., from Greenwich Park. Engraved for the *Complete English Traveller*. (12¼-8 inches.)

The South West Prospect of London. T. BOWLES & T. MELISH, delin.; T. BOWLES, sculp. Coloured. (16¼-11 inches.)

London. View looking West. Cut from the top of a map (?), about 1760. (8½-3¼ inches.)

A West View of London with the Bridge, taken from Somerset Gardens. CANALETI, pinxt. ; E. ROOKER, sculp., 1767. (Republished 1794 by Laurie & Whittle.) (15¾-10¼ inches.)

A View of the Barges conducting his Danish Majesty from Whitehall to the Temple (Sept. 23ᵈ, 1768) in his way to the Mansion House. Inscribed to Christian VII., King of Denmark. (10-7½ inches.)

A Perspective View of the Cities of London and Westminster. Published, 1783, by J. FIELDING. From the *European Magazine.* (9¼-6¾ inches.)

A Prospect of the City of London, from **St.** George's Fields, in **Surrey.** B. COLE, sculp. From the *New Universal Magazine.* (11½-7¼ inches.)

Index to the View of London. With 90 references. Published by J. SWERTNER, 1789. (29½-5 inches.)

A Panorama of London. ' Etched by H. A. Barker at the age of fifteen, who himself took the view from the top of the Albion Mills.' Aquatinted by BIRNIE **(1792).** In 6 sheets. (Each 22-17 inches.)

A Panorama of London. The sheet containing S. Paul's, etc., coloured. (22½-18½ inches.)

View of London taken on the Thames near York Stairs. Drawn and engraved by J. W. EDY, 1792. Coloured. (32-22 inches.)

View from Scotland Yard. Aquatint by T. MALTON, from MALTON'S *Views of London,* 1795. (15½-12 inches.)

A View of Westminster Bridge. S. Paul's in the distance. Three lines of description in French beneath. À PARIS chez Jean, rue Jean de Beauvais, No. 32. (21¾-13¾ inches.)

A View of the Westminster Bridge, London. With inscriptions beneath in English, French, Italian, and German. J. F. LEIZEL, fec., G. B. PROBST, execud. (16½-12¼ inches.)

A North View of London. CANALETI, delin. ; STEVENS, sculpt. Published 1754. Republished 1794 by LAURIE & WHITTLE. (15¾-10¼ inches.)

South Front of the Royal Exchange. S. Paul's in the distance. Aquatint by T MALTON, 1798. From MALTON'S *Views of London.* (15½-12 inches.)

The Royal Exchange of London. S. Paul's in the distance. BOWLES, delin. et sculp., 1751. (16½-10¼ inches.)

The Custom House. Aquatint by T. MALTON, 1799. From MALTON'S *Views of London.* (15-12 inches.)

Somerset Place. S. Paul's in the distance. Aquatint by T. MALTON, 1796. (15-12 inches.)

A View of London, taken from the Bridge near Chelsea. O'NEAL, del.; James ROBERTS, sculp. (7½-6 inches.)

Design for a Stone Bridge to admit Shipping by R. Dodd, 1799. S. Paul's is partially seen through one of the arches. From a *Report* (1800) *upon the Improvement of the Port of London.* J. BASIRE, sculp. (27½-17 inches.)

The Old Soldier, remarkable for constant attendance at S. Paul's, from an original painting. C. MOSLEY, sculp. S. Paul's is seen in the distance. (8¼-8½ inches.)

A View of the City of London, as it appears from under one of the Arches of Westminster Bridge. Printed for R. WILKINSON. (17-11 inches.)

A View of the City of London. (The same plate as the preceding, but coloured.)

VIEWS OF LONDON IN 1800 TO THE PRESENT TIME.

London, from under one of the Arches of Blackfriars Bridge. A coloured aquatint, about 1800 (no margin giving artist and engraver). (39-19¼ inches.)

View of London, taken from Albion Place, Blackfriars Bridge. N. R. BLUCK, del.; J. C. STADLER, sculp. 1802. Coloured. (36-22½ inches.)

London. Engraved by J. CRAIG from a drawing by Lady ARDEN, 1804. (10½-7 inches.)

Blackfriars Bridge. T. SHEPHERD, delin.; H. FINCKE, sculp. (9-7 inches.)

Smithfield Market, from the Barrs. Drawn by T. H. SHEPHERD, engraved by T. BARBER. (8¾-5½ inches.)

London. J. GREIG, del. et sculp. 1805. From Storer and Greig's *Views.* (6-4 inches.)

London. The same plate as above, but etching before the lettering.

London, from the Royal Observatory, Greenwich. Published 1807, by R. PHILLIPS. (7-4½ inches.)

London. A small aquatint; all inscription cut off. (5½-4½ inches.)

A View of London from the Thames, taken opposite the Adelphi. PUGIN and ROWLANDSON, del. et sculp.; J. BLUCK, aquat. From Ackermann's *Microcosm.* 1809. Coloured. (10¾-9 inches.)

Southwark Bridge. From No. 40 of ACKERMANN'S *Repository*. 1812. Coloured. (13·8¾ inches.)

Royal Exchange. With S. Paul's in the distance. T. SUTHER-LAND, sculp. From ACKERMANN'S *Repository*. 1812. Coloured. (5¾-9¼ inches.)

London. A coloured aquatint. View looking towards S. Paul's. Drawn and Engraved by W. PICKETT, 1812. (16¼-11½ inches.)

Frost Fair on the Thames in February, 1814. Woodcut, with three lines of description beneath. (8½-6 inches.)

A View of Frost Fair on the Thames, February, 1814. Woodcut. Published by T. BATCHELAR, 115, Long Alley, Moorfields. (18-13 inches.)

Fair on the Thames, Feb. 1814. Drawn by Luke CLENNELL, engraved by George COOKE. (9¼-6 inches.)

London and Blackfriars Bridge from Hungerford. Drawn by S. OWEN, engraved by W. COOKE. 1811. (9½-6 inches.)

The Intended Iron Bridge, in place of the present London Bridge. (5-3 inches.)

London. A View, partly panoramic, but each sheet forming a complete picture. Drawn and aquatinted by Wm. DANIELL. In 6 sheets : (1) from Greenwich, (2) the Tower, etc., (3) London Bridge, (4) S. Paul's, etc., (5) Somerset House, (6) Westminster. Coloured. (Each 28-20 inches.)

London, from Camberwell, on the South. 1815. (4¾-3 inches.)

London, from the Monument. Lithograph. Published by G. J. Cox, Royal Polytechnic. (7-4½ inches).

London, from Greenwich. Drawn by W. WESTALL, engraved by E. FINDEN. (6¾-4¾ inches.)

London, from Stockwell. From an original drawing by D. COX. Published 1818, by T. MCLEAN. (14½-10 inches.)

View of London. Drawn and engraved by J. S. NEELE and Son. (15-7¼ inches.)

A View of London and the surrounding Country, taken from the top of S. Paul's Cathedral. An aquatint. Circular. (29½ inches.)

Southwark Iron Bridge. S. Paul's in middle distance. J. GENDALL, del. ; T. SUTHERLAND, sculp. Published by ACKERMANN, 1819. Coloured. (19¼-14½ inches.)

London, seen from Blackfriars Bridge. Drawn by L. CLENNELL, engraved by W B. COOKE. (9¼-6 inches.)

London. Drawn by N. WHITTOCK, engraved by J. ROGERS. With border. (9½-7 inches.)

London, from the Shot Tower. Drawn by C. MARSHALL, engraved by W. HENSHALL. From *Select Illustrated Topography of Thirty Miles around London.* (6-9½ inches.)

A View of the Waterloo Bridge. Published 1823, by Richard H. LAURIE, 53, Fleet Street. (17¼-11½ inches.)

Waterloo Bridge. Drawn on Stone by W. WESTALL, A.R.A. 1826. (13½-10¼ inches.)

Waterloo Bridge and S. Paul's. Pencil drawing by E. S. P., 1824. (7¼-4½ inches.)

Lithographic Sketch of the North Bank of the Thames, from Westminster Bridge to London Bridge, showing the proposed Quay and some other Improvements suggested by Lt.-Col. Trench, with a Survey of that part of the River and a Prospectus. 1825.
A panoramic view in ten sheets. (Each 22½-8 inches.)

City Panorama. Bird's-eye View of London and Surrounding Country, taken from the Monument. Will open for the Inspection of the Public, Sept. 1st, 1826. Circular. (9 inches.)

Panorama de Londres. With 24 references in French and English. Circular. (11 inches.)

Panorama of London. Oval. (11-8½ inches.)

London from the River. Coloured aquatint. By W. PICKET, 1827. Showing S. Paul's, Blackfriars Bridge, etc. (15t11 inches.)

A View of the East Side of London Bridge in the Year 1827, from a Drawing by Major G. YATES. · R. MARTIN, lithog. (20½-12½ inches.)

Royal Jennerian **Society** Honorary Diploma, 1835. (Through an arch is seen S. Paul's, etc.) (12½-14¾ inches.)

Blackfriars, from Southwark Bridge. T. S. BOYS del. et lithog. From Boys' *Views of London.* (17¾-7 inches.)

View of the City of London, from the Terrace at Somerset House. W. M. CRAIG, del.; T. DIXON, sculp. (10-7½ inches.)

London. View of principal buildings, with ornamental border, engraved for an Insurance Company. (9-11½ inches.)

The first Carriage, the 'Ariel.' With North View of London. Inscribed to the Directors of the Ærial Transit Company. Published by ACKERMANN 1833, lithograph. (17-14 inches.)

The first Carriage, the 'Ariel.' London from the West, just in front of the Shot Tower, 1843. (12-10½ inches.)

The City of London, View taken in Balloon. From *Excursions Aeriennes.* A French lithograph. (17½-12½ inches.)

Key to the Aeronautical View of London. By R. HAVELL. (22-5½ inches.)

London. A series of 8 embossed views, in colours, from 'London by Day,' at the Colosseum, Regent's Park, and the 8 Key plates. (Each 6-5 inches.)

General View of London, from the Southwark Side. W. H. BARTLETT, del.; E. J. ROBERTS, sculp.. 1843. (9¾-7½ inches.)

London from the Thames. A woodcut. Supplement to the *Pictorial Times*, Dec. 21, 1844. A panoramic view in 4 divisions on 2 sheets. (148-5¼ inches.)

London in the Reign of Queen Victoria. **N.** WHITTOCK, **del.** ; E. WALKER, lith., 1859. (47¼-13½ inches.)

London from Somerset House, looking East. **Drawn by T.** ALLOM ; engraved by T. A. PRIOR. (16¼-9 inches.)

Londres, Vue prise de London Bridge. Etching **by A.** BALLIN. (11-8 inches.)

View of the proposed Line of Railway along the Banks of the Thames from Hungerford Market to London Bridge. Sheet showing S. Paul's. W. RICHARDSON, lithographer. (16-9½ inches.)

Thames Embankment. G. H. ANDREWS, pinx ; T. A. PRIOR. sculp. From the *Stationers' Almanack*, **proof** on India paper. (18¾-10¼ inches.)

Flounder Fishing at Waterloo **Bridge.** A woodcut. S. Paul's **seen** through the arch. (9½-6½ inches.)

London Traffic, as seen from the top of S. **Paul's.** Woodcut, from a drawing by A. ALLOM. (10¾-7½ inches.)

London, from **the top of** S. Paul's Cathedral. A woodcut from the *Graphic,* Sept. 17, 1881. (9-12 inches.)

View of London from S. Paul's, looking Eastward. Woodcut from the *Illustrated London News,* Nov. 19, 1892. (18½-12½ inches.)

OLD S. PAUL'S.

Views.

Old S. Paul's before **the destruction of** the Steeple, **and the** surrounding Houses. **Modern** pen-and-ink drawing. (12¾-8 inches.)

Description of Drawings exhibiting a Restoration of Old S. Paul's **Cathedral, as** it appeared about the **year 1540.** By E. B. FERREY, 1875. **A broad** sheet. Folio.

Saint Paul's Cathedral, before the destruction **of the** Spire, restored from ancient Authorities, by H. W. BREWER, 1891. From the *Builder,* Jan. 2nd, 1892. (15-11 inches.)

Old S. Paul's before the destruction of the Steeple, Paul's **Cross,** S. Faith's, Paul's Walk, East Window, and South View. **Six** woodcuts on one sheet, from *Old England.* (8-12½ inches.)

Vue du dedans de l'Eglise Paroissiale de Sainte Foi, avant le **Feu, de** 1666. From BEEVEREILL'S *Delices de la Grande Bretagne.* (6-5 inches.)

Vue de l'Eglise Cathedrale de S. Paul du côté d'Occident avant le feu de 1666. From BEEVERELL'S *Delices.* (6-5 inches.)

Vue du dedans de la Nef de l'Eglise Cathedrale de S. Paul avant le feu de 1666. From BEEVERELL'S *Delices.* (6-5 inches.)

Plan of S. Paul's Cathedral, 1645. Pub. by COWIE & STRANGE, 1828. (7¾-4½ inches.)

South View of Old S. Paul's, when the Spire was standing ; North View, after the Spire was destroy'd ; South View, after the Spire was destroy'd. Three views on one sheet, from an old *Traveller*, with descriptive letterpress. (8-13 inches.)

S. Paul's. A sheet containing 11 small views of the Old and 5 of the Present Cathedral, with a Prospect of London as before the Fire. D. LOGGAN, fecit, 1724. Sold by J. BOWLES. (18½-15½ inches.)

S. Paul's. A sheet containing 7 views of the Old and 3 of the Present Cathedral, being the upper part of the preceding. (18½-9½ inches.)

The Prospect of the Parochiall Church of St. Faith from West to East under St. Paules. Dan KING, fecit, with portrait of (?) John SELDEN. (6¼-3 inches.)

Monument of Sir Richard de Burley in St. Paul's. LONGMATE, sc. From NICHOLS' *Leicestershire.* (8½-8½ inches.)

Old St. Paul's Cathedral. Three woodcuts on 1 sheet. (5-8¾ inches.)

Inigo Jones's Portico. Old S. Paul's. A woodcut. (2½-2½ inches.)

Bird's-eye View of Old St. Paul's, showing the surrounding Wall, Gates, and Streets ; and Interior of Wren's first Design. Two woodcuts on 1 sheet. (7-11 inches.)

The Cathedral Church of St. Paul, as it was before the Fire of London. A woodcut. (6½-4¼ inches.)

Old St. Paul's Cathedral. A woodcut. (3¾-3 inches.)

Dean Nowell's Monument. J. BASIRE, sculp. From the *Gentleman's Magazine,* 1811. (4¾-7½ inches.)

St. Paul's in Flames. 'Etiam periere Ruinæ,' on scroll at the top. A woodcut. (4-2½ inches.)

Inigo Jones' Portico. Old S. Paul's. H. FLITCROFT, delin. ; H. HULSBERGH, sculp. (15-19¾ inches.)

Restored View of Monuments in the N. Choir Aisle, Old St. Paul's Cathedral. By H. W. BREWER. From the *Builder,* July 4, 1885. (11-14 inches.)

'Paul's Walk,' the Nave of Old St. Paul's, a Restoration. By

H. W. Brewer.   **From the** *Builder,* July 6, 1889   (11-15 inches.)

Geometrical Elevations of the W. Fronts of the Cathedrals of St. Paul's (before the Fire), St. Stephen's Vienna, Strasburgh, Cologne, Mechlin, and the Great Pyramid.   Drawn and etched by T. H. Clarke.   (17¾-14 inches.)

The East Prospect of the Cathedral Church of St. Paul.   From Dugdale's *Monasticon,* 1718 edition, p. 327.   (7-10¼ inches.)

The West Prospect of the Cathedral Church of St. Paul.   Daniel King, sculpsit.   From Dugdale's *Monasticon,* 1718 edition, **p. 325.**   (7-10 inches.)

Plan of the Chapter House and Cloisters of S. Paul's Cathedral, made in 1657, from the Original preserved in the Public Record Office.   A lithograph.   (6½-8½ inches.)

South View of the Chapter House **of** Old **St. Paul's.**   J. D. McQuin, del.; **CHAPMAN, sc.**   (7½-9 inches.)

Complete Series of Plates from Sir William Dugdale's *History of St. Paul's Cathedral,* the First Edition, 1658; and also from the Third Edition, **1818.**

1. Portrait of Sir William **Dugdale.**   Gulielmus Dugdale, ætatis 50, A° 1656.   Wenceslaus Hollar, delin. et sculpsit ; **and,** after Hollar, engraved by W. Finden.

2. Capella Thomæ **Kempe,** London Episcopi. (Between the Nave and the North Aisle.)

MONUMENTS.

3. **Sir John Beauchamp,** 1310.
.**(In the** Nave, south side, under second arch from central tower.)

4. Three monumental brasses : Thomas de **Eure,** Dean, 1389-1400. William **Grene.** Robert **FitzHugh,** Bishop, 1431-143⅚. (On the floor of the Choir, before the High Altar.)

5. John **Donne,** Dean, 1621-31. (In South Aisle of Choir.)

6. John **Colet,** Dean, 1505-19. (In South Aisle of Choir.)

7. William **Hewit,** 1599. (Between Choir and South Aisle.)

8. **Sir** William **Cokayne,** 1626. (In South Aisle of Choir.)

9. Sir Nicholas **Bacon,** Keeper of the Great Seal, 1579. (In Choir, opposite the monument of the Earl of Pembroke, between two pillars, near the High Altar.)

10. Monumental brass of a priest **in cope.** John **Acton,** 1638.

Symon **Edulph**, 1597.
(In South Aisle of Choir.)

11. Monumental brass, a cross.
Thomas Okeford, Vicar, 1508. Monumental brass, priest in cope.

William **Rythyn**, Minor Canon and Almoner, 1400. Monumental brass, priest in cope.

Richard **Lichfeld**, Canon Residentiary, Archdeacon of Middlesex, 1476-149⅔. Monumental brass, priest in cope.
(In South Aisle of Choir.)

12. Three monumental brasses :
William Worseley, Dean, 147⅚-1499.
Roger Brabazon, Canon Residentiary, 1498.
Valentine Carey, Dean, 1614-21 ; Bishop of Exeter, 1621-26.
(In South Aisle of Choir.)

13. Two monumental brasses :
John **Newcourt**, Canon, Dean of Auckland, 1485.
(In South Aisle of Choir.)

14. Henry de **Wengham**, Bishop, 12⁵⁹⁄₆₀-1262.
Eustace de **Fauconberg**, Regis Justiciarius. Bishop, 1221-28.
(In South Aisle of Choir, towards the east.)

15. Sir Christopher **Hatton**, Lord Chancellor, 1591.
(Between two pillars, east of the Altar, on the south side.)

16. Henry de Lacy, Earl of Lincoln, **1310.**
(North side of Lady Chapel.)
Robert de Braybroke, Bishop of London, 138½-1404. Monumental brass.
(Chapel of S. Dunstan.)

17. Roger **Niger**, Bishop of London, 1229-41.
(Between two pillars, north side of Choir.)

18. William, Earl of **Pembroke**, 1569.
(Between North Aisle and Choir, near High Altar.)

19. John, Duke of **Lancaster**, and Constance, his wife, 1399.
(North of High Altar, between two pillars.)
Another plate, with coat-of-arms and other variations from that in Dugdale.

20. King **Sebba** and King **Ethelred**.
(In the north wall of North Choir Aisle.)

21. Monument affixed to north wall of Choir.

22. William Aubrey, LL.D., 1595.
(In the north wall, opposite the Choir.)

23. John de **Chishull**, Bishop, 127¾-12⁷⁸⁄₈₀.
(In north wall of North Aisle of Choir.)

24. Ralph de **Hengham**, Capitalis Justiciarius de **Banco**.
(In North Aisle of Choir.)

25. Sir Simon **Burley**, 1388.
    (In North Aisle of Choir.)

26. John **Mullins, Archdeacon** of London, 1559-91. Monumental brass.
    Sir Simon **Baskerville**, Knight, Doctor in Physic, 1641.
    (In North Aisle of Choir.)

27. Sir John **Wolley**, 1595.
    (In S. George's Chapel.)

28. Sir Thomas **Heneage**, 1594.
    (In the Lady Chapel.)

29. Alexander **Nowell**, Dean, 1560-160½.
    (In the Lady Chapel.)

30. Clausura **circa Altare S. Erkenwaldi** sub Feretro ejusdem.

VIEWS AND PLANS.

31. **Plan of the Church of S.** Faith.
32. **Interior of the Church of S.** Faith, looking East.
33. Chapter **House, from the South.**
34. Ecclesiæ Paulinæ prospectus, qualis **erat** priusquam **ejus** Pyramis e coelo tacta conflagravit.
    (South view, showing the Spire burnt in **1561,** S. Gregory's Church, and Chapter House.)
35. Areæ Ecclesiæ Cathedralis S. Pauli Ichnographia.
    (Ground Plan **of** Old S. Paul's, with the lesser Cloister, Chapter House, and S. Gregory's Church.)
36. **Ecclesiæ Cathedralis S.** Pauli a meridie prospectus.
    (South **view: the tower** has lost its spire; Inigo Jones' Portico is shown.)
37. **Ecclesiæ** Cathedralis S. Pauli a Septentrione prospectus.
    (After the fall of the spire; shows Inigo Jones' Portico.)
38. Ecclesiæ Cathedralis S. Pauli ab Occidente prospectus.
    (Full view of Inigo Jones' Portico.)
39. Ecclesiæ Cathedralis S. Pauli Orientalis facies.
40. Ecclesiæ Cathedralis S. Pauli ab Oriente prospectus.
    (Shows the North Transept.)
41. Navis Ecclesiæ Cathedralis S. Pauli prospectus interior.
    (Looking East.)
42. Partis exterioris Chori ab Occidente prospectus.
    (Shows Screen at entrance of Choir.)
43. Chori Ecclesiæ Cathedralis S. Pauli prospectus interior.
    (The Organ is seen, with its folding-doors, and the Pulpit, both **on** the north side.)
44. Orientalis partis Ecclesiæ Cathedralis S. Pauli prospectus interior.
    (Shows the Lady Chapel, with its screen.)

45. Vignette of S. Paul's Cathedral on Fire in 1666.

45a. The Daunce of Machabree.
(This subject was painted on the walls of the larger Cloister on the north side of the Cathedral.)

Series of Drawings exhibiting a **Restoration of Old S. Paul's Cathedral,** as it appeared about the year 1540, by Mr. EDMUND B. FERREY.

***** These Drawings gained the prize awarded by the Royal Institute of British Architects in 1868, and were presented to the Dean and Chapter by Mr. Ferrey in 1875.

South Elevation, showing Chapter House and Church of S. Gregory. (82½-61 inches.)

West Elevation. (46½-61 inches.)

Longitudinal Section through Choir. (40½-28½ inches.)

East Elevation of Choir. (20-27 inches.)

Transverse Section through Choir. (20-27 inches.)

Ground Plan. (82-48½ inches.)

(Mr. Ferrey has added a printed description of this valuable series of Drawings.)

S. Paul's Cross.

St. **Paul's Cross and Cathedral,** with King James I. and his Court at a Sermon. Engraved by J. STOW from an original picture in the possession of the *Society of Antiquaries.* From WILKINSON'S *Londina Illustrata,* 1811, with letterpress description. (12-17 inches.)

Paul's Cross and Preaching there. From an original drawing in the Pepysian Library, Cambridge. Published 1809, by R. WILKINSON, in the *Londina Illustrata,* with description. (7¾-11 inches.)

St. **Paul's Cross,** as it appeared during the Services performed before James I. and his Court, Sunday, 26th March, 1620. 'This Cross was destroyed in 1643, by order of the Parliament.' A woodcut. (3½-4 inches.)

Dr. Shaw preaching at S. Paul's Cross. From HARRISON'S *History of London.* (4-6½ inches.)

Preaching at Paul's Cross, 1621. W. D. RYE, sc. From Hen. FARLEY'S *St. Paules Church, her Bill for the Parliament.* (6-4½ inches.)

St. **Paul's Cross.** NEVEN, sc.; DEMORAINE, delin. A woodcut. (2½-2½ inches.)

St. **Paul's Cross** in the Reign of James I. From a painting in

the possession of the *Society of Antiquaries*. Engraving **from**
BRAYLEY'S *Londiniana*. (3½-5½ inches.)

Preaching at Paul's Cross. A woodcut. (5¾-4¼ inches.)

Paul's Cross. Particulars of Foundations discovered March 31st,
1879, by Mr. F. C. PENROSE. A woodcut. (7-8 inches.)

Sir C. Wren's earlier Designs for S. Paul's.

Plan of the Structure first intended to be erected for St. Paul's,
taken in 1773 from the Model which is kept in one of the
Galleries, and accurately again examined in 1783. From the
Gentleman's Magazine, 1783. (10¾-7¾ inches.)

Plan of Sr Christopher Wren's first Design of St. Paul's Cathedral.
B. COLE, sculp. (16½-21 inches.)

Section of the Cathedral Church of S. Paul, wherein the Dome is
represented according to a former Design of the Architect.
(28¾-20 inches.)

Section of the Cathedral **Church of** St. Paul, according to the first
Design of S' Christopher **Wren**. H. HULSBERGH, sculp. (22-
17¼ inches.)

View of the Cathedral Church of St. Paul's, according to the first
Design of **the Architect**. J. SCHYNVOET, fecit. (22-16¾
inches.)

Orthography of the Cathedral Church of St. Paul to the South,
according to the first Intention of ye Architect. H. HULSBERGH,
sculp^t. (22-16¾ inches.)

West Front of Sir Chris' Wren's Design for St. Paul's Cathedral,
with Lucern Windows in the Dome and other Variations from
the present Structure. From the original in All Souls' College,
Oxford. Engraved by W. FINDEN for DUGDALE'S *St. Paul's*,
third edition. (9¾-13¾ inches.)

West Front of an unexecuted Plan **for** St. Paul's Cathedral.
From Sir C. Wren's design in All Souls' College. Engraved by
W. FINDEN for DUGDALE'S *St. Paul's*, third edition. (13-9½
inches.)

South View of Wren's first Design. (7-6¼ inches.)

S. PAUL'S *CATHEDRAL—THE PRESENT BUILDING.—EXTERIOR.*

Views from Ludgate Hill, Etc.

West Front of the Cathedral of St. Paul, and the Church of St.
Martin, Ludgate. Painted by W. MARLOW; engraved by T.
MORRIS. Published 1795. (17-22¼ inches.)

West View of St. Paul's Cathedral. Engraved by J. STORER, from a drawing by F. NASH, 1804. (8-11 inches.)

St. Paul's Cathedral. Drawn and engraved by J. C. VARRALL for the *Walks through London*, 1816. (3½-5½ inches.)

Ludgate Hill. From PARTINGTON'S *Views of London.* (2⅓-4¾ inches.)

St. Paul's and Westminster Abbey. Two small views from a Pocket-Book series. (5½-7 inches.)

St. Paul's from Aldersgate Street and from Sermon Lane. Two views by STORER, 1823, with description. (Each 4-6 inches.)

View of St. Paul's from Fleet Street. M^cQUIN, del. (4¾-7¼ inches.)

St. Paul's Cathedral: The Civic Procession on **Lord** Mayor's Day. Painted by D. ROBERTS, engraved by E. GOODALL. *Art Union*, 1844. (16½-13¾ inches.)

St. Paul's Cathedral. The same plate as above, but a proof on India paper.

St. Paul's from Ludgate Hill. T. BOYS, del. et lithog. (12¼-17¼ inches.)

Ludgate Hill. J. D. HARDING, del.; lith., C. HULLMANDEL. (5½-7 inches.)

Ludgate Hill, 1892. A woodcut. (8-6 inches.)

St. Paul's Cathedral, looking up Ludgate Hill. E. WALKER, del. et lith., 1852. (12-16 inches.)

Last few days of St. Paul's. A woodcut. (3¼-4¼ inches.)

A Peep at St. Paul's. A woodcut. (8¾-12 inches.)

A Peep at St. Paul's, and the 'Times' Office from Under-**ground.** Woodcut from the *Graphic*, May 15, 1875. (9-8 inches.)

West Views and Elevations.

Ecclesiæ Cathedralis Sti. Pauli ab Occidente, Descriptio Orthographica. The sheet containing the upper half only. (27½-21 inches.)

The Front, or West End, of the Cathedral Church of St. Paul's. Published in the first yeare of Our Soveraign Lady Queen Ann, 1702. Wm. EMMETT, fecit. Sold by T. BOWLES. (18-25 inches.)

The Front, or West End, of the Cathedral Church of St. Paul's. (The same plate as above, but the inscription has an additional line in French.)

The West Prospect of the Cathedral Church of St. Paul's. Sold by Carington BOWLES, St. Paul's Church Yard. (18-24 inches.)

The West Prospect of the Cathedral Church of St. Paul's. SCHWERT, delin.; R. PARR, sculp. Printed for R. SAYER. (13¾-19¼ inches.)

The West Prospect, etc. Same plate as above. Republished by LAURIE and WHITTLE, 1794.

The Front, or West End, of St. Paul's. T. BOWLES, sculp. Printed for R. WILKINSON. (11¼-12¾ inches.)

The Front, or West End, of St. Paul's. Same plate as above, coloured, but has publication line erased.

The West Prospect of St. Paul's. John KING, del. Coloured. (12-15 inches.)

A Geometrical Elevation of the West-end of St. Paul's Cathedral. J. PASS, del. et sculp., 1799. (7¾-10¼ inches.)

The West Prospect of St. Paul's Church. French and Latin inscriptions beneath. Printed for T. SMITH. (8¾ 10¼ inches.)

Wester-front, of gevel de Nieuwe Hoofdkerk van S. Paulus. Pet. SCHENK exc., Amsteld. (8½-10¼ inches.)

Elevation du Portail de la Cathédrale de St. Paul. With three lines of description in French. (8-13¾ inches.)

The West Prospect of St. Paul's Church. Co. CAMPBELL, delin. From the *Vitruvius Britannicus.* (9½-13¼ inches.)

Elevation of the West Front of St. Paul's Cathedral, according to the former Design for the Towers. (14-12¼ inches.)

St. Paul's Cathedral. Showing the proposed improvements in front. By W. BARBER, 1850. Lithograph. (15¾-14 inches.)

Front of St. Paul's. Published by C. TAYLOR, 1795. (5½-5¾ inches.)

Front of St. Paul's. Same plate as above, with slight variation in shading. (6¼-8 inches.)

The West End of St. Paul's. (4½-6¾ inches.)

St. Paul's Cathedral, from Ludgate Hill. T. H. SHEPHERD, del.; REDAWAY, sculp. From *Mighty London.* (8-10½ inches.)

Front of St. Paul's at London. (5-7½ inches.)

St. Paul's Cathedral. (2¾-4 inches.)

St. Paul's Cathedral. RAWLE, delt.; REEVE, sculp., 1804. (8¾-7 inches.)

St. Paul's. An outline engraving, in circle. (4 inches.)

St. Paul's Cathedral, the Western Front. Drawn by J. ARCHER, engraved by B. WINKLES. From WINKLES' *Cathedrals,* 1835. (6-8 inches.)

North Views and Elevations.

The North Prospect of the Cathedral Church of St. Paul's. Printed for the Proprietor, Carington BOWLES. (27½-19½ inches.)

Ecclesiæ Cathedralis Sti. Pauli a Septentrione descriptio Orthographica. Ex Autographo Architecti. (27¾-20 inches.)

The North Prospect of St. Paul's. J. KING, ex. (15-12 inches.)

North Elevation of the Cathedral Church of St. Paul. Dedicated to Bp. Howley, and the Dean and Chapter of St. Paul's. By G. GLADWIN, 1828. (27-19 inches.)

North Elevation of St. Paul's Cathedral. From an engraving by GLADWIN. Published in 1828. From the *Builder*, January 2, 1892. (15¾-11¼ inches.)

S. Paul's. Drawn by the Editor. From Cathedrals of England and Wales, No. 13, published in the *Builder*, January 2, 1892. (11¼-13¼ inches.)

North-West and South-West Views and Elevations.

The North-West Prospect of the Cathedral Church of St. Paul's. A. d'PULLER, fecit. Printed for I. SMITH, in Exeter Exchange. (34½-22 inches.)

North West Prospect of St. Paul's Cathedral. Margin cut. (17¼-22¾ inches.)

St. Paul's. North West View. H. HULSBERGH, sculp. On title of *Views of all the Cathedrals in England and Wales*. J. SMITH, 1719. (Size of view, 7¾-5 inches.)

The North West Prospect of the Cathedral Church of St. Paul's. J. HARRIS, fecit. (7¼-5¾ inches.)

North-West View of St. Paul's Cathedral. Engraved by J. JACKSON, after a drawing by W. B. CLARKE. Woodcut. (6-5½ inches.)

'London.' Giving a N.W. View of St. Paul's, from a series of views of the Cathedrals. Arms of Bishop and Dean beneath. A. VERE, fecit. (5-5½ inches.)

St. Paul's. N.W. view. Engraved for the *Pocket Magazine*. (6¾-4½ inches.)

Perspective View of St. Paul's Cathedral; also of Westminster Abbey and St. Margaret's Church. Engraved for the *Complete English Traveller*. (15¼-7½ inches.)

View of St. Paul's Cathedral. Pubᵈ by Alexʳ HOGG, 16, Paternoster Row. (10-7 inches.)

View of St. Paul's Cathedral. Engraved for *England Display'd*. (10-7 inches.)

The North West Prospect of the Cathedral Church of St. Paul. Eight lines of description beneath. (8½-7 inches.)

St. Paul's Cathedral, N.W. Drawn and etched by J. C. BUCKLER, 1820. (12-9 inches.)

A North West View of St. Paul's Cathedral. T. M. MÜLLER, sculp. Published 1763; republished 1823, by R. H. LAURIE. (16-10¼ inches.)

The North West Prospect of S. Paul's Cathedral. POILLY, sculp. Paris, Rue St. Jacques. Apparently a S.W. View, but really a 'reverse.' (17-11½ inches.)

Vue de la Cathédrale de St. Paul. A Paris, chez BASSET. A similar plate to the above. (17-11¾ inches.)

North West View of the Cathedral Church of Saint Paul. Drawn and etched by J. BUCKLER, engraved by G. LEWIS, 1814. (26½-20¼ inches.)

North West View. By BUCKLER. Similar to the above, but coloured.

North West View. By BUCKLER. The outline etching.

St. Paul's. N.W. View. From a tradesman's advertisement. A woodcut, 1880. (6-4¼ inches.)

West View of St. Paul's (really a N.W. View). A. P. MOORE, del.; F. C. LEWIS, sculp., 1806. (8¼-7¼ inches.)

La Cathedrale de St. Paul. N.W. View. A French print. No engraver's name. (11½-10½ inches.)

St. Paul's Cathedral Church. A N.W. View, showing the Churchyard without railings. Inscription in English and French. Drawn and engraved by G. GLADWIN, 1835. (18-13½ inches.)

South-West Views of S. Paul's Cathedral.

S. West View of St. Paul's Cathedral. H. S. STORER, del. et sc., 1817. From STORER'S *Cathedrals.* (5-7¼ inches.)

The South West Prospect of St. Paul's Cathedral. H. TERASSON, fecit. Printed and sold by J. BOWLES at the Black Horse in Cornhill, and Tho. BOWLES, next to the Chapter House. (23¼-17½ inches.)

The South West Prospect of St. Paul's Cathedral. The same plate as above, but published by Carington BOWLES, 69, St. Paul's Churchyard.

Side View of St. Paul's. Published by C. TAYLOR, 1795. (6-7¾ inches.)

St. Paul's. Outline, drawn and engraved by J. CONEY. Published for the *Architectural Series of London Churches* by J. BOOTH, 1818. (13¾-10½ inches.)

Eglise de St. Paul. BAUGEON (? sculp.). S.W. View. (6¼-4 inches.)

St. Paul's Cathedral. S.W. View, about 1770. (5-3 inches.)

St. Paul's. S.W. View, with circular top. A tinted lithograph. (11½-9 inches.)

St. Paul's Cathedral, South West View. Drawn and engraved by J. CONEY, 1811. From DUGDALE'S *S. Paul's,* third edition. (17½-13¾ inches.)

St. Paul's Cathedral, 1842. S.W. View. C. W. RADCLYFFE, del. et lith. (8¾-12½ inches.)

St. Paul's Cathedral. S.W. View. Drawn by S. READ. Woodcut from the *Illustrated London News,* January 20, 1883. (19¾-13½ inches.)

East Views and Elevations.

St. Paul's, the East Prospect. Wm. EMMITT, fecit. ; J. SIMON sculpt. (18¼-24 inches.)

The **East Prospect** of the Cathedral Church of St. Paul's. T. PLATT, sculp. **Sold** by Thomas BOWLES. **Top of plate is cut.** (18-22¼ inches.)

The **East Prospect,** etc. **Same plate as above,** but sold (in addition) by John BOWLES, at the Black Horse in Cornhill. (18-24 inches.)

The **East** Prospect, etc. **Same** plate as above, but republished by Carington BOWLES.

The East Prospect of the **Cathedral of St. Paul's.** SCHWERT, delin. ; R. PARR, sculp. **Printed by Robt.** SAYER at the Golden Buck. (14¼-19½ inches.)

The **East Prospect,** etc. Same plate as above, republished 1794 by LAURIE & WHITTLE.

The **East Prospect** of St. Paul's. J. KING, ex. (Coloured.) (11¾-15 inches.)

The **East Prospect** of St. Paul's Church. Inscriptions in French and Latin at bottom. Printed **for** J. SMITH, 1720. (8¾-10¼ inches.)

De Ooster-gevel van de Nieuwe Hoofdkerk van S. Paulus. Pet. SCHENK, Amsteld. (8½-10½ inches.)

Orthographia **Basilicæ** D. Pauli ad Orientem. (13-14¾ inches.)

The East-end of St. Paul's. (4½-6¼ inches.)

South Views and Elevations.

St. Paul's. **Inscription** on ribbon above Dome, which is very incorrectly drawn. A curious view, evidently taken soon after the erection of the Cathedral. (7¾-5½ inches.)

St. Paul's. A **view** very similar to **the above,** but has foreground with figures, and inscription is **at bottom.** (7½-6½ inches.)

St. Paul's. S. View. Woodcut from a pamphlet, 'Appeal for the Completion of St. Paul's.'

The South Prospect of yᵉ Cathedral of St. Paul's. 'The Foundation of this noble Structure began to be layd in yᵉ Year 1670, and was continued wᵗʰ all Dilligence, and now published in the First year of Our Soveraine Lady Queen Anne, 1702. Will. EMMETT, fecit. (26¾-17¾ inches.)

The South Prospect of the Cathedral of St. Paul's. SCHWERT, delin. ; R. PARR, sculp. Published 1794 by LAURIE & WHITTLE. (19¾-13¼ inches.)

The South Prospect of St. Paul's. J. KING, ex.; J. HARRIS, delin. et sculp. (14¾-11¾ inches.)

The South Prospect, etc. Same plate as above, but coloured.

Side Elevation of St. Paul's. (10-7¼ inches.)

The South Prospect of St. Paul's Church. With inscription in French and Latin at bottom. Printed for J. SMITH, 1720. (11¾-8¾ inches.)

L'Eglise de St. Paul. Apparently the same plate as above, but published in Amsterdam, without the English inscription or date.

Hoofdkerk van S. Paulus. Pet. Schenk, exc., Amst. A plate very similar to the above, but has inscriptions in Dutch and Latin, and a Latin dedication to Segismund, King of Poland. (12-8½ inches.)

South-East and North-East Views.

St. Paul's Cathedral from the South East. Engᵈ by WARREN from a drawing by GYFFORD, 1808. (4½-7½ inches.)

St. Paul's Cathedral from the N.E. Showing the scaffolding during the rebuilding in the year 1695. Sutton NICHOLLS, delin. et sculp. This is a reprint. (13-8½ inches.)

St. Paul's Cathedral. A N.E. View, about 1830. (6¾-4¼ inches.)

St. Paul's Cathedral, North Eastern View. Drawn by Hablot Browne, engraved by B. WINKLES. From WINKLES' *Cathedrals.* 1835. (7¼-6 inches.)

St. Paul's Cathedral. N.E. View. G. ADCOCK, sculp., 1828. (7½-5¼ inches.)

St. Paul's Cathedral, South Side from Cannon St. (Really S.E. side.) LAMBERT, delin. et sculp. (10-7½ inches.)

St. Paul's Cathedral. N.E. view. Beneath are views from the South, and of the Choir A woodcut. (5-8¾ inches.)

St. Paul's Cathedral Church. Perspective View of the N. and E. Sides. J. ELMES, delin. ; J. le KEUX, sculp., 1811. From *Fine Arts of the English School.* (13-11¼ inches.)

Dome de la Cathèdrale de St. Paul. Dessiné et lith. par Julus ARNOUT. Imp. Lemercier, à Paris. A N.E. View. (15½-12¼ inches.)

Dome de la Cathèdrale de St. Paul. Same lithograph as above, but coloured.

The South East Prospect of the Cathedral Church of St. Paul's. B. LENS, delineavit ; J. HARRIS, sculpsit. (26-17¾ inches.)

South East Prospect of the Cathedral Church of St. Paul. Dedicated to Joseph, Lord Bishop of Bristol and Dean of St. Paul's, by P. FOURDRINIER. (36½-23½ inches.)

South East Prospect, etc. Same plate as above, but printed for BOWLES and CARVER, 69, St. Paul's Church Yard.

Saint Paul's Cathedral, South East View. In colours. **No** engraver's **name.** About 1830. (21-17 inches.)

St. Paul's, January 18, **1881.** From the corner of Cheapside, representing a snow scene. A chromo-lithograph from *Household Words,* 1883. (6¼-8½ inches.)

East End of St. Paul's. Actually a N.E. view. A proof engraving. (5½-8 inches.)

St. Paul's Cathedral from Watling Street. A woodcut. (3-5¾ inches.)

East End of St. Paul's Cathedral. A N.E. View. Engraved by J. STORER, 1817. From STORER's *Cathedrals.* (5¼-7 inches.)

The New Post Office Savings Bank. Showing S. Paul's from St. Martin's-le-Grand. Lithograph from CASSELL's *London.* (7¾-6½ inches.)

St Paul's from St. Martin's-le-Grand. Drawn by T. GIRTIN, engraved by J. BAILY. Published 1815 by J. GIRTIN. (15¾-21¾ inches.)

St. Paul's from Cheapside. View about 1790. No engraver's name. (7¼-6½ inches.)

General Post Office. View of S. Paul's from **St.** Martin's-le-Grand. W. SIMPSON, del. ; T. PICKEN, lith., 1852. (16-12½ inches.)

The Post Office and St. Paul's, from St. Martin's-le-Grand. Drawn by C. STANFIELD ; engraved by G. COOKE, 1833. From COOKE's *Views of London.* (10-7 inches.)

The Post Office, St. Paul's Cathedral, and Bull and Mouth Inn. Engraved by G. J. EMBLEM, from a drawing by T. ALLOM. *Stationers' Almanack,* 1834. (18¾-10½ inches.)

Views from the River, Etc.

St. Paul's. Showing part of Blackfriars Bridge. Published 1811 by W. DARTON, jun. (5-3½ inches.)

View of London from Waterloo Bridge. Drawn by H. WEST ; engraved by J. SHURY, 1832 (7¼-5 inches.)

London from Blackfriars Bridge. Drawn by CAMPION ; engraved by J. ROGERS (1831). (8-5 inches.)

Black Friars Bridge. From T. MALTON's *Views of London*, 1797. (14½-10¾ inches.)

View of Blackfriars Bridge and St. Paul's, from the Patent Shot Manufactory. Drawn and etched by D. TURNER; aquatinted by SUTHERLAND. Published 1803 by LAURIE and WHITTLE. (16¼-11½ inches.)

St. Paul's Cathedral from Southwark Bridge. Lithograph, printed by G. J. Cox, Royal Polytechnic. (8½-5¼ inches.)

St. Paul's from Southwark Bridge. Same Plate as above, with slight variation in inscription, and without tinted ground.

View of Black Friars Bridge. DAYES, del'; TAGG, sculp', 1796. From HUNTER'S *London*. (10½-7½ inches.)

St. Paul's, Blackfriars Bridge, etc. A coloured aquatint, margin cut. (14¾-10 inches.)

St. Paul's, from the River. Etching by David LAW, signed proof. (18-14 inches.)

St. Paul's Cathedral. View from the River. Etching by I. GAUTIER. (9½-13 inches.)

View of Blackfriars Bridge and St. Paul's Cathedral. A coloured aquatint, margin cut. (24½-16½ inches.)

St. Paul's, with Lord Mayor's Procession by water. A woodcut. Circular. (8 inches.)

St. Paul's, from Southwark Bridge. A photograph. (10¾-8¾ inches.)

The Fire at the City Flour-Mills in Upper Thames Street. A woodcut from the *Illustrated London News*, Nov. 16, 1872. (9½-5½ inches.)

St. Paul's, etc. Emblematic figures of Time and History in the foreground. Frontispiece to an old *Traveller*. (7½-11½ inches.)

St. Paul's from Bankside. W. TOMBLESON, del'. From TOMBLESON's *Views of the Thames*. (8¾-7 inches.)

St. Paul's Cathedral. View of the Southern Front from Southwark Bridge. Drawn by H. BROWNE; engraved by B. WINKLES. From WINKLES' *Cathedrals*, 1835. (6-8 inches.)

St. Paul's, from the Shot Tower. Woodcut, from CASSELL'S *Picturesque Europe.* (6½-7 inches.)

St. Paul's, the View taken from Bank Side. Engraved by RADCLYFFE from a drawing by J. P. NEALE for the *Beauties of England and Wales,* 1815. (6¾-4¾ inches.)

St. Paul's, from Bank Side. Original drawing by J. P. NEALE, 1815. (10-7 inches.)

St. Paul's, etc. With emblematic representation of Commerce and Plenty. Title to a book. R. CORBOULD, del. (7¾-5 inches.)

St. Paul's, from Southwark. In the foreground is a figure in Civic costume. Published by W. MILLER, 1805. (10½-14 inches.)

St. Paul's, from the River. G. GEYANAUD, 1882, from an illustrated paper. (6-9 inches.)

Churches in the City of London. With S. Paul's in the centre. A woodcut. (10½-6¾ inches.)

View of the Observatory erected above the Cross of St. Paul's, from which a Panoramic View of London and its Environs was executed by Mr. T. HORNER. S. RAWLE, sc.ᵗ. (7-10 inches.)

View of the Observatory, etc., 1821. (5¾-9¼ inches.)

Sectional View of the Observatory. (5¼-8½ inches.)

Malton's six Views of the Exterior of St. Paul's; comprising St. Paul's from Ludgate Hill, South Front, West Front, St. Paul's from Cheapside, North-West View, and North Front. Published 1798 by T. MALTON. (Each about 11-15 inches.)

A Parallel of some of the principal Towers and Steeples built by Sir Christopher WREN. Woodcut, from KNIGHT's *Old England.* (7½-5½ inches.)

Tribute to the Memory of Sir Christopher WREN. Comparison of all the buildings erected by him. Drawn by C. R. COCKERELL. (11-8¾ inches.)

INTERIOR VIEWS, ETC.

Plans.

The Foundation, or Ground-plot of St. Paul's Church. Sold by Tho. BOWLES in St. Paul's Church-yard. (16-27¾ inches.)

Plan of the Cathedral of St. Paul's. Dedicated to Sir Robt. Ladbroke, Lord Mayor. SCHWERT, delin.; R. PARR, sculp. (12¾-19¼ inches.)

Plan of the Cathedral Church of St. Paul, with the Vestiges of the Vaults and Peristyle of the Dome. With plan of the High Altar, as designed by WREN. H. HULSBERGH, sculp. (21-29½ inches.)

Plan of St. Paul's, accurately measured from the Building. J. GWYN, delin.; J. GREEN, sculp. Published 1801. In 2 sheets. (Together, 28-51 inches.)

Ichnographic Plan of St. Paul's Cathedral. (11¼-7¾ inches.)

Ground Plan of St. Paul's Cathedral, 1818. Engraved from actual admeasurements by J. CONEY. From DUGDALE's *S. Paul's,* 3rd edition. (9½-14 inches.)

Platte-grond van de Nieuwe Hoofdkerck van S. Paulus. Inscriptions in Dutch and Latin. Pet. SCHENK, Amsteld. (11¾-8½ inches.)

Ground Plan of St. Paul's Cathedral, showing the proposed Increase of Street Accommodation. By W BARBER. (17-12¼ inches.)

St. Paul's Cathedral. Ground-plan, with list of monuments, etc. By J. CLEGHORN, 1836. (6½-10 inches.)

St. Paul's Cathedral Church. Plan of the Basement or Sub-structure. R. ROFFE, sculp. From *Fine Arts of the English School*, 1809. (15¾-10 inches.)

Ground Plan of St. Paul's Cathedral, showing the Basement Story, as also the Groining of the Roofs. By J. CONEY, for the *Architectural Series of London Churches*, 1818. (10½-13½ inches.)

Ground Plan of St. Paul's Cathedral, etc. Same plate as preceding, but a proof on India paper.

St. Paul's Cathedral, Ground Plan. From the *Builder*, Jan. 2nd, 1892. (16-10 inches.)

Ground Plan of Choir, divided centrally by a line running E. and W. The plan S. of the line showing the arrangement of the Choir fittings till 1859; the plan N. of the line showing the arrangement of the Choir fittings from 1859 to 1870. Drawn by C. H. LÖHR. (20-14½ inches.)

Sections.

A Section of the Inside of St. Paul's from East to West. Will. EMMETT, fecit, 1703. (27-17½ inches.)

A Section of the Inside of St. Paul's. (24½-17¼ inches.)

Section of St. Paul's Cathedral, decorated agreeably to the original Intention of Sir Christopher WREN. J. GWYN, delineavit: S. WALE, decoravit; E. ROOKER, sculpsit. Published 1755. (25-33¾ inches.)

Section of St. Paul's Cathedral. Same plate as above, republished 1801, by MOORE, Holborn Hill.

Section of the Cross-Isle of St. Paul's Cathedral to the South. S. GRIBELIN, sculps. (16¾-13 inches.)

Section of part of St. Paul's, showing the Circular Staircase, with the Ascent through the Dome, and from thence to the Observatory. Drawn and etched by T. HORNER. (Measurement, inclusive of side pieces, 50-36 inches.)

Section of the Dome, showing the Decorations. Drawing in pen and ink. (18½-23¾ inches.)

An Exact Section of St. Paul's. (10¾-10 inches.)

St. Paul's Cathedral Church, Section of N. Transept and half of Dome and Elevation of S. Transept and half of Dome. Measured and drawn by A. PUGIN; G. GLADWIN, sculp. (6-8 inches.)

Section through the Nave and Aisles of St. Paul's Cathedral, 1810. S. WARE, del.; J. BASIRE, sculp. From the *Archæologia.* (11¾-11 inches.)

Interior Views, looking towards the East.

The South East Prospect of y⁰ Inside of yᵉ Cathedral Church of St. Paul's. Printed for and sold by Carington BOWLES. (26½-18½ inches.)

The Inside of the Cathedrall Church of St. Paul's. No engraver's name, but probably by J. HARRIS. (22-18¼ inches.)

Ecclesiæ Cathedralis Divi Pauli a Porticu Occidentali Aspectus Interior. Delineavit Robertus TREVITT. Dedication to Sir C. Wren, on ornamental panel at left hand upper corner. (36-19¾ inches.)

A Section of the **Cross Isle from** North to South, with a Prospect of the **Choir and Dome.** Really a perspective view. Will. EMMETT, **sculp.** **Sold by** J. Smith at his **Shop in** Exeter Change. (32-24¼ inches.)

The Inside of St. Paul's Cathedral, **from the West End to the Choir.** Published for STOW's *Survey*, 1754. (16¾-11½ inches.)

The Inside of St. Paul's Cathedral, etc. Same **plate as above.** Republished by R. WILKINSON and **BOWLES** and **CARVER.** Coloured.

An Inside View of St. Paul's. MÜLLER, jun., sculp. Published 1794, by LAURIE and WHITTLE. (15¾-10¼ inches.)

An Inside View of St. Paul's. **Same plate as preceding,** but coloured.

St. Paul's Cathedral. E. T. DOLBY, delt. et lith. 'The grating in the floor below the Organ indicates the burial-place of Nelson and Wellington.'

The South East Prospect of the Inside of the Cathedral Church of St. Paul. Description, in fourteen lines, on scroll in upper right hand corner. (8¾-7 inches.)

Interior of St. Paul's Cathedral. Engraved for **Dr.** HUGHSON's *Description of London.* (6½-4½ inches.)

Interior of St. Paul's, looking East. Woodcut, by J. JACKSON, **after a** drawing by W. B. CLARKE. (5¾-8 inches.)

Views of the Choir.

The Inside of the Choir **of** yᵉ Cathedral Church of **St. Paul's.** B. LENS, delineavit ; J. KIP, sculpsit. (24½-19 inches.)

The Choir of St. Paul's Cathedral. BOWLES, sculpt. Published 1754, for STOW's *Survey.* (16¾-11¼ inches.)

Le Chœur de St. Paul. **A French copy of** the preceding, coloured. À **Paris,** chez DAUMONT. (16¾-10¾ inches.)

A View of St. Paul's Choir, from the Altar.   (9½-7¾ inches.)

The Choir of St. Paul's.   With arms of the Dean beneath.
(4¾-5 inches.)

St. Paul's Cathedral. **The Choir.** Three photographs of the
Choir, from the East, from the West, and the Altar.   (Each
4-5½ inches.)

Views taken from beneath the Dome, etc.

Interior of St. Paul's. Engraved by HOBSON from a drawing by
J. P. **NEALE** for the *Beauties of England and Wales*, 1816.
(5-7½ inches).

Interior View of the Cathedral Church of St. Paul. Drawn and
engraved by J. CONEY. Dedicated to Dean Van Mildert.
(20¼-26½ inches.)

St. Paul's Cathedral. PUGIN and **ROWLANDSON**, delin. et sculp.
From ACKERMANN'S *Microcosm*, 1809, coloured. (9-11¼ inches.)

St. Paul's Cathedral. Showing part of the N. Aisle.   **Water**-
colour drawing, probably by NASH.   (7-9 inches.)

St. Paul's Cathedral. The Whispering Gallery. Drawn by R.
W. BILLINGS; engraved by E. CHALLIS, **1837.**   (4¾-8 inches.)

Interior of St. Paul's from under the Dome. Woodcut, engraved
by J. JACKSON, after a drawing by W. B. COOKE.   (6-8¼ inches.)

Interior of the Dome of St. Paul's Cathedral. Drawn and engraved
by J. CONEY. From **DUGDALE'S** *St. Pauls*, **3rd** edition, 1817.
(9½-14 inches.)

St. Paul's Cathedral. Interior of the Dome, looking towards
the N. Transept. Drawn by H. GARLAND; engraved by W.
WOOLNOTH. From WINKLES' *Cathedrals*, 1835. (5⅞-8¼ inches.)

St. Paul's. Interior of the Dome. An unfinished etching.
(8¾-12 inches.)

Interior of St. Paul's. View taken from the N. Entrance, looking
towards the S. and W. Doors. Drawn by J. CONEY; engraved
by J. SKELTON for the *Architectural Series of London Churches,*
1818.   (10½-13½ inches.)

A Curious Perspective View of the Inside of St. Paul's Cathedral. Printed for R. WILKINSON and BOWLES and CARVER.
(16¾-11¼ inches.)

A Curious Perspective View, etc. Same plate as the preceding;
republished 1794 by LAURIE and WHITTLE.

Suggested Alteration of Segmental Arches, St. Paul's Cathedral. By R. T. CONDER. Woodcut from the *Architect*, July
28, **1883.** (7-10½ inches.)

Views showing the Aisles, Side Chapels, etc.

St. Paul's Cathedral. Three Interior Views by T. MALTON, 1797. View from the West Entrance, Transept from the N. Entrance, and Interior of the Dome. (Each 10-15 inches.)

St. Paul's Cathedral, the Nave and Choir. Drawn by Hablot BROWNE; engraved by W DEEBLE. From WINKLES' *Cathedrals,* **1835.** (5¾-8 inches.)

Inside of St. Paul's Cathedral. Published by C. TAYLOR, 1796. (6-7½ inches.)

The North East View of the Nave of the Cathedral Church of St. Paul From the *Gentleman's Magazine,* 1749. (4½-7¾ inches.)

Interior of the Cathedral Church of St. Paul, with a Representation of the Procession of the Installation of Dr. SUMNER to the Deanery of St. Paul's. Painted by J. HARWOOD; engraved by W. WOOLNOTH, 1824. (23¾-18½ inches.)

Interior of the Cathedral Church of St. Paul. The same plate as the preceding, but an unfinished etching before the lettering or the shield of arms.

A View of the Isle at the Entrance of the North Portico of the Cathedral Church of St. Paul. Delineavit Robertus TREVITT, permissu D. Christophori Wren. (12¼-14¾ inches.)

A View of the Isle, etc. The same plate as the preceding, but coloured.

A View to the Morning Chapel in the Cathedral Church of St. Paul. Robt. TREVITT, delineavit. (10-14½ inches.)

A View to the Morning Chapel, etc. The same plate as the preceding, but coloured.

Cathèdrale de St. Paul (Bas-côté). The Dean's Aisle. Showing the iron gate leading into the Choir. Dessiné et lith. par J. ARNOUT. (10½-15½ inches.)

The Morning Chapel, from the West. A photograph. (4-5½ inches.)

The Morning Chapel, from the East. A photograph. (2¼-3½ inches.)

The Model Room, St. Paul's Cathedral. A woodcut from the *Illustrated London News,* **1852.** (6-4¼ inches.)

The Library, looking East. A photograph. (8-6 inches).

The Library, looking North. A photograph. (8-6 inches.)

St. Paul's Cathedral. Staircase in S.W. Tower, leading to Library. Drawn by R. Stephen AYLING. From the *Builder,* January 2, 1892. (14¾-11¼ inches.)

The Crypt.

The Crypt of St. Paul's. 'Artists' Corner.' A woodcut. (10½-6¾ inches.)

The Artists' Corner in the Crypt of St. Paul's : The Grave of LANDSEER. A woodcut. (8½-6 inches.)

New Chapel for Early Morning Service in the Crypt of St. Paul's Cathedral. A woodcut from the *Graphic*, 16th June, 1877. (8¾-6 inches.)

Sir Christopher Wren's Monument in the Crypt of St. Paul's Cathedral. Drawn and engraved by J. CONEY, 1817. From DUGDALE'S *St. Paul's*, 3rd edition. (14-9¾ inches.)

Tomb of Sir Christopher Wren. A woodcut from KNIGHT'S *Old England*. (3½-2¼ inches.)

The Wellington Chapel, Crypt of St. Paul's Cathedral. A lithograph, published by STANDIDGE and Co. (8½-7 inches.)

The Wellington Tomb in the Crypt of St. Paul's Cathedral. A woodcut. (9¼-6 inches.)

Nelson's Tomb, Crypt of Saint Paul's. Drawn by T. H. SHEPHERD. From *London Interiors.* (7½-10¼ inches.)

View in the Crypt, St. Paul's Cathedral. Showing Nelson's tomb. Engraved by J. STORER, 1817, from STORER'S *Cathedrals.* (7-5¼ inches.)

Sarcophagus, under which the body of Lord Nelson is enclosed, in the Crypt of St. Paul's Cathedral. Etching by J. CONEY, 1817, from DUGDALE'S *St. Paul's*, 3rd edition. (9½-14 inches.)
 (In the Crypt. The sarcophagus, of painted alabaster, is the work of TORREGIANO, and was removed from the Wolsey Chapel at Windsor to S. Paul's. Cardinal Wolsey had intended it for his own monument. See Milman's *Annals*, second edition, p. 485.)

East End of the North Crypt of St. Paul's, dedicated to St. Faith. With effigy of Dr. DONNE, etc. ; by MALCOLM, from the *Gentleman's Magazine*, 1820. (6-6¼ inches.)

The Crypt of St. Paul's Cathedral. Professor Donaldson's proposed Improvement. A woodcut. (9¼-5 inches.)

Furniture and Decorations.

The Marble **Pulpit,** St. Paul's Cathedral. A woodcut. (4¾-7½ inches.)

St. Paul's Cathedral. Specimens of the Ironwork. By R. P. WHELLOCK. A woodcut. (10½-6 inches.)

The Organ in the Choir of St. Paul's, as now arranged. Drawn by R. P. WHELLOCK. A woodcut. (6¾-10¾ inches.)

Details of Organ. By R. P. WHELLOCK. A woodcut. (6½-10¼ inches.)

New Chalice for St. Paul's Cathedral, presented by Dr. W. S. SIMPSON. A woodcut. (4½-7½ inches.)

New Paten for St. Paul's Cathedral, presented by Dr. W. S. SIMPSON. A woodcut. (Circular, 5¼ inches.)

The New Altar **Frontal**, St. Paul's Cathedral, designed by Mr. John MEDLAND. **Illustration from** the *Builder*, July 7, 1888. (13-11½ inches.)

The Reredos. A proposed design giving one **story** only. A water-colour drawing. (9¼-14½ inches.)

The New Reredos, St. Paul's Cathedral. Reprinted from the *Builder*, January 28, 1888. (11¼-15 inches.)

The New Reredos and High **Altar**, St. Paul's Cathedral. From the *Building News*, January 27, 1888. (10½-14½ inches.)

The New Reredos at St. Paul's Cathedral. From the *Illustrated London News*, March 31, 1888. (9¼-12½ inches.)

The New **Altar and Reredos** at St. Paul's Cathedral. From a painting by H. W. BREWER. Woodcut from the *Graphic*, Jan. 28, 1888. (8-12 inches.)

Proposed Decorations. Interior of the Dome; one segment. A photograph. (7½-11¾ **inches.**)

Proposed Decorations. The Apse and Marble Pavement. A photograph. (9-11¼ inches.)

Proposed Decorations. Niche at N. of Apse, etc. A photograph. (4½-10½ inches.)

Proposed Decorations. The Apse. Two photographs. (Each 7¼-11½ inches.)

St. Paul's Cathedral. Gates in N. Aisle. A photograph. (6-8 inches.)

St. Paul's Cathedral. Side Gates leading into Choir. A photograph. (6-8 inches.)

St. Paul's **Cathedral.** Oak Screen at back of South Row of Stalls. Lithograph, 1877. (28-20 inches.)

Three plates of Details of the above screen. (Each 15-22 inches.)

Oak Screen at back of Choir Stalls. A photograph. (8-6 inches.)

Frescoes in the Dome. By Sir James THORNHILL. Eight scenes in the life of S. Paul, engraved by DU BOSC, VANDER GUCHT, and others. (Each 10-17½ inches.)

Copy of full-sized Cartoon for proposed Mosaic Decoration of the Dome. Designed by E. J. POYNTER; the Central Circular Compartment by Sir Frederick LEIGHTON. A chromo-lithograph from the *Builder*, July 5, 1884. (12½-16 inches.)

Decoration for the Dome. The Upper Circular Panel, 'Christ in Judgment,' designed by E. J. POYNTER. From the *Builder*, July 5, 1884. (7-7 inches.)

Decoration for the Dome. The Lower Circular Panel, 'The Resurrection,' designed by Sir Frederick LEIGHTON. From the *Builder*, July 5, 1884. (7-7 inches.)

The Bells.

Great Paul, the New Bell for St. Paul's Cathedral. Five woodcuts from the *Graphic*, May 20, 1882, viz.: Leaving Loughborough, Hung in Foundry for experimental swinging, Position for the first testing of tone, Boring for the Clapper-bolt from the inside, and Boring for the Clapper-bolt from the outside. (9-12¾ inches.)

The Big Bell for St. Paul's, a Rest on the Road, and Arrangements for getting it into the Cathedral. Two woodcuts from the *Illustrated London News*, May 27, 1882. (9-13 inches.)

The Progress of 'Great Paul' from Loughborough to London. Five woodcuts from the *Pictorial World*, 1882. (9-13 inches.)

Testing the Great Bell for St. Paul's Cathedral at Messrs. Taylor and Son's Factory, Loughborough. A woodcut from the *Illustrated London News*, Jan. 14, 1882.

Great Paul's Pilgrimage to St. Paul's Cathedral. Four woodcuts from the *Penny Illustrated Paper*, May 27, 1882. (8-11 inches.)

Great Paul, hung for testing in the Factory. A photograph. (8½-10½ inches.)

Great Paul, on its Trolly. A photograph. (7¼-9¼ inches.)

Great Paul, on the Inclined Plane leading to the W. Door. A photograph. (7¼-9¼ inches.)

Great Paul, on the Road to London. A photograph. (8½-6¾ inches.)

Great Paul, in front of the Doorway, with part removed to effect an entrance for the Bell. A photograph. (9-11¼ inches.)

Raising the Great Bell in the Tower of St. Paul's. Two woodcuts from the *Illustrated London News*, June 3, 1882. (9¼-6 inches.)

Great Paul at St. Paul's Cathedral. Hauling the Bell off the Trolly, and Descending the Inclined Plane. Two woodcuts from the *Graphic*, May 27, 1882. (8¾-8¼ inches.)

The Big Bell for St. Paul's. Procession on the Road to London. A woodcut from the *Illustrated London News*, May 27, 1882. (12¼-4 inches.)

The New Bells and Bell-Cage, St. Paul's Cathedral. A woodcut. B. SLY, del. ; A. BERRY, sc. (6¾-11 inches.)

Pageants before 1800.

Q. Elizabeth's Procession to St. Paul's. A woodcut from KNIGHT's *Old England.* (9-8 inches.)

Procession of James I. to St. Paul's, accompanied by the Prince of Wales and many of the Nobility, on Sunday, March 26, 1620. A woodcut from KNIGHT's *Old England.* (5½-3½ inches.)

A Prospect of the Choir of the Cathedral Church of St. Paul, on the General Thanksgiving the 31st of December, 1706, Her Majesty and both Houses of Parliament present. Long description beneath. Robt. TREVITT, fecit. (39½-24¾ inches.)

The View of the Charity Children in the Strand, upon the vii of July, MDCCXIII., being the day appointed by her late Majesty Queen Anne for a Publick Thanksgiving for the Peace; when both Houses of Parliament made a Solemn Procession to the Cathedral of St. Paul. Descriptions in Latin and English. Hymns on scrolls at two lower corners. G. VERTUE, delin. et sculp., 1715. In 2 sheets. (Together, 50-14¾ inches.)

North Side of the Strand, between Exeter Change and the Maypole, on July 7, 1713, with the assemblage of the Charity Children at the time of the Procession of both Houses of Parliament to St. Paul's Cathedral. From BRAYLEY's *Londiniana.* (15¼-4¼ inches.)

Ticket of Admission for one of the Common Council into the Cathedral Church of St. Paul on Thursday, 23rd of April, 1789, to attend His Majesty on the Solemn Occasion of a Thanksgiving for the Happy Restoration of his Health. COOK, invt. et sculp., 1789. (9½-13¾ inches.)

The Royal Procession in St. Paul's on St. George's Day, 1789, the day appointed for a General Thanksgiving for the King's happy Recovery. View of the Nave. Drawn by E. DAYES; engrav'd by J. NEAGLE. Published by Evans, 1790. (27¼-18½ inches.)

Thanksgiving Visit of George III. to St. Paul's in 1789. Procession up the Nave. A woodcut. (13¼-9½ inches.)

Principal Front of the Bank, showing the Lamps and Transparent Paintings, on the 24th of April, 1789, in consequence of His Majesty's Recovery and Public Visit to St. Paul's. Designed by J. SOANE; P. W. TOMKINS, aquatint, 1790. (29-8 inches.)

Thanksgiving Service for the Recovery of K. George III. View of the Choir. An aquatint. E. DAYES, del.; R. POLLARD, aq. for. (Margin cut.) (25¾-16 inches.)

Thanksgiving Service for the Recovery of K. George III. The same plate as the preceding, but an etching. (25¾-18 inches.)

Their Majesties Procession in St. Paul's, April 23rd, 1789. PRATTENT, sculp. From the *Lady's Magazine.* (6¾-8¼ inches.)

Funeral of Nelson.

Remains of Lord Nelson lying in State in the Painted Chamber at Greenwich Hospital. Engraved by M. MERIGOT from a drawing by C. A. PUGIN; executed during the period of exhibition. (19½-15 inches.)

Funeral Procession of the late Lord Viscount Nelson, from Greenwich to Whitehall, 8th of January, 1806. Engraved by HILL, after PUGIN. (19½-15 inches.)

Funeral Procession of the late Lord Viscount Nelson, from the Admiralty to St. Paul's, 9th of January, 1806. Engraved by MERIGOT, after PUGIN. (19½-15 inches.)

Interment of the Remains of the late Lord Viscount Nelson in the Cathedral of St. Paul, 9th **of January, 1806.** Engraved by LEWIN, after PUGIN. (19½-15 **inches.)**
    The above form a set of four plates, coloured.

An accurate View from **the** House of W. Tunnard, Esq., on the Bankside, on the 8th of January, 1806; when the remains of the great Admiral Lord **Nelson** were brought from Greenwich to Whitehall. A long description beneath. Drawn and etched by **J.** T. SMITH. (18¼-10¾ inches.)

The Funeral Procession of Lord Viscount Nelson, January 9th, 1806. With 6 lines of verse beneath. W. M. CRAIG, del.; E. ORME, excudit; **J.** GODBY, sculpt., 1806, coloured. (17¼-13¼ inches.)

The Ceremony of Lord Nelson's Interment **in St.** Paul's Cathedral, January 9th, 1806. Drawn by W. ORME from a Sketch made on the spot by the Rev. Holt WARING. J. CLARK and **J.** HAMBLE, sculpt. Coloured. (14¾-19 inches.)

An Exact Representation of the Grand Funeral Car, which carried the Remains of Lord **Nelson** to St. Paul's on Thursday, **January** 9th, 1806. Published **by** S. W. FORES. Coloured. **(9¾-10¾** inches.)

Lord Nelson's Coffin, with Description of the Ornaments and Devices thereon. Published by R. ACKERMANN, 1806. Coloured. (16-12½ inches.)

Plan of the Platform and Disposition of the Bannerolls, Trophies, etc., around the Coffin, **at** the Funeral of the much lamented Lord **Nelson.** Published by R. ACKERMANN, 1806. **(10-17** inches.)

Lord Nelson's Funeral Car, Coffin, etc. From the *Lady's Magazine.* (7¼-9 inches.)

The Funeral of Lord Nelson. Showing the procession approaching the W. Door. Published by T KELLY, 1815. (7-9½ inches.)

St. Paul's Cathedral. Monument of Admiral Nelson under

the Dome. Drawn by R. GARLAND; engraved by B. WINKLES. From WINKLES' *Cathedrals*, 1835. (7¾-6¼ inches.)

Sepolcro dell' Ammiraglio Nelson. Questo bassorilievo rappresenta l'Inghilterra la quale con le due altre Provincie viene al porto per ricevere dalla nave il cadavere.

Nel bassorilievo opposto Minerva, Nettuno, e Marte consegnano all' Inghilterra il bambino Nelson.

Nel uno dei lati è l'**Eroe** coronato dalla vittoria nel altro la iscrizione del Parlamento.

Le quattro figure di rilievo simboleggiano le quattro parti del Mondo, e le quattro lapidi son destinate a marcare le rispettive vittorie.

Antonio Canova **invento.** *Bernardino Nocchi dis.* **Pietro** *Fontana incise.*

Monumento ideato 1806, *per collocarsi* **isolato in** *un Tempio rotondo.* (31-25 inches.)

Funeral of Wellington.

Plans and Sections showing the several arrangements made **by** the Commissioners of Her Majesty's Works on the occasion of the *Public Funeral of the late F.M. the Duke of Wellington*, K.G., etc., Nov. 18, 1852.

1. Plan of the Crypt, showing the position of all the Tombs and Graves. (26-19 inches.)
2. General Plan of S. Paul's Churchyard, and Plan of the outworks and barriers.
3. Plan showing the disposition and appropriation of the Waiting and Retiring Rooms.
4. Plans of the Seating and Galleries.
5. Plan, etc., of the Machinery employed at the Horse Guards, and in the Crypt of the Cathedral.
6. Sections of Central Portions of Crypt and elevations of the Machinery.
7. Plan, etc., of the Platform of Western Entrance of S. Paul's, and Machinery connected therewith.

Funeral of **the Duke of Wellington.** Coloured lithograph, showing the grouping round the coffin. (24¼-27¾ inches.)

Funeral of the late Duke of **Wellington** in St. Paul's Cathedral. A woodcut. Supplement to the *Illustrated London News,* Dec. 11, 1852. (20½-30½ inches.)

Wellington's Funeral Car. A woodcut after Sir J. GILBERT. From the *Illustrated London News,* Nov. 27, 1852. (31-21¼ inches.)

Funeral of the Duke of Wellington. The Lying in State at Chelsea Hospital, Nov.; 1852. W. SIMPSON, lith., from a painting by Louis HAGUE. Published by ACKERMANN, 1853. (16-23½ inches.)

Funeral of the Duke of Wellington. The Funeral Car passing the Archway at Apsley House, Nov. 18th, 1852. T. PICKEN, lith. From a painting by Louis HAGUE. Published by ACKERMANN.

Funeral of the Duke of Wellington. The Ceremony in St. Paul's Cathedral, Nov. 18th. W. SIMPSON, lith. From a painting by Louis HAGUE. Published by ACKERMANN.
The three preceding form a set, in colours.

St. Paul's Cathedral during the Interment of the Duke of Wellington, from sketches made on the spot, and lithographed by E. T. DOLBY. (13½-19½ inches.)

The Lying in State at Chelsea Hospital of the Duke of Wellington, from the 11th to 17th Nov. Louis HAGUE, del.; W. SIMPSON, lith. Coloured. (8¼-12½ inches.)

Funeral Car of the Duke of Wellington. Lithograph by DAY and Son, 1852. Coloured. (16-10½ inches.)

The Funeral Car of the Duke of Wellington arriving at St. Paul's Cathedral. E. WALKER, del. et lith. Coloured. (11-8½ inches.)

Arrival of the Funeral Procession of the late Duke of Wellington at St. Paul's. Lithograph, published by BERGER. (17½-7 inches.)

The Interior of St. Paul's Cathedral, prepared for the Funeral of the Duke of Wellington. A woodcut from the *Builder*. (10½-6½ inches.)

The Wellington Monument, St. Paul's Cathedral. A woodcut, from a drawing by R. P. WHELLOCK. (10¼-15¾ inches.)

The Lying in State of the Duke of Wellington. Plan showing trophies, etc. C. R. COCKERELL, direxit. A lithograph, with list at back. (8½-13 inches.)

Mourners. The Horse and Groom of His Grace the late Duke of Wellington, sketched from the Funeral Procession. A. BUTLER, del. et lith., 1852. (12½-9¾ inches.)

Funeral of the Duke of Wellington. The Procession approaching the W. Door. A lithograph. (4¼-6 inches.)

Duke of Wellington's Funeral. Official Programme. A broadside, printed by T. COOPER. (10½-17 inches.)

Official Programme of the Funeral of the Duke of Wellington. A broad-side, published by authority of the Earl Marshal. With woodcut of the Car at the top. (11-18½ inches.)

CEREMONIES AND FUNERALS.

Procession of the Sheriffs to Westminster on **Monday** last. The Procession passing St. Paul's. **A woodcut. Oct. 6,** 1849. (8¾-6 inches.)

A Psalm of Thanksgiving to be sung by the Children of **Christ's Hospital,** on Monday, Tuesday, and Wednesday in Easter Week, according to ancient Custom, for their Founders and Benefactors. A broad-side, printed by H. KENT, 1768. (16½-21½ inches.)

The Anniversary Meeting of the Charity Children in the Cathedral Church of St. Paul. Drawn and engraved by Robt. HAVELL. Coloured. (14¾-18¼ inches.)

The Annual Meeting of the **Charity Children** in St. Paul's Cathedral. E. PUGH, del. ; J. FITTLER, sc., 1804. (6-9 inches.)

St. Paul's Cathedral. Anniversary Meeting **of the** Children of the Charity Schools of **London.** F. MACKENZIE, del. ; W. H. FUGE, sculp. **(6½-9½ inches.)**

The Charity Children at St. Paul's. **(3¾-5½ inches.)**

St. Paul's Cathedral. Meeting of the Charity Children. **G. R.** ROBERTS, pinx. ; **A. H.** PAYNE, sculp. (7¼-10¼ inches.)

The First Evening Service at St. Paul's Cathedral **on Advent** Sunday, Dec. 11, 1858. A woodcut. (9½-7½ inches.)

The Interior of St. **Paul's** Cathedral during the **Service of last** Sunday evening. **A woodcut.** (9¼-13½ inches.)

The Queen's Procession to St. Paul's, Nov. **29, 1820.** Published by T. KELLY, 1821. (5-8½ inches.)

Marriage of Miss Helen Church to the Rev. Francis Paget, at St. Paul's Cathedral, on Wednesday, the 28th ult. A woodcut. From the *Pictorial World*, April 14, **1883.** (9¼-13¼ inches.)

Bach's 'Passion' Music at St. **Paul's** Cathedral. A woodcut. (12-9 inches.)

Apotheosis of Handel. From an original picture by HUDSON in the possession of Dr. **Arnold.** Margin cut. (9-14 inches.)

Plan, showing the Route to be taken by Her Majesty on proceeding in State to St. Paul's, on Tuesday, 27th February, 1872, to offer Thanks for the Recovery of H.R.H. the Prince of Wales. (34-16 inches.)

Thanksgiving Service, 1872. **Large** Scale Plan **of** the Neighbourhood of S. Paul's. From **the** *Ordnance Survey.* (38-26 inches.)

St. Paul's Cathedral. Plan showing the Corridors and Staircases in the Interior of the Cathedral and **the** Arrangement **of** the wooden Structures **and covered** Footways **outside on the Occa-**sion of the Thanksgiving for the Recovery **of the Prince of** Wales, Feb. 27, 1872. (37½-24 inches.)

Ditto.   Gallery Plan, **showing the arrangements for Seating.** (37½-24 inches.)

Ditto.   Ground Plan.   (37½-24 inches.)

Thanksgiving Service, 1872. Facsimiles of Admission Cards, showing to whom allotted.   On **3** sheets.   (Each 37½-24¾ inches.)

Thanksgiving Day. Sketch from Fleet Street, looking up Ludgate Hill.   Woodcut from the *Graphic*, March 6, 1872. (8¾-11¾ inches.)

Thanksgiving Day. Triumphal Arch at Ludgate Circus. **Wood-**cut from the *Illustrated London News*, March **2, 1872.** (13¼-9¾ inches.)

Thanksgiving Day. The Procession passing St. Martin's Church. Woodcut from **the** *Illustrated London News*, March **9,** 1872. (12¼-8¼ inches.)

Thanksgiving Day. The Great Stand on the Site of the Law Courts.   Woodcut from **the** *Illustrated London News*, March **9, 1872.** (12¼-8½ inches.)

Thanksgiving Day. Triumphal Arch in Regent Circus, Oxford Street.   Woodcut from the *Illustrated London News*, March 9, 1872.   (12-8½ inches.)

Thanksgiving Day. Temple Bar decorated.   Woodcut from the *Illustrated London News*, March **9,** 1872.   (8½-12¼ inches.)

Thanksgiving Day. The Procession passing up Ludgate Hill. Woodcut from the *Illustrated London News*, March 9, 1872. (19¼-12¼ inches.)

Funeral of Lord Napier of Magdala.   The Procession leaving the Tower of London.   Woodcut from the *Illustrated London News*, **Jan.** 25, **1890.**

Funeral of Lord Napier. The Crypt of St. Paul's Cathedral, and the Coffin in the Chapel at the Tower.   Two woodcuts from the *Illustrated London News*, Jan. 25, 1890.   (9¼-3½ inches.)

Funeral of Lord Napier. The Body being removed from the Tower and the Ceremony in St. Paul's Cathedral.   Two woodcuts from the *Graphic*, Jan. 25, 1890.   (9-12½ inches.)

Funeral of Lord Napier. The Procession in the Nave of **St.** Paul's Cathedral.   Woodcut from the *Illustrated London News*, Jan. 25, 1890.   (9¼-12½ inches.)

Lord Rosebery unveiling the Bust of the late Sir J. Macdonald, Premier of Canada, in St. Paul's Cathedral yesterday.   Woodcut from the *Daily Graphic*, Nov. **17,** 1892.   (8-8½ inches.)

Monuments in the Present Cathedral.

Dean Milman. (The recumbent figure by WILLIAMSON, the altar tomb by F. C. PENROSE.) A woodcut. (6¾-6¾ inches.)

Admiral **Earl Howe**, Cuthbert Lord **Collingwood**, Sir Ralph **Abercrombie**, and Sir John **Moore**.
The plate contains also a small Interior of St. Paul's.

Captains **Mosse** and **Riou**. Drawn and engraved by S. RAWLE. Frontispiece to the *European Magazine*, vol. **49**. (4½-7 inches.)

Captain **Richard** Rundell **Burgess**. Frontispiece to the *European Magazine*, vol. **44**. (4¾-7 inches.)

Captain **Richard Rundell Burgess**. Published by J. WILLIAMS, 1828. (5¾-9 inches.)

Charles Robert **Cockerell**. A photograph. (4¼-6¼ inches.)

Captain Robert **Faulknor**. From the *Naval Chronicle*, vol. 16. (5¼-8¼ inches.)

Sir Joshua **Reynolds**. Published by J. WILLIAMS, 1828. (5-7¾ inches.)

Captain George **Duff**. From the *Naval Chronicle*, vol. 28. (5¼-8¾ inches.)

Admiral Earl **Howe**. From the *Naval Chronicle*, vol. 27. (6-9 inches.)

Admiral Earl **Howe**. Drawn by BURNEY; engraved by S. RAWLE. Frontispiece to the *European Magazine*, vol. 74. (4¾-8¼ inches.)

Lord **Nelson**. Drawn by BURNEY; engraved by S. RAWLE. Frontispiece to the *European Magazine*, vol. 73. (4¾-8¼ inches.)

Dr. Johnson. Engraved by J. BASIRE, from the *European Magazine*, 1796. (4½-8 inches.)

Dr. Johnson. (5½-7¼ inches.)

Captain **Westcott**. From the *Naval Chronicle*, vol. 18. (6-9 inches.)

Sir Ralph **Abercrombie**. Engraved by WOOLNOTH. (7¼-8 inches.)

Sir Ralph **Abercrombie**. (6-4 inches.)

Sir Samuel **Hood**. Drawing in outline by S. Joseph, 1817. (14½-18 inches.)

(The following engravings, numbered 51 to 68, are from Dugdale's *History of S. Paul's*, 3rd edition.)

No.* 51. Dr. Samuel **Johnson**. (John BACON.)
　　　Sir Joshua **Reynolds**. (John FLAXMAN.)
　　　John **Howard**. (John BACON.)
　　　Sir William **Jones**. (John BACON.)

---

* The numbers refer to the plates in Dugdale. Other plates from his *History of S. Paul's* are enumerated above, pages 178 to 181.

52. Captain Richard Rundell **Burgess.**
Captain George N. **Hardinge.** (C. MANNING.)

53. Captain Robert **Faulknor.** (Charles ROSSI.)
Captain R. Willett **Miller.** (John FLAXMAN.)

54. Earl **Howe.** (John FLAXMAN.)
Lord **Collingwood.** (Richard WESTMACOTT.)

55. Lieutenant-General Sir Ralph **Abercromby.** (Richard
WESTMACOTT.)
Lieutenant-General Sir John **Moore.** (John BACON.)

56. Marquis **Cornwallis.** (Charles ROSSI.)
Captain John **Cooke.**

57. Major-General Thomas **Dundas.** (John BACON, junior.)
Major-General J. R. **Mackenzie.** }
Brigadier-General E. **Langwerth.** } (C. MANNING.)

58. Captain George Blagdon **Westcott.** (Thomas BANKS.)
Major-General Robert **Craufurd.** }
Major-General Henry **Mackinnon.** } (J. BACON, junior.)

59. Lord **Rodney.** (Charles ROSSI.)
Captain James Robert **Mosse.** }
Captain Edward **Riou.** } (Charles ROSSI.)

60. Sir Christopher **Wren's** Monument, in the Crypt.

61. Sarcophagus under which **the Body of Lord Nelson** is
enclosed in the Crypt.

62. Viscount **Nelson.** (John FLAXMAN.)
Captain George **Duff.**

63. Sir Isaac **Brock.** (Richard WESTMACOTT.)
Major-General Bernard Foord **Bowes.** (F. L. CHANTREY.)

64. Major-General Daniel **Hoghton.** (F. L. CHANTREY.)
Lieutenant-Colonel Sir William **Myers,** Bart. (J. KEN-
DRICK.)

65. Sir Samuel **Hood.** (S. Joseph.)
Major-General John Gaspard Le **Marchant.** (James
SMITH and Charles ROSSI.)

66. General Sir Thomas **Picton.** (GAHAGAN.)
Major-General Sir William **Ponsonby. (THEED** and
BAYLY.)

67. Major-General Andrew **Hay.** (H. HOPPER.)
Major-General Arthur **Gore.** (William TALLEMACH **and**
F. L. CHANTREY.)
Major-General John Byrn **Skerritt.** (William TALLEMACH
and F. L. CHANTREY.)

68. Colonel Henry **Cadogan.** (F. L. CHANTREY.)
Major-General Robert T. **Ross.** (J. KENDRICK.)

S. Paul's School.

Invitation Ticket, with view of School and portrait of Dean Colet. 'You are desired to meet yᵉ Gentlemen educated at St. Pauls School in the said School, by Nine of the Clock in the Morning on Tuesday, 25th of January, 1725, being the Feast of the Conversion of St. Paul; from thence to go to the Cathedral of St. Paul, and after Sermon to dine at Mercers Hall in Cheap side.' Signed by the Stewards. (8-13 inches.)

Invitation Ticket, 1727. Underneath is added: 'On receipt of this pay Five Shillings.'

S. Paul's School, about 1720. With a portrait of Dean COLET. (7½-6 inches.)

St. Paul's School. B. COLE, sculp. From MAITLAND'S *London.* (9½-7¼ inches.)

View of St. Paul's School. T. WHITE, sculpt. (7½-5 inches.)

St. Paul's School. Drawn and engraved by J. CRAIG for HUGH-SON's *Walks through London,* 1817. (3½-5¾ inches.)

St. Paul's School. Engraved by B. HOWLETT from a drawing by J. BAKER. From WILKINSON'S *Londina Illustrata,* 1825. With letterpress description. Sixteen pages. (12¾-10 inches.)

St. Paul's School and Dean COLET'S House at Stepney. From the *Gentleman's Magazine,* 1818. (5-7½ inches.)

Old St. Paul's School, founded 1509, as it appeared before the Great Fire. Woodcut from KNIGHT'S *Old England.* (2½-2¼ inches.)

St. Paul's School. Drawn and engraved by S. RAWLE. From the *European Magazine,* 1807. (7-4½ inches.)

St. Paul's School and Merchant **Taylor's School.** B. COLE, sculp. From MAITLAND'S *London.* (9-15 inches.)

St. Paul's School. Engraved by OWEN from a drawing by J. P. NEALE, for the *Beauties of England and Wales,* 1814. (8-5¼ inches.)

St. Paul's School. Drawn by T. H. SHEPHERD; engraved by W. DEEBLE, 1827. From *London in the XIXth Century.* (7½-5 inches.)

St. Paul's School. (4¼-3 inches.)

St. Paul's School. East End of St. Paul's Churchyard. A woodcut. (6½-6¼ inches.)

St. Paul's School. Interior of the School Room. E. and W. Views. Two photographs. (Each 5½-3¾ inches.)

St. Paul's Cathedral Choir School, Carter Lane. Plans, Perspective View, and Details of Sgraffito Work. Three woodcuts from the *Builder,* May 29, 1875. (Each 10½-7 inches.)

The Chapter House.

The Chapter House of the Cathedral Church of St. Paul's. J. HARRIS, delin. et fecit. (22½-18½ inches.)

The Chapter House. Reduced copy of the preceding, with 3 lines of description beneath. PARR. **sculp.** (10-7½ inches.)

Convocation or Chapter House, St. Paul's, in **1701.** A woodcut from KNIGHT's *Old England.* The **date given** (1701) is an error. (4½-3½ inches.)

S. Paul's Churchyard.

The Statue of Her Majesty (Queen Anne) erected at the West End of St. Paul's Anno **1713.** Printed and sold by Carington BOWLES, 69, St. Paul's **Church** Yard. (21-25½ inches.)

The West **Area** of St. Paul's Cathedral. A woodcut. R. P. WHELLOCK, del. ; WALMSLEY, sc. (10¾-6¾ inches.)

St. Paul's Cathedral. West Area Improvements. A woodcut R. P. WHELLOCK, **del.** (11-6¾ inches.)

West Area of St. Paul's Churchyard, as newly arranged. A woodcut. R. P. WHELLOCK, del. (9½-6¾ inches.)

In the Gardens. St. Paul's Cathedral. A woodcut from the *Cottager and Artisan,* October, **1889.** (8¼-11¼ inches.)

Messrs. Cook's Warehouse, St. Paul's Churchyard. A woodcut. 1854. (9¼-7 inches.)

S. PETER'S AT ROME : AND S. PETER'S AS COMPARED WITH S. PAUL'S.

Old Saint Peter's, Rome, about the Year **1450,** restored from ancient Authorities, by H. W. BREWER, **1891.** From the *Builder,* Jan. 2, 1892. (15-9 inches.)

The **Front** of St. Peter's Church at **Rome.** H. TERASSON, fecit. Printed and **sold** by J. BOWLES, **at** the Black Horse in Cornhill, and T. BOWLES, next to ye Chapter House. (23¼-17½ inches.)

La Basilica Vaticana. Showing the W. **Front** and Arcade. With 4 lines of description beneath. G. B. **FALDA,** dis. et fec. G. G. ROSSI, le stampa in Roma. (25·**19 inches.)**

St. Peter's Dome, from the Piazza della Sagrestia. From a water-colour drawing by Mr. John FULLEYLOVE. From the *Builder,* Jan. 2, 1892. (15-10¼ inches.)

Veduta Esteriore del Fianco della gran Basilica Vaticana dalla Parte di Mezzo Giorno. Published by J. ROSSI in Rome, 1763. (27¼-18¼ inches.)

Veduta dell' Esterno della gran Basilica di S. Pietro in Vaticano. Etching by PIRANESI. (24-16 inches.)

Prospetto della Basilica Vaticana, Architettura di Carlo Maderno. Published by ROSSI, in Rome, 1705. (18¼-27¼ inches.)

Veduta Interiore della gran Basilica di S. Pietro. Published by ROSSI, in Rome. (26¾-19½ inches.)

S. Peter's. Veduta interna della Basilica di S. Pietro in Vaticano. PIRANESI, fecit. Coloured engraving. (23¼-16 inches.)

St. Peter's Church. After PIRANESI. (14¾-10 inches.)

Ichnography of St. Peter's at Rome and St. Paul's, drawn on the same Scale. Two woodcuts, from an old magazine. 8vo.

Plans of the Magnificent Cathedrals of St. Peter at Rome and St. Paul, with Views of those Churches. From the *London Magazine.* (7½-9¾ inches.)

Geometrical Elevations of the West Fronts of St. Peter's, St. Paul's, and other Buildings, to one Scale. Drawn and etched by T. H. CLARKE; aquatinted by R. HAVELL, 1831 (18¼-13 inches.)

A Parallel View between New St. Paul's and St. Peter's at Rome, with View of Old St. Paul's, A.D. 1240. E. BROWN, del.; H. ADLARD, sculp. (8-10½ inches.)

The Cathedral Churches of St. Peter's at Rome and St. Paul's. A woodcut. (7¾-4¾ inches.)

Ground Plans of the outer Walls of all the most celebrated Churches in Europe. From the *Gentleman's Magazine*, Supplement to vol. 84. (7½-4½ inches.)

MISCELLANEOUS VIEWS.

Altar of Diana, discovered in Foster Lane. From ARCHER'S *Reliques of Old London.* (11-9 inches.)

Roman Altar found in Foster Lane, Cheapside, in excavating for the New Goldsmith's Hall. A. SHAW, del.; J. BASIRE, sculp. From the *Archæologia,* vol. xxiv. (11¼-8¼ inches.)

Panier Alley, Pie Corner, East Cheap, and **Bennett's Hill.** Four views of the sculptured figures, on 1 sheet. J. PASS, sculp., 1814. (8¼-10½ inches.)

Interior of St. Mildred, Bread Street, **Sir C.** Wren, architect. Pencil drawing by R. PAYNE, 1881. (10¾-18 inches.)

A Plan of London House, now in the Possession of Mr. Jacob ILIVE, Dec., 1747. From WILKINSON'S *Londina Illustrata,* 1814. (10-12¼ inches.)

Chertsey. Plan of **the** Abbey and surrounding Buildings. From an early drawing. (13½-9¾ inches.)

Old Church at **Chertsey.** From the *Gentleman's Magazine*, 1807. (6¾-4½ inches.)

Cowley's House at **Chertsey.** A woodcut, with description beneath. (4½-7 inches.)

View of **Chertsey.** From an old *Traveller*. (7-6 inches.)

The Porch House, **Chertsey.** Drawn by J. C. BARROW, from an original by Mr. DANIEL; engraved by G. J. PARKYNS. (14½-11½ inches.)

Remains of **a** Tile Pavement recently found within the Precincts of **Chertsey** Abbey. Description, list, and 10 coloured plates of tiles, by Henry SHAW, 1857. (Each about 10-9 inches.)

Barking Abbey Gateway. J. GREIG, **del. et** sculp. (8-7 inches.)

Part of a Stone Slab **in Barking** Church. Drawn, etched, and published by FISHER, 1809. (8½-12 inches.)

Barking, Essex. Engraved by J. **STORER from a** drawing by S. PROUT, 1804. (10¼-7¾ inches.)

Rubbing **from the** Brass of Thomas **Mordon, at Barking.** (23-27½ inches.)

The North West Prospect **of** Westminster Abby, with the Spire as design'd by Sir Christopher **Wren.** J. JAMES, del.; P. FOUR-DRINIER, sculp. (20-16¾ inches.)

Remains of the Manor House, denominated 'The Lordship of **Toten** Hall,' now vulgarly called Tottenham Court, and occupied by the Adam and Eve Tea House and Gardens. A Lordship belonging to the Deans of S. Paul's. From WILKINSON'S *Londina Illustrata,* **1813.** (10¼-12½ inches.)

Visitation Mandate from Archbishop Boniface to the Dean and Chapter of S. Paul's, 1253. Frontispiece to the Rev. T. HUGO'S **paper** upon the Mandate. (11-7 inches.)

Specimens of Bookbinding **and** facsimiles **of Seals,** from originals in the Library. Three facsimiles in colours. (8½-12 inches.)

Old London Signs, Tablets, etc. Drawings of one hundred and one subjects, with a description.

A Royal Procession passing S. Paul's Cathedral. Water colour drawing from the original painting at Windsor Castle.

Portrait of **King Richard II.** From the original in Westminster Abbey. John CARTER, **del. et sculp.,** 1786. Published by N. Smith, **Oct. 28,** 1791.

MISCELLANEOUS.

CONTENTS.

———•◦•———

SERIES OF PLATES

FROM MR. W. LONGMAN'S 'HISTORY OF THE THREE CATHEDRALS DEDICATED TO S. PAUL IN LONDON.

Steel Engravings engraved by H. Adlard (from Mr. Ferrey's Designs).

OLD S. PAUL'S.

Plate **A.** Ground Plan (Old S. Paul's).
    „   **B.**   West Elevation   „
    „   **C.**   South Elevation   „
    „   **D.**   East Elevation   „
    „   **E.**   Transverse Section (Old S. Paul's).
    „   **F.**   Longitudinal Section   „

Full-Page Woodcuts engraved by G. Pearson.

OLD AND NEW S. PAUL'S.

S. Paul's Cathedral (the present Building). **From a print** in the *Gardner Collection*, drawn by J. BUCKLER, F.S.A., and engraved by G. LEWIS.

South-West View of Old S. Paul's. Supposed to be taken from present Doctors' Commons. Compiled by F. WATKINS, from drawings by E. B. FERREY, Architect.

Interior of the Nave of Old S. Paul's. From a print in the *Gardner Collection*, after HOLLAR.

A Bird's Eye View of Old S. Paul's, showing the Surrounding Wall, Gates, and Neighbouring Streets. Compiled by F. WATKINS, from drawings by E. B. FERREY, Architect.

SIR CHRISTOPHER WREN'S UNEXECUTED DESIGNS.

Design for S. Paul's, made by Sir Christopher WREN immediately before the Great Fire. From Sir Christopher WREN's drawing in the *All Souls' Collection* at Oxford.

View of the Cathedral Church of S. Paul's, according to the first Design (after the Great Fire), of the Architect, Sir Christopher

WREN, Knt. ('Kensington model.') From a print in the *Gardner* **Collection**, engraved by SCHYNVOET.

Ground Plan of S. Paul's, according to the First Design (after the Great Fire) of Sir Christopher WREN. From a print in the *Gardner Collection*, engraved by B. COLE.

Ground Plan of East End of S. Paul's, according to a Tentative Design (No. 21 of the *All Souls' Collection*) made by Sir Christopher WREN, showing Communion Table and Reredos.

Interior View of Sir C. WREN'S First Design (after the Great Fire). Drawn by J. GOODCHILD from the model now in the Kensington Museum.

The Last Design made for **S.** Paul's by Sir Christopher WREN. From WREN'S drawing in the *All Souls' Collection*.

'Former Design' for **S.** Paul's by Sir Christopher WREN. Original title : **'A section** of the Cathedral Church of St. Paul, showing the Dome, according to a former Design by Sir Christopher WREN.' From a print in the *Gardner Collection*.

Section of the Dome of S. Paul's. From Sir Christopher WREN'S 'former Design,' with separate enlarged portion from another drawing of the same, showing the continuity of the supports of **the Dome** according to the Indian method.

MODERN S. PAUL'S.

Ground Plan of the Cathedral. **From an** original drawing by Mr. PENROSE, Surveyor to St. Paul's, with (dotted) lines, from a **former** drawing by Sir Christopher WREN, showing his intentions as to the position of the surrounding railing.

Projection of Old (shaded) upon the Plan of **New S.** Paul's. From Sir Christopher WREN'S drawing in the *All Souls'* Collection, Oxford.

UNEXECUTED DESIGN.

Plinth of the Cathedral, with and without a Balustrade. Taken from original drawings in the *Gardner Collection*.

Thomas Bird's Sculpture of the Conversion of S. Paul, in the Pediment of the Western Front of the Cathedral. From the model preserved in the Cathedral Library.

Dome of S. Paul's.

Interior of the Cathedral, looking East.

Ground Plan of Crypt of the Cathedral. From an **original** drawing by Mr. PENROSE, Surveyor to S. Paul's.

One of the Campaniles of the Cathedral.

Ground Plan of S. Paul's according to a Design with Surrounding Arcades and a Baptistery. From a drawing by Sir Christopher WREN in the Vestry of the Cathedral.

Proposed Ornamentation on Spandrels of Arches around the Dome of Modern Cathedral. From an old engraving in the *Gardner Collection*, by William EMMETT.

Woodcuts engraved by G. Pearson.

Clustered Pillars and Triforium Arcade.

S. Paul's Cross.

Inigo Jones's Portico (from HOLLAR).

Copy of a Woodcut on the Title-page of *Maroccus Extaticus*.

Sir Paul Pindar's House in Bishopsgate Street.

Old S. Paul's Cathedral on Fire.

Lud-gate on Fire.

Model of Baldachino preserved in S. Paul's Cathedral.

East End of S. Paul's, as altered by Sir Christopher WREN from the ' Kensington model' Design.

Phœnix over Southern Portico.

Steps at Western Entrance, as originally Planned by Sir Christopher WREN, and as now intended to be carried out.

Pendentives or Spandrels.

Cantalever Cornice round **Inner Dome**.

Section, showing Inner and Outer Domes, with the Conical Wall.

Stairs, as they formerly existed, leading up to the Lantern, between the Inner and Outer Domes. From an original drawing in the *Gardner Collection*.

Ground Plan of Pronaos, showing **Recess for** the Great Doors under Western Portico.

Section showing Buttresses.

Pier Arches of the Nave, showing the Archivolts, rising above the Architraves.

Comparative Sizes of S. Peter's and S. Paul's Cathedrals.

Diagram showing Construction **of Internal Dome, Cone of Brick-work**, and Outer Dome.

Clerestory **Windows** above the Attic Order.

Diagram of the Arch, turned from an Attic Order

SERIES OF PLATES

ISSUED BY THE SOCIETY FOR PHOTOGRAPHING
RELICS OF OLD LONDON.

1. **Oxford Arms Inn.** Entrance.
2, 3.   „   „   The Inn Yard.
4.   „   „   Upper Gallery.
5.   „   „   Staircase.
6.   „   „   Galleries.
7, 8. **Old Houses** in Wych **Street.**
9, 10.   „   in Drury Lane.
11. **Lincoln's Inn.** Gate House.
12.   „   Old Square.
13, 14. **S. Bartholomew the Great.** The Church.
15.   „   „   The Green Churchyard.
16.   „   „   Church and Boys' School.
17, 18.   „   „   **North side and Poors'**
Churchyard.
19. **Temple Bar.**
20. **Houses** in Leadenhall Street.
21. **Old Houses** in Gray's Inn Lane.
22. **Shop** in Brewer Street, Soho.
23. **Sir Paul Pindar Inn,** Bishopsgate Street.
24. **Staple Inn,** Holborn Front.
25, 26. **Canonbury Tower.**
27-29. **Barnard's Inn.**
30, 31. **Old Houses,** Aldersgate Street.
32. **Shaftesbury House,** Aldersgate Street.
33, 34. **Christ's Hospital.**
35. **Churchyard** of S. Lawrence, Pountney.
36. **Old Houses** in Great Queen **Street.**
37. **Charterhouse.** General Views from Charterhouse Square.
38, 39.   „   Wash-house Court.
40.   „   The Cloisters.
41-44.   „   **The Great Hall.**
45.   „   **The Grand Staircase.**
46.   „   The Governors' Room.
47.   „   Entrance to the Chapel.
48.   „   Founder's **Tomb.**

97. Inner Temple Gate House.
98.   „   „   Churchyard Court.
99.   „   „   5, King's Bench Walk.
100. Middle Temple Gate House.
101.   „   „   Fountain Court.
102.   „   „   Hall.
103. Gray's Inn. Field Court.
104.   „   Hall.
105. Clement's Inn. Garden House.
106. Clifford's Inn.
107. Staple Inn. Hall.
108. Six small subjects :

    1. **Guy**, Earl of Warwick.
    2. Stone in Panyer Alley.
    3. Pelican, Aldermanbury.
    4. Queen Elizabeth, Ludgate.
    5. Wooden Midshipman, Leadenhall Street.
    6. Royal Arms, Old London Bridge.

109. S. John's Gate, Clerkenwell.
110. Old Houses in the Strand.
111. Great S. Helen's, Bishopsgate Street.
112. Tennis Court, James Street, Haymarket.
113. Emmanuel Hospital, Westminster.
114. Queen Anne's Gate.
115. Chimney **Piece**. Sessions House, Clerkenwell.
116.   „   „   **Court** House, S. Andrew's, Holborn.
117.   „   „   Tallow Chandlers' Hall.
118. **Court Room**. New River Company.
119. **Doorway**. 26, Queen Square, Westminster.
    „   9, Grosvenor Road.
    „   17, Delahay Street.
120. Five small subjects :

    1. The **Chained Bear**, 6, Lower Thames Street.
    2. London Stone.
    3. Hour Glass, S. Alban's, Wood Street.
    4. The Boy, Pie Corner.
    5. Figures from the Clock, S. Dunstan in the West.

ENGRAVED PORTRAITS OF BISHOPS OF LONDON.

Accession.	Bishop.	Painter.	Engraver.	
1502	Warham ...	Holbein ...	Vertue ...	1737.
1522	Tunstall ...	—	Fourdrinier.	
1540	Bonner ...	—	Cooper.	
1550	Ridley ...	Vander Werff	Trotter.	
1559	Grindal ...	Lens... ...	Vander Gucht.	
	„ ...	Skelton ...	Fittler ...	Original at Lambeth.
1570	Sandys ...	—	Trotter.	
	„ ...	—	Æ.	
	„ and wife ...	—	—	Original at Bishopsthorpe.
1577	Aylmer ...	—	White.	
1597	Bancroft ...	—	Vertue.	
1604	Vaughan ...	—	Æ.	
1610	Abbot ...	—	Simon Passæus	1616.
	„ ...	—	J. Houbraken.	
1611	King ...	—	Simon Passæus.	
1621	Mountain...	—	G. Y. ...	1659.
1628	Laud ...	Vandyke ...	Jas. Watson...	1779.
1633	Juxon ...	—	—	Original at Longleat.
	„ ...	—	Vertue ...	Proof.
1660	Sheldon ...	—	Hollar.	
	„ ...	—	—	Mezzotint.
1663	Henchman	Lely.		
	„ ...	Lely... ...	—	Photograph.
1675	Compton...	Oil Painting, attributed to Sir James Thornhill.		
	Compton...	D. Loggan ...	D. Loggan ...	1679.
	„ ...	J. Rily ...	J. Beckett.	
1714	Robinson...	M. Dahl ...	G. Vertue ...	Bp. of Bristol.
1723	Gibson ...	J. Ellys ...	G. Vertue ...	1727.
1748	Sherlock ...	Van Loo, 1740	S. Ravenot ...	1756.
	„ ...	Van Loo, 1740	McArdell ...	1757.
1762	Osbaldeston	T. Hudson ...	McArdell.	
1764	Terrick ...	Nat. Dance ...	Edw. Fisher...	1770.
1777	Lowth ...	R. E. Pyne ...	J. K. Sherwin	1784.
1787	Porteus ...	H. Edridge...	C. Picart ...	1809.
1813	Howley ...	Owen ...	Reynolds ...	Proof.

PORTRAITS *OF DEANS OF* S. *PAUL'S.*

Accession.	Dean.	Painter.	Engraver.	
1505	Colet ...	—	R. Houston.	
„	...	Holbein.		
1560	Nowell.			
„	...	—	Harding ...	Original at Brasenose.
1602	Overall ...	—	R. White.	
1621	Donne ...	M. Droeshout	Martin.	
„	...	—	Lombart.	
	Steward ...	G. P. Harding	J. Stow ...	1822.
1661	Barwick ...	—	G. Vertue.	
1664	Sancroft ...	—	R. White.	
„	...	—	—	The seven Bishops.
„	...	D. Loggan ...	D. Loggan ...	1680, *ad vivum.*
1678	**Stillingfleet**	Mrs. **Beale.**		
„		Lely	A. Blooteling	**Proof.**
„		Lely	„	**Later state.**
1689	Tillotson ...	R. White ...	R. White.	
„	...	Mrs. Beale ...	„	
„	...	Sir Godfrey Kneller ...	G. Vertue.	
„	...	Sir Peter Lely	A. Blooteling.	
1691	Sherlock ...	R. White ...	R. White.	
1750	Secker ...	T. Willes ...	J. McArdell.	1747.
„	...	T. Hudson ...		
1766	Cornwallis ...	Nath. Dance	Edw. Fisher ...	1679.
1768	Newton ...	Sir Joshua Reynolds ...	Jos. Collyer ...	1782.
„	...	„ ...	Thos. Watson	1775.

CANONS AND *PREBENDARIES OF S. PAUL'S.*

Accession.		Painter.	Engraver.	
1672	Holder ...	D. Loggan ...	—	*ad vivum.*
1705	Pelling, John	—	J. McArdell ...	**Prebendary.**
1842	Hale, Arch-deacon of London	Thos. A. Woolnoth ...	W. Walker ...	1850.
1856	Melvill, Canon.			

MASTER OF **THE** CHORISTERS.

1813	Hawes, William.	

SEALS OF BISHOPS OF LONDON.
(*Sulphur Casts.*)

1108-1128. Richard de Beames. I.
1152-1162. Richard de Beames. II.
1163-1188. Gilbert Folliott.
1189-1198. Richard FitzNeal. (Two.)
1199-1221. William of S. Mary Church. (Two.)
1221-1228. Eustace de Fauconberg. (Two.)
1229-1241. Roger Niger. (Two.)
1244-1259 Fulk Bassett. (Three.)
1260-1262. Henry de Wengham. (Two.)
1274-1280. John Chishull.
1306-1313. Ralph Baldock.
1319-1338. Stephen Gravesend.
1340-1354. Ralph Stratford. (Two.)
1362-1375. Simon Sudbury. (Two.)
1382-1404. Robert Braybrook. (Two.)
1407-1421. Richard Clifford.
1426-1431. William Gray.
1436-1448. Robert Gilbert.
1450-1489. Thomas Kemp.
1496-1501. Thomas Savage.
1522-1530. Cuthbert Tunstall.
1540-1549. Edmund Bonner.

SEALS *OF THE* DEAN AND *CHAPTER AND* OTHER *MEMBERS* OF THE *CATHEDRAL.*

Dean and Chapter. Twelfth century.
       ,,   ,,   Thirteenth century. Two large seals and two small.
       ,,   ,,   1335.
Precentor. Two seals.
Archdeacon of London.
Minor Canons. **Two seals: about** 1394.
    (The original **silver seals are** still in the **possession of the** College.)
Official : Sede Vacante.
Negociant.

AUTOGRAPH SIGNATURES EXHIBITED IN THE *LIBRARY.*

KINGS AND QUEENS OF ENGLAND.

Charles I.	Mary II.	George III.
Charles II.	William III.	Victoria.
James II.		

KING OF TAHITI.

Kamehameha, 1863.

ARCHBISHOPS AND BISHOPS.

Archbishop Cranmer.	Bishop Juxon.
„ Laud.	„ Henchman.
„ Sheldon.	„ Compton.*
„ Sancroft.	„ Morley (Winchester).
„ Sterne (York).	„ Crew (Durham).

LITERARY MEN.†

Izaak Casaubon. [18 C. 1-4.]
Izaak Walton. (Iz. Wa.) [38 E. 50.]
Hamon l'Estrange. [24 G. 26.]
Dr. Bentley.

Sir Christopher Wren.

MEDALS

CHIEFLY RELATING TO S. PAUL'S CATHEDRAL. EXHIBITED IN THE LIBRARY.

[The figures attached to each entry indicate the measurement of the diameter of the medal in inches and tenths.]

1. Obverse : CAROLVS . AVGVSTISS . ET . INVICTISS . MAG . BRIT FRAN . ET . HIB . MONARCHA . 1633.
      (Equestrian figure of Charles I. to the left.)
    Reverse : SOL . ORBEM . REDIENS . SIC . REX . ILLVMINAT VRBEM.
      (View of London, the sun shining in its splendour. London Bridge is seen, and the tower of S. Paul's.)
   Silver (1-7).

2 Obverse : WREN.
      (Youthful bust, to the right.)
    Reverse : CHRISTOPHER WREN ARCHITECT . MDCCX. SI MONV-MENTVM REQVIRIS CIRCVMSPICE.
      (S. Paul's Cathedral.)
   Bronze (2-4). B.WYON . F.

3. Obverse : CHRISTOP . WREN . EQVES . AUR . ET . ARCHITECT . OBIIT . A.D. 1723 . ÆT . 91.
      (Bust of Sir C. Wren to the left.)

---

* See volumes marked 36 C 56, 13 F 6-8, 18 D 12, 20 D 2, etc.
† These autographs are not now exhibited. They are to be found on the title-pages of books in the library.

Reverse : INCEPT . A.D. 1675 . AEDES . PAVLI . LOND . PERFECT .
1711 . VNVM . PRO . CVNCTIS . FAMA . LOQVATVR
OPVS.
(West Front of S. Paul's.)
Bronze (4-1). C. D. CAAB. scvlp.

4, 5, 6. Obverse : GEORGIVS . III. MAGN . BR . FR . ET . HIB . REX.
(Head of George III., to the right.)
Reverse : LÆTITIA . CVM PIETATE.
DEO . OPT . MAX REX PIENTISS . PRO . SALVTE .
REST . VSLM . APRIL . 23 1789.
Bronze (2-2), and two copies in silver.

7. Obverse : GOD . SAVE . THE . KING. G. III. 1788.
(Head of George III., to the right.)'
Reverse : VISITED . S. PAULS . 23 . APRIL . 1789.
(Arms of the City of London.)
White metal (1-4).

8. Obverse : GEORGIVS . III. REX.
(Head of George III., to the right.)
Reverse : VISITED S. PAULS . 23 . APRIL . 1789.
(Arms of the City of London.)
Bronze (1-2).

9. Obverse : GEORGIVS . III. DEI . GRATIA.
(Head of George III., to the right.)
Reverse : ROYAL . THANKSGIVING . AT . ST. PAUL'S . DEC. 19 .
1797.
(An altar, surmounted by the crown, sword, and
sceptre, inscribed : HOWE . ST. VINCENT . DUNCAN.)
Bronze (1-4). Milton.

10. Obverse : REGNO . PACEM . OBTVLIT . SUPER . PACE . RATA . DIE
. 27 . MARTII.
(Warrior crowned by Victory.)
Reverse : DEO . GLORIAM . REFERT . PAX . CELEBRATA . DIE . 1 .
JVNII . MDCCCII.
(N.W. view of S. Paul's.)
Bronze (2-0), also in white metal.

11. Obverse : MY . SOUL . DOTH . MAGNIFY . THE . LORD . MARCH .
27 . 1802.
(Peace welcoming a kneeling figure.)
Reverse : WE . PRAISE . THEE . O . GOD . THANSGIVING . JVNE . 1.
(Figure of Piety ; on the left S. Paul's ; on the
right medallion portrait.)
Bronze (1-6).

12. Obverse : GEORGIVS IIII. D . G . BRITANNIARVM . REX . F . D .
1820.
(Head of George IV., to the left.)

Reverse : SOCIETY . **OF** . **PATRONS** . **OF** . **CHARITY** . SCHOOLS .
INSTITUTED . A.D. 1700.
(S. Paul's Cathedral, **West Front.**)

Silver (2-2).

13. Obverse : WEALTH . AND . INDEPENDENCE.
(Plenty with a cornucopia scattering flowers.)
Reverse : THE . CONSTITUTION . 1821.
(On the left, S. Paul's ; on the right, Westminster
Abbey.)

Bronze (1-9).

14. Obverse : THE FIRST STONE OF THE NEW LONDON BRIDGE WAS
LAID BY JOHN GARRATT ESQ^R LORD MAYOR OF
LONDON . ON THE 14TH OF MARCH . 1824 AND
OPEN'D BY THEIR MAJESTIES AUGUST **1ST,** 1831.
Reverse : CARRIAGE **WAY** 33½ FEET.   LENGTH **OF** BRIDGE
732 FT.   CENTRE ARCH . 150.   SIDE ARCH , **140.**
(London Bridge, with S. Paul's.)

Bronze **(1-2).**

15. **Visit of the** Queen to the Guildhall **upon her accession** to the
Throne, 1837.
Obverse : VICTORIA . REGINA.
(Crowned head, to the left.)
Reverse : IN HONOUR OF HER MAJESTY'S **VISIT TO** THE COR-
PORATION OF LONDON, 9TH NOVEMBER, 1837.
(South **Front** of Guildhall.)

Bronze (2-2).   B. Wyon.

16. Visit of the Sultan of Turkey to the City.
Obverse : ABDULAZIZ . OTHOMANORVM . IMPERATOR . LONDINIUM
INVISIT . MDCCCLXVII.
(Head of the Sultan, to the right.)
Reverse : (The City of London receiving Turkey with emblems
of hospitality.   **In** the background, on **the** left,
S. Paul's ; on **the** right, the Mosque of Sultan
Achmet at Constantinople.   On **an** altar between
the two figures : WELCOME.)

Bronze (3-1).   J. S. and A. B. Wyon.

17. Opening of the Holborn Valley Viaduct and Blackfriars Bridge,
1869.
Obverse : **VICTORIA** . D . G . BRIT . REGINA . F . D.
(Head of Queen Victoria, to the left.)
Reverse : HOLBORN VIADUCT . BLACKFRIARS . BRIDGE 1869.
(Views of the Viaduct and Bridge, with the City
Arms in the centre, supported on the left by the
City of London, and on the right by Britannia.)

Bronze (3-1).   Two copies.   G. S. Adams, sc.

18. National Thanksgiving for Recovery of the Prince of Wales.
Obverse : I WAS GLAD WHEN THEY SAID UNTO ME, LET US GO
INTO THE HOUSE OF **THE** LORD.
(The Queen and the Prince of Wales welcomed
by two figures.)

Reverse : NATIONAL THANKSGIVING FOR THE RECOVERY OF
H.R.H. THE PRINCE OF WALES. 17 FEB., 1872.
(The interior of S. Paul's at the time of the
Thanksgiving Service.)

Bronze (3·1). Two copies.

19. Obverse : ALBERT EDWARD PRINCE OF WALES, BORN NOV. 9,
1841.
(Head of the Prince of Wales, to the left.)

Reverse : ST. PAUL'S CATHEDRAL LONDON, 1872.
(N.W. view of S. Paul's.)

Bronze (1·0). Two copies.

20. Obverse · NASSER-ED-DEEN SHAH OF PERSIA.
(Head of the Shah.)

Reverse : (The City of London personified, holding a scroll
inscribed 20TH JUNE . 1873. On the left S. Paul's
Cathedral ; on the right the arms of the City of
London and of the Shah.)

Bronze (3·1). A. B. Wyon.

21. Obverse : ALBERT EDWARD, PRINCE OF WALES, PRESIDENT.
(Head of the Prince, to the left.)

Reverse : ANNUAL INTERNATIONAL EXHIBITION OF ALL FINE ARTS
INDUSTRIES AND INVENTIONS. A.D. MDCCCLXXIV.
(View of Albert Hall.)

Bronze (2·1). G. Morgan, sc.

22. Jubilee medal.
Obverse : REGINA . 1837 . VICTORIA . IMPERATRIX . 1887.
(Heads of the Queen, at the two dates.)

Reverse : ANNUS . JUBILAEUS . 1887.
(An allegorical subject.)

Bronze (3·2).

23. Obverse : ST. PAUL'S CATHEDRAL LONDON.
(N.W. exterior view.)

Reverse : FOUNDED VII CENTURY. BURNT XI CENTURY. REBUILT
IN STONE XII AND XIII CENTURY. AGAIN BURNT
1666. REBUILT IN ITS PRESENT STATE 1672-1713.
CHRISTOPHER WREN.
(Interior, looking East. View of Aisles and Nave.)

Bronze (2·5). J. Weiner, of Brussels.

24. Obverse : ST. PAUL'S CATHEDRAL . LONDON.
(N.W. exterior view.)

Reverse : (The interior of S. Paul's, showing the Nave and
Choir.)

Bronze (2·5). Josh. Davies, Birmingham.

25. Charity Schools at S. Paul's.
Obverse : MAY NATIONAL EDUCATION EVER FLOURISH.
(N.W. exterior view.)

Reverse : MONITOR'S MEDAL.
(Crown lying on the Bible.)

Bronze (1·9).

15

TOKENS.

26. Obverse : LONDON AND BRIGHTON HALFPENNY.
(West Front of S. Paul's.)

Reverse : PAYABLE AT THE WAREHOUSE OF I. SPITTLE LONDON,
OR OF I. KIRBY, OR R. LASHMAR, BRIGHTON.
(A shield with two dolphins.)

Bronze (1-2). Five copies.

27. Obverse : SISE LANE HALFPENNY, 1795.
(Britannia. S. Paul's on the **left**.)

Reverse : KING. LORDS. COMMONS.
(In a triangle held by two hands and surmounted
by a crown, the word CONSTITUTION.)

Bronze (1-2). Two copies.

28. Obverse : **R.** YOUNG, **DEALER IN COINS, NO. 18, LUDGATE ST.,**
LONDON.
(A star, **enclosing** : HONI SOIT QUI MAL Y PENSE.)

Reverse : (West Front **of S. Paul's.**)

Bronze **(1-4).**

MISCELLANEOUS OBJECTS OF INTEREST IN THE LIBRARY.

Cast of a **Danish Monumental Stone**, found in August, 1852,
at the S.E. of S. Paul's Churchyard, 18 feet below the present
level, with a Runic inscription

KONA LET LEKIA STIN THENSI AUK TUKI.

That is, as deciphered by Professor Browne :

KONA AND **TUKI** CAUSED **LAY** THIS STONE.

Presented to the Library by **Dr.** W. Sedgwick Saunders.
The original stone is in the Guildhall Library.
[See *supra*, page 79.]

Cast of the **Tonsure Plate used by the Clergy of S. Paul's**
Cathedral in the Thirteenth Century.
The original plate is in the British Museum. It has been
figured and described by the Librarian in the *Journal* of the
British Archæological Association for 1882, **pp.** 278-290.

Two Books in the Library still retain **their** ancient **Chains** ; and a
third chain is exhibited in the **Glass Case in** the middle of the
Library.

A very fine series **of Drawings** of **Old** S. Paul's Cathedral,
presented by Mr. Edmund B. Ferrey, Architect.
[These are framed and glazed, and are placed on the walls
of the Trophy Room.]

Model of Sir Christopher Wren's first design for S. Paul's Cathedral. [In the triforium over the North Aisle of the Nave, at the West End.]

Thomas Bird's Model for the Pediment of the West Front of the Cathedral. On a brass plate affixed is the inscription :

'This Model of part of the West end of S. Paul's Cathedral was presented to the Vicar of Shiplake, A.D. 1835, by Mr. J. Plumbe, of Henley-on-Thames, who had purchased it from Badgmore House, once the residence of Richard Jennings, the Master Builder of that Cathedral.'

Archbishop Laud's Conference with Fisher. The Archbishop's own copy, with his arms on the side.

Palais du Vatican. Chapelle Sixtine. Fresques de Michel Ange. A large and important series of photographs, numbered 1 to 121.

APPENDIX.

CONTENTS.

DESIDERATA.

DESIDERATA.

BOOKS ILLUSTRATING THE HISTORY OF S. PAUL'S CATHEDRAL.

1501. **Catherine** [of Aragon], Queen Consort of Henry VIII., King of England [Divorce].
The traduction & mariage of the princesse (. . . Kateryne doughter to . . . the kinge and quene of Spayne, etc.). [Being a programme of ceremonies appointed to be observed at the landing of the Princess, her entry into London, and her marriage with Arthur, Prince of Wales.] B.L., MS. Notes. R. Pynson [London, 1501]. 4to.
[British Museum copy is imperfect ; wanting sig. a3 and 4, and b3 and 4 ; title-page mutilated. Without pagination.]

1533. **Frith** (John). A boke made by J. F. prisoner in the Tower of London, answeringe unto M. mores lettur which he wrote agenst the first litle treatyse that J. F. made concerninge the sacramente of the body and bloude of christ unto which boke are added . . . the articles of his examinacion before the bishoppes of London, Winchestur and lincolne, in Paules church at London, for which J. F. was condempned ād after burēt in smithfelde the fourth daye of Juli . . . 1533. B.L. C. Willems, Monster. 1533. 8vo. (Without pagination.)

1566. **Desainliens** (Claude). The Frenche Littelton. A most easie, perfect and absolute way to learne the frenche tongue : newly set forth by C. Holliband [*i.e.*, C. Desainliens] teaching in Paules Churchyarde by the signe of the Lucrece, etc. T. Vautroullier, London, 1566. 16mo.

1595. **Bankes** (a Vintner in Cheapside). Maroccus Extaticus. Or, Bankes Bay Horse in a Trance. A Discourse set downe in a merry Dialogue, between Bankes and his beast : Anatomizing some abuses and bad trickes of this age. By J. D. the wier-

---

* The titles of these books are, with one or two exceptions, taken from the 'Catalogue of Books in the Library of the British Museum, printed in England, Scotland, and Ireland, and of books in English printed abroad, to the year 1640.' By George Bullen, Keeper of the Department of Printed Books. Three volumes. 8vo. London, 1884.

drawer of Hadley, and H. R., head Ostler of Bosomes Inne.
Printed for Cuthbert Burby [London], 1595.   4to.
[Banks' horse was the subject of an allusion in Shakespeare's
Love's Labour's Lost, Act I., sc. 2.   J. D. for John Dando, and
H. R. for Harry Runt, are pseudonyms.]

1604.   **The Meeting of Gallants at an Ordinarie** : or, The
Walkes in Powles.   B.L.   Printed by T. C. and solde by M.
Lawe, London, 1604.   4to.

1622.   **Farley** (Henry).   Portland-Stone in Paules-Church-yard.
Their Birth, their Mirth, their Thankefulnesse, their Advertisement.
[In verse.]   Printed by G. E. for R. M., London, 1622.   16mo.
(Without pagination.)

1631.   **Charles I.**, King.   His Majesties Commission giving power
to enquire of the Decayes of the Cathedral Church of St. Paul,
in London, and for the repairing of the same.   (10 April, 1631.)
R. Barker. . . . and the Assignes of J. Bill, London.   4to.,
1631.

1712.   **A Well-Timber'd POEM**, on Her Sacred Majesty ; Her
Marble STATUE, and its Wooden Enclosure in Saint Paul's
Church-yard.   8vo., London, 1712.
[A copy is in the Guildhall Library.]

PAUL'S CROSS SERMONS.

1553.   **Brooks**, James (Bishop of Gloucester).   A Sermon [on S.
Matt. ix. 18] very notable, fruictefull and Godlie, made at Paules
crosse, the xii. daie of Novēbre in the first yere of Quene Marie
. . . by J. Brokis &c.   B.L.   R. Caly.   8vo., London, 1553.

1554.   The same Sermon, newly imprinted and somewhat augmented.
B.L.   R. Caly.   8vo., London, 1554.

1565.   **Jewel** (John).   A Replie unto M. Hardinges Answeare [to
the Bishop's Sermon on 1 Cor. xi. 23, 'pronounced at Paules
Crosse . . . 1560'] by perusinge whereof the discrete and dili-
gent Reader may easily see the weake and onstable groundes
of the Romaine Religion, whiche of late hath beene accompted
Catholique.   H. Wykes.   Folio, London, 1565.

1570.   **Fox** (John), the Martyrologist.   A Sermon of Christ crucified
[on 2 Cor. v. 20, 21] preached at Paules Crosse the Friday before
Easter, commonly called Good fryday, etc.   (The Prayer in this
Sermon made for the Church, and all the states thereof.   A
postscripte to the papistes.)   B.L.   J. Daye.   4to., London,
1570.
Newly recognised by the Authour.   B.L.   J. Daie.   8vo.,
London, 1575.
Another edition.   B.L.   MS. Notes.   J. Day.   8vo., London,
1577

Another edition. B.L. Printed by the Assignes of R. Day. 8vo., London, 1585.

Another edition. B.L. Printed for the Company of Stationers. 8vo. [London], 1609.

1571. **Fox** (John), the Martyrologist. De Christo Crucifixio concio (on 2 Cor. v. 20, 21). Joan Foxi. Apud J. Dayum, Londini, 1571, Octob. 1. 4to.

1571. **B., E.** A Sermon [on 2 Tim. iii. 16] preached at Pauls Crosse on Trinity Sunday, 1571. By E. B. B.L. J. Awdely. 16mo., London, 1576.

1580. **Chaderton** (Laurence). An excellent and godly sermon [on Matt. vii. 21-23] . . . preached at Paules Crosse the xxvi. day of October, An. 1578, etc. B.L. C. Barker. 8vo., London, 1580.
(Fifty-eight leaves, without pagination. Register, A.-H. ii.)

1578. **Stockwood** (John). A Sermon [on Acts x. 1-8] preached at Paules Crosse . . Wherin . . is . . prooved, that it is the part of all those that are fathers, householders, and schole-maisters, to instruct all those under their governement, etc. B.L. H. Bynneman for G. Byshop. 8vo. London [1578].

1578. **White** (Thomas). A Sermō [on Zeph. iii.] preached at Pawles Crosse on Sunday the thirde of November 1577, in the time of the plague by T. W[hite]. B.L. F. Coldock. 8vo., London, 1578.

1581. **Bisse** (James). Two Sermons [on S. John vi. 27] preached the one at Paules Crosse the eight of Januarie 1580, the other at Christes Church in London the same day in the after noone. T. Woodcocke. 8vo., London, 1581.

1585. Another edition of this Sermon. R. Waldegrave for T. Woodcoke. 8vo., London, 1585.

1589. **A most godly . . . Sermon** [on Titus iii. 1] preached at Pauls Crosse the 17. of November . . 1583. B.L. T. Orwin for T. Chard. 8vo., London, 1589. (Without pagination.)

1589. **White** (Thomas) (Founder of Sion College). A Sermon [on S. Luke iii. 10-14] preached at Paules Crosse the 17. of November An. 1589. In joyfull remembrance . . for the peaceable yeres of her Majesties . . Raigne over us, now 32. R. Robinson and T. Newman. 8vo. [London], 1589.

1591. **Babington** (Gervase) (successively Bishop of Llandaff, of Exeter, and of Worcester). A Sermon [on S. John vi. 37] preached at Paules Crosse . . . in Mychaelmas tearme last, 1590. [Edited by H. Wilkinson.] B.L. T. Este. 8vo., London, 1591.

1592. **Fisher** (William). A Godly Sermon preached at Paules Crosse [on Malachi iii. 16, 17]. B.L. E. Allde, for E. Aggas. 8vo., London, 1592. (Without pagination).

1593. **Playfere** (Thomas). Hearts Delight. A Sermon [on Ps. xxxvii. 4] preached at Pauls Crosse . . . in Easter Terme, 1593. J. Legatt. 8vo., London, 1611.

   *** Another edition. J. Legatt. 8vo., London, 1617.

1594. **Dove** (John). A Sermon [on 1 John ii. 18] preached at Pauls Crosse the 3. of November 1594, intreating of the second comming of Christ, and the disclosing of Antichrist, etc. P. Short, for W. Jaggard. 16mo. [London, 1594].

1594. **Lewes** (R.) A Sermon [on Gen. xxvii. 1-10] preached at Paules Crosse, . . . concerning Isaac and his Testament, disposed by the Lord to Jacobs comfort, though it were intended to Esau by his father, etc. B.L. J. Barnes. 8vo., Oxford, 1594. (Without pagination.)

1595. **Hill** (Adam). The Crie of England. A Sermon [on Gen. xviii. 21] preached at Paules Crosse in September 1593. E. Allde for B. Norton. 8vo., London, 1595.

1596. **J. T.** (minister of Gods Word). A Sermon [on S. James iv. 8] preached at Paules Crosse . . . by I. T. minister of Gods Word. Printed by the Widow Orwin for R. Ockold. 8vo., London, 1596. (Without pagination.)

1597. **Dove** (John). A Sermon [on Ezekiel xxxiii. 11] preached at Paules Crosse, the sixt of February, 1596, etc. [Printed for R. Dexter. London, 1597.] 8vo.

1601. **Dove** (John). Of Divorcement. A sermon [on S. Matth. xix. 9] preached at Pauls Crosse the 10. of May, 1601. Printed by T. C. 8vo., London, 1601.

1603. **H., J.** Gods universal right proclaimed. A Sermon [on Ps. xxiv. 1, 2] preached at Paules Crosse, the 27. of March, 1603, being the next Sunday after Her Majesties departure ; by J[ohn] H[ayward]. Imprinted . . . for C. Burby. 8vo., London, 1603.

1607. **Wilkinson** (Robert). Lots Wife. A Sermon at Paules Crosse [on S. Luke xvii. 32]. By R. W. [*i.e.*, Robert Wilkinson]. F. Kyngston. 4to., London, 1607.

1607. **Pelling** (John). A Sermon [on 1 S. Pet. v. 7] of the Providence of God. Preached at Paules Crosse, etc. N. Okes, for N. Butter. 4to., London, 1607.

1608. **Price** (Daniel). The Marchant. A Sermon [on S. Matt. xiii. 45, 46] preached at Paules Crosse on Sunday the 24. of August, being the day before Bartholomew faire 1607. J. Barnes. 4to., Oxford, 1608.

1609. **Tynley** (Robert). Two Learned Sermons. The one, of the mischievous subtiltie . . . the other of the false Doctrines, and refined Hæresis of the Romish Synagogue. Preached, the one at Paules Crosse the 5. of November 1608 [on Psalm cxxiv. 1-8]; the other, at the Spittle the 17. of April, 1609 [on S. Matt. vii.

15, 16]. In the first are examined divers passages of that lewde English Libell written by a Prophane Fugitive against the Apologie for the Oath of Allegiance. In the second are answered many of the arguments published by R. Chambers, Priest, concerning Popish miracles, etc. W. Hall for T. Adams. 4to., London, 1609.

1608. **Rainolds** (John). Doctor Reignolds his letter to Sir F. Knollis concerning Doctor Bancroft's sermon at Paules Crosse, 9. Feb. 1588. 8vo., 1608.

1608. **Hall** (Joseph). Pharisaisme and Christianity: Compared and set forth in a Sermon at Pauls Crosse, May 1. 1608, by J. H[all]. Upon Matth. 5. 20, etc. M. Bradwood for S. Macham. 8vo., London, 1608.

Another edition. Printed by H. L. for S. Macham. 8vo., London, 1609.

1609. **Wheatlie** (William). A Caveat for the Covetous; or, a Sermon preached at Paules Crosse . . out of Luke 12. 15. Printed by T. C. for T. Man and M. Lawe. 12mo., London, 1609.

1609. **Stock** (Richard). A Sermon [on Isai. ix. 14-16] preached at Paules Crosse, the second of November, 1606. Printed by T. C. for E. Weaver and W. Welby. 12mo., London, 1609.

1609? **A Sermon** [on Psal, lxix. 33] preached at Pauls Crosse the third of Sept. 1609. 4to. [London, 1609?].

(Imperfect, wanting title-page and dedication.)

1609. **Loe** (William). The Joy of Jerusalem : and Woe of the Worldlings. A Sermon [on S. John xvii. 9] preached at Pauls Crosse etc. T. Haveland for C. Knight and J. Harrison. 8vo., London, 1609. (Without pagination.)

1610. **Sclater** (William) (Vicar of Pitminster). A threefold Preservative against three dangerous diseases of these latter times: 1. Non-proficiency in grace; 2. Fals-hearted hypocrisie; 3. Backsliding in Religion. Prescribed in a Sermon [on Heb. vi. 4-6] at Pauls Crosse, Sept. 17, 1609. Imprinted by S. S. for H. Bonian and W. Walley. 4to., London, 1610. (Without pagination.)

1610. **Myriell** (Thomas). The Devout Soules Search; with the happie issue of Comfort found. In a Sermon [on S. Mark xvi. 6] preached at Paules Crosse, Jan. 14, 1610. Printed by T. C for J. Budge. 8vo., London, 1610.

1611. **Gardiner** (Samuel). The Foundation of the Faythfull. In a sermon [on 2 Tim. ii. 19] deliuered at Paules Crosse, the 17 of Januarie, 1610 [O.S.]. Imprinted by W. W. for T. Manne, 8vo., London, 1611. (Without pagination.)

Imperfect, wanting sig. D7, D8.

1612. **Milles** (Robert). Abrahams suite for Sodome. A Sermon [on Gen. xviii. 32] preached at Pauls Crosse the 25. of August, 1611 &c. W. Stansby; for M. Lawe. 8vo., London, 1612. (Without pagination.)

1612. **Hall** (Joseph). An Holy Panegyrick. A Sermon [on 1 Sam. xii. 24, 25] preached at Paules Crosse upon the Anniversarie Solemnitie of the . . . Inauguration of . . . King James, Mar. 24, 1613. By J. H[all] D.D. J. Pindley, for S. Macham. 8vo., London, 1613.

1615. **Hoskins** (John). Sermons preached at Pauls Crosse and else-where. 4 parts. By John Hoskins, Fellow of New College, Oxford. W. Stansby for N. Butter. 4to., London, 1615.
    (Each part has a distinct title-page, pagination, and register.)

1616. **Adams** (Thomas). The Sacrifice of Thankefulnesse. A Sermon [on Psal. cxviii. 27] preached at Paules Crosse the third of December . . 1615 . . By T. A. Whereunto are annexed five other of his sermons, &c. T. Purfoot for C. Knight. 4to., London, 1616.

1616. **Price** (Sampson). Ephesus Warning before her Woe. A Sermon [on Rev. ii. 5] preached at Pauls Crosse. G. Eld for J. Barnes. 4to., London, 1616.

1616. **Sutton** (Thomas), D.D. (Fellow of Queen's College, Oxford). Englan[ds] first and secon[d] Summo[ns] two Sermons [on Hos. iv. 1-3, and Rev. iii. 15, 16] preached at Paules Crosse . . . Jan. 3, 1612 . . [and] Feb. 5, 1615. The second impression, perused and corrected by the authour. N. Okes for M. Law. 8vo., London, 1616.

1616. **Jackson** (William). The Celestiall Husbandrie : or the Tillage of the soule . . . In a Sermon [on Hosea x. 12] at Pauls Crosse the 25 of February 1616 . . . Much inlarged, etc. W. Jones, . . . sold by E. Weaver. 4to., London, 1616.

1617. **Richardson** (Charles). The Price of our Redemption. A Sermon [on S. Matt. xx. 28] preached at Paules Crosse, the sixt of Aprill last, 1617. W. Butler. 8vo., London, 1617.

1622. **Ley** (Roger). The Bruising of the Serpents Head. A Sermon [on S. Luke xi. 21-23] preached at Pauls Crosse, etc. J. Dawson for N. Bourne. 4to., London, 1622.

1623. **Adams** (Thomas). The Barren Tree. A Sermon [on S. Luke xiii. 7] preached at Pauls Crosse &c. A. Mathewes for J. Grismand. 4to., London, 1623.

1624. **Lawrence** (John). A Golden Trumpet, to rowse up a drowsie Magistrate : or a patterne for a Governors Practise, drawne from Christs comming to . . and weeping over Hierusalem. As it was sounded at Pauls Crosse the 11 of April, 1624. [On S. Luke xix. 41.] J. Haviland. 4to., London, 1624.

1626. **Five Sermons** upon Severall Occas.ons preach'd at Pauls Crosse, and at Saint Maries in Oxford. Printed for J. Parker. 4to., London, 1626.

Another edition. J. Hartland. 4to., London, 1637.

1626. **Holyday** (Barten). A Sermon [on Psal. xviii. 48, 49] preached at Pauls Crosse, August the 5th 1623 by Barten Holyday. W. Stansby for N. Butter. 4to., London, 1626.

SERMONS PREACHED IN S. PAUL'S CATHEDRAL.

1490? **Innocents' Day.** In die Innocenciŭ S[er]mo pro episcopo puerorum [on Ps. c. 12]. Eng. B.L. [Wynkyn de Worde, London, 1490?]. 4to.

(Twelve leaves, without pagination, sig. a, b.; double columns.)

1509. **Fisher** (John), Cardinal, Bishop of Rochester. This sermon folowynge was compyled & sayd in the Cathedrall chyrche of saynt Poule within yᵉ cyte of London by the ryght reverende fader in god Johñ bysshop of Rochester, the body beynge present of the moost famouse prynce Kynge Henry the vij., etc. B.L. Wynkyn de Worde. 8vo., London, 1509.

(Without pagination or catchwords. Twelve leaves, sig. A, B. The title-page is partly occupied by a woodcut, and has an ornamental heraldic device on the verso.)

1535. **Matthew** (Simon). A Sermon [on 1 S. Pet. v. 6] made in the Cathedrall churche of saynt Paule at London, the 27 day of June, anno. 1535. B.L. T. Berthelet. 8vo., London, 1535. (Without pagination.)

1548. **Latimer** (Hugh), Bishop of Worcester. A notable Sermõ [on Rom. xv. 4] of yᵉ reverende father Maister Hughe Latimer, whiche he preached in yᵉ Shrouds at paules churche in Londõ, on the xviii daye of Januarye. B.L. J. Daye, . . . and William Seres. 8vo., London, 1548. (Without pagination.)

1564. **Grindal** (Edmund), successively Bishop of London, Archbishop of York and of Canterbury. A Sermon [on S. Matth. xxiv. 44] at the funeral solemnitie of . . . Prince Ferdinandus, the late Enperour of most famous memorye, ho!den in the Cathedrall Churche of Saint Paule in London, the third of October 1564 etc. B.L. J. Day. 4to., London, 1564. (Without pagination.)

1564. **Grindal** (Edmund). Concio Funebris in obitum Augustæ memoriæ Ferdinandi Cæsaris recens defuncti . . . in Ecclesia Cathedrali D. Pauli habita Octob. 3, anno 1564, per reverendum D. Episcopum London. D. Edmundum Grindallum.

Ex Anglico, in Latinum conversa, per J. Foxum. Excusum per J. Dayum. 4to., Londini, 1564. (Without pagination.)

1603? **Hooke** (Christopher). A Sermon preached in Paules Church in London [on 1 S. John iii. 1-3]: and published for the instruction and consolation of all that are heavie harted etc. B.L. E. Allde. 8vo., London [1603?]. (Without pagination.)

1609. **Morley** (Henry). The Cleansing of the Leper : discoursed and opened, first in certaine lectures within the Cathedrall Church of Saint Paul in London ; upon occasion of that great visitation of the plague in . . . 1603. And now thought meete to be published &c. H. L. for C. Knight. 8vo., London, 1609.

1623. **Squire** (John). A Sermon on the second Commandement [Exod. xx. 4 6] preached in Saint Pauls Church, Januarie 6, 1623. Printed by W. S. for N. Newbery. 4to., London, 1624.

1629. **Walker** (William, Pastor of Chiswick). A Sermon [on Rom. ii. 22] preached in St. Pauls-Church in London . . . Novemb. 28, 1628. B. Alsop and T. Fawcet, for R. Allot. 4to., London, 1629.

1635. **Gore** (John). The Oracle of God. A Sermon [on 2 Cor. xii. 9] . . . preached in the Cathedrall Church of St. Paul . . . on the 20, day of December . . . 1635. T. Cotes for T. Alchorn. 4to., London, 1636.

1635. **Gore** (John). Unknowne Kindnesse. A Sermon [on Ps. cxli. 5] preached in the Cathedrall Church of St. Paul . . . 1635. T. Cotes for T. Alchorne. 12mo., London, 1635.

1635. **Gore** (John). The Way to be Content. A sermon [on Philip. iv. 11] preached in the Cathedrall Church of St. Paul . . . the 26 day of May . . . 1634. T. Cotes for T. Alchorne. 4to., London, 1635.

1635. **Gore** (John). A Winter Sermon [on Psalm cxlvii. 16-18] preached in the Cathedrall Church of St Pauls . . . upon Shrove Sonday . . . 1634 . . . being a time of extraordinary snow and floods. T. Cotes for T. Alchorn. 4to., London, 1635.

1637. **Squire** (John). A Thanksgiving for the Decreasing and Hope of the Removing of the plague : being a Sermon [on Psal. l. 15] preached at St Pauls . . . 1. January, 1636. Printed by B. A. and T. F. for J. Clark. 4to., London, 1637.

1637. **Squire** (John). Three Sermons : two of them appointed for the Spittle, preached in St. Paul's Church by J. Squier . . . and J. Lynch, etc. R. Young for H. Blunden. 4to., London, 1637.

1638. **Gore** (John). The God of Heaven. A Sermon [on Psalm lxxiii. 25] . . . Preached in the Cathedrall Church of St Pauls . . . the 23 of September . . . 1638. T. Cotes for T. Alchorn. 4to., London, 1638.

PLAYS ACTED BY THE CHILDREN OF PAUL'S.

1584. **Lilly** (John). Campaspe. Played before the Queenes Maiestie on new yeares day, at night, by her Maiesties Childrē, and the Children of Paules. [A tragi-comedy in five acts and in prose.] T. Cadman. 4to., London, 1584. (Without pagination.)

Another edition in British Museum with manuscript notes. T. Orwin for W. Broome. 4to., London, 1591.

1591. **Lilly** (John). Sapho and Phao. [A comedy in five acts and in prose.] Played beefore the Queenes Majestie on Shrove-tewsday, by her Majesties Children, and the Boyes of Paules. T. Cadman. 4to., London, 1584. (Without pagination.)

Another edition. T. Orwin for W. Broome. 4to., London, 1591.

1591. **Lilly** (John). Endimion, the Man in the Moone, etc. [A Comedy in five Acts and in prose.] J. Charelwood for the Widdowe Broome. 4to., London, 1591.

1592. **Lilly** (John). Gallathea. [A Comedy in five acts and in prose.] As it was playde before the Queenes Majestie at Greene-wiche . . . By the Chyldren of Paules. J. Charlewoode for the Widow Broome. 4to., London, 1592. (Without pagination.)

1600. **Dodypoll** (Doctor). The Wisdome of Doctor Dodypoll. As it hath bene sundrie times acted by the Cnildren of Powles. [A Comedy in five acts and in verse.] T. Creede for R. Olive. 4to., London, 1600.

1601. **Drum** (Jacke). Jacke Drums Entertainment: or, the Comedie of Pasquill and Katherine. [In five acts and in prose and verse.] Printed for R. Olive. 4to., London, 1601.

1607. **Middleton** (T.). Michaelmas Terme. As it hath been . . . acted by the children of Paules. [A comedy in five acts, and in verse and prose.] Printed for A. L. 4to., London, 1607. (Without pagination.)

1607. **Smith** (Wentworth?). The Puritaine, or the Widdow of Watling-streete. [In five acts, in prose and verse.] Acted by the Children of Paules. Written by W. S. [*i.e.*, Wentworth Smith (?), frequently but erroneously attributed to W. Shakespeare]. G. Eld. 4to., London, 1607. (Without pagination.)

1608. **Middleton** (Thomas). A Tricke to catch the Old-one. [A comedy in five acts and in prose.] As it hath beene often in Action, both at Paules, and the Black-Fryers . . . Composde by T. M[iddleton]. Printed by G. E[ld]: and are to be sold by Henry Rockytt. 4to., London, 1608.

NOTE.

The works enumerated on pages 231 to 239 are not at present in the Library. But it has been thought desirable to include them as Desiderata in this catalogue, partly with a view to render this attempt at a bibliography of S. Paul's Cathedral somewhat more complete, and partly with the hope that possessors of rare books included in these lists may be induced to enrich the already valuable collection by supplying its deficiencies.

It will be observed that in some cases the books still needed are earlier or later editions of works already acquired.

The following list, to the year 1731, is taken chiefly from a work entitled *A Complete List of the Stewards, Presidents, etc., belonging to the Royal Corporation for the Relief of the Poor Widows and Children of Clergymen, from the Grant of the Charter by King Charles II., July 1, 1678* (8vo., London, 1733). In this work (compiled by William Freeman, A.B., Lecturer of S. Botolph's, Aldersgate) it is stated that the first sermon was preached in 1655, at S. Paul's, by the Rev. George Hall, M.A., Minister of S. Botolph's, Aldersgate, and afterwards Bishop of Chester. No subsequent meeting is mentioned until the year 1674, with which the following list commences. We are told elsewhere that 'the custom of preaching to the Sons of the Clergy began in Dr. Manton's time: Dr. Hall preached the first Sermon to them, as Dr. Manton did the second. See Works, vol. iii.'— *Gentleman's Magazine*, lv., 164. It is probable that a meeting for this charitable purpose may have been held from the year 1655, though with occasional interruptions. The festival clearly originated prior to the charter being granted to the Corporation of the Sons of the Clergy in 1678, as from 1674 there appear to have been stewards and a treasurer annually appointed; and Bishop Spratt, in his sermon preached in 1678, speaks of 'these friendly and charitable meetings' as having been '*for several years* renewed, with no just offence to any, though with the grief and envy perhaps of some, who are not of our household of faith, but to the comfort of all that are; for the present benefit and relief of many, and with well-grounded hopes and presages of much greater things for the future.' In 1702, Dr. White Kennett recommended that 'an account should be drawn up of the first meeting of this Society, of the several benefactions to it,

16

and of the manifold good services done by it.' It is to be regretted that this suggestion was not then attended to.

J. H. M.[1]

Sermons marked thus * are in the Cathedral Library.
Sermons marked thus † were not printed.

AT S. PAUL'S CATHEDRAL.

| 1655* | George Hall ... | ... | *Minister of S. Botolph's, Aldersgate Street.*[2] |

AT S. MICHAEL'S, CORNHILL.

| 1674 | †John Dolben ... | ... | *Bishop of Rochester.* |
| 1675 | †John Pearson ... | .. | *Bishop of Chester.* |

AT BOW CHURCH, CHEAPSIDE.

1676	†Peter Gunning	...	*Bishop of Ely.*
1677	†John Fell ...	...	*Bishop of Oxford.*
1678*	Thomas Spratt	...	*Bishop of Rochester.*
1679 1680	†William Lloyd	...	*Bishop of S. Asaph.*
1681	†Thomas Tennison	...	*Vicar of S. Martin's-in-the-Fields.*
1682	Arthur Bury ...	...	*Rector of Exeter College, Oxford.*[3]
1683	William Beveridge	...	*Archdeacon of Colchester.*[4]
1684	Francis Turner	...	*Bishop of Ely.*
1685	†Edward Pelling	...	*S. Martin's, Ludgate.*
1686	Henry Dove ...	...	*S. Bride's.*
1687 1688 1689	†Adam Littleton	...	*Rector of Chelsea.*
1690	†Thomas Linford	...	*Afternoon Preacher at Gray's Inn.*
1691	Thomas Tennison	...	*Bishop of Lincoln, elect.*
1692	Edward Fowler	...	*Bishop of Gloucester.*
1693	Edward Lake ...	...	*Rector of S. Mary-at-Hill.*
1694	†Thomas Manningham		*Canon of Windsor.*
1695	Thomas Whinsop	...	*Rector of S. Mary's, Abchurch.*
1696*	Zaccheus Isham	...	*Rector of S. Botolph's, Bishopsgate.*

AT S. PAUL'S CATHEDRAL.

| 1697 | George Stanhope | ... | *Chaplain in Ordinary to his Majesty.* |
| 1698 | †Francis Atterbury | ... | *Lecturer of S. Bride's.*[5] |

---

[1] This note is due to Mr. J. H. Markland, who about the year 1830 was the treasurer of the festival. I am permitted to print this list by the courtesy of the Registrar, Sir Paget Bowman.

[2] See *supra*, p. 102.

[3] Printed in Dr. Bury's *Constant Communicant*, second edition, 8vo. In the *Gentleman's Magazine*, vol. lv., p. 63, it is stated that Dr. George Rust, Bishop of Dromore, was the preacher in 1682.

[4] Printed in the fourth volume of his *Thesaurus Theologicus*, 8vo.

[5] In 1698, music was, for the first time, introduced at this festival.

1699	William Assheton	... *Rector of Beckenham.*
1700*	Richard West ...	... *Fellow of Magdalen College, Oxford.*
1701	†Thomas Lamplugh	... *Afterwards Prebendary of York.*
1702	White Kennett	... *Archdeacon of Huntingdon.*
1703*	Nathaniel Resbury	... *Rector of S. Paul's, Shadwell.*
1704	Lilly Butler ...	... *S. Mary's, Aldermanbury.*
1705*	Thomas Spratt	... *Archdeacon of Rochester.*
1706*	Roger Altham...	... *Rector of S. Botolph's, Bishopsgate.*
1707*	Charles Trimnell	... *Rector of S. James's, Westminster.*
1708	Philip Bisse ...	... *Fellow of New College, Oxford.*
1709*	Francis Atterbury	... *Dean of Carlisle, and Preacher at the Rolls.*
1710*	Thomas Sherlock	... *Master of the Temple.*[1]
1711*	Nathaniel Marshall	... *Rector of Finchley.*
1712	George Bell ...	... *Chaplain to the Lord Privy Seal.*
1713*	Henry Sacheverell	... *Rector of S. Andrew's, Holborn.*
1714*	Edmund Chishull	... *Chaplain in Ordinary to his Majesty.*
1715	William Savage ...	... *Rector of S. Andrew's, Wardrobe.*
1716*	Thomas Bisse ...	... *Preacher at the Rolls.*
1717*	William Lupton	... *Preacher of Lincoln's Inn.*
1718	John Rogers ...	... *Rector of Wrington, Somersetshire.*
1719*	Joseph Smith ...	... *Rector of S. Dionis Backchurch.*
1720	Joseph Trapp ...	... *Rector of Dauntsey, Wilts.*
1721	Daniel Waterland	... *Master of Magdalene College, Cambridge.*
1722*	Powlett St. John	... *Rector of Yeldon, Bedfordshire.*[2]
1723	William Delaune	... *President of S. John's College, Oxford.*[3]
1724	Samuel Edgley	... *Vicar of Wandsworth, Surrey.*
1725*	Joseph Roper ...	... *Rector of S. Nicholas, Cole Abbey, London.*
1726*	Sir John Dolben, Bart.	*Prebendary of Durham.*
1727*	Michael Hutchinson ...	*Minister of Hammersmith.*
1728	Robert Kilburn	... *Prebendary of S. Paul's.*
1729	Ralph Brideoake ...	... *Archdeacon of Winchester.*
1730*	Thomas Spateman	... *Prebendary of S. Paul's.*
1731	Robert Warren	... *Rector of S. Mary's, Stratford-le-Bow.*
1732*	Henry Stebbing	... *Preacher of Gray's Inn.*
1733	Thomas Mangey	... *Prebendary of Durham.*
1734-5*	George Lavington	... *Canon Residentiary of S. Paul's.*
1735-6*	Philip Barton ...	... *Canon of Christ Church, Oxford.*
1737*	William Berryman	... *Rector of S. Andrew Undershaft.*
1738	Edmund Martin	... *Dean of Worcester.*

[1] Reprinted 1852, for the benefit of the Charity, by Joshua Watson, Esq., D.C.L. See *supra*, p. 114.

[2] Printed in a volume of Fourteen Sermons on Practical Subjects, 8vo., p. 209. 1737.

[3] Printed also in a volume of Twelve Sermons, 8vo., p. 268. 1723.

1739*	Edward Banyer	... *Afternoon Preacher at Gray's Inn.*
1740*	Edmund Bateman	... *Archdeacon of Lewes.*
1741*	Edward Yardley	... *Archdeacon of Cardigan.*
1742	Isaac Maddox	... *Bishop of S. Asaph.*
1743	Edward Cobden	... *Archdeacon of London.*[1]
1744	Andrew Trebeck	... *Rector of S. George's, Hanover Square.*
1745	Henry Hervey Ashton	*Rector of Shotley, Suffolk.*
1746*	Samuel Nichols	... *Afterwards Master of the Temple.*
1747	†Francis Ayscough[2]	...
1748	†Thomas Hayter	... *Archdeacon of York.*
1749	Sir G. Williams, Bart.	... *Vicar of Islington, Middlesex.*
1750	†Henry Stebbing	... *Fellow of Catherine Hall, Cambridge.*
1751*	Arnold King ...	... *Rector of S. Michael's, Cornhill, London.*
1752*	James Townley	... *Rector of S. Benedict's, Gracechurch, London.*
1753*	Thomas Ashton	... *Rector of S. Botolph's, Bishopsgate.*[3]
1754*	John Butler ...	... *Chaplain to the Princess Dowager of Wales.*
1755*	Samuel Salter ...	... *Master of the Charterhouse.*[4]
1756*	Thomas Church	... *Vicar of Battersea, and Prebendary of S. Paul's.*
1757*	Gloucester Ridley	... *Minister of Poplar.*
1758	James Ibbetson	... *Archdeacon of S. Alban's.*
1759	Stotherd Abdy	... *Rector of Theydon Garnon, Essex.*
1760	William Dodwell	... *Archdeacon of Berks.*
1761*	John Burton ...	... *Fellow of Eton.*[5]
1762	George Horne	... *Fellow of Magdalen College, Oxon.*
1763	Thomas Franklin	... *Vicar of Ware, Hertfordshire.*
1764	Richard Hind...	... *Rector of Sheering, Essex.*
1765*	James Halifax...	... *Vicar of Ewell, Surrey.*
1766	†Cutts Barton ...	... *Dean of Bristol.*
1767	Richard Eyre ...	... *Rector of Bright Waltham, Berks.*
1768	Robert Pool Finch	... *Rector of S. Michael's, Cornhill, London.*
1769*	Thomas Percy	... *Vicar of Easton Maudit, Northamptonshire.*
1770	Peter Whalley ...	... *Rector of S. Gabriel's, Fenchurch Street, London.*
1771	William Parker	... *Rector of S. James's, Westminster.*[6]
1772	Thomas Morrell	... *Rector of Buckland, Herts.*

[1] Printed in a volume of Poems, and Twenty-eight Sermons, 4to., p. 53. 1757.
[2] At this rehearsal Prince George and Prince Edward were present.
[3] Printed in a volume of Twenty-one Sermons, 8vo., p. 27. 1770.
[4] Preached extempore.
[5] Printed in vol. ii. of Occasional Sermons, 8vo., p. 97. 1766.
[6] The Rev. Mr. Tilson, of Richmond, Surrey, gave £200 to try the experiment of a rehearsal of the music in a church or chapel at the west end of the town. S. George's, Hanover Square, was the church selected.

1773	Samuel Glasse	...	*Chaplain in Ordinary to his Majesty.*
1774	†Josiah Tucker	...	*Dean of Gloucester.*
1775	Andrew Burnaby	...	*Vicar of Greenwich.*[1]
1776	Beilby Porteus	...	*Rector of Lambeth.*
1777	James Cornwallis	...	*Dean of Canterbury.*
1778	John Warren ...	...	*Prebendary of Ely.*
1779	Robert Richardson	...	*Rector of S. Anne's, Westminster.*
1780	John Law ...	...	*Archdeacon of Rochester.*
1781*	Robert Markham	...	*Rector of S. Mary's, Whitechapel.*
1782	William Jones...	...	*Rector of Paston, Northampton shire.*
1783	Richard Kay ...	...	*Archdeacon of Nottingham.*
1784	†Samuel Carr ...	...	*Rector of Finchley, Middlesex.*
1785*	Thomas Jackson	...	*Prebendary of Westminster.*
1786*	Samuel Horsley	...	*Archdeacon of S. Alban's.*
1787	Anthony Hamilton	...	*Archdeacon of Colchester.*
1788	Phipps Western	...	*Canon Residentiary of Wells.*
1789*	William Vincent	...	*Sub-Almoner to his Majesty.*
1790	Durand Rhudde	...	*Rector of Brantham and Wenham, Suffolk.*
1791	Joseph Holden Pott	...	*Archdeacon of S. Alban's.*
1792*	Richard Nicoll	...	*Chancellor of Wells.*
1793*	Griffith Griffith	...	*Rector of S. Mary-le-Bow, London.*
1794*	William Langford	...	*Canon of Windsor.*
1795*	Charles P. Layard	...	*Prebendary of Worcester.*
1796*	Thomas Rennell	...	*Prebendary of Winchester.*
1797*	George Gretton	...	*Vicar of Dartmouth, Devonshire.*
1798*	Gerard Andrewes	...	*Rector of S. James's, Westminster.*
1799*	Charles Moss ...	...	*Canon Residentiary of S. Paul's.*
1800	H. W. Majendie	...	*Bishop of Chester.*
1801*	William L. Bowles	...	*Rector of Dumbleton, Gloucester shire.*
1802	George Henry Law	...	*Prebendary of Carlisle.*
1803*	George H. Glasse	...	*Rector of Hanwell, Middlesex.*
1804	Robert Hodgson	...	*Rector of S. George's, Hanover Square.*
1805*	Charles Barker	...	*Canon Residentiary of Wells.*
1806	Robert Price ...	...	*Prebendary of Durham.*
1807*	William Coxe ...	...	*Archdeacon of Wilts, and Canon Residentiary of Sarum.*
1808*	Francis Randolph	...	*Prebendary of Bristol.*
1809*	Sir Henry Rivers, Bart.		
1810*	J. S. Clarke ...	...	*Vicar of Preston, Sussex.*
1811*	William Douglas	...	*Prebendary of Westminster.*
1812	Charles Burney	...	*Rector of S. Paul's, Deptford.*
1813	Hon. Henry Ryder	...	*Dean of Wells.*
1814	Henry Phillpotts	...	*Prebendary of Durham.*
1815	George Mathew	...	*Vicar of Greenwich.*

[1] Printed in a volume of Occasional Sermons, 8vo., p. 39.   1777.

1816*	John Cole ...	... *Rector of Exeter College, Oxford.*
1817*	Laurence Gardner	... *Minister of Curzon Chapel, London.*
1818*	D. W. Garrow	... *Rector of East Barnet, Herts.*
1819*	Charles Goddard	... *Archdeacon of Lincoln.*
1820*	Robert Stevens	... *Rector of S. James's, Garlick Hythe.*
1821	Thomas Rennell	... *Vicar of Kensington.*
1822	Charles J. Blomfield	... *Archdeacon of Colchester.*
1823	George D'Oyly	... *Rector of Lambeth, and Sundridge, Kent.*
1824	John B. Jenkinson	... *Dean of Worcester.*
1825	James Henry Monk	... *Dean of Peterborough.*
1826*	Christopher Benson	... *Prebendary of Worcester.*
1827	John Hume Spry	... *Rector of S. Marylebone.*
1828*	P. N. Shuttleworth	... *Warden of New College, Oxford.*
1829*	Charles Webb Le Bas	*Rector of S. Paul's, Shadwell.*
1830*	Edmund Goodenough	*Prebendary of Westminster.*
1831*	George Chandler	... *Dean of Chichester.*[1]
1832	William Dealtry	... *Prebendary and Chancellor of Winchester.*
1833	George Davys ...	... *Dean of Chester.*
1834*	John Merewether	... *Dean of Hereford.*[2]
1835	George Pellew	... *Dean of Norwich.*
1836*	Hugh N. Pearson	... *Dean of Salisbury.*
1837	Thomas Calvert	... *Warden of Manchester Collegiate Church.*
1838*	John Lonsdale	... *Preacher of Lincoln's Inn.*
1839*	Lord John Thynne	... *Prebendary of Westminster.*
1840	W. T. P. Brymer	... *Archdeacon of Bath.*
1841*	W. Hale Hale	... *Archdeacon of London.*
1842	Samuel Wilberforce	... *Archdeacon of Surrey.*
1843*	George Butler	... *Dean of Peterborough.*
1844*	Henry Melvill	... *Principal of E. I. College, Haileybury.*
1845	R. W. Jelf ...	... *Canon of Christ Church.*
1846*	J. Giffard Ward	... *Dean of Lincoln.*
1847*	Henry Howarth	... *Rector of S. George's, Hanover Square.*
1848	Thomas Dale ...	... *Vicar of S. Pancras.*
1849*	Edward M. Goulburn	... *Perpetual Curate of Holywell, Oxford.*
1850	Charles Musgrave	... *Archdeacon of Craven.*
1851*	Charles John Vaughan	*Headmaster of Harrow School.*[3]
1852	G. B. Blomfield	... *Rector of Stevenage, Herts.*
1853	John Sinclair ...	... *Archdeacon of Middlesex.*
1854	John Bird Sumner	... *Lord Archbishop of Canterbury.*[4]

[1] Second edition, printed in 8vo. 1832.
[2] Queen Adelaide was present at this Festival.
[3] Printed also in a volume of Sermons, 8vo., p. 177. 1851.
[4] His Royal Highness, the late Prince Consort, was present at this the Bicentenary Festival.

1855	Charles A. Thurlow ...	*Chancellor of Chester.*
1856	James Amiraux Jeremie	*Regius Prof. of Divinity, Cambridge.*
1857	Henry Alford	*Dean of Canterbury.*
1858	Thomas Garnier ...	*Rector of Trinity Church, Marylebone.*
1859	Daniel Moore	*Incumbent of Camden Church, Camberwell.*
1860	Archibald Boyd ...	*Incumbent of Paddington, and Hon. Canon of Gloucester.*
1861	William Carus ...	*Canon of Winchester.*
1862	Anthony W. Thorold ...	*Rector of S. Giles-in-the-Fields.*
1863	Hon. Augustus Duncombe	*Dean of York.*
1864	Walter Farquhar Hook	*Dean of Chichester.*
1865	Harvey Goodwin ...	*Dean of Ely.*[1]
1866	William G. Humphry ...	*Prebendary of S. Paul's.*
1867	J. R. Woodford ...	*Vicar of Kempsford, Gloucestershire.*
1868	John Saul Howson ...	*Dean of Chester.*
1869	Thomas James Rowsell	*Rector of S. Margaret's, Lothbury.*
1870	Henry Parry Liddon ...	*Canon of S. Paul's.*
1871	J. C. Miller	*Canon of Worcester.*
1872	James Moorhouse ...	*Vicar of Paddington.*
1873	Francis J. Holland ...	*Minister of Quebec Chapel.*
1874	William Connor Magee	*Bishop of Peterborough.*[2]
1875	Frederic W. Farrar ...	*Headmaster of Marlborough College.*
1876*	William Boyd Carpenter	*Vicar of S. James's, Lower Holloway.*
1877	Ernest R. Wilberforce	*Vicar of Seaforth, Liverpool.*
1878	James Fleming ...	*Canon of York.*
1879	Edward Carr Glyn ...	*Vicar of Kensington.*
1880	Charles Marson ...	*Vicar of Clevedon, Somerset.*
1881	Henry Montagu Butler	*Headmaster of Harrow School, and Prebendary of S. Paul's.*
1882	Edward White Benson	*Bishop of Truro.*
1883	S. Reynolds Hole ...	*Prebendary of Lincoln and Vicar of Caunton, Notts.*
1884	Arthur J. Mason ...	*Vicar of Allhallow's, Barking.*
1885	Randall T. Davidson ...	*Dean of Windsor.*
1886	John Gott	*Dean of Worcester.*
1887	J. E. C. Welldon ...	*Headmaster of Harrow School.*
1888	John G. Richardson ...	*Vicar of S. Mary's, Nottingham.*
1889	Charles J. Ridgeway ...	*Vicar of Christ Church, Lancaster Gate.*
1890	Edward S. Talbot ...	*Vicar of Leeds.*
1891	William C. E. Newbolt	*Canon of S. Paul's.*
1892	Alfred George Edwards	*Bishop of S. Asaph.*

[1] His Royal Highness the Prince of Wales was present at this Festival.
[2] The Sermon was preached extempore, and not published.

SOCIETY FOR THE PROPAGATION OF THE GOSPEL.

1702	Richard Willis	...	...	*Dean of Lincoln.*
1703	†William Lloyd	...	...	*Bishop of Worcester.*
1704	Gilbert Burnet	...	...	„ *Salisbury.*
1705	John Hough	...	...	„ *Lichfield and Coventry.*
1706	John Williams	...	...	„ *Chichester.*
1707	William Beveridge	...	...	„ *S. Asaph.*
1708	William Stanley	...	...	*Dean of S. Asaph.*
1709	Sir William Dawes	...	...	*Bishop of Chester.*
1710	Charles Trimnell	...	...	„ *Norwich.*
1711	William Fleetwood	...	...	„ *S. Asaph.*
1712	White **Kennet**	...	...	*Dean of Peterborough.*
1713	John Moore	...	...	*Bishop of Ely.*
1714	George Stanhope	...	...	*Dean of Canterbury.*
1715	St. George Ash	...	...	*Bishop of Clogher.*
1716	**Thomas** Sherlock	...	...	*Dean of Chichester.*
1717	Thomas Hayley	...	...	*Residentiary of Chichester.*
1718	Philip Bisse	...	...	*Bishop of Hereford.*
1719	Edward Chandler	...	...	„ *Lichfield and Coventry.*
1720	Samuel Bradford	...	...	„ *Carlisle.*
1721	Edward Waddington	...	...	*Afterwards Bishop of Chichester.*
1722	Hugh Boulter	...	...	*Bishop of Bristol.*
1723	John Waugh	...	...	*Dean of Gloucester.*
1724	Thomas Green	...	...	*Bishop of Ely.*
1725	John Wynne	...	...	„ *S. Asaph.*
1726	Joseph Wilcocks	...	...	„ *Gloucester.*
1727	John Leng	...	...	„ *Norwich.*
1728	Richard Reynolds	...	...	„ *Lincoln.*
1729	Henry Egerton	...	...	„ *Hereford.*
1730	Zachary Pearce	...	...	*Afterwards Bishop of* **Rochester.**
1731	John Denne	...	...	*Archdeacon of Rochester.*
1732	George Berkeley	...	...	*Dean of Londonderry.*
1733	Richard Smalbroke	...	...	*Bishop of Lichfield and* **Coventry.**
1734	Isaac Maddox	...	...	*Dean of Wells.*
1735	Francis Hare	...	...	*Bishop of Chichester.*
1736	John Lynch	...	...	*Dean of Canterbury.*
1737	Nicolas Claggett	...	...	*Bishop of S. David's.*
1738	Thomas Herring	...	...	„ *Bangor.*
1739	Joseph Butler	...	...	„ *Bristol.*
1740	Martin Benson	...	...	„ *Gloucester.*
1741	Thomas Secker	...	...	„ *Oxford.*
1742	Henry Stebbing	...	...	*Chancellor of Salisbury.*
1743	Matthias Mawson	...	...	*Bishop of Chichester.*
1744	John Gilbert	...	...	„ *Llandaff.*
1745	Philip Bearcroft	...	...	*Secretary of the Society.*
1746	Matthew Hutton	...	...	*Bishop of Bangor.*

1747	John Thomas ...	... *Bishop of Lincoln.*	
1748	Samuel Lisle ...	... ,, *S. Asaph.*	
1749	William George ...	... *Dean of Lincoln.*	
1750	Richard Trevor ...	... *Bishop of S. David's.*	
1751	John Thomas ...	,, *Peterborough.*	
1752	Richard Osbaldistone ...	,, *Carlisle.*	
1753	Edward Cresset ...	,, *Llandaff.*	
1754	Robert H. Drummond ...	,, *S. Asaph.*	
1755	Thomas Hayter ...	,, *Norwich.*	
1756	Frederick Cornwallis ...	,, *Lichfield and Coventry.*	
1757	Edmund Keene ...	,, *Chester.*	
1758	James Johnson ...	,, *Gloucester.*	
1759	Antony Ellis ...	,, *S. David's.*	
1760	Sir William Ashburnham	,, *Chichester.*	
1761	Richard Newcome ...	,, *Llandaff.*	
1762	John **Hume** ...	,, *Oxford.*	
1763	John Egerton ...	,, *Bangor.*	
1764	Richard Terrick ...	,, *Peterborough.*	
1765	Philip Yonge ...	,, *Norwich.*	
1766	William Warburton ...	,, *Gloucester.*	
1767	John Ewer ...	,, *Llandaff.*	
1768	John Green ...	,, *Lincoln.*	
1769	Thomas Newton ...	,, *Bristol.*	
1770	Frederick Keppel ...	,, *Exeter.*	
1771	Robert Lowth ...	,, *Oxford.*	
1772	Charles Moss ...	,, *S. David's.*	
1773	Jonathan Shipley ...	,, *S. Asaph.*	
1774	Edmund Law ...	,, *Carlisle.*	
1775	**Shute** Barrington ...	,, *Llandaff.*	
1776	John Hinchcliffe ...	,, *Peterborough.*	
1777	William Markham ...	... *Archbishop of York.*	
1778	Brownlow North ...	... *Bishop of Worcester.*	
1779	James York ...	,, *S. David's.*	
1780	John Thomas ...	,, *Rochester.*	
1781	Richard Hurd ...	,, *Lichfield and Coventry.*	
1782	John **Moore** ...	,, *Bangor.*	
1783	Beilby **Porteus** ...	,, *Chester.*	
1784	John Butler ...	,, *Oxford.*	
1785	John Ross · ...	,, *Exeter.*	
1786	Thomas Thurlow ...	,, *Lincoln.*	
1787	John Warren ...	,, *Bangor.*	
1788	James Cornwallis ...	,, *Lichfield and Coventry.*	
1789	Samuel Halifax ...	,, *Gloucester.*	
1790	Lewis Bagot ...	,, *Norwich.*	
1791	Edward Smallwell ...	,, *Oxford.*	
1792	George Pretyman ...	,, *Lincoln.*	
1793	John Douglas ...	,, *Salisbury.*	
1794	William Cleaver ...	,, *Chester.*	
1795	Samuel Horsley ...	,, *Rochester.*	
1796	Richard Beadon ...	,, *Gloucester.*	

1797	Charles Manners Sutton		*Bishop of*	*Norwich.*
1798	Edward Venables Vernon		,,	*Carlisle.*
1799	Spencer Madan ...	...	,,	*Peterborough.*
1800	Henry R. Courtney	...	,,	*Exeter.*
1801	Ffol. H. W. Cornewall	...	,,	*Bristol.*
1802	John Buckner ...	...	,,	*Chichester.*
1803	John Randolph ...	...	,,	*Oxford.*
1804	Henry W. Majendie	..	,,	*Chester.*
1805	George Is. Huntingford...		,,	*Gloucester.*
1806	Thomas Dampier	...	,,	*Rochester.*
1807	George Pelham ...	...	,,	*Bristol.*
1808	Thomas Burgess	...	,,	*S. David's.*
1809	John Fisher ...	...	,, ·	*Salisbury.*
1810	Henry Bathurst ...	...	,,	*Norwich.*
1811	John Luxmore ...	...	,,	*Hereford.*
1812	Samuel Goodenough	...	,,	*Carlisle.*
1813	William L. Mansell	...	,,	***Bristol.***
1814	Bowyer Sparke ...	...	,,	*Ely.*
1815	William Jackson	...	,,	*Oxford.*
1816	George Henry Law	...	,,	*Chester.*
1817	William Howley ...	...	,,	*London.*
1818	John Parsons ...	...	,,	*Peterborough.*
1819	Henry Ryder ...	...	,,	*Gloucester.*
1820	Edward Legge ...	...	,,	*Oxford*
1821	Herbert Marsh ...	...	,,	*Peterborough.*
1822	William Van Mildert	...	,,	*Llandaff.*
1823	John Kaye ...	...	,,	*Bristol.*
1824	William Carey ...	...	,,	*Exeter.*
1825	Christopher Bethell	...	,,	*Gloucester.*
1826	Robert James Carr	...	,,	*Chichester.*
1827	Charles James Blomfield		,,	*Chester.*
1828	John B. Jenkinson	...	,,	*S. David's.*
1829	Charles R. Sumner	...	,,	***Winchester.***
1830	**Robert Gray** ...	...	,,	***Bristol.***
1831	**Hugh Percy** ...	...	,,	*Carlisle.*
1832	**George Murray** ...	...	,,	*Rochester.*
1833	**Edward Copleston**	...	,,	*Llandaff.*
1834	**John Bird Sumner**	...	*Archbishop of Canterbury.*	
1835	**Richard Bagot** ...	...	*Bishop of Oxford.*	
1836	**James Henry Monk**	...	,,	*Gloucester.*
1837	**Edward Maltby** ...	... ,,	,,	*Durham.*
1838	Henry Phillpotts...	...	,,	*Exeter.*
1839	Joseph Allen ...	...	,,	*Ely.*
1840	William Otter ...	...	,,	*Chichester.*
1841	Charles T. Longley	...	,,	*Ripon.*
1842	Edward Denison	..	,,	*Salisbury.*
1843	†Edward Stanley ...	...	,,	*Norwich.*
1844	Thomas Musgrave	...	,,	*Hereford.*
1845	George Davys ...	...	,,	*Peterborough.*
1846	Connop Thirlwall	...	,,	*S. David's.*

1847	Henry Pepys ...	...	*Bishop of Worcester.*
1848	Ashurst T. Gilbert	,,	*Chichester.*
1849	†John Lonsdale ...	,,	*Lichfield.*
1850	Samuel Wilberforce	,,	*Oxford.*
1851	Thomas Vowler Short	,,	*S. Asaph.*
1852	S. A. McCoskry ...	,,	*Michigan, U.S.*
1852	Samuel Wilberforce	,,	*Oxford (Jubilee).*
1853	James Prince Lee	,,	*Manchester.*
1854	†Richard Whateley	...	*Archbishop of Dublin.*
1855	†Renn D. Hampden	...	*Bishop of Hereford.*
1856	†John Graham ...	,,	*Chester.*
1857	†Walter Kerr Hamilton ...	,,	*Salisbury.*
1858	†William Higgin ...	,,	*Derry.*
1859	†Lord Auckland ...	,,	*Bath and Wells.*
1860	†Montague Villiers	,,	*Carlisle.*
1861	†Robert Bickersteth	,,	*Ripon.*
1862	†James Colquhoun Campbell ...	,,	*Bangor.*
1863	†Marcus Gervaise Beresford		*Archbishop of Armagh.*
1864	†John Jackson ...	...	*Bishop of Lincoln.*
1865	†Joseph C. Wigram ...	,,	*Rochester.*
1866	†Henry Philpott ...	,,	*Worcester.*
1867	Charles James Ellicott ...	,,	*Gloucester and Bristol.*
1868	†E. Harold Browne ...	,,	*Ely.*
1869	†George Augustus Selwyn	,,	*Lichfield.*
1870	†Harvey Goodwin ...	,,	*Carlisle.*
1871	†James Fraser ...	,,	*Manchester.*
1872	†Frederick Temple ...	,,	*Exeter.*
1873	William Alexander ...	,,	*Derry.*
1874	†James Russell Woodford ...	,,	*Ely.*
1875	†James Atlay ...	,,	*Hereford.*
1876	†John Fielder Mackarness	,,	*Oxford.*
1877	†Lord Arthur Charles Hervey ...	,,	*Bath and Wells.*
1878	†Robert Bickersteth ...	,,	*Ripon.*
1879	†William Basil Jones ...	,,	*S. David's.*
1880	†Thomas Legh Claughton	,,	*S. Alban's.*
1881	Richard Durnford ...	,,	*Chichester.*
1882	Harvey Goodwin ...	,,	*Carlisle.*
1883	†Ernest Rowland Wilberforce ...	,,	*Newcastle.*
1884	G. T. Bedell ...	,,	*Ohio.*
1885	†Boyd Carpenter ...	,,	*Ripon.*
1886	Edward King ...	,,	*Lincoln.*
1887	W. S. Perry ...	,,	*Iowa, U.S.*
1888	W. C. Doane ...	,,	*Albany, U.S.*
1889	†Francis John Jayne ...	,,	*Chester.*
1890	William Connor Magee ...	,,	*Peterborough.*
1891	William Alexander ...	,,	*Derry.*
1892	Edgar Jacob ...	...	*Canon of Winchester.*

SOCIETY FOR PROMOTING CHRISTIAN KNOWLEDGE.

1704*	Richard Willis ...	... Dean of Lincoln.
1705	George Stanhope	... „ Canterbury.
1706	White Kennet ...	... Archdeacon of Huntingdon.
1707*	Francis Gastrel ...	... Canon of Christchurch.
1708*	Robert Moss ...	... Afterwards Dean of Ely.
1709*	Samuel Bradford	... Afterwards Bishop of Rochester.
1710	George Smalridge	... „ „ Bristol.
1711*	Andrew Snape ...	... Afterwards Canon of Windsor.
1712	Lord Willoughby de Broke	Afterwards Dean of Windsor.
1713*	Sir William Dawes	... Bishop of Chester.
1714*	John Robinson	... „ London.
1715	William Wake	... „ Lincoln.
1716*	Edmund Gibson	... „ Lincoln.
1717*	William Talbot ...	.. „ Salisbury.
1718	William Lupton ...	... Prebendary of Durham.
1719	Thomas Sherlock	... Dean of Chichester
1720	Dr. Knight	...
1721	Nathanael Marshall	... Afterwards Canon of Windsor.
1722*	Hugh Boulter	... Bishop of Bristol.
1723	Daniel Waterland	... Master of Magdalen College, Cambridge.
1724	Thomas Wilson ...	... Bishop of Sodor and Man.
1725	William Berriman	... Fellow of Eton.
1726*	Thomas Mangey	... Prebendary of Durham.
1727	— Watson ...	...
1728	Thomas Yalden ...	... Prebendary of Chumleigh, Devon.
1729*	John Rogers ...	...
1730	Samuel Peploe ...	... Bishop of Chester.
1731	Joseph Wilcox ...	... „ Gloucester.
1732	Henry Stebbing ...	... Preacher at Gray's Inn.
1733*	Robert Clavering	... Bishop of Peterborough.
1734	John Heylyn ...	... Afterwards Prebendary of Westminster.
1735	Zachary Pearce ...	... Bishop of Rochester.
1736	John Denne	... Archdeacon of Rochester.
1737	John Thomas ...	...
1738	John Conybeare ...	... Dean of Christchurch.
1739	Nicolas Clagett ...	... „ S. David's.
1740	John Thomas ...	... „ Peterborough.
1741	Isaac Maddox ...	... Bishop of S. Asaph.
1742	Joseph Trapp ...	... Rector of Harlington.
1743*	Thomas Secker ...	... Bishop of Oxford.
1744	Matthew Hutton ...	... „ Bangor.
1745	Joseph Butler ...	... „ Bristol.
1746*	George Lavington	... Residentiary of S. Paul's.

1747	Richard Trevor ...	...	*Bishop of S. David's.*
1748	Philip Bearcroft ...	...	*Secretary of S.P.G.*
1749	Samuel Squire ...	...	*Archdeacon of Bath.*
1750	Edward Yardley ...	...	„ *Cardigan.*
1751	Thomas Church ...	...	*Prebendary of S. Paul's.*
1752	John Chapman ...	...	*Archdeacon of Sudbury.*
1753	Robert H. Drummond ...		*Bishop of S. Asaph.*
1754	John Cobden ...	...	*Archdeacon of London.*
1755*	Thomas Hayter ...	...	*Bishop of Norwich.*
1756	Samuel Nicolls ..	...	*Master of the Temple.*
1757	Glocester Ridley	...	*Afterwards Prebendary of Salisbury.*
1758*	William Dodwell	...	*Residentiary of Salisbury.*
1759*	John Burton ...	...	*Fellow of Eton.*
1760	Thomas Ashton ...	...	*Fellow of Eton.*
1761*	Thomas Negus ..	...	*Rector of S. Mary's, Rotherhithe.*
1762*	Frederick Cornwallis	...	*Bishop of Lichfield and Coventry.*
1763*	Patrick Delany ...	...	*Dean of Down.*
1764	Sir Peter Rivers, Bart.	...	*Rector of Woolwich.*
1765	Thomas Newton ...	...	*Bishop of Bristol.*
1766	Josiah Tucker ...	...	*Dean of Gloucester.*
1767	Edmund Keene ...	...	*Bishop of Chester.*
1768	William Worthington	...	*Prebendary of York.*
1769	Philip Yonge ...	...	*Bishop of Norwich.*
1770	Richard Eyre ...	...	*Rector of Bright Waltham, Berks.*
1771*	James Hallifax ...	...	„ *Cheddington, Bucks.*
1772	Edward Bentham ...	...	*Regius Professor of Divinity, Oxford.*
1773	John Green ...	...	*Bishop of Lincoln.*
1774*	Robert Pool Finch	...	
1775	Newton Ogle ...	...	*Dean of Winchester.*
1776	Dr. Kaye... ...	...	*Sub-Almoner to his Majesty.*
1777	Jonathan Shipley ...	...	*Bishop of S. Asaph.*
1778	Anthony Hamilton	...	*Archdeacon of Colchester.*
1779*	Robert Markham	...	*Rector of S. Mary's, Whitechapel.*
1780	John Butler ...	...	*Bishop of Oxford.*
1781	William Parker ...	...	*Rector of S. James's, Piccadilly.*
1782	Beilby Porteus ...	...	*Bishop of Chester.*
1783*	George Horne ...	...	*Dean of Canterbury.*
1784*	William Vincent	...	*Sub-Almoner to his Majesty.*
1785*	James York ...	...	*Bishop of Ely.*
1786*	John Hinchcliffe	...	„ *Peterborough.*
1787*	James Chelsum ...	...	*Rector of Droxford, Hants.*
1788*	Lewis Bagot ...	...	*Bishop of Norwich.*
1789*	Samuel Halifax ...	...	„ *S. Asaph.*
1790*	Brownlow North ...	...	„ *Winchester.*
1791*	Samuel Glasse	...	*Chaplain in Ordinary to his Majesty.*
1792*	John Warren ...	...	*Bishop of Bangor.*
1793*	Samuel Horsley ...	...	„ *S. Asaph.*

1794* Joseph Holden Pott   ... *Archdeacon of St. Alban's.*
1795* Henry R. Courtenay   ... *Bishop of Bristol.*
1796* George Is. Huntingford ... *Warden of Winchester College.*
1797* John Law   ... *Archdeacon of Rochester.*
1798* Henry Whitfield   ... *Rector of S. Margaret's, Lothbury.*
1799* Thomas Rennell   ... *Master of the Temple.*
1800* John Buckner   ... ... *Bishop of Chichester.*
1801* Thomas Lewis **O'Beirne**   ,,   *Meath.*
1802* John Randolph ...   ... ,,   *Oxford.*
1803* Robert Gray   ... ... ,,   *Bristol.*
1804* George Pretyman   ... ,,   *Lincoln.*
1805* George Pelham ...   ... ,,   *Bristol.*
1806* John Fisher   ... ... ,,   *Exeter.*
1807* George Owen Cambridge   *Archdeacon of Middlesex.*
1808* John Chappel Woodhouse *Dean of Lichfield.*
1809* Charles Daubeny   ... *Archdeacon of Salisbury.*
1810* Henry Bathurst ...   ... *Bishop of Norwich.*
1811* Herbert Marsh ...   ,,   *Peterborough.*
1812* Whittington Landon   ... ***Provost** of Worcester.*
1813* George Henry Law   ... *Bishop of Chester.*
1814* William Howley ...   ... *Archbishop of Canterbury.*
1815* Charles Henry Hall   ... *Dean of Christchurch.*
1816* Robert Hodgson   ... ,,   *Chester.*
1817* **Christopher** Bethell   ... *Bishop **of** Bangor.*
1818* James **Hook**   ... ... *Archdeacon **of** Huntingdon.*
1819* William Stanley Goddard *Prebendary of S. Paul's.*
1820* William Van Mildert   ... *Bishop of Durham.*
1821* Henry Ryder   ... ... ,,   *Gloucester.*
1822* John Kaye   ... ... ,,   *Lincoln.*
1823* Reginald Heber ...   ... ,,   *Calcutta.*
1824* William Carey   ... ... ,,   *Exeter.*
1825* Richard Mant   ... ... ,,   *Down and **Connor**.*
1826* Charles R. Sumner   ... ,,   *Winchester.*
1827* Charles James Blomfield   ,,   *London.*
1828* John B. Jenkinson   ... ,,   *S. David's.*
1829* Edward Copleston   ... ,,   *Llandaff.*
1830* James Henry Monk   ... ,,   *Gloucester and Bristol.*
1831* John Inglis   ... ... ,,   *Nova Scotia.*
1832* Hugh Percy   ... ... ,,   *Carlisle.*
1833* Edward Grey   ... ... ,,   *Hereford.*
1834* John Bird Sumner   ... *Archbishop of Canterbury.*
1835* Robert James Carr   ... *Bishop of Worcester.*
1836* Lord John George **Beres**-
    ford   ... ... *Archbishop of Armagh.*
1837* William Otter   ... ... *Bishop of Chichester.*
1838* George Murray ...   ... ,,   *Rochester.*
1839* Edward Maltby ...   ... ,,   *Durham.*
1840* Richard Bagot   ... ... ,,   *Bath and Wells.*
1841* Joseph Allen   ... ... ,,   *Ely.*
1842* Charles T. Longley   ... ,,   *Ripon.*

1843* Edward Denison ... *Bishop of Salisbury.*
1844* Connop Thirlwall ... „ *S. David's.*
1845* George Davys ... ... „ *Peterborough.*
1846 Henry Pepys ... ... „ *Worcester.*
1847 Ashurst T. Gilbert ... „ *Chichester.*
1848 John Lonsdale ... ... „ *Lichfield.*
1849 Samuel Wilberforce ... „ *Oxford.*
1850 Thomas Vowler Short ... „ *S. Asaph.*
1851 John Bird Sumner ... *Archbishop of Canterbury.*
1852 Renn D. Hampden ... *Bishop of Hereford.*
1853 John Graham ... ... „ *Chester.*
1854 James Price Lee ... „ *Manchester.*
1855 Alfred Ollivant ... ... „ *Llandaff.*
1856 John Jackson ... ... „ *Lincoln.*
1857 No sermon is printed in report ; probably none delivered.
1858 Walter Kerr Hamilton ... *Bishop of Salisbury.*
1859 Henry Montagu Villiers ... „ *Carlisle.*
1860 No sermon is printed in report.
1861 Lord Auckland ... ... *Bishop of Bath and Wells.*
1862 Charles Baring ... ... „ *Durham.*
1863 William Thomson ... *Archbishop of York.*
1864 Robert Bickersteth ... *Bishop of Ripon.*
1865 James Colquhoun Camp-
    bell ... ... „ *Bangor.*
1866 James Colton Wigram ... „ *Rochester.*
1867 Harvey Goodwin ... „ *Carlisle.*
    .*. From this date no sermons were preached till
1879 Joseph Barber Lightfoot, *Bishop of Durham.* Sermon
    preached in November at S. Martin-in-the-Fields, on the
    opening of the Society's New House in Northumberland
    Avenue.

CataLogVs LiбrorVM eCCLesIae

s. PaVLI

eXpLICIt FeLICIter

In Ipso

beatI PaVLI

PATRONI NOSTRI FESTO.

17

INDEX.

⁎ *This Index contains about 2,694 references. Every reference has been carefully compared with the text since the Index has been in type.*

THE END.

Elliot Stock, Paternoster Row, London.